Mastering
Risk Modelling

ONE WEEK LOAN

This book is accompa
Cl
ROM(s)

i

FT Prentice Hall

FINANCIAL TIMES

In an increasingly competitive world, we believe it's quality of thinking that will give you the edge – an idea that opens new doors, a technique that solves a problem, or an insight that simply makes sense of it all. The more you know, the smarter and faster you can go.

That's why we work with the best minds in business and finance to bring cutting-edge thinking and best learning practice to a global market.

Under a range of leading imprints, including Financial Times Prentice Hall, we create world-class print publications and electronic products bringing our readers knowledge, skills and understanding which can be applied whether studying or at work.

To find out more about our business publications, or tell us about the books you'd like to find, you can visit us at **www.pearsoned.co.uk**

PEARSON

Prentice Hall

market editions

Mastering
Risk Modelling

A practical guide to modelling
uncertainty with Excel

First Edition

ALASTAIR L. DAY

FT Prentice Hall
FINANCIAL TIMES

An imprint of **Pearson Education**

London • New York • Toronto • Sydney • Tokyo • Singapore
Hong Kong • Cape Town • Madrid • Paris • Amsterdam • Munich • Milan

PEARSON EDUCATION LIMITED

Head Office:
Edinburgh Gate
Harlow CM20 2JE
Tel: +44 (0)1279 623623
Fax: +44 (0)1279 431059

First published in Great Britain in 2003

© Pearson Education Limited 2003

The right of Alastair L. Day to be identified as Author
of this Work has been asserted by him in accordance
with the Copyright, Designs and Patents Act 1988.

ISBN 0 273 65978 2

British Library Cataloguing in Publication Data
A CIP catalogue record for this book can be obtained from the British Library.

10 9 8 7 6 5 4 3 2 1

Typeset by Mathematical Composition Setters Ltd, Salisbury, Wiltshire.
Printed and bound in Great Britain by Bell & Bain Limited, Glasgow.

The Publishers' policy is to use paper manufactured from sustainable forests.

About the author

Alastair Day has worked in the finance industry for 20 years in treasury and marketing functions. He worked originally for the NFC negotiating funding and administering leases and switched to marketing finance upon the privatization of NFC in 1980. During the 1980s he was a director of a leasing company which grew rapidly based on vendor programmes in the IT, print and machine tool industries. The directors sold the company to a PLC at the end of the decade. In 1990 he established Systematic Finance plc as a consultancy and financial lessor concentrating on the computer and communications industries.

Alastair has a degree in Economics and German from London University, an MBA from the Open University Business School, and is an associate lecturer in corporate finance with the OUBS. Other publications include books such as *Mastering Financial Modelling* and *The Financial Director's Guide to Purchasing Leasing* published by Pearson Education, other books and a range of software products. In addition, he develops and presents public and in-house courses on a range of topics including financial modelling, leasing, financial and credit analysis, and other corporate finance topics.

Acknowledgements

I would like to thank my wife, Angela Miles, for her support and assistance with this book. In addition, Laurie Donaldson of Pearson Education has provided valuable support and backing for this project.

Contents

Contents

Conventions

- The main part of the text is set in Garamond, whereas entries are set in Courier. For example:

    Enter the Scenario Name as `Base Case`

- Items on the menu bars also shown in Courier. For example:

    Select `Tools, Goalseek`

- The names of functions are in Courier capitals. This is the payment function, which requires inputs for the interest rate, number of periods, present value and future value. For example:

    `=PMT(INT,NPER,PV,FV,TYPE)`

- Cell formulas are also shown in Courier. For example:

    `=IF($C$75=1,IF($B25>C$22,$B25-C$22-C$23,`
    `-C$23),IF($B25<C$22,C$22-$B25-C$23,-C$23))`

- Equations are shown in italics. For example, net present value:

$$NPV = \frac{(Cash\ flow)^{N}}{(1+r)^{N}}$$

- Genders. The use of 'he' or 'him' refers to masculine or feminine and this is used for simplicity to avoid repetition.

Overview

WHO NEEDS THIS BOOK?

Business has always meant taking risks in order to secure a return. In the last century, this was often a game of chance where outcomes could not be accurately predicted. Developments in computing and theory have led to a big change in how risk and reward is perceived.

Financial modelling has come into its own since the original development of Visicalc and Lotus 1-2-3 as the preferred tool for financial calculations. The omnipresence of Microsoft Office means that techniques can be demonstrated more simply in Excel than with hand-held financial calculators.

Banks and financial institutions increasingly use risk management tools to manage portfolios and assess client credit risk. Additionally, risk modelling plays a part in structured and project finance. In the corporate sector, directors of UK public companies are tasked with disclosing the main risks facing the company as part of the risk management process. This book mixes theory with practice and introduces a number of Excel templates as the basis for more complex risk models.

The requirement for financial modelling is certain to develop further in future owing to:

- advances in computer technology and speed on the desktop;
- the continued development of more specific risk software (e.g. @RISK);
- more historic data being available for analysis within organizations;
- the use of models being a required skill for financial executives and business students alike.

The key objectives of this book are to:

- provide financial managers with practical templates for applying risk and uncertainty to Excel;
- improve financial managers' abilities with Excel;
- demonstrate a systematic method of developing Excel models for fast development and error checking;

- provide a library of basic templates for further development as an illustration of the methods.

This book aims to assist two key groups:

- Excel users with a basic understanding of model design and a wish to extend their Excel modelling skills;
- practitioners who want to be able to build more complex models using advanced Excel features.

The areas of responsibility are:

- CFOs and finance directors;
- financial controllers;
- analysts;
- accountants;
- corporate finance personnel;
- treasury managers;
- risk managers;
- middle office staff;
- general managers;
- personnel in banks, corporates and government who make complex decisions and who could benefit from a modelling approach;
- academics, business and MBA students.

Therefore, people interested in this book range from a company accountant who wants to be able to understand investment risk to managers who require more complex models.

The book is international in its outlook and will provide examples relevant to both the UK and overseas.

HOW TO USE THIS BOOK

- Install the Excel application templates using the simple SETUP command. There is a key to the file names at the back of the book.
- Work through each of the chapters and the examples.
- Use the book, spreadsheets and templates as a reference guide for further work.
- Practice and improve your efficiency and competence with Excel.

Alastair L Day
www.financial-models.com

Introduction

File: FT4_01.xls

SCOPE OF THE BOOK

Mastering Financial Modelling, an earlier book, provides an introduction to Excel financial modelling and shows how to use Excel in a disciplined manner to develop applications. Since spreadsheet models are often poorly planned and developed, it provides a specific method for developing applications. This book develops these ideas to include risk analysis and to show how techniques can be added to simpler models in order to:

- make the models more comprehensive;
- accept that the real world is uncertain and models should be able to cope with a range of possible outcomes;
- derive more useful management information;
- understand how the model 'flexes' with change;
- act as a further method of checking the model's outputs.

Financial modelling is the term often used for applications from simple spreadsheets to complex models. In this book, the term *financial model* is used to denote a dedicated spreadsheet written to solve a business problem. The basic need is to answer a business problem such as the minimum budgeted cash flow over the next 12 months, the net present value of an investment or the price of an option. The spreadsheet does not simply hold data but is organized as an analysis tool. The objective is often to represent a closed system such as the investment in new equipment, together with forecast revenue and expenditure. The model therefore represents a computer program written to solve the problem, which is different to using the spreadsheet only for holding data or adding up a few numbers. The model could be written in Visual Basic or C++ but it is usually quicker, easier and more intuitive to develop a model in Excel.

Models underpin decisions and the basic risk process could be described as:

- defining objectives, since you need to be clear about objectives and output answers or reports;
- identifying all possible courses of action to weigh up advantages and disadvantages;
- assembling data or variables that are relevant and understanding the extent of the accuracy and relevance of the data available;
- building the computer models to assist and organize any decisions;
- assessing the decision and comparing options by using the data outputs;
- implementing a decision and monitoring the subsequent variances to the original plan;

- monitoring the effect of decisions and if the project fails ensuring that lessons can be learnt.

However much effort is expended on the 'correct' variables for the model, there must always be some potential for error or variance since a model is only a best guess of the likely outcomes. Risk here is often considered to be the potential downside resulting from a business decision.

The advantage of Excel is that most people have had some exposure to the language and are comfortable with the interface and commands. Since there is a similarity of presentation within the Microsoft Office suite, users can write simple spreadsheets quickly. The disadvantages of such a free approach are when decisions need to be taken or when an application needs to be distributed or maintained. Whilst you can write fragments of code for your own use, any files for use by others should be clear and auditable. In particular, the disadvantages of many Excel models are as follows:

- wide range of abilities on the part of the authors;
- most people use less than 10 per cent of capability (e.g. they may never have used the statistical or array functions or inserted a pivot table);
- a lack of standard structure or design method making auditing all but impossible;
- a poor structure leads to a lack of clarity and confusing output reports;
- it is easy to make mistakes since errors can lie undetected (for years!) – users are often overconfident about their abilities and often assume their code is error free;
- Excel is not a programming language and therefore there are no standards for naming cells or documenting the work;
- duplication of effort arises since most users do not develop templates for specific types of applications;
- spreadsheets do not cope well with text (but then there is the option of Microsoft Word).

Companies usually assume that executives are proficient in Excel since they have qualified in finance, but this is not always the case. Financial modelling demands a disciplined approach just like any other programming language. Since Excel does not have to be compiled before use, people often produce disorganized designs with little regard for future development or maintenance. For instance, dates can be hard coded and of course will work this year, but next year you have to search through the model and change all entries. Similarly, authors often mix numbers and formulas in the same cell so that others cannot work out where to input data and of course the author finds it impossible to check for mistakes. Due to a lack of clear objectives, the model may also not even produce a clear answer to the original question.

Most financial models consist of input variables, calculations and some kind of output. The objectives of modelling should include some of the following:

■ analyzing and processing data into information;

■ modelling a considered view or forecast of the future (e.g. project cash flows);

■ processing data quickly and accurately into clear and relevant management information;

■ testing assumptions in a 'safe' environment before mistakes are made (e.g. project scenarios);

■ supporting management decision making through a structured approach.

Simple model

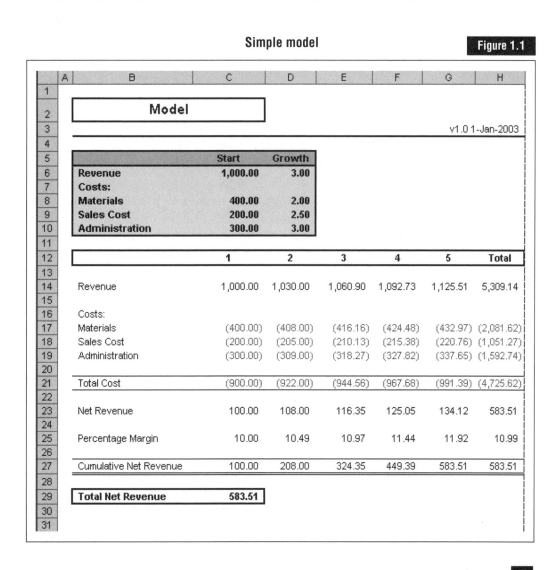

Figure 1.1

(Modelling often produces too much information and one objective may be to reduce the detail in summaries.);

- understanding more precisely the variables or rules in a problem to ensure that the whole system is modelled;

- learning more about processes and the behaviour of variables, in particular the importance of key variables and how they behave;

- discovering the sensitivity and risk inherent in the model.

EXAMPLE MODEL

Figure 1.1 shows a simple example of revenue and costs. The inputs are shown tinted grey and the schedule below calculates the net revenue at the end of the five-year period. This is the sum of cells C27:H27.

This is a deterministic or input–calculation–output model since the inputs or variables are fixed. For example, sales growth is 3 per cent from a base of 1000. These figures represent the best estimate of the value of each input variable but they are still single points rather than ranges.

OBJECTIVES OF RISK MODELLING

The deterministic model above may not provide all the answers. The future is uncertain and there are factors that are within the organization's control and those, such as the weather, over which it has no control. Whilst analysts may wish to control or know the future, risk modelling seeks to apply mathematical theory to the problem. In the simple problem above, the organization may wish to know how likely it is to achieve the forecast net revenue. Corporate finance theory advises that organizations and individuals are rational and risk averse. This means that they take a defined risk for a desired return. Translated into this example, this could be rephrased as the forecast net revenue and the possible variance or standard deviation. There would be no point in accepting this budget if possible results ranged from 100 to 700 since a result of 100 would be unacceptable. The managers may then wish to know what the chance is of the forecast net revenue falling below 200. Modelling could help to uncover the risk and uncertainty in the budget.

To illustrate the concept of return and variance, Figure 1.2 shows the result of 1000 random numbers on the Normal_Distribution2 sheet based on a mean of 584 and a standard deviation of 50. The data were generated using the random number generator in `Tools, Data Analysis`.

Normal distribution

Figure 1.2

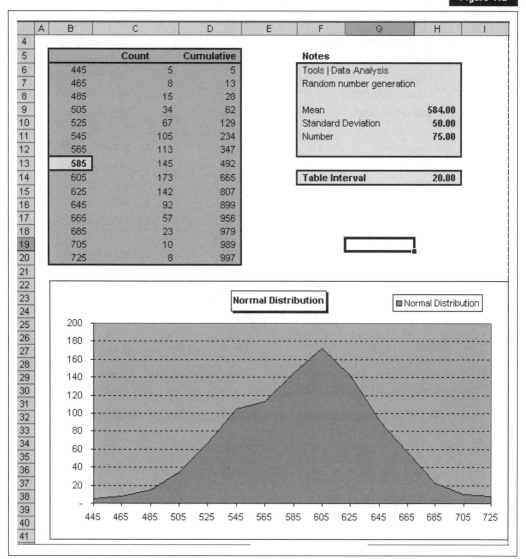

The table uses a FREQUENCY function as an array to count the values within pre-defined ranges.

```
=FREQUENCY($C$6:$C$80,$E$6:$E$20)
```

Note that the distribution has extended tails on either side of the mean. Analysis concentrates on the downside and the number of potential results that fall below a required level. Table 1.1 uses Tools, Data Analysis, Descriptive Statistics to generate a description of the distribution.

Table 1.1	Descriptive statistics	
Mean		582.9898481
Standard error		1.592886606
Median		586.2308387
Mode		557.862761
Standard deviation		50.37149731
Sample variance		2537.287741
Kurtosis		0.167480937
Skewness		–0.084604382
Range		328.1966201
Minimum		426.6767336
Maximum		754.8733537
Sum		582989.8481
Count		1000
Largest (1)		754.8733537
Smallest (1)		426.6767336

Risk models provide:

- an understanding of risk since a single answer may not be enough for decision making;
- multiple answers to better understand the range of outcomes;
- the inclusion of elements of risk or uncertainty (e.g. future cash flows);
- the chance to test inherently inaccurate forecasts;
- likely outcomes under a number of different assumptions or scenarios;
- information on the behaviour of key variables.

Modelling helps to identify risk since you need to be able to test all the variables. Sales forecasts are notoriously optimistic and so what happens if you downgrade the timescale when an item of equipment starts to generate revenue? The percentage is a variable that must be modelled to gauge its effect on the eventual answer.

Alternatively risk could be divided into:

- *risk*, which can be measured and is subject to probability mathematics;
- *uncertainty*, which consists of random events or variables (e.g. the weather) or which emanates from a lack of knowledge about the system being modelled. In the latter case variables are not included in the model.

The notion that risk exists in all business decisions is therefore key; however, risk may not always be negative since simple analysis may lead to missed opportunities. Analysis may confirm that the potential downside is minor or that a project is too pessimistic and greater sales growth is possible. One approach is to review the impact and likelihood as a matrix and try to group and prioritize risks. The approach then hinges on two questions:

- What is the source of the risk?
- What is its likely impact and likelihood?

Management can then concentrate on those variables that fall in the top right-hand box of the matrix shown in Figure 1.3.

Excel provides techniques and functions for generating multiple answers and dealing with uncertainty. These include:

- Data tables, which are one- or two-dimensional grids of possible answers. Since most models include a few key variables, this allows more information of how a model 'flexes' with variation in key variables.

- Scenarios which allow the inclusion of individual cases within the model (e.g. best case, worst case).

- What if analysis involving the use of several scenarios with probabilities assigned to them. For example, you could value a company based on several future scenarios of market penetration and assign probabilities to each scenario. A single net present value (NPV) could then be transformed into an expected net present value (ENPV) based on probability.

- Decision trees using probability mathematics and utility theory to place a value on decisions.

- Optimization techniques such as Solver where the desired result is known but there is uncertainty about the inputs required.

- Simulation techniques involving the generation of large numbers of

Impact-likelihood matrix

Figure 1.3

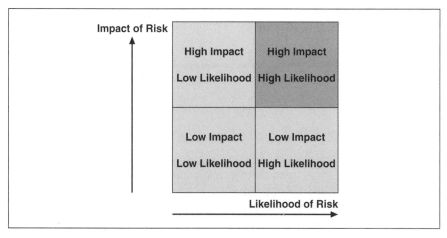

possible scenarios to find the range of possible results. Simulation is considered in more detail in Chapter 5.

One other factor in modelling is perhaps the perception of risk in the process. In only relatively few circumstances are the probabilities and possible outcomes completely clear and risk is bounded by perception. Modelling is one part of the process and you have to look at the perception of risk and the potential upsides and downsides. One individual may be less risk averse than another, which will have an effect on the process and the outcome.

SUMMARY

This chapter has introduced some ideas of risk and uncertainty and the objective in the following chapters is to demonstrate how single answer deterministic models can be made more useful and provide better management information. The following chapters provide a number of techniques and discuss several applications:

- projects and investments
- financial analysis
- credit and credit risk
- portfolios
- equity valuation
- fixed income
- derivatives.

Review of model design

File: FT4_02.xls

INTRODUCTION

A book on modelling would not be complete without a chapter on model design. Modelling should help with crystallizing the variables in a particular problem and clarifying the calculations and outputs required. As stated, models are often ill thought out and therefore may not answer the problem or be flexible enough for further development. As institutions develop larger libraries of Excel models, it is becoming increasingly important to build in future maintenance into modelling.

DESIGN OBJECTIVES

Users should develop a systematic method for developing spreadsheet models. Initial questions should include:

- What is the overall objective of the model?
- What reports or outputs are needed?
- What is the key question to be answered?
- Who will use it?
- What are the components of the problems and how can the problem be sub-divided into smaller sections?
- What should be the overall structure of the model?

The rule is to spend more time on initial planning in order to save time later. The aims should be:

- A clear layout with easily visible inputs, calculations and outputs. Users need to understand the structure quickly otherwise they tend to get frustrated. Badly designed models can cloud thinking rather than enhance understanding.
- A clear area for user inputs, in one place with a distinctive input colour.
- Easy-to-understand workings with areas set aside for derivation of interim variables.
- Simplicity in the formation of cell formulas. Some spreadsheet users appear to think it is good practice to make the cell formulas as complex as possible. This only makes the model difficult to understand and more costly to maintain.
- Consistency in approach and method. You will notice that all the spreadsheets in this book follow a consistent design method. The method has

been developed over a number of years and it works. For example, there is always a cell name called 'Version' or 'Contact', and a title at the top left of every sheet (see Figure 2.1).

- Ease of use so that users do not have to understand the full structure of the model. For example, it is always useful to have a management summary close to an inputs area. As you change variables, you get immediate feedback on the answer. This saves clicking along several sheets to the answer.

- Future ease of maintenance and modification through a modular design. This means that you can add more features as needs change without a complete redesign.

- To reduce code as far as possible by not calculating any answer more than once. For example, you calculate the dates for the top of the schedule on the first schedule and then look them up on all other schedules. This is true also of text labels where the first instance should be entered and then further instances looked up from the first. The objective is always to reduce the amount of 'hard coding' to ensure that all changes cascade through the model.

- In most cases, a single point model does not provide enough information. A model should demonstrate how the answer varies when you change key variables.

- Moving on from variances, the model should cope with levels of risk and uncertainty. This book provides techniques for widening the scope of models with risk techniques.

Figure 2.1   **Standard layout**

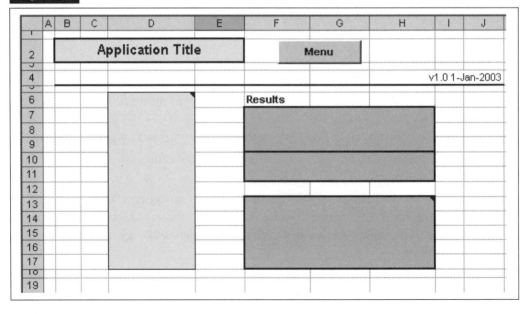

- Precise and clear management reporting through the use of sensitivity or charts in order to demonstrate clear analysis. The ultimate answer needs to be clear and accessible to any user. You should bear in mind that different users have varying priorities.

COMMON ERRORS

Below is a checklist of common spreadsheet errors encountered when auditing and checking models. This list is not exhaustive, but merely serves to confirm the weaknesses exposed by poor design and method.

- No form of layout with inputs, calculations and outputs clearly marked. A common mistake is not to put all the inputs together and mark the areas as inputs, calculation and output.
- No version number or author name to show the exact version being used. It is a good idea to have a version number and record the differences between one date and another. In a few months' time models should produce the same answers as today. It is a good idea to have a sheet in a model to record changes from one version to another as a form of document control.
- No menu system or macro-driven buttons for easy navigation around a workbook.
- No inputs section since it is always clearer to set up an inputs area or sheet and bring together all the key variables.
- No specific colour for inputs and results. This book uses bold for inputs and grey boxes for outputs. This improves understanding since you expect certain elements on all sheets. In Excel, blue cells are always inputs.
- No use of names for key variables since it is usually clearer to name the main variables in the inputs section. Formulas throughout the rest of the workbook are then easier to understand.
- No borders or shading leading to a bland design. You can quickly include simple borders and colours to improve the appearance if you keep the Formatting toolbar visible. The models in this book all follow the same principles of tint and appearance.
- No data validation of inputs to allow users to enter any value. Using `Data`, `Validation`, you can allow different data types and set maximums and minimums or other operators (see Figure 2.2).
- A mixture of number formats used on the same sheet with differing numbers of decimal places. Users also often use numbers and decimals as percentages on the same sheet. You can save custom number formats (see Figure 2.3), which can be useful, for example for adding inputs. It is

Figure 2.2

Data validation

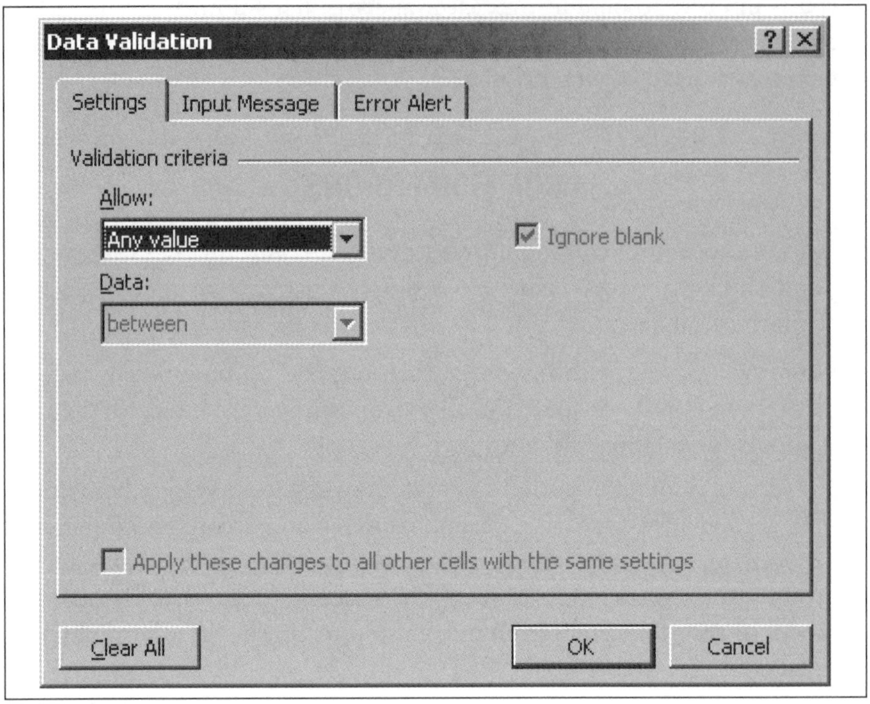

possible to use the syntax to create new formats using these rules:

> Syntax: `"Positive";"Negative";"Zero";"Text"`

For example, 12 months could be entered as #0 "Months".

- Users often mix numbers and formulas in the same cells. The calculation area of the model should have no 'hard' inputs and the only input numbers should be in the inputs area. Any mixture leads to auditing and consistency problems as below

> `=E16*1.05*1.02`

- More than one formula per line is a common problem since again it makes spreadsheets hard to understand. On a cash flow model with months as the column headers, you expect the same formula for each month rather than a mixture.

- Cell formulas can be overwritten with numbers where users have not checked sheets for consistency and allowed errors.

- Labels are sometimes hard coded and it makes sense to make labels as dynamic as possible. For example, it makes more sense to label a cell with a dynamic label such as 'Price with a volatility of 20 per cent' rather than 'Price'.

- No use of graphics in reporting in order to show clearly the results. Most

Custom number formats

Figure 2.3

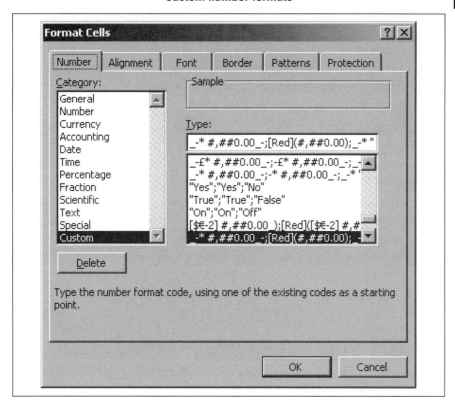

people are usually inefficient in understanding grids of data and the important results are best confirmed by graphics.

■ No commenting of individual cells to show workings or provide explanations. This can be achieved by `Insert`, `Comment` or the use of `Data`, `Validation`. In the latter case, you select the second tab for input message. Here you can insert a message, which will be displayed when you click on the cell.

■ No conditional formatting to highlight answers or change the cell formatting dependent on the answer. This is a useful feature of Excel since you can establish rules for each cell.

■ No use of functions to reduce the amount of code and the possibility of errors. Whilst you can calculate monthly rentals, such as the formula below, it is usually better to use a built-in function such as PMT:

```
=1/((1-(1/((1+Monthly_Rate)^Term__Months)))
/Monthly_Rate)
```

■ Sheets are often not set up for printing. Good design means thinking about the output and making sure that the information can be printed out.

- Management reporting or summary is often unavailable. For example a complex model usually contains too much information to be accessible to users of different levels. A summary demonstrates the answers to key questions without the levels of detail in the rest of the model. For example, a project finance model could contain a summary of the costs and potential net revenues to fund debt and equity. The important ratios such as return on equity and debt service covers could also be shown.

- Following on from management reporting, sensitivity analysis helps to show the behaviour of the model to changes in variables. Forecasts are often too optimistic and you need to test the model to ensure that the inputs are sensible.

- Documentation or explanation on how the model works is often omitted. For the purposes of maintenance, details of variables, key calculations, structure of the model and any other relevant information can be presented as notes on a separate sheet in the workbook.

EXCEL FEATURES

The model is FT4_02.xls as shown in Figure 2.4. Each of the sections in this chapter is covered on a sheet in the model. Open the file and click along the bottom to see the progression of sheets.

This is a simple net present value model which adds up the cash flows for a period and multiples them by a 10 per cent discount factor. The net present value in cell C14 is gained by adding up the discounted cash flows.

Figure 2.4 **Original present value model**

	A	B	C	D	E	F	G	H	I
1		Present Value							
2									
3			0	1	2	3	4	5	
4									
5		Capital value	-100000						
6		Cash flows		28000	28000	28000	28000	28000	
7									
8		Total	-100000	28000	28000	28000	28000	28000	
9									
10		Factor	1.00	0.91	0.83	0.75	0.68	0.62	
11									
12		Net cash flow	-100000	25454.55	23140.5	21036.81	19124.38	17385.8	
13									
14		NPV	6142.03						
15									

Options view

Figure 2.5

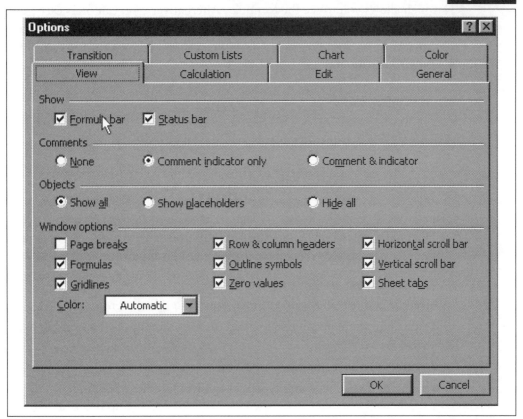

Original model formula

Figure 2.6

	A	B	C	D	E
1		Present Value			
2					
3			0	1	2
4					
5		Capital value	-100000		
6		Cash flows		28000	28000
7					
8		Total	=SUM(C5:C7)	=SUM(D5:D7)	=SUM(E5:E7)
9					
10		Factor	=1/(1+10%)^(C3)	=1/(1+10%)^(D3)	=1/(1+10%)^(E3)
11					
12		Net cash flow	=C8*C10	=D8*D10	=E8*E10
13					
14		NPV	=SUM(C12:H12)		
15					

If you go to `Tools Options View`, you can select `View Formulas`, which allows you to see the formulas. Alternatively you can press `Ctrl` and `'` together and this toggles between view formulas and normal view. As you can see this is only producing a net present value based on the cash flows using the formula:

$$Period\_Factor = \frac{(1)}{(1 + 10\%)^{Period\_Number}}$$

Figure 2.6 shows the formulas view displaying all the cell references.

FORMATS

The model is presently a mixture of inputs and calculations (see Figure 2.7) and the first job is to reorganize the layout. This involves:

- inserting lines and moving the inputs;
- referring to the inputs in the cash flows and calculations;
- labelling where possible to look up the values in inputs, for example B9 is now =C3;
- correcting the factors with an input;
- using different fonts and typefaces to break up the monotony.

Figure 2.7   **Formats**

	A	B	C	D	E	F	G	H	I
1		Present Value							
2									
3		Capital value	100000		Management Summary				
4		Periodic cash flow	28000		NPV	6142.03			
5		Discount rate	10%						
6									
7			0	1	2	3	4	5	
8									
9		Capital value	-100000						
10		Periodic cash flow		28000	28000	28000	28000	28000	
11									
12		Total	-100000	28000	28000	28000	28000	28000	
13									
14		Factor	1.00	0.91	0.83	0.75	0.68	0.62	
15									
16		Net cash flow	-100000	25454.55	23140.5	21036.81	19124.38	17385.8	
17									
18		NPV	6142.03						
19									

Layout

Figure 2.8

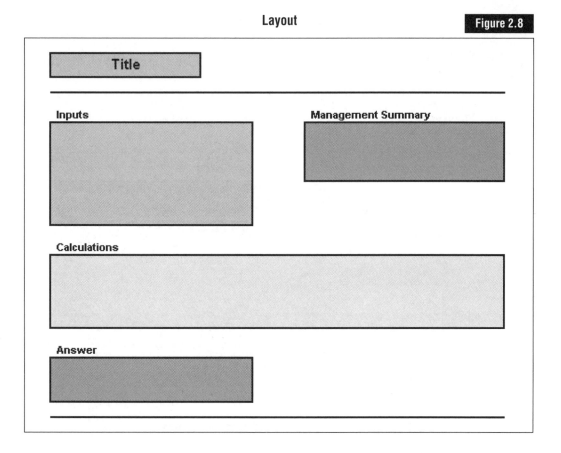

The title, inputs, summary and answer are now clear in a bold typeface and the model follows a defined layout (see Figure 2.8).

NUMBER FORMATS

The number formats are inconsistent with no separators and two different sets of decimal places.

Go to Format, Format Cells, Number to change the default settings (see Figure 2.9).

You can experiment with different custom formats where positive, negative and zero is separated by semi-colons. Colours are in square brackets. Text is enclosed in inverted commas (e.g. Format) so that 'years' is added to the number: 0 "years". You insert your custom format in the Type box or amend an existing format.

This extract in Figure 2.9 shows the accounting format with positive numbers slightly set to the left and negative numbers in red with brackets

Figure 2.9 **Custom format cells**

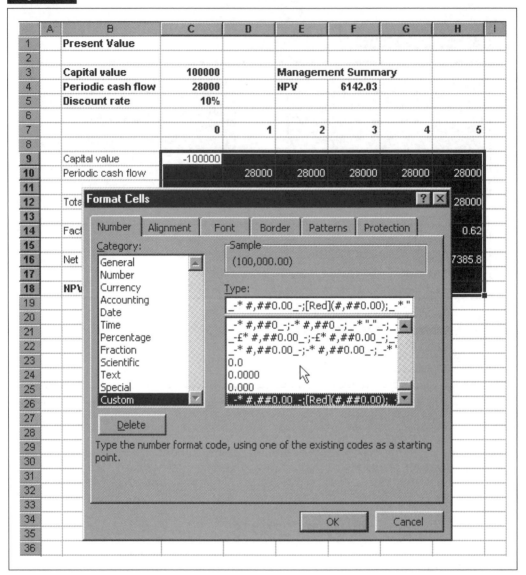

around them. Zero is a dash to avoid confusion or schedules of zeros. This type of format is easy to read on laser printers whereas a minus sign is often hard to read on negative numbers.

Accounting style format: `_-* #,##0.00_-;[Red]`
`(#,##0.00);_-* "-"_-`

The effect is to control the view of the numbers to a maximum of two decimal places.

LINES AND BORDERS

Lines and borders assist in breaking up the cell code and make the model look more interesting for the audience both on the screen and in printed output. It is best to keep the Formatting toolbar visible (see Figure 2.10). Go to `View`, `Toolbars`, `Formatting` to show this toolbar. This saves always going to `Format`, `Cells`, `Borders` etc. to add lines.

Figures 2.11 and 2.12 show highlighting cells and then applying a border from the toolbox. Thick lines are placed around the main sections and double lines to indicate a total.

Formatting toolbar

Figure 2.10

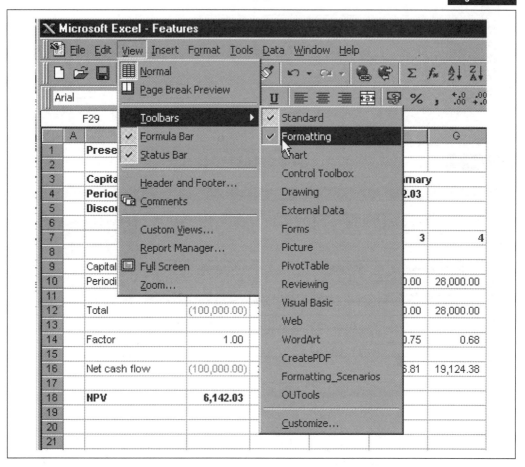

Figure 2.11   Borders

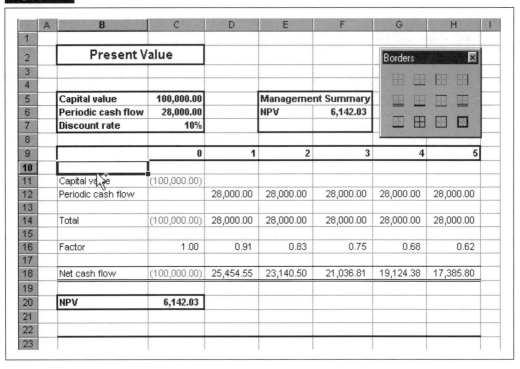

	A	B	C	D	E	F			I
1		Present Value							
2									
3		Capital value	100,000.00		Management Summar				
4		Periodic cash flow	28,000.00		NPV	6,142.03			
5		Discount rate	10%						
6									
7			0	1	2	3	4	5	
8									
9		Capital value	(100,000.00)						
10		Periodic cash flow		28,000.00	28,000.00	28,000.00	28,000.00	28,000.00	
11									
12		Total	(100,000.00)	28,000.00	28,000.00	28,000.00	28,000.00	28,000.00	
13									
14		Factor	1.00	0.91	0.83	0.75	0.68	0.62	
15									
16		Net cash flow	(100,000.00)	25,454.55	23,140.50	21,036.81	19,124.38	17,385.80	
17									
18		NPV	6,142.03						
19									

Figure 2.12   Completed borders

	A	B	C	D	E	F	G	H	I
1									
2		Present Value							
3									
4									
5		Capital value	100,000.00		Management Summary				
6		Periodic cash flow	28,000.00		NPV	6,142.03			
7		Discount rate	10%						
8									
9			0	1	2	3	4	5	
10									
11		Capital value	(100,000.00)						
12		Periodic cash flow		28,000.00	28,000.00	28,000.00	28,000.00	28,000.00	
13									
14		Total	(100,000.00)	28,000.00	28,000.00	28,000.00	28,000.00	28,000.00	
15									
16		Factor	1.00	0.91	0.83	0.75	0.68	0.62	
17									
18		Net cash flow	(100,000.00)	25,454.55	23,140.50	21,036.81	19,124.38	17,385.80	
19									
20		NPV	6,142.03						
21									
22									
23									

COLOUR AND PATTERNS

Colours and patterns also help to define inputs and outputs. In Figure 2.13 a neutral colour is used for the inputs and grey for the answers although the screen colours do not show up here. These colours are personal, but it is important to be consistent in the use of colours and formats.

Colours

Figure 2.13

	A	B	C	D	E	F
1						
2		**Present Value**				
3						
4						
5		Capital value	100,000.00		Management Summa	
6		Periodic cash flow	28,000.00		NPV	6,142.
7		Discount rate	10%			
8						
9			0	1	2	3	4	5
10						
11		Capital value	(100,000.00)			
12		Periodic cash flow		28,000.00	28,000.00	28,000.00	28,000.00	28,000.00
13						
14		Total	(100,000.00)	28,000.00	28,000.00	28,000.00	28,000.00	28,000.00
15						
16		Factor	1.00	0.91	0.83	0.75	0.68	0.62
17						
18		Net cash flow	(100,000.00)	25,454.55	23,140.50	21,036.81	19,124.38	17,385.80
19						
20		NPV	6,142.03			
21						
22						
23						

Fill Color — No Fill — Gray

SPECIFIC COLOUR FOR INPUTS AND RESULTS

Specific colours for inputs show where data is required. The author always uses blue for inputs, green or black for totals and red or black for calculated results (see Figure 2.14). Colour should be used sparingly as the effect can be too garish for most tastes.

With limited colour, the model becomes much clearer for the user and forces the author to keep inputs together for the sake of consistency. The model is now organized and easier for user input than the original model.

Figure 2.14

Font colours

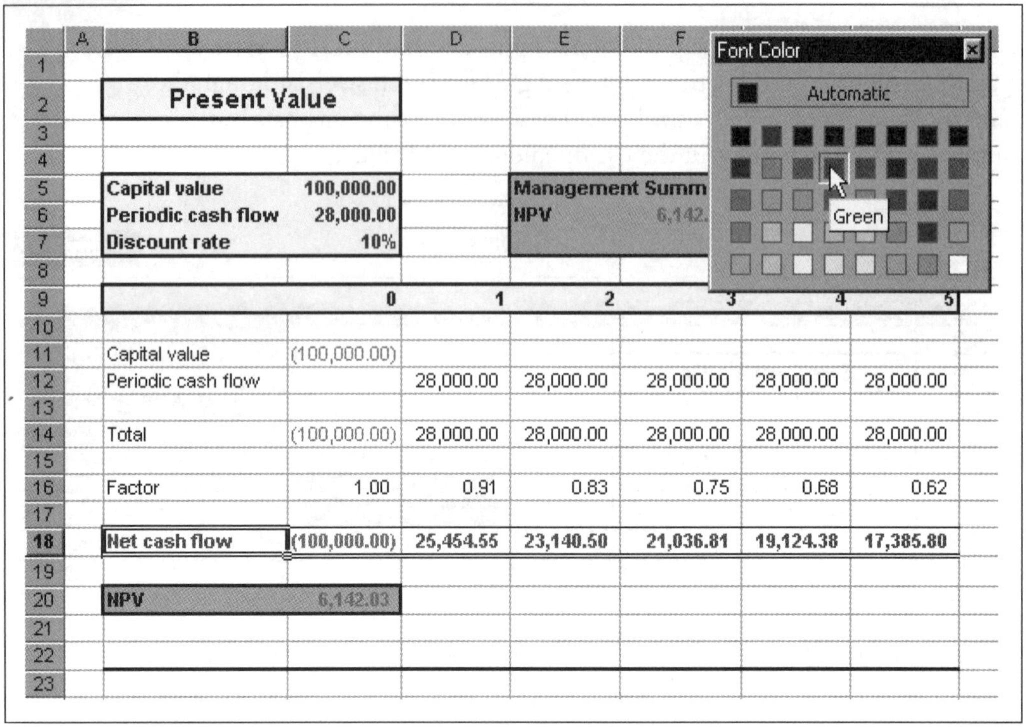

	A	B	C	D	E	F	
1							
2		**Present Value**					
3							
4							
5		Capital value	100,000.00		Management Summ		
6		Periodic cash flow	28,000.00		NPV	6,142.	
7		Discount rate	10%				
8							
9				0	1	2	
10							
11		Capital value	(100,000.00)				
12		Periodic cash flow		28,000.00	28,000.00	28,000.00	28,000.00	28,000.00
13							
14		Total	(100,000.00)	28,000.00	28,000.00	28,000.00	28,000.00	28,000.00
15							
16		Factor	1.00	0.91	0.83	0.75	0.68	0.62
17							
18		Net cash flow	(100,000.00)	25,454.55	23,140.50	21,036.81	19,124.38	17,385.80
19							
20		NPV	6,142.03				
21							
22							
23							

Font Color — Automatic — Green — 0 1 2 3 4 5

DATA VALIDATION

Data validation allows you to set limits for cells so that if you want a date, the user can only enter a date, or if you want a seven-character text string, the user has to enter this to proceed. This is accessed using Data, Validation on the main menu bar (see Figure 2.15).

In this case, it would be a good idea to limit the three inputs as follows:

Capital value	Positive number greater than zero
Periodic cash flow	Positive number greater than zero
Discount rate	Positive number between 0 and 1, i.e. 100 per cent.

The dialog box has three tabs (see Figure 2.16): for settings, an input message when the cursor is close to the cell, and the error alert to be shown on incorrect entry. You can choose not to show the Input Message by de-selecting the box.

The Error Alert (see Figure 2.17) shows if you enter a wrong figure and will not let you proceed until you comply with the validation terms. This

Validation settings

Figure 2.15

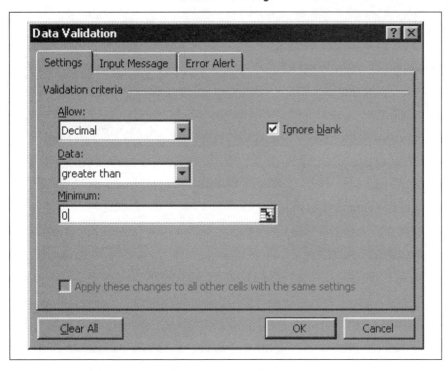

Validation input message

Figure 2.16

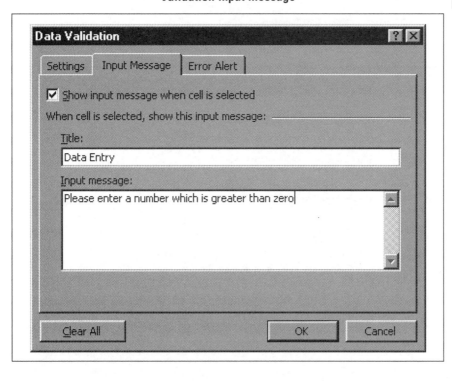

Figure 2.17

Validation error alert

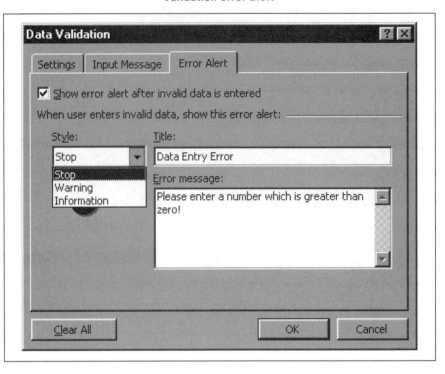

Figure 2.18

Paste special validation

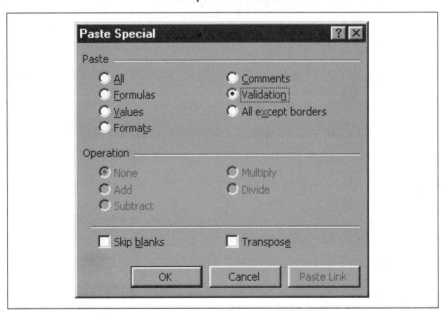

Validation error

Figure 2.19

	A	B	C	D	E	F	G	H	I
1									
2		**Present Value**							
3									
4									
5		Capital value	100,000.00		Management Summary				
6		Periodic cash flow	28,000.00		NPV	(77,119.42)			
7		Discount rate	120%						
8									
9				0	1	2	3	4	5
10									
11		Capital value	(100,000.00)						
12		Periodic cash flow		28,000.00	28,000.00	28,000.00	28,000.00	28,000.00	
13									
14		Total	(100,0(						0
15									
16		Factor							2
17									
18		Net cash flow	(100,0(						1
19									
20		NPV	(77,119.42)						
21									
22									
23									
24									

Data Entry Error ✕

✖ Please enter a discount rate between 0% and 100%.

[Retry]   [Cancel]

means that the capital value should always be a positive figure, errors are avoided and auditing becomes easier.

Since the periodic cash flows share the same validation, you can Copy and then Edit, Paste Special, Validation rather than typing in all the parameters again (see Figure 2.18).

The final validation is simply to ensure that the discount rate is less than 100 per cent. The effect is to narrow the inputs and hopefully ensure that a user will get the correct answers. If he tries to enter a discount rate of 120 per cent, the error message shown in Figure 2.19 appears.

Again this is simply looking at the model from a user standpoint and trying to coach the users on what they are required to do to get satisfactory answers.

CONTROLS – COMBO BOXES AND BUTTONS

A further tool to speed up inputs and assist users can be found on the Forms toolbar under View, Toolbars. These are the same controls, which you also find in Access or Visual Basic. In this example, you might wish to allow the user to input a discount rate between 8 per cent and 12 per cent at 0.5 per cent intervals. This cannot be done by validation and a different approach is needed. Validation will only permit an upper or lower value.

The first stage is to insert a workings area at the bottom of the sheet and to cut and paste the discount rate into it (see Figure 2.20). This is to ensure that the model continues to function when a control is placed at cell C7.

The Workings box shows an interval and then rates starting at 8 per cent and incrementing by the amount of the interval (see Figure 2.21).

The finished workings box shows the discount rates between 8 per cent and 12 per cent. The interval is not 'hard coded' and is dependent on cell C26. Whilst these are variables, most users do not need this detail and so these items are placed in the workings area and clearly marked.

The combo box control returns a number for the index of the selection. Here there are eight possible selections and the index number will be placed

Figure 2.20　　　　　　　　　　　**Combo workings 1**

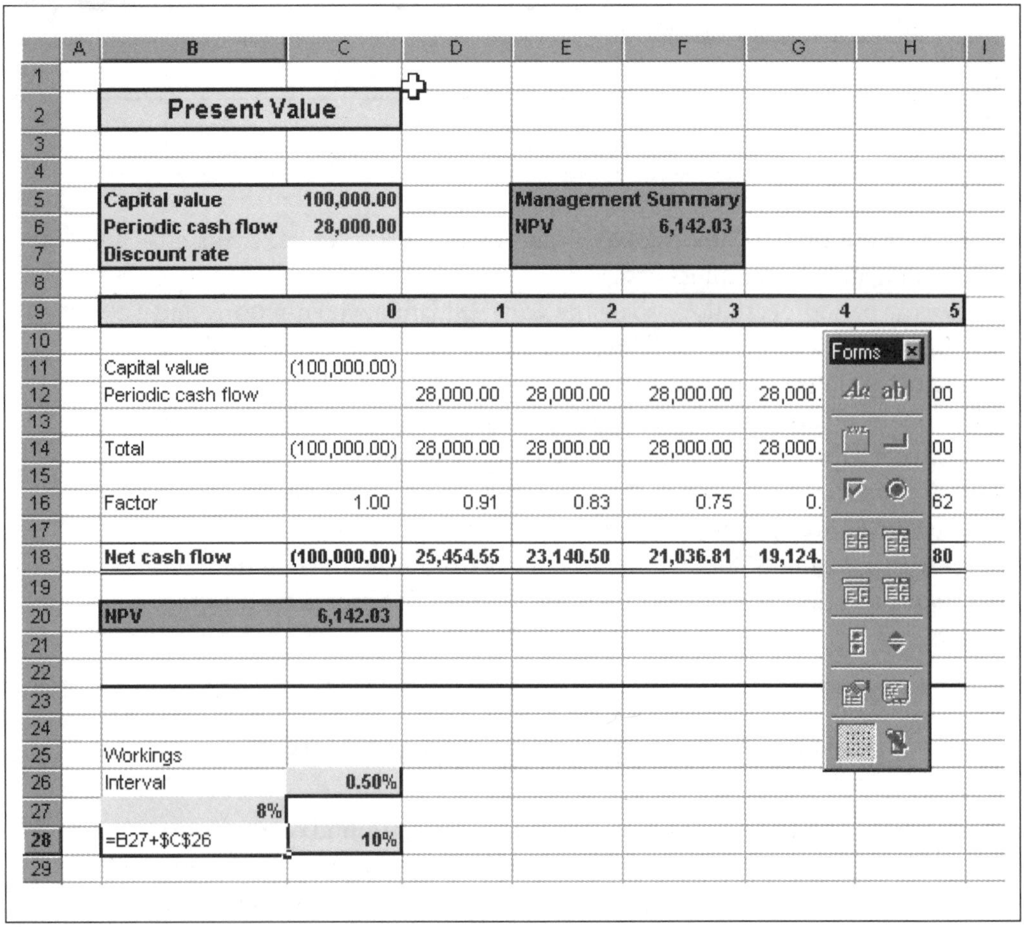

Combo workings 2

Figure 2.21

	A	B	C	D	E	F	G	H	I
4									
5		Capital value	100,000.00		Management Summary				
6		Periodic cash flow	28,000.00		NPV	6,142.03			
7		Discount rate							
8									
9			0	1	2	3	4	5	
10									
11		Capital value	(100,000.00)						
12		Periodic cash flow		28,000.00	28,000.00	28,000.00	28,000.00	28,000.00	
13									
14		Total	(100,000.00)	28,000.00	28,000.00	28,000.00	28,000.00	28,000.00	
15									
16		Factor	1.00	0.91		0.75	0.68	0.62	
17									
18		Net cash flow	(100,000.00)	25,454.55	23,14	036.81	19,124.38	17,385.80	
19									
20		NPV	6,142.03						
21									
22									
23									
24									
25		Workings							
26		Interval	0.50%						
27		8%	1						
28		8.500%	10%						
29		9.000%							
30		9.500%							
31		10.000%							
32		10.500%							
33		11.000%							
34		11.500%							
35		12.000%							
36									
37									

in cell C27. If you click on the Combo Box in the toolbar, you can draw a combo box in cell C7.

You have to tell the control where to get the input information from and where to put the result. Here the discount rates that need to be displayed are in B28:B35 and the result should be placed in cell C27 (see Figure 2.22).

The final stage is to link the discount rate cell C28 with the index cell C27. Since C28 will now be calculated, the colour has been changed to red to avoid confusion. This requires a simple function called Offset from the Lookup group, accessed by selecting Insert, Function.

The Offset function allows you to nominate a starting call and then go down by X rows and across by Y columns and return the value (see Figure 2.23). Here the example should start at cell B27 and go down by the

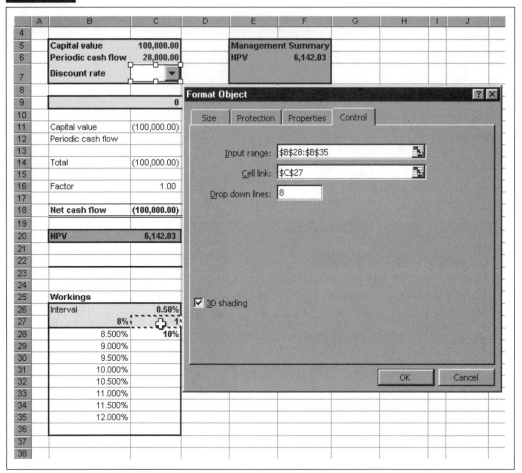

Figure 2.22 **Format control**

number of rows returned by the control. You start at B27 and go down by C27 and no columns (see Figure 2.24). This should return the discount rate to be used in the present value calculations.

The combo box controls the user input and makes it faster to select the individual discount rates (see Figure 2.25). Note that a user could still input data to cells B27, C26 and C27. The combo box runs a macro or routine to update the cell, but does not protect it.

There are other controls in the toolbox that you could use to make the inputs more intuitive. For example, spinners and scrollbars allow you to increment a value by one click and provide an input variable for specifying the click value.

The ScrollBar sheet shows the inclusion of these two controls as an alternative. Here you select an upper and lower value and an incremental value. The solution is slightly more complex since the control does not

Paste function

Figure 2.23

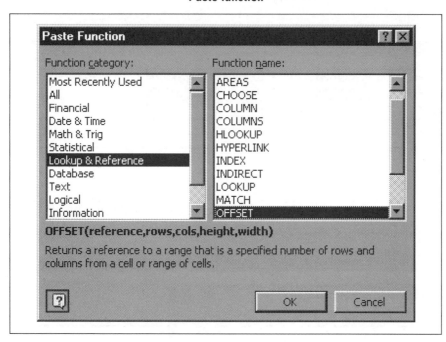

Offset

Figure 2.24

Figure 2.25   **Working combo box**

	A	B	C	D	E	F	G	H	I
		C28	▼	=	=OFFSET(B27,C27,0)				
4									
5		Capital value	100,000.00		Management Summary				
6		Periodic cash flow	28,000.00		NPV	6,142.03			
7		Discount rate	10.00% ▼						
8									
9				0	1	2	3	4	5
10									
11		Capital value	(100,000.00)						
12		Periodic cash flow		28,000.00	28,000.00	28,000.00	28,000.00	28,000.00	
13									
14		Total	(100,000.00)	28,000.00	28,000.00	28,000.00	28,000.00	28,000.00	
15									
16		Factor	1.00	0.91	0.83	0.75	0.68	0.62	
17									
18		Net cash flow	(100,000.00)	25,454.55	23,140.50	21,036.81	19,124.38	17,385.80	
19									
20		NPV	6,142.03						
21									
22									
23									
24									
25		Workings							
26		Interval	0.50%						
27		8%	4						
28		8.50%	10%						
29		9.00%							
30		9.50%							
31		10.00%							
32		10.50%							
33		11.00%							
34		11.50%							
35		12.00%							
36									
37									

accept fractions. You therefore have to calculate the eventual discount rate from the position of the scroll bar.

The scroll bar is set to accept values from 1 to 8 and to increment by one. The cell link is cell C26 and the Offset function in cell C27 uses this index number (see Figure 2.26).

Scroll bar

Figure 2.26

	A	B	C	D	E	F	G	H	I
1									
2		**Present Value**							
3									
4									
5		Capital value	100,000.00			Management Summary			
6		Periodic cash flow	28,000.00			NPV		11,795.88	
7		Select:	◀		▶				
8		Discount rate	8.00%						
9									
10				0	1	2	3	4	5
11									
12		Capital value	(100,000.00)						
13		Periodic cash flow		28,000.00	28,000.00	28,000.00	28,000.00	28,000.00	
14									
15		Total	(100,000.00)	28,000.00	28,000.00	28,000.00	28,000.00	28,000.00	
16									
17		Factor	1.00	0.93	0.86	0.79	0.74	0.68	
18									
19		**Net cash flow**	**(100,000.00)**	**25,925.93**	**24,005.49**	**22,227.30**	**20,580.84**	**19,056.33**	
20									
21		NPV	11,795.88						
22									
23									
24		**Workings**							
25		Interval	0.50%						
26		8%	0						
27		8.50%	8.00%						
28		9.00%							
29		9.50%							
30		10.00%							
31		10.50%							
32		11.00%							
33		11.50%							
34		12.00%							
35									
36									

CONDITIONAL FORMATTING

Conditional formatting allows you to display cells differently depending on the value in the cell. This means fonts, borders and patterns. In this example, it could be useful to introduce a management test to show if the project succeeds or fails and then display the result accordingly (see Figure 2.27).

There is now a new cell C7, which defines the management test requiring a minimum net present value of 7000. The formatting is set using the Format button to pink when the value is greater than or equal to the value in cell C7. The result is shown in Figure 2.28, where, at 9.5 per cent the project achieves the goal.

You can add further formats by clicking on Add and also copy using Edit, Paste Special, Formats.

Figure 2.27	Conditional Formatting

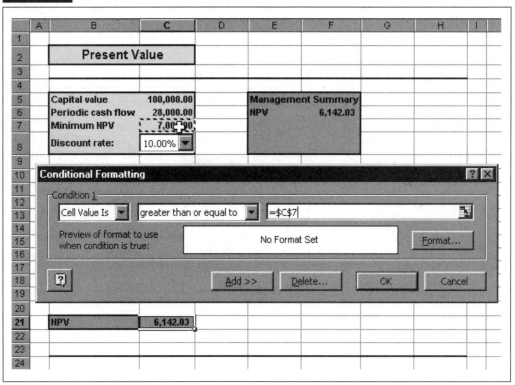

NPV result

Figure 2.28

	A	B	C	D	E	F	G	H	I
1									
2		**Present Value**							
3									
4									
5		Capital value	100,000.00		Management Summary				
6		Periodic cash flow	28,000.00		NPV	7,511.85			
7		Minimum NPV	7,000.00						
8		Discount rate:	9.50%						
9									
10			0	1	2	3	4	5	
11									
12		Capital value	(100,000.00)						
13		Periodic cash flow		28,000.00	28,000.00	28,000.00	28,000.00	28,000.00	
14									
15		Total	(100,000.00)	28,000.00	28,000.00	28,000.00	28,000.00	28,000.00	
16									
17		Factor	1.00	0.91	0.83	0.76	0.70	0.64	
18									
19		Net cash flow	(100,000.00)	25,570.78	23,352.31	21,326.31	19,476.08	17,786.37	
20									
21		NPV	7,511.85						
22									
23									
24									

USE OF FUNCTIONS AND TYPES OF FUNCTIONS

The model already includes the function Offset, but the net present values could more easily by calculated using the NPV (net present value) function. At present, there is code in cells C17 to H19, which means there are potentially 12 mistakes. The goal should be to reduce code in order to reduce the potential for errors. The solution at present is equivalent to using Excel instead of a set of discount tables.

You can use Insert, Function from the Menu Bar or the Standard toolbar and functions are divided into sections for easy reference. Select Financial Functions and scroll down to NPV (see Figure 2.29).

The NPV function discounts outstanding cash flows and so the years one to five are selected. You then add the cash flow at period 0.

```
=NPV(C25,D15:H15)+C15
```

Figure 2.29   **NPV function**

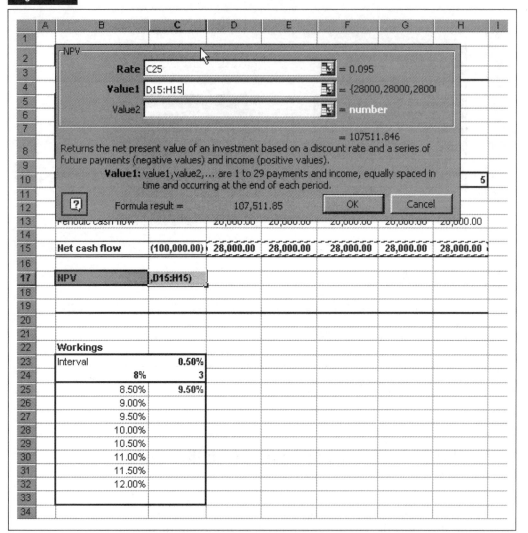

This results in the correct answer of 7511.85 at the discount rate of 9.5 per cent.

Notice the spreadsheet is now much simpler with a reduction in the necessary rows. You can always obtain help on the functions by pressing the Question Mark (see Figure 2.30). Within the Help for the selected function, you can view a listing of alternative functions by selecting See Also.

Function detail

Figure 2.30

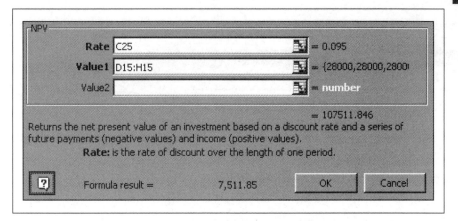

ADD-INS FOR MORE FUNCTIONS

The typical installation of Excel contains the basic functions, but more functions are available in the Analysis Toolpak. For example, NPV assumes that each period contains the same number of days. XNPV allows you to enter dates when the cash flows are received (the Valuation file discussed in Chapter 19 uses this function).

To ensure that you have access to extended functions go to Tools, Add-Ins, Analysis Toolpak. Tick this item and press OK to install it. The Toolpak will then be available every time you open Excel. If it is not available as an add-in, you will need to reinstall Excel using the original Office disks.

The next sheet uses the XNPV function and EDATE, which is a date function that advances the date by multiples of one month at a time (see Figure 2.31). You provide a start date and then the number of months to be advanced. Since the interval is a variable, there is a new control in the inputs area which points towards a set of workings to derive the number of months for the EDATE function in cells D13 to H13.

Again you add the initial cash flow and the result is 7502.58, which compares with the previous answer of 7511.85.

Figure 2.31 **XNPV and EDATE**

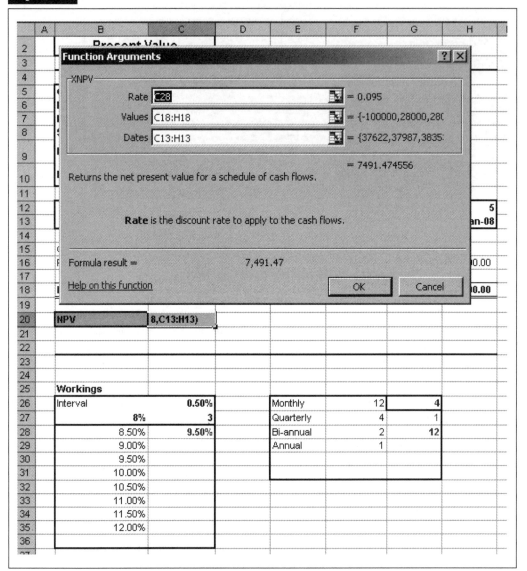

TEXT AND UPDATED LABELS

You could improve the clarity of the model by allowing the labels to update and providing some text on the result. If the net present value is above the limit, then you could have a label informing the user. The Text sheet in the model provides two improvements:

- it shows the discount rate in the label
- it provides feedback on the calculated net present value.

Cell B20 is now an updated label. The Text function converts numbers to text following the number formats. This will display the percentage to two decimal places. The ampersand (&) is used to join or concatenate the text strings.

```
="NPV at "&TEXT(C31,"0.00%")
```

The management feedback uses an IF function to display one text string if the project is above the limit and another if it is below. In order to reduce the code, the IF statement substitutes a zero above or below depending on the net present value.

```
="NPV is "&IF(C20>=C7,"above","below")&" the
limit of "&TEXT(C7,"#,##0")
```

The spreadsheet will now inform the user of the discount rate used and provide a comment of the answer (see Figure 2.32). Excel takes the decision rather than the user having to spend time reviewing the result.

Text labels

Figure 2.32

	A	B	C	D	E	F	G	H
1								
2		**Present Value**						
3								
4								
5		Capital value	100,000.00		Management Summary			
6		Periodic cash flow	28,000.00		NPV at 9.50%		7,491.47	
7		Minimum NPV	7,000.00		NPV is above the limit of 7,000			
8		Start date	1-Jan-03					
9		Interval	Annual ▼					
10		Discount rate:	9.50% ▼					
11								
12			0	1	2	3	4	5
13			1-Jan-03	1-Jan-04	1-Jan-05	1-Jan-06	1-Jan-07	1-Jan-08
14								
15		Capital value	(100,000.00)					
16		Periodic cash flow		28,000.00	28,000.00	28,000.00	28,000.00	28,000.00
17								
18		Net cash flow	(100,000.00)	28,000.00	28,000.00	28,000.00	28,000.00	28,000.00
19								
20		NPV at 9.50%	7,491.47		NPV is above the limit of 7,000			
21								
22								

RECORDING A VERSION NUMBER, AUTHOR, ETC.

As detailed in Chapter 1, there should be some documentation as part of the model. With complex models, it is good practice to record version numbers, author name and contact details together with notes on how the model works. As a model develops over time, you can record the changes between one version and another. This is particularly important if you find a major error. In addition, it means that a version reference is at the top of every sheet that you printed out (see Figure 2.33).

This section could of course run to several pages with diagrams and notes. It is, of course, better to put the notes in the model and you can always hide a sheet by selecting Format, Sheet, Hide.

Figure 2.33   **Documentation**

	A	B	C	D	E	F	G	H
37								
38		Documentation						
39		Version Number	v1.0 1-Jan-2003					
40		Author	Alastair Day					
41		Company	Systematic Finance plc					
42		Contact	Tel: +44 (0)1483 532929					
43								
44		Notes	This is simple net present model designed to show the implementation of					
45			various Excel features on a simple model.					
46								
47								
48								
49								
50								
51								

USING NAMES

Names can make formulas easier to understand: for example rather than using cell C28, you can have PeriodInterestRate. The standard cells above such as Version, Author, etc. would also be better standardized across all your models such that =Version will always insert the version number. The files with this book use several standard names such as Author, Company, Version and Product.

You can use Insert, Name, Define to define names; alternatively, Excel will create multiple names using the labels to one side of the selected cells (see Figures 2.34 and 2.35). This creates the names in the left-hand column (e.g. Start_date).

Create names

Figure 2.34

	A	B	C	D	E	F	G	H
1								
2		**Present Value**						
3							v1.0 1-Jan-2003	
4								
5		Capital value	100,000.00		Management Summary			
6		Periodic cash flow	28,000.00		NPV at 9.50%		7,491.47	
7		Minimum NPV	7,000.00		NPV is above the limit of 7,000			
8		Start date	1-Jan-03					
9		Interval	Annual ▼					
10		Discount rate:	9.50% ▼					
11								
12			0	1	2	3	4	5
13			1-Jan-03	1-Jan-04	1-Jan-05	1-Jan-06	1-Jan-07	1-Jan-08
14								
15		Capital value	(100,000.00)					
16		Periodic cash flow		28,000.00	28,000.00	28,000.00	28,000.00	28,000.00
17								
18		Net cash flow	(100,000.00)	28,000.00	28,000.00	28,000.00	28,000.00	28,000.00
19								
20		NPV at 9.50%	7,491.47		NPV is above the limit of 7,000			
21								
22								
23		Systematic Finance plc : Tel: +44 (0)1483 532929						

Apply names

Figure 2.35

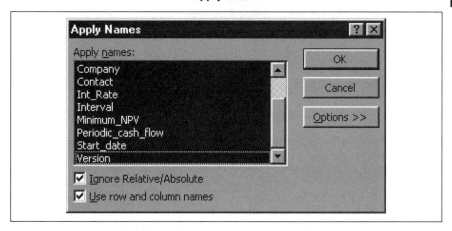

The function is now easier to understand since it refers to the periodic interest rate in cell C20.

```
=XNPV(Int_Rate,C18:H18,C13:H13)
```

If you copy a sheet containing names, then the new sheet will continue to refer to the original sheet. Similarly, if you copy a sheet to a new workbook,

Excel creates a link between the two workbooks. You can always check for links by selecting Edit, Links. If this is the case, you have to remove them manually and reinsert the cell formulas.

PASTING A NAMES TABLE

It is useful to paste a list of names as part of the documentation to provide an audit trail. You select Insert, Name, Paste, Paste List. (See Figure 2.36.)

Figure 2.36   **Names list**

	A	B	C	D	E	F	G	H	I
51		Names List							
52		Annual_Rate	=Names!$C$31						
53		Author	=Names!$C$40						
54		Capital_value	=Names!$C$5						
55		Company	=Names!$C$41						
56		Contact	=Names!$C$42						
57		Int_Rate	=Names!$C$28						
58		Interval	=Names!$G$28						
59		Minimum_NPV	=Names!$C$7						
60		Periodic_cash_flow	=Names!$C$6						
61		Start_date	=Names!$C$8						
62		Version	=Names!$C$39						
63									
64									
65									

COMMENT CELLS

Commenting cells allow notes to be placed against cells to provide background or help the user. Go to Insert Comment or right mouse click on a cell. Enter a text message and then format the font size and colours (see Figures 2.37 and 2.38).

You can control how Comments are viewed using Tools, Options, View. You can turn them off, show the indicator or have the comment permanently visible. In the second case, the cell displays a red triangle at its top right-hand corner. Again, comments can assist in explaining important formulas or telling the user what to do. For example, some people use numbers for percentages and then divide by 100 in code. A comment could inform a user to insert a number rather than a percentage.

Comments

Figure 2.37

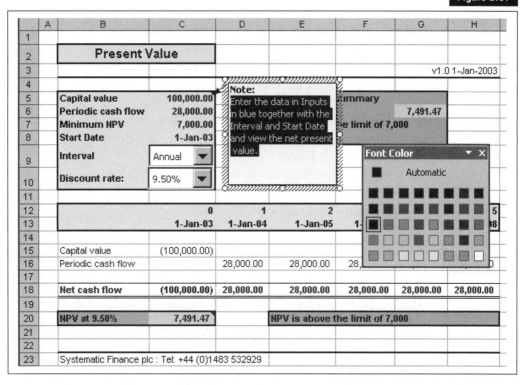

Comments options

Figure 2.38

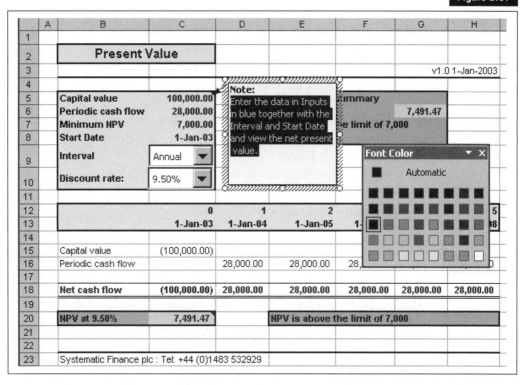

GRAPHICS

Graphics assist in management reporting and showing a user important results. The example now adds a cumulative cash flow and graphs the pattern. You can use the Chart Wizard icon on the Standard toolbar or `Insert Chart`. (See Figure 2.39.)

This is just charting a single series and so a column graph will produce a clear printout. On the second step, click the `Series` rather than the `Data Range` tab. You can then click, `Add Series` to add the name of the series, values and labels (see Figure 2.40).

This will plot the cumulative cash flow values with the dates as the X labels across the chart (see Figure 2.41). The name is also in code as Graphics!$B$20. If you click on Next, the chart title and legend titles are

Figure 2.39	Chart types

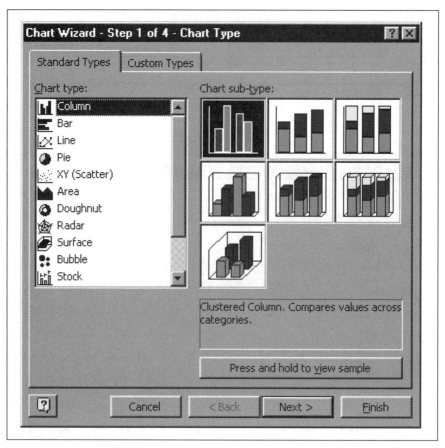

Source data

Figure 2.40

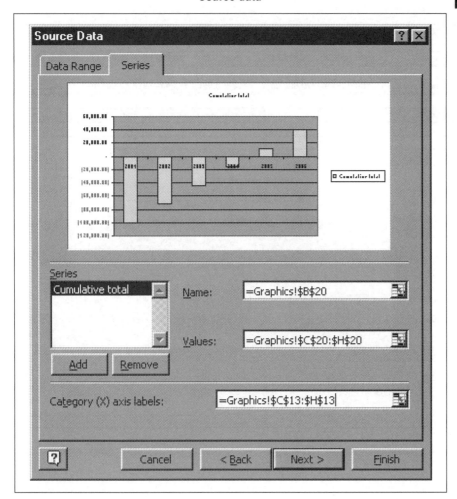

displayed. Excel will not allow you to enter a cell reference against the name, but you can do this when you have finished the Wizard.

If you right click the X axis, it can be formatted so that the tick marks are low as an option in Patterns. The chart title is entered as =Graphics! $B$20 so that it updates itself. This is important since you do not want labels to be 'hard-wired'. The objective is always to reduce the hard coding and allow changes to cascade.

Payback is a non-time value of money method of investment appraisal. Essentially, you check how long it takes to get your money back. Figure 2.41 shows clearly that this will happen in year four.

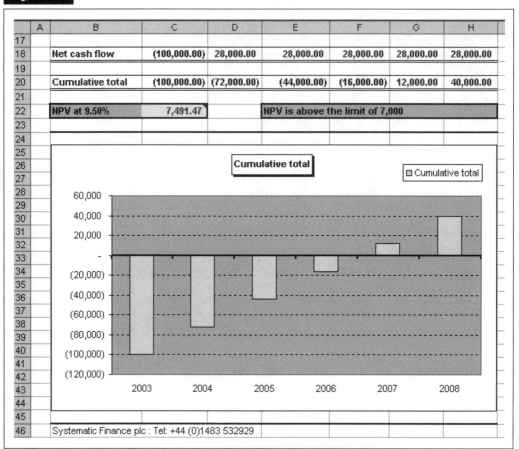

Figure 2.41   **Cumulative chart**

	A	B	C	D	E	F	G	H
17								
18		Net cash flow	(100,000.00)	28,000.00	28,000.00	28,000.00	28,000.00	28,000.00
19								
20		Cumulative total	(100,000.00)	(72,000.00)	(44,000.00)	(16,000.00)	12,000.00	40,000.00
21								
22		NPV at 9.50%	7,491.47		NPV is above the limit of 7,000			

Systematic Finance plc : Tel: +44 (0)1483 532929

DYNAMIC GRAPHS TO PLOT INDIVIDUAL SERIES

A single chart is very useful, but a dynamic graph would allow you to review any of the rows. This is a simple example but this approach would be useful for examining individual lines in a cash flow or company analysis.

The steps are:

- Set up a combo box with the inputs as the labels to the individual lines and a cell link to update (F25).

Dynamic chart

Figure 2.42

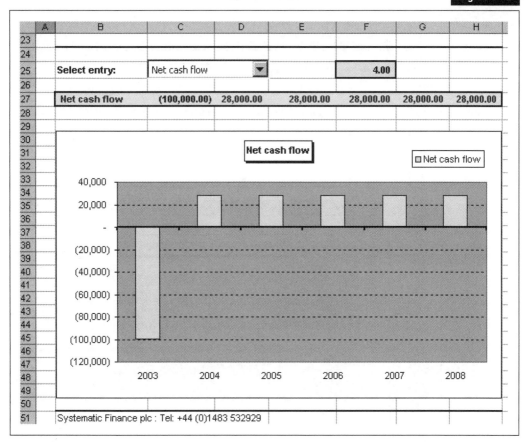

- Use an Offset function to look up the relevant line using the cell link from the control. The Offset function starts from row 14 and moves down by the number in cell F25.

- Point the chart at the look-up lines and ensure that the series and chart names are not hard-coded. The name of the series is cell B27 to ensure that it updates. The formula in cell B27 is:

```
=OFFSET(B14,$F$25,0)
```

Figure 2.42 displays the combo box with each of the available rows.

In the file, there is also a sheet called Dynamic_Graph_Example, which puts together a table of figures, a combo control, an Offset function and a graph to display the results (see Figure 2.43).

Figure 2.43

Dynamic graph

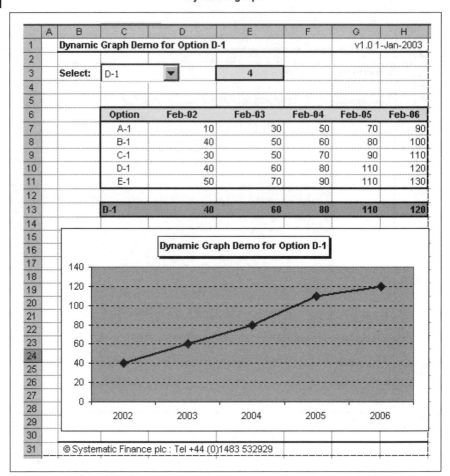

	A	B	C	D	E	F	G	H
1		Dynamic Graph Demo for Option D-1					v1.0 1-Jan-2003	
2								
3		Select:	D-1	▼	4			
4								
5								
6			Option	Feb-02	Feb-03	Feb-04	Feb-05	Feb-06
7			A-1	10	30	50	70	90
8			B-1	40	50	60	80	100
9			C-1	30	50	70	90	110
10			D-1	40	60	80	110	120
11			E-1	50	70	90	110	130
12								
13		D-1		40	60	80	110	120

DATA TABLES

The model so far has produced a single point answer: the capital and cash flows discounted at 9.5 per cent result in a net present value. The model would be more powerful if you could display the net present values for a range of discount rates simultaneously on the same sheet. This can be achieved by the array function Table, which can be found under the toolbar `Data, Table`.

The steps are:

- Set up a grid with an interval as an input.
- Enter the function.
- Graph the results.

The dynamic graph has been moved down on the Data_Tables sheet to make room for the data or sensitivity table (see Figure 2.44). The grid consists of an interval and then a row of discount rates in line 29. The 9.5 per cent is an absolute and is marked as an input. The cells on either side are plus or minus the interval. Cell B30 looks up the answer in cell C22. When complete the data table will show the net present value at each of these interest rates.

The next stage is to highlight the grid area and enter the data table (see Figure 2.45).

Cell C81 in this interim version is the periodic discount rate derived from the combo box. Excel inserts the figures in the grid and the answer of 7502.58 at 9.5 per cent is visible. This shows the sensitivity of the final answer to changes in the discount rate (see Figure 2.46).

Sensitivity table

Figure 2.44

	A	B	C	D	E	F	G	H
1								
2		**Present Value**						
3								v1.0 1-Jan-2003
4								
5		Capital value	100,000.00		Management Summary			
6		Periodic cash flow	28,000.00		NPV at 9.50%		7,491.47	
7		Minimum NPV	7,000.00		NPV is above the limit of 7,000			
8		Start Date	1-Jan-03					
9		Interval	Annual ▼					
10		Discount rate:	9.50% ▼					
11								
12			0	1	2	3	4	5
13			1-Jan-03	1-Jan-04	1-Jan-05	1-Jan-06	1-Jan-07	1-Jan-08
14								
15		Capital value	(100,000.00)					
16		Periodic cash flow		28,000.00	28,000.00	28,000.00	28,000.00	28,000.00
17								
18		Net cash flow	(100,000.00)	28,000.00	28,000.00	28,000.00	28,000.00	28,000.00
19								
20		Cumulative total	(100,000.00)	(72,000.00)	(44,000.00)	(16,000.00)	12,000.00	40,000.00
21								
22		NPV at 9.50%	7,491.47		NPV is above the limit of 7,000			
23								
24								
25		Sensitivity Table for the Discount Rate						
26								
27		Interval	0.50%					
28								
29			8.50%	9.00%	9.50%	10.00%	10.50%	11.00%
30		7,491.47	10,319.09	8,890.59	7,491.47	6,120.96	4,778.30	3,462.74
31		Variance to 7,491	(2,827.61)	(1,399.11)	-	1,370.51	2,713.18	4,028.73

Figure 2.45   **Table function**

	A	B	C	D	E	F	G	H
11								
12			**0**	**1**	**2**	**3**	**4**	**5**
13			**1-Jan-03**	**1-Jan-04**	**1-Jan-05**	**1-Jan-06**	**1-Jan-07**	**1-Jan-08**
14								
15		Capital value	(100,000.00)					
16		Periodic cash flow		28,000.00	28,000.00	28,000.00	28,000.00	28,000.00
17								
18		**Net cash flow**	**(100,000.00)**	**28,000.00**	**28,000.00**	**28,000.00**	**28,000.00**	**28,000.00**
19								
20		**Cumulative total**	**(100,000.00)**	**(72,000.00)**				0,000.00
21								
22		**NPV at 9.50%**	**7,491.47**					
23								
24								
25		**Sensitivity Table for the Discount Rate**						
26								
27		**Interval**	**0.50%**					
28								
29			8.50%	9.00%	9.50%	10.00%	10.50%	11.00%
30		7,491.47	10,319.09	8,890.59	7,491.47	6,120.96	4,778.30	3,462.74
31		Variance to 7,491	(2,827.61)	(1,399.11)	-	1,370.51	2,713.18	4,028.73

Dialog box overlay:
Table | ? X
Row input cell: [ ]
Column input cell: [ ]
OK   Cancel

Table is an array function, which means that you cannot alter individual cells within the group. If you try to alter any of cells C31 to H31, you will get an error message. Similarly, if you copy a data table from one sheet to another, only the values will be pasted. You have to highlight the grid and reinput the table on the new sheet.

Rather than create a further chart, this example uses the existing 'dynamic graph' and increases the inputs to line 31. Line 31 is simply a variance to the original answer. The Offset function merely requires the rows to index down by and so no other programming changes are necessary.

Data tables can be single-dimensional, as above, or two-dimensional. There are often two dominant variables in a model and this approach allows you to 'flex' the variables. It is important to use a grid to set out the table and best not to hard code the interval. This means that you can always change the interval quickly and see on any printouts the interval used. In addition, it is best practice to input the current value for the variable in the middle so you can see the values on either side. Some applications with the book then use a macro to update the input values on the table by copying down the values from the inputs area.

Composite table

Figure 2.46

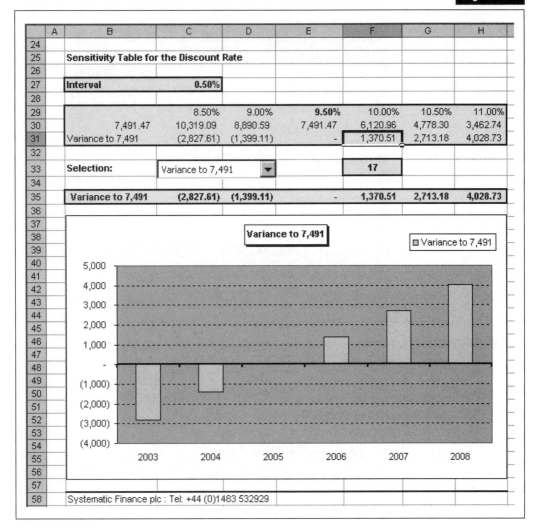

SCENARIOS

If there were several versions of this simple example project, producing multiple spreadsheets would be wasteful and potentially introduce errors. Similar spreadsheets tend to diverge over time and be more difficult to maintain. Scenarios provide the facility to 'remember' inputs so that you can load them at any time. As an added bonus, Excel will produce a management report based on the scenarios.

Scenarios are accessed using `Tools, Scenarios, Add` (see Figure 2.47). There are saved cases on the Scenarios sheet.

Figure 2.47

Add scenario

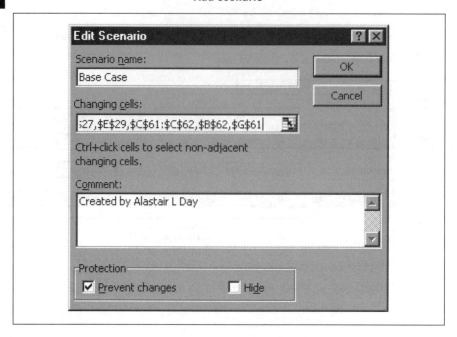

You can select multiple cells by separating them with a comma (or a semi-colon in continental Europe). When you have selected them, Excel allows you to review the values in each of the cells before saving them. Press Show to display the scenario.

There are further examples on the sheet which vary only the capital value and periodic cash flow. If you press Tools, Scenarios, Summary and select cells C22 and E22 as the result cells, Excel produces the management report shown in Figure 2.48.

It is always best to start from a Base Case and vary these inputs rather than developing further scenarios. Here Worst Case and Best Case vary only two cells from the original scenario. It is therefore clearer what exactly changes from the initial estimate.

Only one cell is named on this sheet: this is Scenarios!$C$22, which shows as a name in line 17 rather than a cell reference. This is a static or values only report, which will not change if the underlying values change. If the model changes, you have to run the report again. It also acts like an audit trail since you could print this out and keep it in a file to show what inputs produce the range of results.

Scenario report

Figure 2.48

		Current Values:	Base Case	Worst Case	Best Case
Scenario Summary					
Changing Cells:					
	$C$5	100,000.00	100,000.00	103,000.00	99,000.00
	$C$6	28,000.00	28,000.00	27,000.00	28,500.00
	$C$7	7,000.00	7,000.00	7,000.00	7,000.00
	$C$8	1-Jan-03	1-Jan-01	1-Jan-03	1-Jan-03
	$C$27	0.50%	0.50%	0.50%	0.50%
	$E$29	9.50%	9.50%	9.50%	9.50%
	$C$61	0.50%	0.50%	0.50%	0.50%
	$C$62	3	3	3	3
	$B$62	8%	8%	8%	8%
	$G$61	4	4	4	4
Result Cells:					
	NPV	7,491.47	7,491.47	7,491.47	7,491.47
	Limit	NPV is above the limit of 7,000	NPV is above the limit of 7,000	NPV is above the limit of 7,000	NPV is above the limit of 7,000

Notes: Current Values column represents values of changing cells at time Scenario Summary Report was created. Changing cells for each scenario are highlighted in gray.

SPREADSHEET AUDITING

There are a number of techniques which can be used separately or together to check the inputs and calculations in a model. It is of course important that any model is free of errors which could arise from:

- technical design, such as high-level analysis of ideas or principals;
- conceptual errors, for example, flaws in logic, rationale or mechanisms;
- user errors, such as individual cell coding errors or overwritten cells;
- compounded errors, such as errors on errors, especially in distributed models.

The methods described below include:

- manual review
- show formulas (also known as formula auditing mode)
- audit toolbar
- pattern matching to ensure consistency

- FIND for hidden errors
- known test data
- data to all inputs
- chart – known patterns
- add-ins such as PopTools or Spreadsheet Detective described at www.financial-models.com.

Using some of the design techniques earlier in the chapter reduces the opportunity for errors, for example:

- design method in segregating inputs and calculations;
- splitting out workings;
- keeping individual cell coding as simple as possible;
- self-checking, such as making sure a balance sheet adds up on both sides.

A manual review often reveals simple errors and other features such as the spell checker will show up text errors. Other methods involve other features in Excel.

| Figure 2.49 | | Show formulas | |

	A	B	C	D
1				
2		Present Value		
3				
4				
5		Capital value	100000	
6		Periodic cash flow	28000	
7		Minimum NPV	7000	
8		Start Date	37622	
9		Interval	Annual	
10		Discount rate:	9.50%	
11				
12			0	1
13			=C8	=EDATE(C13,$G$63)
14				
15		=B5	=-C5	
16		=B6		=$C$6
17				
18		Net cash flow	=SUM(C15:C17)	=SUM(D15:D17)
19				
20		Cumulative total	=C18	=C20+D18
21				
22		="NPV at "&TEXT(C66,"0.00%")	=XNPV(C63,C18:H18,C13:H13)	
23				
24				

View formulas

This function is called Tools, Formula Auditing, Formula Auditing Mode on later versions of Excel. Viewing formulas shows the formulas and if there are constant values these cells will not change (see Figure 2.49). You can select View Formulas at Tools, Options, View. Alternatively you can press Cntrl and ' to toggle between the two views. This is a good check on the quality of the underlying sheet and will reveal overwritten cells or inconsistencies.

Using the above example, the errors again become apparent. The errors in cells G10 and H10 show up against cell F10, which contains the correct code.

Audit toolbar

The audit toolbar can be displayed by pressing on the menu-bar Tools, Auditing, Show Auditing Toolbar. The example shown in Figure 2.50 is in the data table sheet, which traces the derivation of the net present value.

You can trace precedents and dependants for a cell (see Figure 2.51). The

Auditing toolbar

Figure 2.50

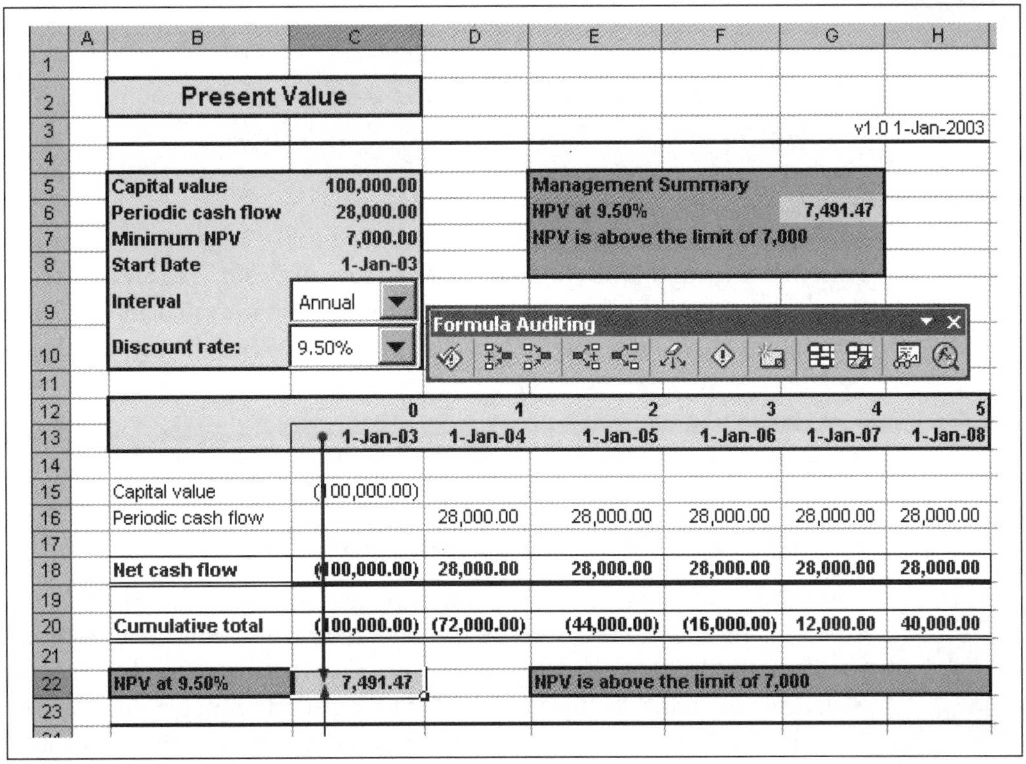

Figure 2.51　　　　　　　**Dependants and precedents**

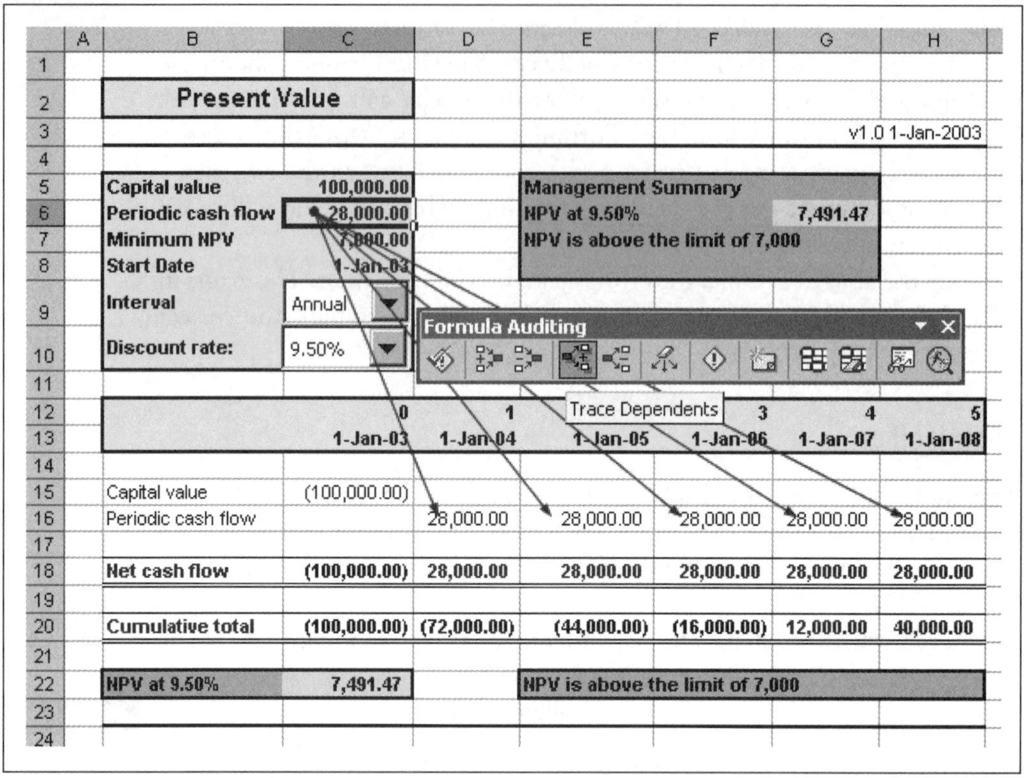

NPV at cell C22 is derived from the dates, cash flows and discount rate. The arrow from below refers to the frequency of the periods.

Pattern matching

Pattern matching allows you to search for constants, formulas, arrays, etc. In the above example, this would highlight the errors in the calculations. Select cell B15 to H20 and access Edit, Go To, Special to display this dialog box (see Figure 2.52). Formula errors are shown in Figure 2.53.

If you highlight formulas, Excel shows them. You would expect to see formulas in the cash flows rather than anything hard coded from above.

Use known data with an entry to every input cell

You need to enter data to every entry cell to ensure that the results are as expected. In an accounts spreading model, you could enter data to every possible cell and make sure that the balance sheet balances and that the cash flow agrees with the change in cash. With the current example, there is data in each of the inputs, but it is always a good idea to see what happens if

Edit go to special

Figure 2.52

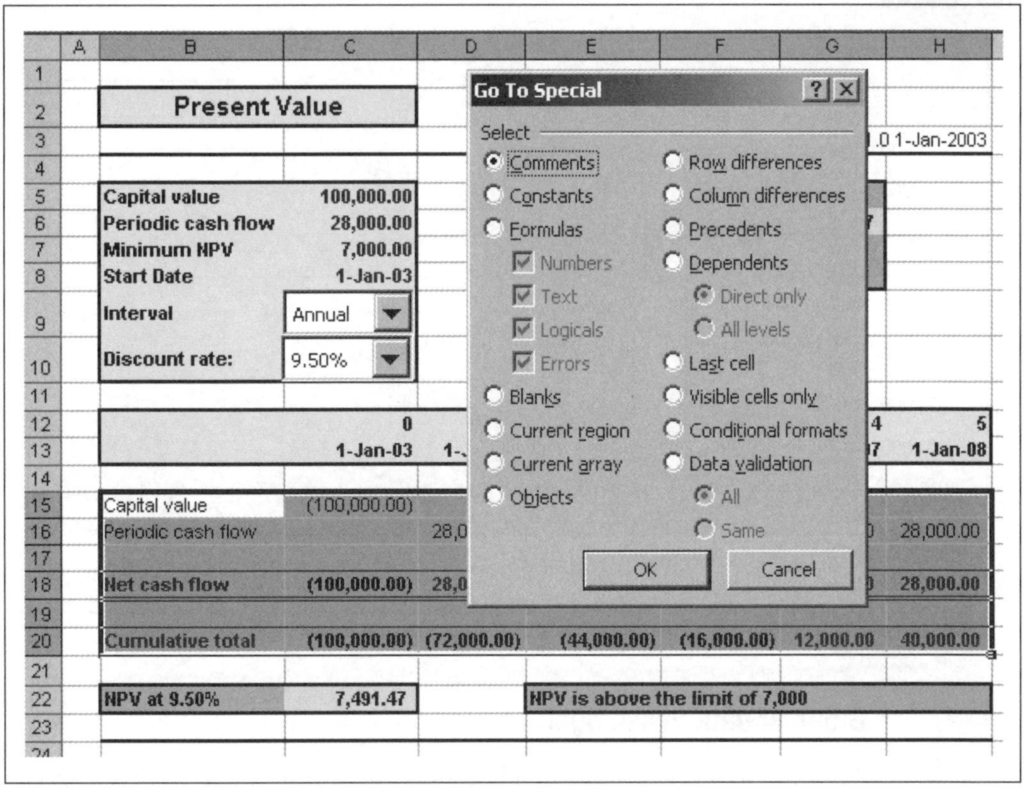

Formula errors

Figure 2.53

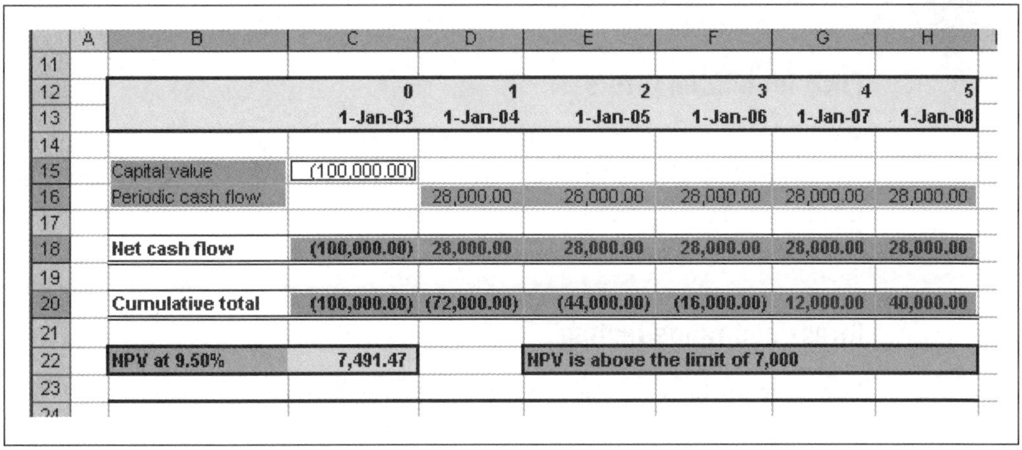

unusual data were entered. Users can always be relied on not to follow instructions. Techniques such as data validation obviously help in avoiding 'rubbish in, rubbish out'.

Figure 2.54 **Graph check**

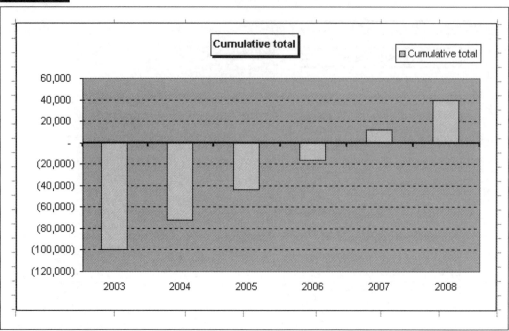

Graph or data 'looks right'

The cumulative cash flow graph is smooth with no kinks as expected (see Figure 2.54). If the series were curved then this could point to an error in the calculations. People are better in assessing pictures than grids of numbers and can 'see' errors more quickly.

FIND for hidden errors

You can use Edit, Find to look for errors such as N/A or Div/0 since errors are not always obvious. You could also do the same by choosing Edit, Go To, Special, Formulas, Errors. While you should find errors by other means, this is useful for checking entire sheets.

Stress and range testing

You need to be sure that unusual inputs will not cause errors or answers which appear to be correct, but which are incorrect. Users are easily upset by a page of errors, which they have to audit. There are a number of things to look for:

- Extremes in range of inputs. This can be controlled through validation or using controls to limit the range of inputs.

- Test the likely range of results to make sure that the model can display them. For example a column should be able to display the potential range of numbers.
- Negative numbers where positive numbers are expected.
- Text in place of numbers and vice versa.
- Large or small numbers to test the number of decimal places required.
- Decimals in place of integers to ensure validation and use by continental European versions of Excel.
- Numbers in place of decimals.
- Dates in wrong order (31/12/00, 12/31/00) to test for US and other date formats.
- Blank inputs and checks for subsequent errors in formulas. The function ISBLANK can help to identify problems and suppress errors.
- Zero inputs to correct #Div/0 errors. This can be rectified by ISERROR functions or IF statements such as: =IF(Income!J10<>0,(Income!J 24/Income!J10)*100,0)

SUMMARY

This chapter reviews a distinct design method for spreadsheet applications. Models for distribution or use by third parties require a rigorous and disciplined approach and this chapter suggests a number of points for good design and a list of useful features. The application discussed in the chapter progresses using a number of features to show the importance of design. You will note that the quality of presentation and the management information produced progressively improves. Finally, there are a number of auditing techniques to ensure consistency in the design and coding of the model. It is important that models can be checked and these techniques provide a framework for auditing.

3

Risk and uncertainty

File: FT4_03.xls

INTRODUCTION

The methodology in the previous chapter suggests developing a single-point model and segregating areas of a workbook into:

- inputs
- calculations
- outputs.

Correct design ensures that all inputs are visible and all have been modelled. This means you can change the inputs and note the immediate effect on the output. The next aspect to address is sensitivity to a change of key variables.

The simple model derives a single result and thereby limits the analysis. The result neither provides information on the potential variance nor backs up decision making. In business modelling, risk is always present since forecasts are inherently inaccurate. You can sub-divide risk into two components:

- risk
- uncertainty.

RISK

In corporate finance, you need to be able to explore the potential upsides and downsides, and to understand how the anticipated result could vary. With any project, you want to understand how likely you are to fail to reach a minimum target or alternatively the effect on the result of important variables.

Risk can be defined as the chance of making a loss; this could be making a loss on an asset sale or the possibility of machine failure. Alternatively, you could describe a risk in quantitative terms such as a 30 per cent possibility of a loss. In finance, you are normally more concerned with downsides since any upside always seems a remote possibility. In order to control risk, you first have to be able to describe and measure it and then decide if the anticipated return is worth the risk. Whilst some individuals may differ in the perceptions, it is usually assumed that decision makers are rational and weigh up the potential pros and cons.

The Capital Asset Pricing Model (CAPM) is a useful example of risk and return. Portfolio theory shows how the risk in a portfolio can be mitigated by diversification based on standard deviation and correlation. The CAPM formula deals with individual risk and the beta score is a measure of individual stock risk against the market. The formula is:

$$Return = R_f + \beta * R_p$$
$$R_f = Risk\ free\ rate$$
$$\beta = Measure\ of\ risk$$
$$R_p = Risk\ premium$$

This formula defines the return that investors should demand and is defined by the return on the share against the market index. Investors can deposit funds at the risk-free rate or in a diversified portfolio at the market rate. This means that there is a basic return to be gained with no chance of a loss. The premium is therefore a measure of the extra return to be derived from taking the market risk. In the example below, a share with beta of one produces a result of 10 per cent.

$$R_f = 5\%$$
$$\beta = 1.0$$
$$R_p = 5\%$$
$$Return = 5\% + (1 \times 5\%) = 10\%$$

The variance is therefore the variability against the market: a beta of more than one indicates a greater than market risk and the opposite is true of a beta of less than one.

Figure 3.1 shows the prices for ten shares over a five-year period against an index. The values are converted into logarithms and plotted against each other. The beta is therefore the correlation of the share's return with the

Figure 3.1

Share (stock) prices

No.	Month	Index	AAA	BBB	CCC	DDD	EEE	FFF	GGG	HHH	III	JJJ
0	Jan-98	1,153.1	356.2	362.0	180.5	256.8	498.0	729.3	175.3	187.1	171.8	50.1
1	Feb-98	1,202.1	379.8	368.8	185.8	247.2	540.0	757.4	184.3	206.2	175.8	50.5
2	Mar-98	1,146.6	349.8	367.3	176.3	246.3	528.0	757.9	190.3	201.5	176.8	55.9
3	Apr-98	1,208.8	370.0	375.3	185.3	257.7	547.0	785.9	185.3	224.2	176.8	60.9
4	May-98	887.3	299.5	286.3	128.8	222.5	340.0	530.1	140.3	162.7	120.8	39.0
5	Jun-98	796.3	266.4	258.8	120.3	214.9	335.0	471.1	121.3	142.7	105.8	40.6
6	Jul-98	870.2	281.1	287.3	143.8	206.4	382.0	529.8	129.3	164.1	112.8	40.6
7	Aug-98	915.8	298.9	293.8	143.8	219.7	392.0	526.2	138.3	176.8	135.8	39.7
8	Sep-98	908.1	302.6	292.3	145.3	243.4	391.0	528.6	139.3	169.4	154.1	40.6
9	Oct-98	896.8	291.5	278.8	145.3	260.6	370.0	479.4	126.3	157.4	151.8	39.0
10	Nov-98	928.2	275.9	266.3	155.3	275.8	369.0	482.4	129.3	164.7	158.8	57.3

v1.0 1-Jan-2003

β estimation

Figure 3.2

	No.	Month	Index	Index Returns	Selection:	AAA	AAA Returns
69							
70							
71	0	Jan-98	1,153.10			356.18	
72	1	Feb-98	1,202.10	0.042		379.77	0.064
73	2	Mar-98	1,146.60	(0.047)		349.75	(0.082)
74	3	Apr-98	1,208.80	0.053		369.97	0.056
75	4	May-98	887.33	(0.309)		299.51	(0.211)
76	5	Jun-98	796.31	(0.108)		266.42	(0.117)
77	6	Jul-98	870.22	0.089		281.12	0.054
78	7	Aug-98	915.84	0.051		298.89	0.061
79	8	Sep-98	908.08	(0.009)		302.57	0.012
80	9	Oct-98	896.75	(0.013)		291.54	(0.037)
81	10	Nov-98	928.19	0.034		275.91	(0.055)

market. The formula is cell E73 (see Figure 3.2) is:

```
= LN(D73/D72)
```

Columns D and H can then be plotted as a scatter graph with a trend line through the series to illustrate the slope (see Figure 3.3).

For company AAA, the slope of the trend line from the function SLOPE, is 1.06. It is highly correlated with market movements. The other shares in this example portfolio show a range of variance with the index. The beta table is shown in Figure 3.4.

The beta is therefore a historic score of risk, which shows that some shares in this collection have been more volatile than the market and therefore investors should demand a higher return. Risk can therefore be measured and, in theory, the past should broadly equal the future.

The model sheet is a simple real estate model. This is a buy for let model where you invest in property and receive rental income. The first section shows all the variables where the cost inputs are percentages of the purchase price (see Figure 3.5).

There are a significant number of variables which can be multiplied out to produce returns and profits. These include both the one-off costs of purchasing and refurbishing a property, but also the on-going costs of maintaining and letting it. Since the owners' funds will be leveraged through a form of loan or mortgage, the cost of borrowing is a significant cost to be placed against the gross rental yield. In addition, the percentage voids or rent-free periods could also be a significant factor. Lastly, property may afford the benefit of capital growth over and above the rental income.

The objective of the model is to calculate the projected annual income and the owners' return on the equity investment. The second profit measure

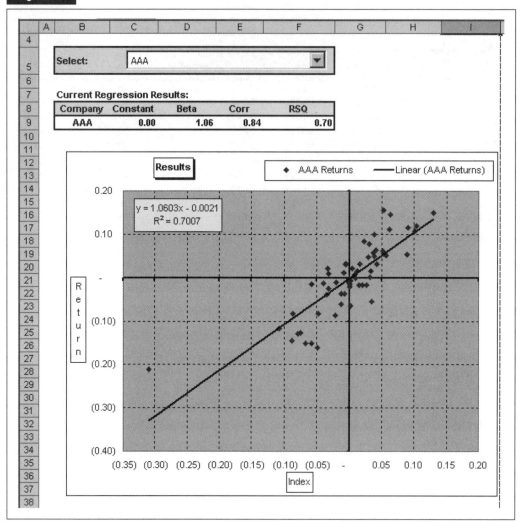

Figure 3.3 β **scatter chart**

includes the benefit of capital growth and there is an overall yield measure from income and capital.

The answer is a yield on income of 2.65 per cent or 10.10 per cent including capital growth (see Figure 3.6). Whilst there are financial and non-financial risks, property rental has inherent risks which could significantly lower the yield. For example:

- maintenance and other regular costs;
- assumed rental per month and the state of the rental market in the area;
- capital growth on the property;
- voids defined as the number of days when the property lies empty;
- interest rate to be paid on loans.

β table

Figure 3.4

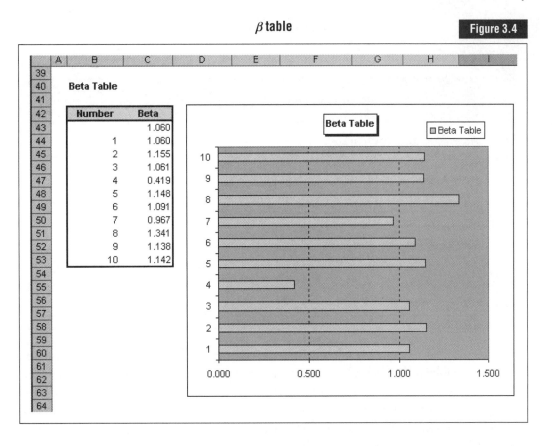

Inputs

Figure 3.5

	Inputs	Costs
Purchase Price	100,000.00	(100,000.00)
Stamp Duty / Tax	1.00	(1,000.00)
Other Costs	0.75	(750.00)
Reburbishment Costs	2.00	(2,000.00)
Letting Fees	1.175	(1,175.00)
Building Insurance	0.300	(300.00)
Gas Safety	0.050	(50.00)
Inventory	0.060	(60.00)
Maintenance	0.500	(500.00)
Assumed Rental per Month	666.67	
Capital Growth	4.00	
Voids %	10.00	
Mortgage Period (yrs)	25.00	
Interest Rate %	5.51	(307.34)
Mortgage Percentage %	50.00	(2,731.07)

Figure 3.6   Estate schedule

	Cost	Rental %	Gross Yield	Annual Rental	Annual Costs	Mortgage Per Annum	Net Rental Income
Property Cost	(100,000.00)						
Initial Costs	(3,750.00)	0.6667	8.0000	8,000.04	(2,085.00)	(3,688.11)	2,226.93
Total Investment	(103,750.00)						
Plus Mortgage	50,000.00						
Voids				(800.00)			
Net Income				**7,200.04**	**(2,085.00)**	**(3,688.11)**	**1,426.93**

	Net	Yield %
Net Investment	**(53,750.00)**	
Net Letting Income	**1,426.93**	**2.65**
Capital Growth	**4,000.00**	
Total Income	**5,426.93**	**10.10**

The model only allows single-point entry and the inputs are best guesses. Given the cyclical nature of the property market, it is fair to say that there are significant risks or alternatively variables not fully modelled. For example, interest rates could rise and rents fall in a depressed economy. This could make it hard to find suitable tenants and therefore voids could rise. These factors together would then significantly impact on the overall yield.

Figure 3.7   Probability

	Return	A	B	Variance	Expected A	Expected B
1.00	(50.00)	-	-	-	-	-
2.00	(40.00)	-	5.00	(5.00)	-	(200.00)
3.00	(30.00)	-	5.00	(5.00)	-	(150.00)
4.00	(20.00)	5.00	10.00	(5.00)	(100.00)	(200.00)
5.00	(10.00)	10.00	10.00	-	(100.00)	(100.00)
6.00	-	20.00	10.00	10.00	-	-
7.00	10.00	30.00	10.00	20.00	300.00	100.00
8.00	20.00	20.00	10.00	10.00	400.00	200.00
9.00	30.00	10.00	10.00	-	300.00	300.00
10.00	40.00	5.00	15.00	(10.00)	200.00	600.00
11.00	50.00	-	15.00	(15.00)	-	750.00
Total		**100.00**	**100.00**	**-**	**1,000.00**	**1,300.00**

Expected Return A	**1,000.00**	
Expected Return B	**1,300.00**	
Variance	**(300.00)**	

Based on historic experience, it could be possible to plot both the average and variability in these factors in order to quantify the chance of a significant loss.

Risk is also allied to theories of probability. Supposing that an investor could invest in shares and over one year the expected probabilities and returns are shown in Figure 3.7.

Figure 3.7 shows the possible returns in column C and the expected probabilities for shares A and B in columns D and E. Columns G and H are the probability return for shares A and B multiplied by the return. Share B suggests a much wider range of returns than A and the higher adjusted return is a profit of 1300. Share A possesses a narrower range and therefore appears to present the less risk.

The range shows up clearly on a probability chart, where option B displays a flat distribution whereas A is a more normal bell curve distribution (see Figure 3.8). The profit or loss at each point is set out in Figure 3.9 and this shows the possibility of a significant loss on share B.

The return can therefore be expressed as an amount and a range or probability. There is always the option of not investing and the perception of risk may be important. In most situations, the outcomes are not completely clear and perception of risk is affected by subjective factors: for example, it depends on how you perceive losses or gains. In addition, the concept of risk adversity may not always be correct. Some individuals are risk takers while others will always opt for safety.

Probabilities

Figure 3.8

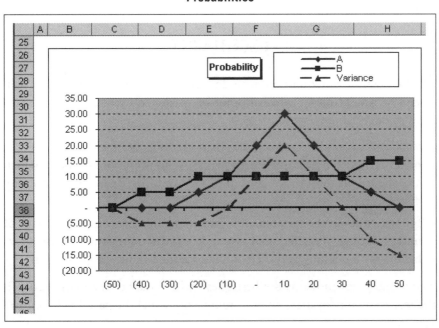

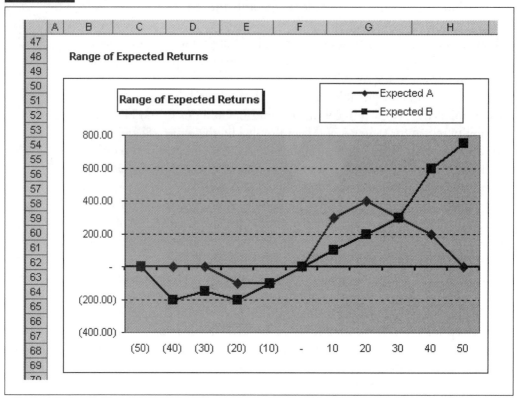

Figure 3.9 — Range of expected outcomes

UNCERTAINTY

All the possible outcomes on a model cannot be predicted and there will always be uncertainty – which cannot be predicted exactly. There are two areas of uncertainty:

- Random or unexpected events that are outside the control of the organization: for example, earthquakes or multiple occurrences, which are the result of chance and do not conform easily to probability distributions.

- Ignorance about the variables or inputs to the model arising from a lack of understanding. Further analysis and information could reveal more factors for modelling and thereby increase the validity of the system.

The single-point model is the best guess, which may or may not occur. In the real estate model above the future may not equal the past due to unforeseen events.

RESPONSE TO RISK

A generic model for responding to risk is:

■ Identify sources of risk in a project or organization (see Figure 3.10), in particular the financial risks where an organization may be more skilled in dealing with this form of operational risk.

■ Describe risks and how they impact on the organization using some form of probability impact diagram. The questions could be: why might it happen? and what would lessen the impact?

■ Analyze and understand relative importance which could include risk mapping.

■ Mitigate and control, through structuring or other changes to operations, to increase the controllable elements.

■ Accept or reject residual or incontrollable risk.

■ In a credit or project model you would need to price accordingly to ensure a 'correct' risk/return ratio.

■ Build up a database, monitor and learn for the future.

Risk response   Figure 3.10

Risk Response

Identify sources of risk

Describe risks

Analyze and understand relative importance

Mitigate and control

Accept or reject residual or uncontrollable risk

Price accordingly

Monitor and learn

Risk mapping should reveal the potential severity and possible frequency with which potential problems could occur. The response on a project could be:

■ Increase the size of the project as the original plan could be too cautious.

■ Do nothing, since the potential cost of dealing with risk outweighs the perceived benefits.

- Collect more data on the problem to better understand the potential downsides.
- Add a contingency to the planning and thereby allow for risk.
- Reduce or build in an abandonment option as a less risky approach.
- Share the risk with a partner or contractor in return for lesser fees.
- Transfer risk through an insurance contract.
- Eliminate risks by redesigning the plan to reduce uncertainty.
- Cancel project or financing since the potential losses are perceived to be too high or uncontrollable.

The above list could give an organization the opportunity to examine the basis for trying to control risk and later chapters explore credit, project and other scenarios.

METHODS

The discussion of risk and uncertainty above shows that a single-point answer may not reveal the prospect of loss inherent in any business decision. The methods for dealing with risk can be summarized as follows:

- sensitivity analysis using data tables and charts;
- scenario analysis and scenario manager;
- manual scenarios using functions;
- decision trees;
- simulation.

Figure 3.11   **Sensitivity table**

	A	B	C	D	E	F	G	H	I
38									
39		Sensitivity Table to Voids % Across and Mortgage Percentage % Down							
40									
41		Interval Across	2.50						
42		Interval Down	15.00						
43									
44		2.65	2.50	5.00	7.50	**10.00**	12.50	15.00	17.50
45		5.00	5.41	5.21	5.01	4.81	4.60	4.40	4.20
46		20.00	5.06	4.82	4.58	4.35	4.11	3.87	3.63
47		35.00	4.56	4.27	3.98	3.68	3.39	3.10	2.81
48		**50.00**	3.77	3.40	3.03	**2.65**	2.28	1.91	1.54
49		65.00	2.38	1.86	1.34	0.83	0.31	(0.21)	(0.72)
50		80.00	(0.78)	(1.62)	(2.47)	(3.31)	(4.15)	(4.99)	(5.84)
51		95.00	(14.77)	(17.06)	(19.34)	(21.63)	(23.91)	(26.20)	(28.48)
52									

Sensitivity analysis

This technique uses data tables in Excel as one- or two-dimensional grids to show multiple answers on the same sheet. In the real estate example, the percentage of voids is plotted against the degree of leverage. This helps to show the effect on the yield before capital growth.

Figure 3.11 illustrates the losses increasing with leverage as the percentage of voids increases. Tables of numbers are not easy to interpret and therefore a chart always helps to show the degree of change. Figure 3.12 demonstrates the gross and net yield and the line series is the middle row in the table.

Sensitivity chart

Figure 3.12

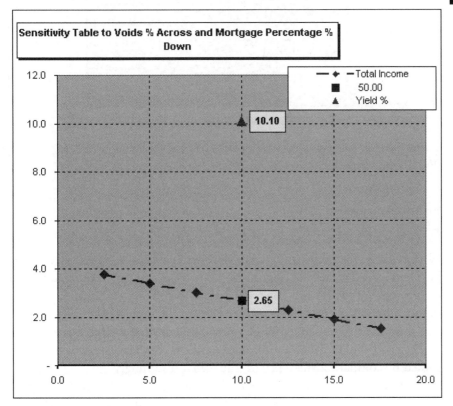

Scenarios

Scenario planning can be a powerful tool for 'thinking the unthinkable'. There are always different views of the future and history reminds us that the future cannot be fully explained or controlled. There are many techniques

Figure 3.13   Scenario Manager

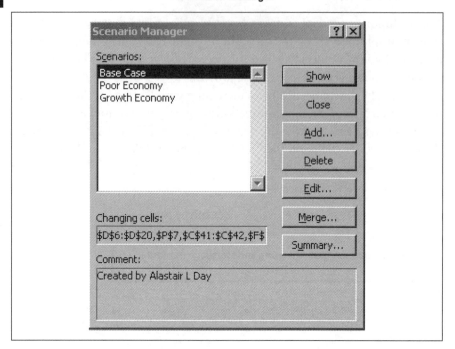

for gaining ideas such as:

■ brain storming;

■ mental mapping;

■ panels of experts such as in the Delphi technique.

Within Excel, the built-in Scenario Manager allows for different views to be held and loaded at will (see Figure 3.13). You can use it to save an audit trail of previous inputs or as a considered view to different futures. Saving the inputs means that you can always get back to the same answer. This can be useful in ensuring the integrity of a previously created model. For example, you can test the model at a future date and ensure that it has not been corrupted by comparing answers with the scenario summary.

There are three saved scenarios in the model to show the effect of a poor or growth economy on the result. This focuses the decision makers' attention on the possibility of falling rents, lowered occupancy and increased borrowing costs. The Summary button produces a management report of the inputs and outputs.

The report provides a concise report and in this case demonstrates how an adverse economy removes any possibility of a positive return on the investment (see Figure 3.14).

Figure 3.15 confirms the findings from the scenario report.

Scenario report

Figure 3.14

Scenario Summary				
	Current Values:	Base Case	Poor Economy	Growth Economy
Changing Cells:				
Purchase_Price	100,000.00	100,000.00	100,000.00	100,000.00
Stamp_Duty___Tax	1.00	1.00	1.00	1.00
Other_Costs	0.75	0.75	0.75	0.75
Reburbishment_Costs	2.00	2.00	2.00	2.00
Letting_Fees	1.175	1.175	1.175	1.175
Building_Insurance	0.300	0.300	0.300	0.300
Gas_Safety	0.050	0.050	0.050	0.050
Inventory	0.060	0.060	0.060	0.060
Maintenance	0.500	0.500	0.500	0.500
Assumed_Rental_per_Month	675.00	666.67	600.00	675.00
Capital_Growth	5.00	4.00	2.00	5.00
Voids	7.50	10.00	20.00	7.50
Mortgage_Period__yrs	25.00	25.00	25.00	25.00
Interest_Rate	5.50	5.51	7.00	5.50
Mortgage_Percentage	50.00	50.00	50.00	50.00
$P$7	0	0	0	0
$C$41	2.50	2.50	2.50	2.50
$C$42	15.00	15.00	15.00	15.00
$F$44	7.50	10.00	20.00	7.50
$B$48	50.00	50.00	50.00	50.00
Result Cells:				
Net_Invested	(53,750.00)	(53,750.00)	(53,750.00)	(53,750.00)
Net_Income	1,722.98	1,426.93	(565.68)	1,722.98
Yield	3.21	2.65	(1.05)	3.21
Income_after_Growth	6,722.98	5,426.93	1,434.32	6,722.98
Net_Yield	12.51	10.10	2.67	12.51

Notes: Current Values column represents values of changing cells at
time Scenario Summary Report was created. Changing cells for each
scenario are highlighted in gray.

Scenario comparison

Figure 3.15

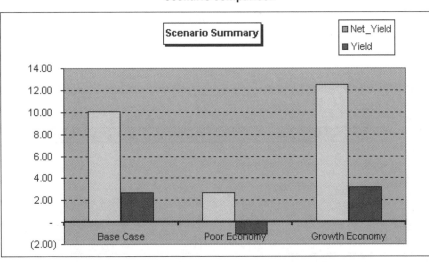

Manual scenarios

You can also use functions such as OFFSET, CHOOSE or LOOKUP to load different sets of variables. The advantage is the visibility of all the variables. The example on the Manual_Scenarios sheet uses a combo box to generate the index number in cell H5 (see Figure 3.16). Row 16 contains OFFSET functions to look up the rows above based on the index number.

Decision trees

Decision trees are used to select the best course of action in situations where you face uncertainty and many business decisions fall into this category. You face a complex problem that seems to make it impossible to choose the right option. Although you do not know the exact outcome, you may have some information about the range of possible outcomes and how likely each is to occur. This information can be used to select the option that is most likely to yield favourable results. Modelling provides the framework to consider the quantitative factors and uses Bayes theorem to apply the probabilities.

Simulation

Scenario analysis allows you to keep different views of the world on the same sheet. You can load, for example, base case, optimistic and pessimistic. While this offers advantages over a single answer, there are times when there are significant elements of risk to be captured in a model. In the real estate model, there are single inputs such as voids or the mortgage percentage for deriving the expected yields.

For each variable you could probably define a minimum, maximum and most likely, as in a triangular distribution. If there are ten variables, then

Figure 3.16

Manual scenarios

	A	B	C	D	E	F	G	H
4								
5		Choose	Scenario 2			▼		2
6								
7		Factor:	Inflation					
8								
9			1	2	3	4	5	6
10		Scenario 1	5.00	5.00	5.00	5.00	5.00	5.00
11		Scenario 2	7.00	7.00	7.00	7.00	7.00	7.00
12		Scenario 3	9.00	9.00	9.00	9.00	9.00	9.00
13		Scenario 4	11.00	11.00	11.00	11.00	11.00	11.00
14		Scenario 5	13.00	13.00	13.00	13.00	13.00	13.00
15								
16		**Choose**	**7.00**	**7.00**	**7.00**	**7.00**	**7.00**	**7.00**

there are 10^3 possible states and therefore it quickly becomes impossible to model all possibilities. Another example is a bonds portfolio of 100 instruments where there could be eight possible credit states for each bond on expiry of a time period. Again there could be 100^8 possible combinations on expiry.

In a simulation model, you specify the probability distribution of each uncertain variable. The model generates random numbers within the distribution and produces a large number of possible scenarios. The resulting histogram of results provides information on the mean score, standard deviation, percentiles and other statistics. Simulation is dealt with in more detail in Chapter 5.

SUMMARY

The presence of risk in business underlines the need for initial analysis and identification of all key variables in a business problem. The problem should drive the modelling and not the other way around. Objectives should be clear to allow for risk identification, assessment, mitigation and inclusion. Simple techniques include tables and scenarios for identifying a range of possible outcomes.

Project finance

File: FT4_04.xls

INTRODUCTION

This chapter introduces a project finance model as an example of the design method outlined in Chapter 2 and an illustration of the range of risks associated with financing a project. The text below outlines the risk process in financing and then provides a generic model for projects. The aim is to show the process of identifying the sources of risk and the modelling approach as a complete model. The eventual model is complete with all the elements of a finished model and aims to illustrate both the range of risks and also the modelling approach including all the possible variables.

Project finance is the creation of a separate entity for a project that can stand apart from the sole business of the sponsor. The brief could be to design, construct and operate, for example, a power station or infrastructure improvement. Generally, the future cash flows can be forecasted and used as security for the project financing. The objectives are:

- to establish a vehicle to receive capital in the form of equity and debt;
- to expend the funds on constructing assets;
- to generate a revenue stream to pay back the loans; and
- to provide an acceptable return to the equity participants and demonstrate the security in the project to debt participants.

REQUIREMENTS

The difference between project finance and a traditional loan is that the former depends on the ability of the project to generate sufficient funds for loan repayment. Usually the loans are without recourse to the sponsor's balance sheet. In a traditional loan the borrower is responsible for repayments, whereas the project vehicle is 'ring fenced' from other assets from the sponsors.

Therefore, project finance is a means of raising finance, which seeks to bring together specialist parties and allocate risk and reward in accordance with the level of each participant's involvement. Financial engineering and sensible structuring seeks to allocate the potential gains and losses between the parties. Funders need to examine carefully the sources of risk since there is no diversification of risk as there would be when a company undertakes a range of projects. In addition, projects are typically sizeable and perhaps too large for one participant to accept all the risk. The key elements are as follows:

Figure 4.1

Basic project structure

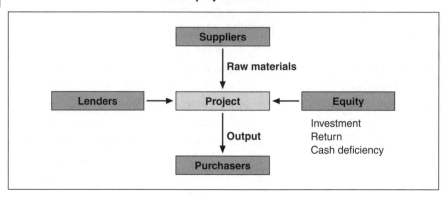

- a stand-alone vehicle to hold all the contracts and manage the project;
- long-term contracts to purchase outputs to act a security for debt;
- contracts for the design, construction and operation of project assets;
- a market for the output (e.g. electricity from a power station and road tolls from a road construction);
- mechanisms and covenants for injecting further funds in the event of future financial problems.

The basic project structure is shown in Figure 4.1.

Whilst a company seeking a loan can show the bank an operating history and annual reports, a project plan can only point to future profitability and cash flow. The funds are required today in anticipation of positive cash flows in the future based on use of the assets. There are a number of feasibility factors to take into account, for example:

- technology and implementation of technical processes;
- economic factors to allow a project to generate sufficient cash flow and there may be factors such as political upheavals which cannot be anticipated;
- availability of raw materials and other inputs together with effective management.

ADVANTAGES

Project financing arrangements usually include mutual interests in structuring over and above separate financing for allocating risk and reward. Advantages include:

- pooling of benefits between the interested parties;
- means of spreading risk among specialists in particular fields (e.g. financiers, constructors and operators);

- a fixed life arrangement releasing excess cash flow to equity participants after debt servicing has been covered, which could allow higher returns than from traditional financing;
- the project vehicle manages the cash flows to lenders, equity participants and sponsors to ensure that debt providers are paid directly from project flows without recourse to a stand-alone company;
- increased debt capacity and increased gearing possible by securing the projected cash flows;
- lower cost of capital than traditional finance due to increased leverage and risk premiums;
- economies of scale greater than two corporations acting separately;
- contractual arrangements for resolving disputes and potentially lower legal costs.

RISKS

Figure 4.2 summarizes the sources of risk in an example project.

Project risks

Figure 4.2

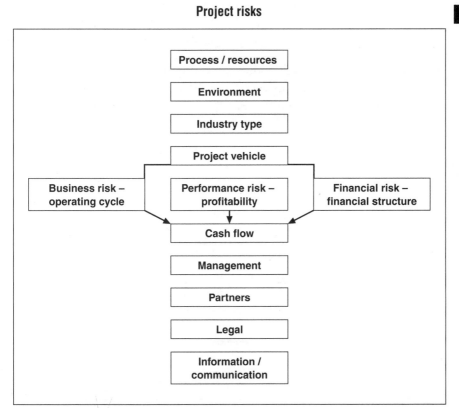

The methodology is initially to describe risks in order to analyze and then mitigate the risk through structuring and other methods. This list details some of the elements to be modelled, which are in effect the key elements of credit analysis:

- Environment and macro factors are those that an organization cannot directly control. A simple model is the STEEPV model (see Figure 4.3). In a long-term project shifts in politics, taxation or other factors can have profound effects on demand and cash flow. These factors are a source of uncertainty:
  - social and lifestyle developments that affect demand and costs;
  - technological changes, where an industrial process can be rendered expensive or unsustainable in the face of advances in technology.
- Economic and activity cycles, which affect future demand for goods and services and the availability of raw materials.
- Environmental factors especially for power and oil and gas projects. This is important during the project's life and demands are made upon the operators to clean up sites on expiry of the project.
- Political climate and support through changes of government both at home and in any country where the project operates (e.g. changes in tax methods, rates of corporate tax and environmental legislation).
- Values and other 'soft' factors, which develop over time. Each decade exhibits certain values such as the 'green 1990s'.

- Industry type, since each industry exhibit different risk factors in its ability to insulate itself against future change. A road scheme and an industrial plant require a different approach and demand for product can vary over time.

Figure 4.3   **STEEPV**

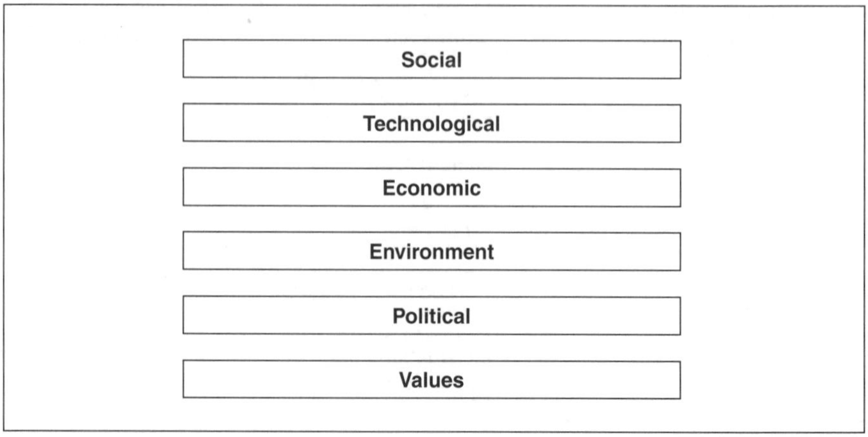

Social

Technological

Economic

Environment

Political

Values

- Choice of project vehicle could be important. There are advantages to limited companies, unlimited and limited partnerships, joint interest ownership or an off-balance-sheet vehicle. Each method has tax, accounting and legal consequences. The elements are:
  - Business risk is efficiency in the operating cycle. Ratios such as debtor, creditor or inventory days demonstrate the measure of management control over working capital. It is obviously important that a project can generate cash in order to service the loans.
  - Performance risk means profitability and margin such as gross and net profit margins. Profit is dependent on accounting standards and conventions and therefore it is important to review accounting policies, such as the depreciation period for assets. For example, long depreciation periods enhance earnings in the early stages. Other return ratios combine the balance sheet and the income statement, such as the return on equity, return on assets or return on investment.
  - Financial risk emanates from the financial structure and the level of debt to equity. Since interest has to be paid on debt, whereas dividends can be suspended, higher leverage brings more financial risk. Similarly, a company needs working capital and the structure of the balance sheet should provide for both short- and long-term capital.
- Cash flow should be evident if business, performance and financial risk are controlled. A company producing profits should also produce cash. It is also important that there is both volume and a lack of volatility in cash flow in order to meet commitments.

Sample ratios are set out in Figure 4.4, which lists analysis ratios for each of the factors above.

Other factors are less easy to quantify, especially over time, but nevertheless these factors have to be considered for their impact on the overall plan:

- Management makes all the strategic decisions rather than the banks. In a structured finance transaction, depth of management is important and must have all the necessary skills to deliver on the covenants. There is, of course, the truism that managements rather than companies fail.
- Partners may also provide future instability given that many projects last for ten or 20 years. In a cogeneration scheme, there are sponsors, construction companies and other specialists, banks, equity investors, raw material suppliers and customers for the generated power. The cash flows are only as sound as the partners' ability to manage all the processes.
- Legal considerations are always a factor across national borders and therefore the documentation should confirm the understanding of all parties and deal with all ambiguities in order to reduce the latitude for interpretation. The contracts must not only be in place, but also be capable of

Figure 4.4

Ratios

Line	Year	2005 1	2006 2	2007 3
	Core Ratios			
R-10	Return on Sales (NPAT/Sales %)	1.28	7.04	11.74
R-11	Asset Turnover (Sales / Total Assets)	0.68	0.85	1.03
R-12	Asset Leverage (Total Assets/Equity)	2.37	2.21	1.99
R-13	Return on Equity (NPAT/Equity %)	2.06	13.27	24.18
	Profitability			
R-17	Gross Profit / Sales (%)	57.05	56.04	55.29
R-18	Net Operating Profit / Sales (%)	8.70	15.61	20.78
R-19	Profit before Tax / Sales (%)	1.83	10.06	16.77
R-20	Profit after Tax / Sales	0.87	6.01	12.14
R-21	Return on Capital Employed (ROCE)	6.96	16.17	27.86
R-22	Return on Invested Capital (ROIC)	6.09	12.00	18.51
R-23	Return on Assets (ROA)	5.93	13.32	21.48
	Operating Efficiency			
R-27	Inventory Days	-	1.00	2.00
R-28	Trade Receivables (Debtor) Days	91.25	91.25	91.25
R-29	Creditors Days	110.46	101.44	94.94
R-30	Funding Gap Debtors+Inventory-Creditors	19.21	9.19	1.69
	Financial Structure			
R-34	Current Ratio	1.24	1.37	1.37
R-35	Quick Ratio (Acid Test)	1.24	1.37	1.37
R-36	Working Capital (Thousands)	4.15	7.49	9.60
R-37	Gross Gearing (%)	115.59	97.79	75.29
R-38	Net Gearing (%)	112.56	91.67	64.29
R-39	Gearing - Debt to Equity Ratio	50.36	45.03	34.92
R-40	Solvency	126.59	281.27	518.26
R-41	Debt Service Ratio	3.12	1.86	2.27
	Cashflow Ratios			
R-45	EBITDA / Sales (%)	22.01	26.70	30.22
R-46	Net Operating Cash Flow/Sales	2.59	14.04	17.52
R-47	Free Cash Flow/Sales	9.46	19.59	21.53

enforcement through the courts. This is especially true of acceptance, cost and negligence clauses.

- Information, knowledge management and communication are becoming more important as a separate area, since most companies depend on management information systems and their ability to leverage knowledge into competitive advantage. This is also true of a project, especially in cost control and gaining a deep understanding of the underlying business.

Analysis of the above factors should reveal the list of factors which will eventually become inputs for a financial model. The aim is to investigate, as thoroughly as possible, all the variables to save revisions to the financial model at a later stage. Key considerations are:

- the significant sources of risk and uncertainty associated with each stage of an investment;
- the causes of each risk;
- any links between factors and how risks could be grouped for classification and analysis.

Figure 4.5 shows the response sequence.

Response

Figure 4.5

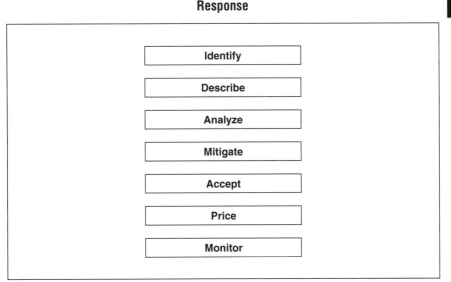

Only risks that are identified can be evaluated and then managed. Risk matrices are helpful in assessing the impact and probability and highlighting factors for subsequent sensitivity analysis (see Figure 4.6). Whilst there are a large number of inputs and rule to the model, there are usually a small number of input variables, which are clearly significant. For example, what happens to financial ratios and benefits of the project if construction were delayed by six months? Experience from earlier projects can help to outline difficulties and areas of concern.

Figure 4.6	Impact–likelihood 4 × 4 matrix

Figure 4.6 Impact–likelihood 4 × 4 matrix

(Matrix)

Impact axis (vertical): Very High, High, Medium, Low

Likelihood axis (horizontal): Low, Medium, High, Very High

- Very High Impact / Low Likelihood (top-left cell)
- Very High Impact / Very High Likelihood (top-right cell)
- Low Impact / Low Likelihood (bottom-left cell)
- Low Impact / Very High Likelihood (bottom-right cell)

RISK ANALYSIS

Analysis of significant risks can take qualitative and quantitative forms using some of these methods:

- likelihood or frequency of occurrence per year or 100 years as a way of expressing likelihood;
- potential consequence (with respect to one or more of the factors or related cash flows) if the risk occurs;
- most likely frequency of the risk occurring during the whole lifetime of the project;
- possible timing of the risk's impact;
- risk scores.

It is sometimes beneficial to allot a score for the likelihood and one for the impact and then combine the figures as a score. Risk with the highest scores can then be identified by these two factors and selected for further analysis. Combinations of risks can be evaluated together as one factor. Examples of occurrences are:

- once and for all chance of occurrence;
- average rate of occurrence over the duration of the project;

- variable rate of occurrence;
- extent of occurrence (e.g. per kilometre of road);
- probability of each of a series of possible values or ranges of values over the life of the investment (i.e. a probability distribution).

RISK MITIGATION

Project modelling assists with the risk analysis by providing a closed system for evaluating the inputs and likely outputs. All the costs and likely revenues can be calculated and then 'stress-tested' to see if the results are acceptable. Example outputs are:

- net present value (NPV);
- internal rate of return or modified internal rate of return;
- payback or discounted payback;
- cover ratios on the funding to ensure that there are sufficient funds to repay debts;
- maximum borrowing and other financial covenants;
- maximum possible tariff or optimum tariff required to cover debt and produce returns.

There are various phases to any project through construction, commissioning, operation and closure, and with long-term cash flows the level of error increases over time. Risk mitigation could include a number of techniques such as:

- insurance;
- risk sharing through partnerships;
- structuring;
- financial engineering.

The above discussion seeks to demonstrate the degree of complexity in a project model and the risk faced at each stage of the process. The next section outlines the Excel model.

FINANCIAL MODEL

The file, FT4_04, is an example feasibility model which brings together the main variables in a project with the objective of providing two key results. The model contains a construction schedule to be funded through debt equity and then repayments against a forecast revenue and cost structure. Investors need to be certain of a return on their investment while bankers need reassurance that loans can be repaid in full and on time. The audience is therefore a range of stakeholders with different agendas and varied risk appetites and the model needs to flexible enough to incorporate all the variables so that their contribution can be tested. By performing stress or sensitivity analysis, the model should reveal more information on the sources of risk and uncertainty, and assist with the structuring of the equity and debt injection.

It is assumed that analysis has been carried out and reveals areas for further research which are:

- plant completion date and the time required to rise to peak production;
- interest costs and loan structure, where interest rates are higher than planned;
- equity/debt gearing percentage;
- cost of construction rising in local currency;
- contingencies and possible overruns in construction and other costs adding to the strain on cash and the loans to be serviced, especially in the early stages, thereby reducing the cash available to investors;
- tax rates and retrospective changes in the nature and timing of tax payments;
- other costs such as management fees;
- production volumes and selling prices failing to meet initial expectations;
- costs of raw materials altering drastically due to economic shock or times of political instability;
- overhead costs rising above planned levels;
- escalators and inflation rates over the period reducing the selling price in real terms.

The model needs to be able to incorporate all these factors and store a number of individual cases. The organization must develop a number of individual scenarios to be considered and tested rather than adopt a solitary view of the future. Experience shows that macro factors increase in importance over time together with the possibility of seemingly random events. Therefore the cases have to encompass both a poor and a more positive economic outlook. The result of each case will be a cash flow with related financial statements and ratio analysis in order to assess:

- NPV of the project at the risk adjusted weighted average cost of capital or a nominated hurdle rate;

- internal rate of return to investors;
- debt service capacity of the project.

The organization of the model naturally splits into a number of sheets or areas. This makes it easier for co-workers and other users to understand and will make maintenance easier in the future. Adding more schedules will not require a fundamental redesign of the underlying workbook. The schedules are:

- menu;
- control area to look up individual scenarios from input sheets;
- input sheets for construction, timing, production, costs, contingencies and all the other variables;
- financial schedules – income statement and balance sheet;
- analysis – cash flow, ratios and sensitivity;
- management analysis – dynamic chart for line-by-line examination;
- management summary – annual summary and single-page report;
- explanation, user help and notes.

Figure 4.7 shows a model structure.

Model structure   Figure 4.7

Menu	Menu sheet - macro driven
Control / Inputs	Inputs and assumptions
Inputs – Scenarios	Individual scenarios
Production Scenarios	Production scenarios
Construction	Capital expenditure
Borrowing	Loan and equity requirement
Project_Output	Quantity, revenue and costs
Income_Statement	Profit and loss
Balance_Sheet	Balance sheet
Cash flow	Derived FRS1 cash flow
Dividend_Cash flow	
Ratios	Annual ratio analysis
Sensitivity	WACC calculations
	Sensitivity tables and charts
Management_Analysis	Dynamic charts for any line on any schedule
Schedule	Data only - do not delete
Management_Summary	Single page flash report
Annual_Summary	Summary of cash flows for each year

The only inputs allowed are on the Control, Inputs and Sensitivity sheets and these are always marked in blue on the screen. The model is based on the App_Template and follows exactly the same style and design method (see Figure 4.8). This includes:

- use of colour – green for headings and totals, red for negative numbers, black for positive numbers;
- formats such as the use of a dash for zero;
- borders to break up sections of the schedule and highlight totals and answers;

Figure 4.8   **Layout**

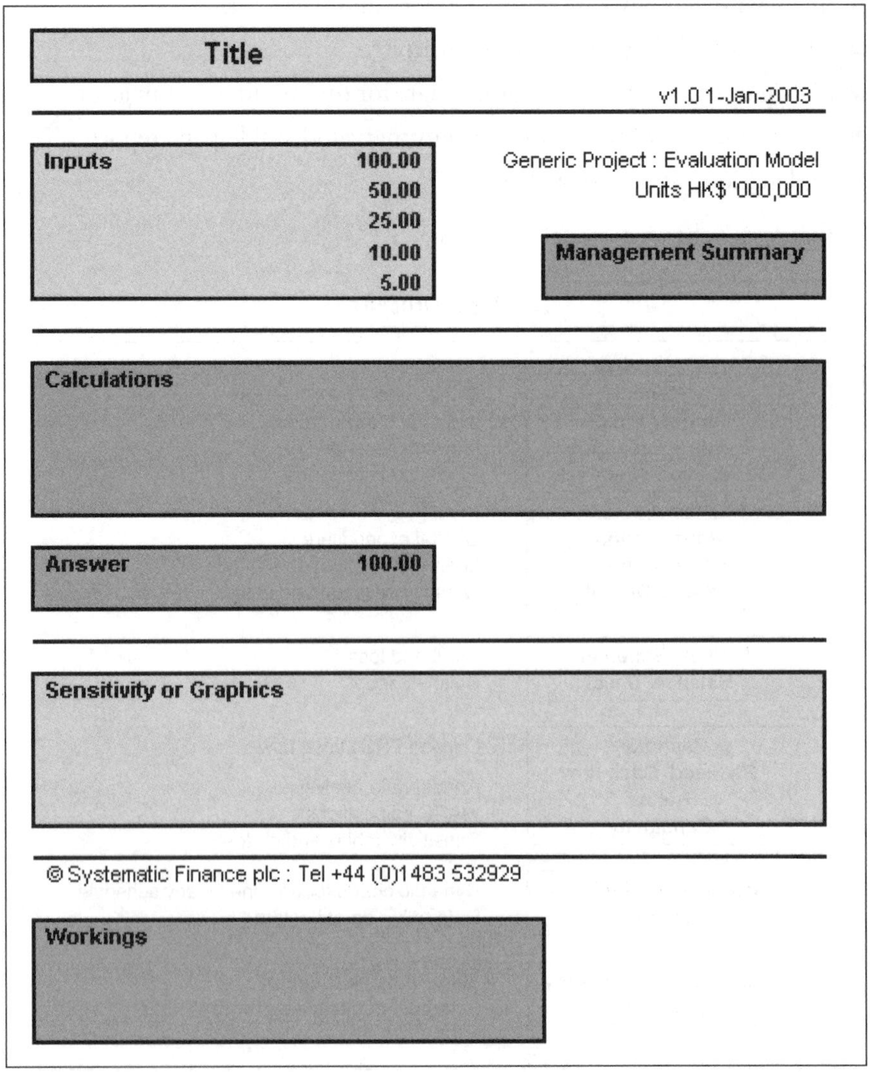

Title

v1.0 1-Jan-2003

Inputs   100.00   Generic Project : Evaluation Model
              50.00   Units HK$ '000,000
              25.00
              10.00   Management Summary
               5.00

Calculations

Answer   100.00

Sensitivity or Graphics

© Systematic Finance plc : Tel +44 (0)1483 532929

Workings

■ version numbers, units and project title in the same positions on each schedule.

INPUTS

It is important to adopt a consistent style for spreadsheet models and all the models in this book follow the same pattern. This makes them easier to understand and faster to develop with fewer errors. The menus sheet below includes a combo control and assigned macro to access any sheet on the list. This is called GetSheetNames, which loops through and updates the list of sheets starting at row 50 and then selects the sheet number from the combo box. Excel uses index numbers internally so that Worksheets(1) is the first sheet in the workbook. A full list of macros is given on the Macro sheet as part of the documentation.

```
Sub GetSheetNames()

Dim Number, Counter, SheetName(25)
Dim IndexNumber

On Error GoTo Error:

Application.Calculation = xlCalculationManual

Application.ScreenUpdating = False    'Turn off
screen updating
Worksheets(1).Select    'Select first sheet -
always the menu
Range("B51:B69") = ""    'Zero existing list

Range("B50").Select    'Start at the top of the
list
Number = ActiveWorkbook.Sheets.Count    'Count
number of sheets in book

For Counter = 1 To Number    'Loop through each
sheet
SheetName(Counter) = Worksheets(Counter).Name
'Put in the name of the sheet

ActiveCell.Offset(1, 0).Range("A1").Select
ActiveCell.FormulaR1C1 = Worksheets(Counter).Name
```

```
Next Counter

Error:
Range("A2").Select
On Error Resume Next
IndexNumber = Range("C50")   'Access the sheet
number you selected
Sheets(IndexNumber).Select
Range("A2").Select
Application.ScreenUpdating = True   'Turn on
screen updating

Application.Calculation = xlAutomatic

End Sub
```

Figure 4.9 shows a project menu. The menu also contains a number of standard inputs such as the name of the application and the author. Again these are standard names that are used on all workbooks developed by the author.

Version	= Menu!$C$15
Product	=Menu!$C$6
Author	=Menu!$C$7
Company	=Menu!$C$8
Telephone	=Menu!$C$9
Fax	=Menu!$C$10
Email	=Menu!$C$11
Web	=Menu!$C$12
Objective	=Menu!$C$14
Contact	=Menu!$B$28

There are a large number of inputs for this model in order to provide future flexibility:

- Basic inputs – project name, revision, dates, currency, units (millions, thousands, etc.).
- Funding costs, period, fees and degree of leverage (debt to equity split). Since the model will produce the cash available to debt and equity, the degree of leverage may be important in increasing the NPV of the project.
- Escalators for future costs and revenues since prices are expected to rise.
- Predicted products, output quantities and sale price per unit.
- Costs for materials and establishment divided up into individual costs.
- Capital expenditure split into construction and subsidiary costs together

Project menu

Figure 4.9

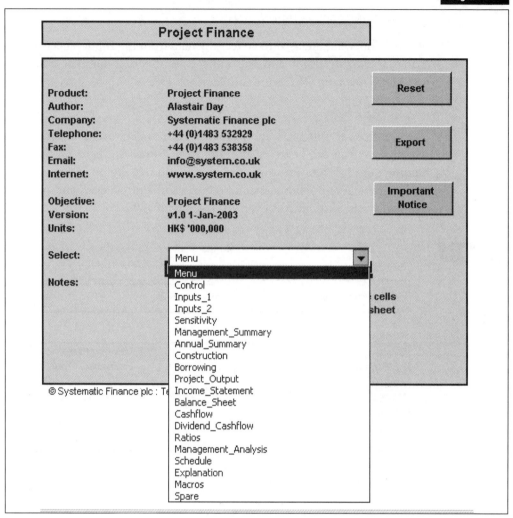

with potential cost overruns and an option to include or discard. There are also inputs for post-completion capital expenditure.

- Cash and other starting balances for the balance sheet and cash flow. These would normally remain at zero.

The Control sheet uses a combo box at the top to look up information on the Inputs_1 and the Inputs_2 sheets which hold up to ten scenarios. This means that the individual scenarios are always visible. Whilst you can use the Scenario Manager in Excel, this method is often used on project models for the individuals cases. The control workings are at the bottom on Inputs_1 and the cell link is named Scenario_No. The data is derived from the cell inputs across the top entered by the user and looked up using the TRANSPOSE array function. The formula is as below and entered as an array using Control, Shift and Enter together.

{=TRANSPOSE($D$9:$M$9)}

OFFSET functions are used to collect the data from the Inputs sheets with a changing starting point and the same column offset number from the named cell Scenario_No. For example in cell D8:

=OFFSET(Inputs_1!C8,0,Scenario_No)

The Control sheet incorporates problems such as delays and contingencies so that the effects can be tested at a later stage. Similarly, there is a choice of funding out of cash or using an annuity method (see Figure 4.10).

The construction table uses combo boxes for contingencies and provides totals with and without cost overruns (see Figure 4.11).

| Figure 4.10 | Inputs |

| Select Scenario: | Evaluation Model 1 ▼ |

Key Inputs & Results

Client	Generic Project
Reference	Evaluation Model 1
Start Date	1-Jan-03
Company Year End	31-Dec-03
Years to Operation	2.0 years
Currency	HK$
Units	Millions

Rates

Interest Rate Loans	10.00%
Debt Funding (% of total)	50.0%
Dividend Payout	50.0%
Project Delay (% of Yr up to 1 year)	0.0%
Equipment Life (8-12 years)	10.0 years
Corporate Tax	30.0%
Management Fees	5.00%

Loan Repayment Method

% Cash Flow Dedication	Cash	50.0%
Annuity	Annuity	10.0 years
Number of Years	Years	10.0 years
CAPEX Percentage in First Year		75.0%
Loan Repayment Method		Cash 50.0% ▼
Selected		Cash
Cash Flow Dedication to Servicing Loan		50%

Expenditure

Figure 4.11

Capital Expenditure/Construction

Item	Amount	Contingency 20.0%	Total
Property, Plant & Equipment	50.00	No ▼	50.00
Construction Costs	25.00	No ▼	25.00
Infrastructure	10.00	No ▼	10.00
Legal Costs	0.50	No ▼	0.50
Establishment Costs	0.50	No ▼	0.50
Pre-Completion Capex Over/Under Run	20.0%		
Total Capital Cost - No Increase	86.00		
Total Capital Cost with Contingency	86.00		

It is important to be able to review answers on an input sheet so that you do not have to tab to the other end of the model every time you change an entry. This summary table provides the main return numbers from the cash flow (see Figure 4.12). There are also minimum and maximum rules for return and gearing and the model uses an IF statement and conditional formatting to show up the answer.

The formula in K16 is =IF(J16<I16,"Fail","Pass") and column J uses MAX or MIN functions to select a case for cover, gearing and NPV.

Inputs_1 sheet is set out in columns to mirror the first page of the Control sheet whereas Inputs_2 sheet is in rows to accommodate the extra expenditure during the operating period (see Figure 4.13).

Summary

Figure 4.12

Results: Leveraged IRRs

			Equity NPV after Tax	
Equity Div before Tax	R20	183.2%	10% S32	98.5
Equity after Tax	R21	28.4%	15%	58.6
Project after Tax	R22	19.3%	20%	36.6
Project beforeTax	R23	24.4%	25%	23.8

WACC	16.7%
Net Present Value	33.06

Management Tests

Min Interest Cover Ratio	1.00	1.33	Pass
Minimum NPV at 16.66%	25.00	33.06	Pass
Maximum Gearing	75.00	51.54	Pass
Min After Tax Equity Return	20.00	28.37	Pass

Figure 4.13 **Inputs sheet**

Selected Scenario		Evaluation Model 1	
Key Inputs & Results		**1**	**2**
Client		Generic Project	Generic Project
Reference		Evaluation Model 1	Evaluation Model 2
Start Date		1-Jan-03	1-Jan-03
Company Year End		31-Dec-03	31-Dec-03
Years to Operation		2.0 years	2.0 years
Currency		HK$	HK$
Units		Millions ▼	Millions ▼
Rates			
Interest Rate Loans		10.00%	10.00%
Debt Funding (% of total)		50.0%	55.0%
Dividend Payout		50.0%	55.0%
Project Delay (% of Yr up to 1 year)		0.0%	0.0%
Equipment Life (8-12 years)		10.0 years	10.0 years
Corporate Tax		30.0%	30.0%
Management Fees		5.00%	6.00%
Loan Repayment Method			
% Cash Flow Dedication	Cash	50.0%	60.0%
Annuity	Annuity	10.0 years	10.0 years
Number of Years	Years	10.0 years	10.0 years
CAPEX Percentage in First Year		75.0%	80.0%
Loan Repayment Method		Cash 50.0% ▼	Cash 60.0% ▼
Selected		Cash	Cash
Cash Flow Dedication to Servicing Loan		50%	60%

SENSITIVITY AND COST OF CAPITAL

The Sensitivity schedule calculates a weighted average cost of capital (WACC) for the project using the Capital Asset Pricing Model (CAPM). The procedure is as follows:

- input for the risk-free rate, risk premium, historic equity beta, historic debt equity ratio, any extra hurdle rate premium, tax rate and predicted debt equity ratio;

- the model un-leverages the equity beta by multiplying the beta by (1 – debt/equity ratio);

- the resulting asset beta is divided by (1 – forecast debt/equity ratio);

- the cost of equity can then be calculated from extra hurdle rate + risk free rate + risk premium * equity beta;
- the cost of debt is the cost multiplied by (1 − tax rate);
- the WACC is then the cost of equity multiplied by its weighting plus the cost of debt multiplied by its weighting;
- there is also the option of including inflation in the calculation using the Fisher formula: [(1 + interest rate) * (1 + inflation)] − 1.

In this example, the cost of capital is 15.50 per cent to reflect the risk on the organization in the beta, leverage in the debt/equity ratio, inflation and a hurdle premium to incorporate the extra risk in the project relative to the organization (see Figure 4.14).

The slider control updates the forecast debt/equity ratio and is linked to a macro to update the inputs for the data tables shown in Figure 4.15. This is an alternative to the button at the top of the page since the outputs below are axes for the data tables further down the sheet:

- equity beta
- project debt/equity ratio
- inflation adjusted WACC percentage.

Cost of capital inputs   Figure 4.14

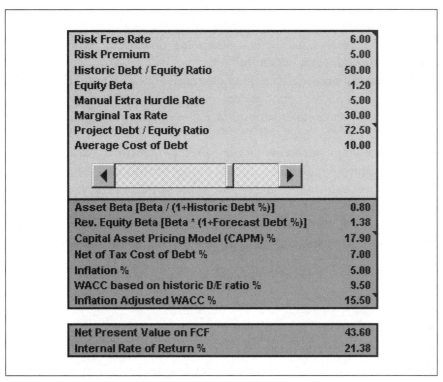

Risk Free Rate	6.00
Risk Premium	5.00
Historic Debt / Equity Ratio	50.00
Equity Beta	1.20
Manual Extra Hurdle Rate	5.00
Marginal Tax Rate	30.00
Project Debt / Equity Ratio	72.50
Average Cost of Debt	10.00

Asset Beta [Beta / (1+Historic Debt %)]	0.80
Rev. Equity Beta [Beta * (1+Forecast Debt %)]	1.38
Capital Asset Pricing Model (CAPM) %	17.90
Net of Tax Cost of Debt %	7.00
Inflation %	5.00
WACC based on historic D/E ratio %	9.50
Inflation Adjusted WACC %	15.50

| Net Present Value on FCF | 43.60 |
| Internal Rate of Return % | 21.38 |

| Figure 4.15 | Data table |

Sensitivity of Net Present Value on FCF to Project Debt / Equity Ratio Across and Equity Beta Down

| Interval Across | 5.00 | Project Debt / Equity Ratio - Across |
| Interval Down | 0.10 | Equity Beta - Down |

	43.60	57.50	62.50	67.50	72.50
0.90	36.67	40.31	44.25	48.50
1.00	34.60	38.35	42.42	46.84
1.10	32.57	36.43	40.63	45.21
1.20	30.58	34.54	38.87	**43.60**
1.30	28.64	32.69	37.14	42.01
1.40	26.74	30.88	35.44	40.45
1.50	24.88	29.10	33.77	38.92

The other tables display the sensitivity of the WACC to the project debt/equity ratio and the beta together with the effect on the NPV of the WACC.

CONSTRUCTION, BORROWING AND OUTPUT

The construction amounts, borrowings capacity and output are laid out in the Control schedule. These sheets show the workings on a periodic basis where the phasing of the construction affects the requirement for borrowings. After construction, there is also some new minor expenditure for repairs, maintenance and additions.

The depreciation per annum is an input cell on the Control schedule and the total capital for the period is depreciated at the rate. In the example, the rate used is 10 per cent per annum since the equipment life is ten years (see Figure 4.16).

The borrowings and equity ratio are fixed so that the construction determines the capital requirement. Interest during construction is capitalized on the Loan sheet to form the total requirement. The debt percentage is subject to a loan over ten years. The objective is to allow the debt requirement and equity to cascade through the model based on the construction costs. The model uses equity first and then loans, but a model could be made more complex with different loan facilities offering varied expiry dates and interest rates. Other methods of equity injection could include:

- percentage of total capital (debt and equity);
- equity injected into the capital as required;
- equity paid at certain times such as completing milestones or key stages;
- percentage of construction costs after escalation and contingencies.

Construction schedule

Figure 4.16

Generic Project : Evaluation Model 1

Line	Year	Reference	2003 -2	2004 -1
	Capital Expenditure		75.00%	25.00%
CP-11	Property, Plant & Equipment	CN79	37.5	13.1
CP-12	Construction Costs	CN80	18.8	6.6
CP-13	Infrastructure	CN81	7.5	2.6
CP-14	Legal Costs	CN82	0.4	0.1
CP-15	Establishment Costs	CN83	0.4	0.1
CP-16	**Total before Contingency**		**64.5**	**22.6**
CP-18	Contigency	CP16*CN42	-	-
CP-19	Management Fees	(CP16+18)*CN23	3.2	1.1
CP-20	**Total after Contingency**		**67.7**	**23.7**
CP-22	CAPEX Adjustment/Saving	CP27*CN29	-	-
CP-23	**Total CAPEX (Unescalated) - Pre Completion**		**67.7**	**23.7**
	Capital Cost Schedule - Post Completion			
CP-26	CAPEX - before Contingency	CN89*(1+CN35)^CN51	-	-
CP-27	Contigency	CP26*CN42	-	-
CP-28	Management Fees	(CP26+27)*CN23	-	-
CP-29	**Total CAPEX - Post Completion/Contingency**		-	-
CP-31	**Total Project Capital Cost**		**67.7**	**23.7**

In the extract from the Loan funding schedule, the debt/equity split of 50 per cent is maintained and repayments are scheduled on a cash or annuity basis (see Figure 4.17). The interest rates come from the Control sheet so that the schedule calculates the key information:

- interest payable both pre- and post-completion;
- principal repayment;
- cash flow available to repay interest and principal;
- balance carried forward to the next period.

This model is limited to two products denoted on the Control schedule. The purpose of this sheet is to provide a link between the initial inputs and the accounting sheets. The figures are presented without escalators to show an excess or deficit from the basic revenue and costs. The revenue is simply the number multiplied by the price per unit. At the bottom, the costs are escalated based on the increases in the Control sheet and the period number (see Figure 4.18).

Figure 4.17	Borrowings schedule

Generic Project : Evaluation Model 1

Line	Year	Reference	2003 -2	2004 -1	2005 1
	Funding Required during Construction				
L-10	Pre Completion Capital Costs	CP23	67.7	23.7	-
L-11	Interest During Contruction or Delay	L10*CN17	3.4	8.0	-
L-12	Facility and Commitment Fees	(L10:11)*CN90+((L10:11)-L31)*CN!	1.2	0.1	0.1
L-13	Increase in Working Capital	B40	-	-	10.0
L-14	Startup/Delay Expenses	S18	-	-	-
L-15	**Total Funding Required**		**71.1**	**31.7**	**10.0**
L-17	Provided by Debt	50.0%	35.6	15.8	5.0
L-18	Provided by Equity	50.0%	35.6	15.8	5.0
	Loan Drawdown/Repayment Schedule				
L-21	Opening Balance	L26	-	35.6	51.4
L-22	Add Loan Drawdowns	L17	35.6	15.8	5.0
L-23	**Closing Balance - Total**		**35.6**	**51.4**	**56.4**
L-25	Less Principal Repayment				-
L-26	**Closing Balance - Total**		**35.6**	**51.4**	**56.4**

Figure 4.18	Output

Generic Project : Evaluation Model 1

Line	Year	Reference	2003 -2	2004 -1	2005 1	2006 2	2007 3
	Revenue Schedule - No Inflation						
PJ-10	Product 000	CN54*(1-CN20)			100	150	200
PJ-11	Product 111	CN55*(1-CN20)			100	100	100
PJ-12	**Total Output**				**200**	**250**	**300**
PJ-14	Price per Unit - Product 000	PJ10	0.3	-	0.3	0.3	0.3
PJ-15	Price per Unit - Product 111	PJ11	0.5	-	0.5	0.5	0.5
PJ-16	**Total Revenue**		-	-	**75.0**	**87.5**	**100.0**
	Cash Operating Schedule - No Inflation						
PJ-19	Fixed Labour Expenses	CN65			7.5	7.5	7.5
PJ-20	Variable Labour Expenses	CN66			5.0	6.3	7.5
PJ-21	Materials	CN67			20.0	25.0	30.0
PJ-22	Corporate Overheads	CN68			0.3	0.3	0.3
PJ-23	Insurance	CN69			3.7	3.4	3.0
PJ-24	Land Rates & Taxes	CN70			0.2	0.2	0.2
PJ-25	Administration	CN71			1.5	1.5	1.5
PJ-26	Marketing	CN72			1.5	1.5	1.5
PJ-27	Repairs and Maintenance	CN73			1.9	1.7	1.5
PJ-28	Input Materials	CN74			7.0	7.0	7.0
PJ-29	Utilities	CN75			10.0	10.0	10.0
PJ-30	Contingency Items	PJ20:29	0.0%		-	-	-
PJ-31	**Cash Expenses after Contingency**				**58.6**	**64.2**	**69.9**
PJ-33	**Excess / (Deficit)**		-	-	**16.4**	**23.3**	**30.1**

ACCOUNTING SCHEDULES

All the schedules so far provide the data for the accounting schedules for presenting the likely profitability, net worth, cash flow and financial analysis. These schedules use standard layouts which could also be incorporated into budget, loan analysis, equity valuation, management buy out and other models involving forecasts and accounting statements, such as:

- income statement
- balance sheet
- ratios
- cash flow.

Each of the lines is labelled with its source and uses data from loan and cost schedules. The result from the income statement is the accounting profit in each of the periods (see Figure 4.19). Workings at the bottom show the calculation of tax for both the income and cash flow schedules.

Income statement

Figure 4.19

Generic Project : Evaluation Model 1							
Line	Year	Reference	2003 -2	2004 -1	2005 1	2006 2	2007 3
P-09	Revenues	PJ40	-	-	82.7	101.3	121.6
P-10	Less: Fixed Labour Expenses	PJ19			7.9	8.3	8.7
P-11	Variable Labour Expenses	PJ20			5.5	7.2	9.1
P-12	Materials	PJ21			22.1	28.9	36.5
P-13	Corporate Overheads	PJ22			0.3	0.3	0.3
P-14	Insurance	PJ23			4.1	3.9	3.6
P-15	Land Rates & Taxes	PJ24			0.2	0.2	0.2
P-16	Administration	PJ25			1.7	1.7	1.8
P-17	Marketing	PJ26			1.7	1.7	1.8
P-18	Repairs	PJ27			2.1	2.0	1.8
P-19	Input Materials	PJ28			7.7	8.1	8.5
P-20	Utilities	PJ29			11.0	11.6	12.2
P-21	Contingency	PJ30			-	-	-
P-22	Depreciation	CP42			10.4	10.5	10.7
P-23	**Total Operating Costs**		-	-	**74.6**	**84.5**	**95.2**
P-25	**Operating Profit**		-	-	**8.1**	**16.8**	**26.4**
P-27	Less: Interest Expenses	L34			5.4	5.6	5.5
P-28	**Profit before Tax**		-	-	**2.7**	**11.2**	**20.9**
P-30	Less: Corporate Tax	P41	-	-	0.8	3.4	6.3
P-31	**Net Profit after Tax**		-	-	**1.9**	**7.9**	**14.6**
P-33	Dividends	C30	-	-	6.2	6.6	9.5
P-34	**Retained Earnings**		-	-	**(4.3)**	**1.3**	**5.2**

The balance sheet self-checks at the bottom and demonstrates the accounting valuation for the project at each period end (see Figure 4.20). The income statement and balance sheet are linked since increased loans feed through to higher interest payment in the income statement, less profit to pay dividends and therefore less cash and net worth in the balance sheet.

There are two cash flow statements. The first restates the income statement and balance sheet in the standard annual accounts format. This divides trading from non-trading cash and displays totals for the net operating cash flow and the cash inflow or outflow before financing. New capital as debt or equity is isolated and the statement reconciles back to the change in cash on the balance sheet. The second cash statement calculates the cash available for paying dividends, which is set in the Control schedule as 50 per cent of the cash available. The elements are shown in Figure 4.21. Again the schedule self-checks to the change in bank on the balance sheet.

Figure 4.20 | **Balance sheet**

Generic Project : Evaluation Model 1

Line	Year	Reference	2003 -2	2004 -1	2005 1	2006 2
B-09	Cash/Bank	C31	(1.2)	(1.4)	4.8	11.4
B-10	Accounts Receivable (Debtors)	B37	-	-	20.7	25.3
B-11	**Total Current Assets**		**(1.2)**	**(1.4)**	**25.4**	**36.7**
B-13	Fixed Assets - Equipment	CP40	72.4	104.2	104.2	105.4
B-14	Depreciation				10.4	21.0
B-15	**Fixed Assets - Written Down Value**		**72.4**	**104.2**	**93.7**	**84.4**
B-17	**Total Assets**		**71.1**	**102.8**	**119.2**	**121.1**
B-18						
B-19	Accounts Payable (Creditors)	B38	-	-	10.7	12.3
B-20	Current Portion Long Term Debt	L29	-	-	0.9	1.8
B-21	Provision for Tax	P30-C19	-	-	-	-
B-22	**Total Current Liabilities**		-	-	**11.6**	**14.1**
B-24	Non Current Liabilities					
B-25	Long Term Debt	L28	35.6	51.4	55.4	53.6
B-26	**Total Liabilities**		**35.6**	**51.4**	**67.1**	**67.7**
B-28	Equity - Shareholders' Equity	L39	35.6	51.4	56.4	56.4
B-29	Retained Earnings	L47	-	-	(4.3)	(3.0)
B-30	**Total Equity**		**35.6**	**51.4**	**52.1**	**53.4**
B-32	**Total Liabilities and Equity**		**71.1**	**102.8**	**119.2**	**121.1**
	CheckSum: No Errors		-	-	-	-

Dividend cash flow

Figure 4.21

Generic Project : Evaluation Model 1

Line	Year	Reference	2003 -2	2004 -1	2005 1	2006 2	2007 3
C-09	Operating Profit	P25	-	-	8.1	16.8	26.4
C-10	Add back Depreciation/Amortisation	CP42	-	-	10.4	10.5	10.7
C-11	**Operating Cash Flow (EBITDA)**		-	-	**18.5**	**27.3**	**37.0**
C-13	Less: Increase in Working Capital	B40	-	-	10.0	3.0	3.3
C-14	Capex - Pre Completion	CP23	67.7	23.7			
C-15	Capex - Post Completion				-	1.2	1.3
C-16	Interest - Pre Completion	L11	3.4	8.0	-		
C-17	Interest on Debt				5.4	5.6	5.5
C-18	Establishment/Commitment Fees	L12	1.2	0.1			
C-19	Corporate Tax				0.8	3.4	6.3
C-20	**Net Operating Cash Flow**		**(72.4)**	**(31.8)**	**2.3**	**14.2**	**20.7**
C-22	Financing Sources - Debt	L17	35.6	15.8	5.0	-	-
C-23	Financing Sources - Equity	L18	35.6	15.8	5.0	-	-
C-24	**Total Financing Sources**		**71.1**	**31.7**	**10.0**	**-**	**-**
C-26	Financing Uses - Loan Principal Repmt	L25	-	-	-	0.9	1.8
C-27	**Net Financing Cash Flow**		**71.1**	**31.7**	**10.0**	**(0.9)**	**(1.8)**
C-29	Cash Flow available for Dividend	C20+C27	(1.2)	(0.1)	12.3	13.2	18.9
C-30	Less Dividend 50.0%				6.2	6.6	9.5
C-31	**Net Cash Flow**		**(1.2)**	**(0.1)**	**6.2**	**6.6**	**9.5**
	Change in Bank	B9		(0.1)	6.2	6.6	9.5
	CheckSum: No Errors			-	-	-	-

The equity and debt providers need the financial analysis of the project. The equity providers need to know the returns relative to the risk. In particular the key areas are:

- profitability and return such as return on equity, profit margin and return on assets;
- financial structure such as gearing, interest coverage and solvency;
- operating cycle such as working capital, debtors, creditors and inventory days;
- cash flow such as net operating cash flow to sales.

The model provides the standard ratios grouped around the core ratios. Again all the derivations of the ratios are shown on the schedule (see Figure 4.22). The return ratios are calculated on a pre- and post-tax basis.

Debt providers may be more interested in cover ratios. The financial model needs to derive the maximum amount of debt that the project cash

Figure 4.22   **Ratios**

Generic Project : Evaluation Model 1

Line	Year	Reference	2003 -2	2004 -1	2005 1	2006 2	2007 3
	Core Ratios						
R-10	Return on Sales (NPAT/Sales %)	P31/P9			2.30	7.75	12.04
R-11	Asset Turnover (Sales / Total Assets)	P9/B17			0.69	0.84	0.96
R-12	Asset Leverage (Total Assets/Equity)	B17/B30			2.29	2.27	2.16
R-13	Return on Equity (NPAT/Equity %)	P31/B30			3.64	14.72	24.99
	Profitability						
R-17	Gross Profit / Sales (%)	(P9-(P10:12))/P9			57.14	56.12	55.36
R-18	Net Operating Profit / Sales (%)	P25/P9			9.80	16.59	21.68
R-19	Profit before Tax / Sales (%)	P28/P9			3.28	11.08	17.20
R-20	Profit after Tax / Sales	P31/B17			1.59	6.48	11.59
R-21	Return on Capital Employed (ROCE)	P25/(B30+B25)			7.53	15.71	24.60
R-22	Return on Invested Capital (ROIC)	(P25-P30)/(B25+B20+B30)			6.72	12.36	17.91
R-23	Return on Assets (ROA)	P25/B17			6.80	13.88	20.87
	Operating Efficiency						
R-27	Inventory Days	B13/P11			-	-	-
R-28	Trade Receivables (Debtor) Days	B10/P9*365			91.25	91.25	91.25
R-29	Creditors Days	B19/(P10:12)			110.16	101.21	94.77
R-30	Funding Gap Debtors+Inventory-Creditors	R29-R28-R27			18.91	9.96	3.52
	Financial Structure						
R-34	Current Ratio	B11/B22			2.18	2.60	2.68
R-35	Quick Ratio (Acid Test)	(B11-Inv)/B22			2.18	2.60	2.68
R-36	Working Capital (Thousands)	B11-B22			13.80	22.56	32.10
R-37	Gross Gearing (%)	(B20+B25)/B30			108.17	103.86	91.59
R-38	Net Gearing (%)	(B20+B25-B9)/B30			99.02	82.55	56.01
R-39	Gearing - Debt to Equity Ratio	B25/(B25+B30)			51.54	50.12	45.36
R-40	Solvency (Interest Coverage)	P25/P27			150.34	300.69	483.35
R-41	Debt Service Ratio	(P25+C10-P30)/(C17+C26)			3.29	3.67	4.24

flow could safely support. The important ratios here are:

- Gross gearing (%) $(B20 + B25)/B30$
- Net gearing (%) $(B20 + B25 - B9)/B30$
- Gearing – debt to equity ratio $B25/(B25 + B30)$
- Solvency (interest coverage) $P25/P27$
- Debt service ratio $(P25 + C10 - P30)/(C17 + C26)$

There are variants of these ratios. For example earnings before interest, taxation, depreciation and amortization (EBITDA) or net operating cash flow could be used instead of operating profit for interest coverage. The project must be able to demonstrate both quantity and quality of cash flow and therefore in its simplest form must cover the interest payments. Debt providers also require repayment of principal and the debt service ratio includes both interest and debt in the formula:

(Operating profit + Depreciation + Amortization − Dividends)/
(Interest + Principal repayment)

An alternative formula is:

EBITDA/(Interest + (Principal/(1 − Tax rate)))

Where any of these ratios fall below one, the project is not generating sufficient cash to service its debts. A good model should survey the data and include decision making. The extract from the Control sheet shown in Figure 4.23 includes individual coverage tests to ensure that the model 'passes' at each stage. The minimum or maximum is extracted using the functions MIN and MAX to highlight the periods where coverage is at a minimum. Since forecasts notoriously become less accurate the further into the future you project, it is obviously important to critically review the coverage and returns from the later periods. The model therefore assists in demonstrating the key ratios for the client, advisers, debt and equity providers. This extract is on the Control sheet.

Return ratios

Figure 4.23

Results: Leveraged IRRs				Equity NPV after Tax		
Equity Div before Tax	R51	183.2%		10%	S32	98.5
Equity after Tax	R52	28.4%		15%		58.6
Project after Tax	R53	19.3%		20%		36.6
Project before Tax	R54	24.4%		25%		23.8

WACC	15.5%
Net Present Value	43.60

Management Tests

Min Interest Cover Ratio	1.00	1.33	Pass
Minimum NPV at 15.50%	25.00	43.60	Pass
Maximum Gearing	75.00	51.54	Pass
Min After Tax Equity Return	20.00	28.37	Pass

MANAGEMENT ANALYSIS AND SUMMARIES

The complete model is included in this chapter to demonstrate the number of variables, possible inputs and therefore the level of risk to be borne by each party. On account of the detail, the model needs schedules to summarize and report on the findings. These schedules are called:

- Management Summary
- Annual Summary
- Management Analysis.

The Management Summary brings together the internal rates of return from the Control schedule together with the components of the weighted average cost of capital from the Sensitivity sheet (see Figure 4.24). The table of management tests is repeated to demonstrate the acceptability of the cash flows.

Figure 4.25 is a summary of the capital costs and the loans and equity mix. The construction requirements are matched by an equal amount of debt and equity.

The Sensitivity chart illustrates how the NPV of the project changes as the cost of capital increases or declines (see Figure 4.26). The slope of the lines gives a good indication of the responses since the NPV rises by 20 to around 50 if the cost of capital is reduced to 15 per cent. If the WACC rises above 21.5 per cent, then the project attains a negative NPV.

The Annual Summary picks key lines from the other schedules to summarize output, revenue, cash and ratios on a periodic basis (see Figure 4.27). This is a single page report for showing exactly how the cash flows and how this affects the cover and return ratios.

Schedules of figures are difficult to understand and therefore the model

Figure 4.24

Management Summary

Results

Equity Div before Tax	183.2%
Equity after Tax	28.4%
Project after Tax	19.3%
Project before Tax	24.4%

Project Equity Beta	1.20
Manual Extra Hurdle Rate	5.0%
Project Debt / Equity Ratio	72.5%
Capital Asset Pricing Model (CAPM) %	17.9%
Net of Tax Cost of Debt %	7.0%
WACC	15.5%
Net Present Value	43.60

Management Tests

	Rule	Achieved	
Min Interest Cover Ratio	1.00	1.33	Pass
Minimum NPV at 15.50%	25.00	43.60	Pass
Maximum Gearing	75.00	51.54	Pass
Min After Tax Equity Return	20.00	28.37	Pass

Capital Costs and Loans

Figure 4.25

Capital Costs and Loan	
Property, Plant & Equipment	50.63
Construction Costs	25.31
Infrastructure	10.13
Legal Costs	0.51
Establishment Costs	0.51
Management & Contingency	4.35
Interim Interest	11.34
Increase in Working Capital	9.98
Total Required	112.75

Loan	56.37
Loan Cost	10.00
Method	Cash 50.0%
Equity	56.37
Total Funding	112.75

Sensitivity

Figure 4.26

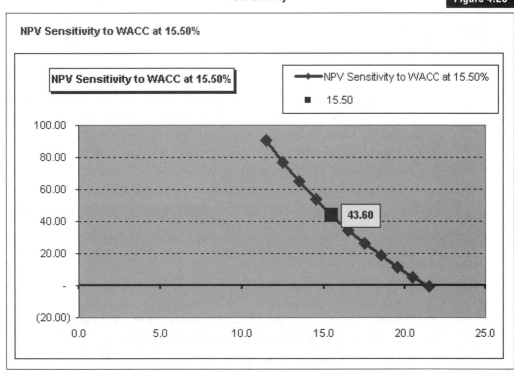

NPV Sensitivity to WACC at 15.50%

Figure 4.27 **Annual Summary**

Generic Project : Evaluation Model 1

Line	Year	Reference	2003 -2	2004 -1	2005 1	2006 2
S-09	Output Product 000				100.0	150.0
S-10	Output Product 111				100.0	100.0
S-11	**Total Output**		-	-	**200.0**	**250.0**
S-13	Price Per Unit - Product 000	PJ14	0.3	0.3	0.3	0.3
S-14	Price per Unit - Product 111	PJ15	0.5	0.5	0.6	0.6
S-15	**Total Revenue**		-	-	**82.7**	**101.3**
S-17	Operating Costs	PJ31	-	-	(74.6)	(84.5)
S-18	Operating Cashflow	S15+S17	-	-	8.1	16.8
S-19	Project Finance Loan	50%	35.6	15.8	5.0	
S-20	Equity Injection	50%	35.6	15.8	5.0	
S-21	**Total Sources of Cash**		**71.1**	**31.7**	**18.1**	**16.8**
S-23	Capital Expenditure	CP31	(67.7)	(23.7)	-	(1.2)
S-24	Capitalised Interest	L11	(3.4)	(8.0)	-	
S-25	Working Capital	B40	-	-	(10.0)	(3.0)
S-26	Establishment/Commitment Costs	L12	(1.2)	(0.1)	(0.1)	
S-27	Interest Payments	L34			(5.4)	(5.6)
S-28	Corporate Taxes	P53			(0.8)	(3.4)
S-29	Loan Repayments	Cash			-	(0.9)
S-30	**Total Uses of Cash**		**(72.4)**	**(31.8)**	**(16.3)**	**(14.1)**
S-32	Net Cashflow after Tax	S21+S30	(1.24)	(0.15)	1.78	2.67
S-33	Cumulative Cashflow		(1.24)	(1.39)	0.39	3.05
S-34	Cover Ratios - Interest	(S32-S27-S29)/S27			1.33	1.65
S-35	Principal Cover	(S29+S32)/S29			-	3.81
S-36	Debt Service Cover	(S32+S27+S29)/(S27+S29)			1.33	1.41
S-37	PV Cumulative Cashflows Cover	NPV(CN16,L57/S19)			0.12	0.25

provides an additional method of reporting using a dynamic chart. The objective is to copy any sheet to the Schedule sheet and then look up these values on the Management Analysis sheet (see Figure 4.28). This saves producing multiple charts and provides the user with the flexibility of examining almost any line in the model.

The first stage is to choose a schedule using the control box and this updates the cell link at D61. There is a macro assigned to the control called CopyDataSheet. This performs the following:

- selects Management Analysis sheet;
- updates the sheet names at B50 on the Menu sheet;
- selects the sheet number selected by the control;
- copies rows 9 to 75 (since row 75 is the maximum row of any schedule);
- goes to the Schedule sheet and paste specials the values;
- pastes to A9 the name of the sheet that has been copied and pasted.

Management Analysis

Figure 4.28

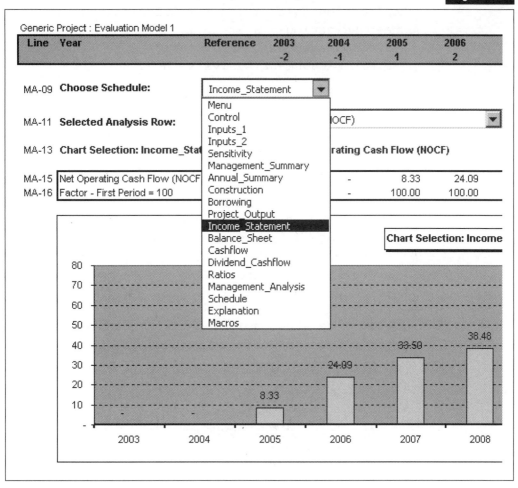

The full text of the macro is as follows:

```
Sub CopyDataSheet()
'
' CopyDataSheet Macro
' Macro developed by Alastair L Day
' Excel uses index numbers for sheets so this
macro copies a sheet number given by the control
and paste specials the values into the Schedule
sheet
' The second control then selects a row on the
Schedule sheet for a chart

Dim Sheet_Selection
Dim Number, Counter, SheetName(25)
```

```
Application.ScreenUpdating = False
Application.Calculation = xlCalculationManual
Sheet_Selection =
Range("Management_Analysis!d61")
'Select Management Analysis sheet

'Update the sheet names at B50 on the Menu sheet
Worksheets(1).Select   'Update list of schedules
on menu sheet
Range("B50").Select
Number=ActiveWorkbook.Sheets.Count

For Counter = 1 To Number
    SheetName(Counter) = Worksheets(Counter).Name
    ActiveCell.Offset(1, 0).Range("A1").Select
    ActiveCell.FormulaR1C1 =
    Worksheets(Counter).Name
Next Counter

'Select the sheet selected by the control
    Application.Worksheets(Sheet_Selection).
    Select

'Copy rows 9 to 75
    Rows("9:75").Select
    Application.CutCopyMode = False
    Selection.Copy

'Go to the Schedule sheet and paste special the
values
    Range("b9").Select
    Sheets("Schedule").Select
    Range("A9").Select
    Selection.PasteSpecial Paste:=xlValues,
    Operation:=xlNone, SkipBlanks:= False,
Transpose:=False
    Range("A9").Select
    Application.CutCopyMode = False

    Range("b2") =
    Application.Worksheets(Sheet_Selection).Name

'Paste to A9 the name of the sheet you just
copied and pasted
```

```
Sheets("Management_Analysis").Select
Range("A9").Select

Application.StatusBar = False
Application.ScreenUpdating = True
Application.Calculation = xlAutomatic
End Sub
```

The second control then selects a line number on the Schedule sheet using a simple OFFSET formula based on the cell link at cell D63 (see Figure 4.29). Again, the user sees the actual line text and can decide easily which line is needed. This is the formula in cell G15:

```
=IF(ISERROR(OFFSET(Schedule!G8,$D$63,0)),0,OFFSET
(Schedule!G8,$D$63,0))
```

Select line

Figure 4.29

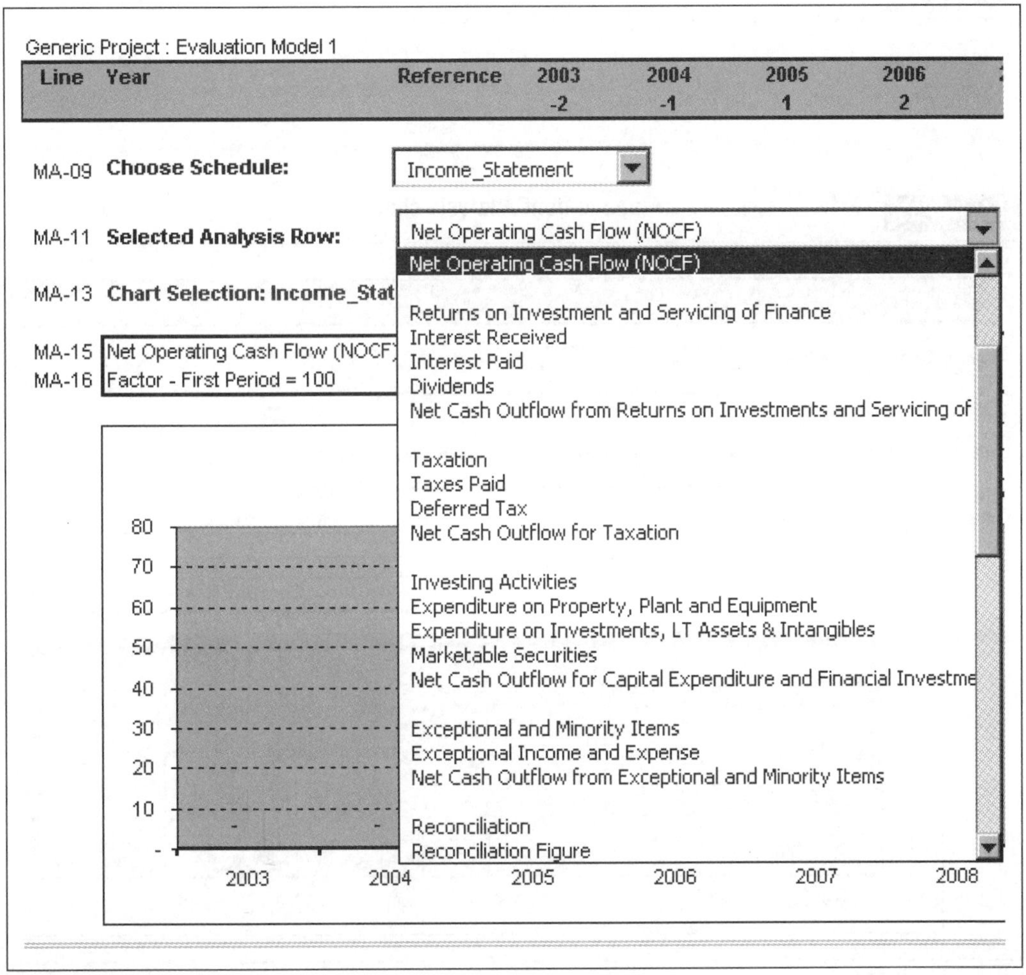

The data is changed on row 15 and row 16 includes a factor analysis. The first data point defaults to 100 and all subsequent points are restated as a factor. Minus 20 per cent would be 80 and plus 25 per cent would be 125. This is often a better way of presenting percentage changes than using just the percentage difference.

The finished Management Analysis chart shows the net operating cash flow from the cash flow schedule (see Figure 4.30). Here you can see the trend of the forecast results and examine the changes using multiple scenarios updated from the Control sheet.

You can select other schedules and the text in the second control will automatically update if calculation is set to automatic (Tools, Options, Calculation). Since the macro suppresses the screen updates, you do not notice the macro running. Figure 4.31 shows the return on sales from the Ratios schedule.

The Schedule sheet merely contains values correct to 13 decimal places and the sheet always remains unprotected since the macro needs access to the sheet to update the values (see Figure 4.32).

Figure 4.30 **Management Analysis chart**

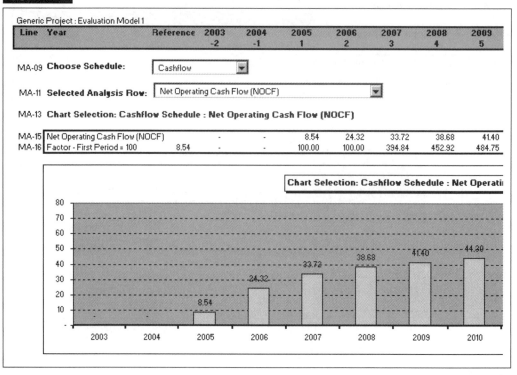

Ratio analysis

Figure 4.31

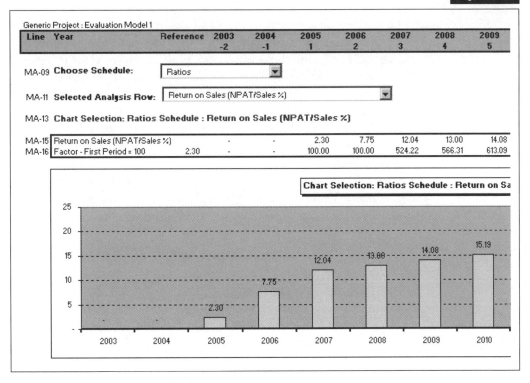

Schedule values

Figure 4.32

Generic Project : Evaluation Model 1

Line	Year	Reference	2003 -2	2004 -1	2005 1	2006 2
	Core Ratios					
R-10	Return on Sales (NPAT/Sales %)	P31/P9			2.30	7.75
R-11	Asset Turnover (Sales / Total Assets)	P9/B17			0.69	0.84
R-12	Asset Leverage (Total Assets/Equity)	B17/B30			2.29	2.27
R-13	Return on Equity (NPAT/Equity %)	P31/B30			3.64	14.72
	Profitability					
R-17	Gross Profit / Sales (%)	(P9-(P10:12))/P9			57.14	56.12
R-18	Net Operating Profit / Sales (%)	P25/P9			9.80	16.59
R-19	Profit before Tax / Sales (%)	P28/P9			3.28	11.08
R-20	Profit after Tax / Sales	P31/B17			1.59	6.48
R-21	Return on Capital Employed (ROCE)	P25/(B30+B25)			7.53	15.71
R-22	Return on Invested Capital (ROIC)	(P25-P30)/(B25+B20+B30)			6.72	12.36
R-23	Return on Assets (ROA)	P25/B17			6.80	13.88

SUMMARY

Project finance and its basic methodology allow risk to be shared amongst participants. The financial model sets out all the model sections together with the extra variables and contingencies to explore the potential cost overruns and other variables. Rather than just producing basic cover ratios, the model provides much more flexibility for examining up to ten scenarios in the Control and Inputs schedules and the variables cascade through the model. The Management Analysis and summaries provide the user with a means of extending the understanding of the risk inherent in the project. Macros and controls allow you to review multiple lines on all the schedules to demonstrate the potential downsides of the project.

Simulation

Files: FT4_05_01.xls
and FT4_05_02.xls

INTRODUCTION

The project finance model in the previous chapter introduced a single-point model and then layered on scenarios and other risk techniques. Whilst you can add scenarios and multiply the answers by the assumed probability to derive a weighted outcome, there comes a point when it is inefficient to add more and more manual scenarios. The solution is to explicitly model uncertainty and build it into the model. The project model contained inputs for sales growth and demand as single points as a best guess. In the real world, you may be less certain about an exact figure and the desired input could be a range or a distribution. The simulation on the Monte Carlo simulation model accepts distributions as inputs, runs the model through large numbers of theoretical scenarios and produces an output also as a distribution.

On the one hand, the single-point model produces answers such as the net present value (NPV) or the return to investors. On the other hand, the simulation model answers questions such as 'How likely is the company to achieve cash flow covers on loan repayments of three times?' or 'What percentage chance is there that the unit will make a profit?' This could be a great benefit since you do not have to build the physical system to understand the possible outcomes. The programming is often simpler than trying to model a number of discrete scenarios.

Uncertainty grows with time and estimating the interplay between variables using single-point models fails to take into account the potential forecasting errors. Errors increase with time as shown by the error bars. Figure 5.1 shows errors bars increasing with time. Similarly with time, factors may increase in importance or factors arise which have not been modelled. Therefore a model which incorporates the uncertainty to be found in empirical situations may provide more management information about potential risks.

The structure of a simulation model is very similar to a single-point model and it is usual to build in simulation as an extra layer on the existing model. Most of the calculations and variables remain the same except that certain variables will now be represented by probability distributions instead of a single value.

Probability modelling is not a new concept. The mathematics behind Monte Carlo came out of the Manhattan Project to build the atomic bomb during World War II. The work is largely credited to Stanislaw Ulam, an Austrian-born mathematician, along with computer pioneer and scientist John von Neumann. Simulation models offered a way of arriving at approximate solutions to complex problems associated with the random neutron

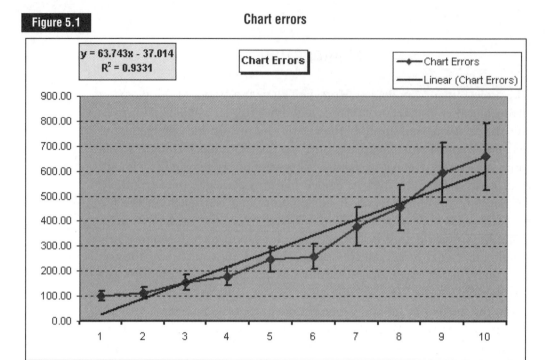

Figure 5.1   **Chart errors**

diffusion in nuclear weapons material. One report says that Ulam named the method 'Monte Carlo' after a relative fond of sneaking off to Monaco's casinos. Nevertheless, the name does underline the fact that this is a probability and not a certainty model.

This chapter deals with simulation methods within Excel, however there are a number of commercial add-ons to Excel for automating the process. These are:

- @RISK at www.palisade.com
- Crystal Ball at www.crystalball.com
- Pop Tools statistical add-in at www.dwe.csiro.au/vbc/poptools/index.htm.

BUILDING BLOCKS

There are several building blocks to simulation models consisting of random numbers and probability distributions. The golden rule is that all iterations generated by the model must be possible so that the model replicates possible events that could feasibly occur in the real world. If you follow this rule, you will have a greater chance of producing a model that is both accurate and realistic. For example, a very common mistake is to produce a model that inadvertently calculates the mean of the answer, rather than developing a model that produces a large number of scenarios, from which the spreadsheet calculates the mean. For a simple illustration, consider the modelling of a variable (X) that has a 50 per cent chance of being Normal(100, 33) and a 50 per cent change of being Normal(70, 5). A normal distribution can be described by its mean and standard deviation so that in the example above the mean is 100 and the standard deviation 33. This could be incorrectly modelled as follows:

$$X = Normal(100, 3) * 0.5 + Normal(70, 5) * 0.5$$

or correctly as a discrete distribution:

$$X = Discrete(\{Normal(100, 3), Normal(70, 5)\}, \{0.5, 0.5\}).$$

The first formula is wrong because it generates values that could not occur and does not generate a lot of those that would occur. There is a 50 per cent chance of each discrete set of events with a different mean and standard deviation.

Random numbers

Excel is capable of generating random numbers between 0 and 1 using the RAND function. Alternatively, the RANDBETWEEN allows you to produce discrete numbers between a high and low figure. Each time you press F9, the sheet updates with new values. With RAND, approximately 10 per cent of the numbers will be between 0 and 0.1 eventually, although smaller samples will give anomalies. More numbers will be generated in certain bins and you need larger samples to generate truer randomness. Two statistical theories underline the methodology in simulation.

Strong law of large numbers

This states that the larger the sample size the closer the distribution to the theoretical distribution. As you run more trials then the randomness starts to disappear and the outliers become less important. The distribution starts to attain a much more concise shape.

Central limit theorem

This states that a mean of set of variables drawn independently from same distribution will be normally distributed. Based on the Strong law above, it means that if you take variables at random from a non-normal distribution, the selected values will be approximately normally distributed.

This can be expressed as formula where the mean of n variables (n should be large), with same distribution f(x), will be normally distributed:

$$\bar{x} = Normal(\mu, \sigma/\sqrt{n})$$

where μ = mean and σ standard deviation of the f(x) distribution from which the n samples are drawn. If you multiply both sides by n, then the sum of n variables drawn independently from the same distribution is given by:

$$\Sigma = n\bar{x} = Normal(n\mu, \sqrt{n}\sigma)$$

The file, FT4_05_01.xls contains a sheet called Dice which reproduces throwing two dice up to 2000 times. The data are on the sheet called Dice_Data (see Figure 5.2). The combinations of scores range from two to 12 but numbers such a seven are easier to attain since there are more combinations of dice that produce this result.

If you only create 50 trials, there are not enough trials to create the theoretical distribution under the two theorems above. Each time you press F9, you will obtain a different set of values. Figure 5.3 shows excess scores at the upper end of the scale. Further trials would improve the shape of the distribution since there should be a peak at seven since this is the most likely combination.

As you increase the number of trials the shape of the histogram changes until with 2000 trials the shape is closer to a normal bell curve. The histograms for 2000, 1000 and 50 trials are shown together represented as percentages of the total sample (see Figure 5.4). The larger sample clearly

Figure 5.2

Dice data

No	First	Second	Total	Mean	Standard Deviation
1	5	3	8	8.0000	-
2	4	4	8	8.0000	-
3	3	3	6	7.3333	1.1547
4	3	3	6	7.0000	1.1547
5	4	6	10	7.6000	1.6733
6	4	4	8	7.6667	1.5055
7	4	1	5	7.2857	1.7043
8	4	1	5	7.0000	1.7728
9	4	3	7	7.0000	1.6583
10	5	3	8	7.1000	1.5951
11	4	2	6	7.0000	1.5492
12	2	6	8	7.0833	1.5050
13	2	3	5	6.9231	1.5525
14	5	5	10	7.1429	1.7033
15	4	6	10	7.3333	1.7995
16	6	3	9	7.4375	1.7877
17	4	2	6	7.3529	1.7657
18	3	1	4	7.1667	1.8865
19	5	6	11	7.3684	2.0333
20	2	1	3	7.1500	2.2070

Fifty trials

Figure 5.3

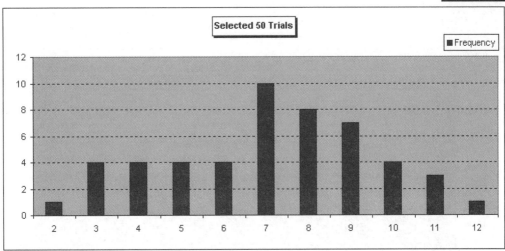

Comparison of trials

Figure 5.4

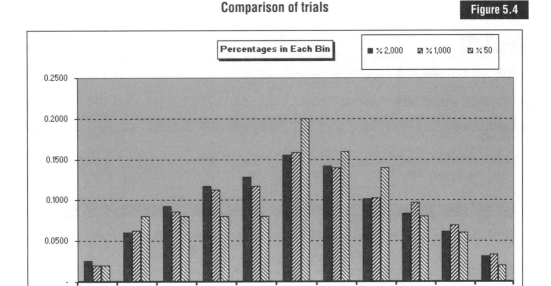

results in a more normal distribution and this is confirmed by the variance chart showing the difference of 50 and 1000 trials to 2000 trials (see Figure 5.5).

Figure 5.6 contains all the data for the histograms. The Dice_Data sheet produces the random numbers and scores which have to be counted and presented as frequency plots. There is also a requirement to show scores of less than 2000 to demonstrate how the distribution changes with more trials. Cell E7 contain an input for the row number. This is used in cell E10

Figure 5.5

Variance to 2000 trials

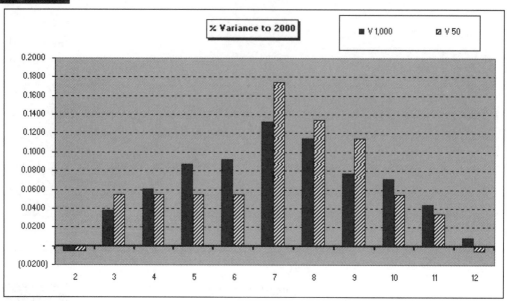

Figure 5.6

Data

							% Variance to 2000	
Low	1							
High	6							
Select Row	50							
	2,000	**1,000**	**50**	**% 2,000**	**% 1,000**	**% 50**	**V 1,000**	**V 50**
Mean	7.0470	7.0620	7.3000				0.0150	0.3420
Standard Deviation	2.4051	2.4075	2.2246				0.0023	(0.1532)
Kurtosis	(0.6221)	(0.5930)	(0.4340)				0.0290	0.1726
Skew	0.0198	(0.0260)	(0.0475)				(0.0458)	(0.1432)

				Percentages in Each Bin			Variance % to 2000	
Combined Score	**2,000**	**1,000**	**50**	**% 2,000**	**% 1,000**	**% 50**	**V 1,000**	**V 50**
2	37	15	0	0.0185	0.0150	-	(0.0035)	(0.0185)
3	122	71	3	0.0610	0.0710	0.0600	0.0525	0.0415
4	169	93	3	0.0845	0.0930	0.0600	0.0745	0.0415
5	237	120	4	0.1185	0.1200	0.0800	0.1015	0.0615
6	291	136	8	0.1455	0.1360	0.1600	0.1175	0.1415
7	354	159	8	0.1770	0.1590	0.1600	0.1405	0.1415
8	268	133	9	0.1340	0.1330	0.1800	0.1145	0.1615
9	200	99	8	0.1000	0.0990	0.1600	0.0805	0.1415
10	152	81	2	0.0760	0.0810	0.0400	0.0625	0.0215
11	113	63	4	0.0565	0.0630	0.0800	0.0445	0.0615
12	57	30	1	0.0285	0.0300	0.0200	0.0115	0.0015
Total	2000	1000	50	1.000	1.000	1.000	0.797	0.797

to create an offset number for an average function. This means that you can look at any combination between 1 and 2000.

```
E10 =AVERAGE(Dice_Data!E7:OFFSET(Dice_Data!E$7,
Dice!E$9-1,0))
```

The same method is used to count the scores in the bins from two to 12 and create the data for the histograms.

```
E17 =FREQUENCY(Dice_Data!$E$7:OFFSET
(Dice_Data!$E$7,$E$9-1,0),$B$17:$B$27)
```

Figures 5.7 and 5.8 show how the mean and standard deviation develop during the 2000 trials. The initial variation disappears and the means and standard deviations move closer to their theoretical results.

Mean

Figure 5.7

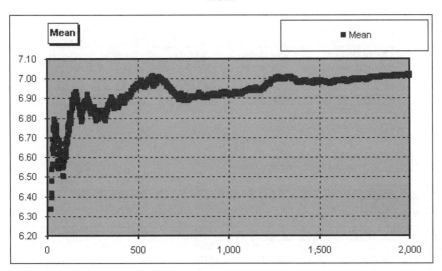

Standard deviation

Figure 5.8

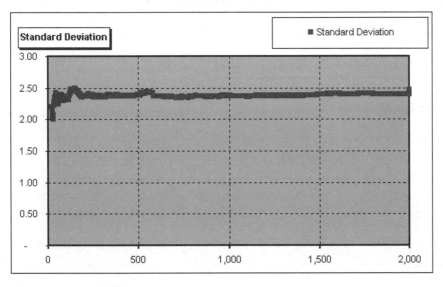

PROCEDURE

The procedure is to decide on the structure of the model and the variables to be modelled. The example here is called Rental in the file FT4_05_02.xls. This shows a simple, single-point model looking at the margin from renting housing units (see Figure 5.9). The maximum number of units for rent is 25 and the minimum 22. The average selected is 22 at a rental of 2000 per month. The expenses are 40,000 and the resulting margin 4000.

The Sensitivity table shows the risk from renting fewer properties or an increase in costs (see Figure 5.10). If occupancy is lower at 20 units, the

Figure 5.9   **Inputs**

	Start	Low	High	Result
No of Units	22 Units	20 Units	25 Units	
Rental per month	2,000.00			
Expenses	40,000.00	1,000.00		
Net Margin	4,000.00			

Figure 5.10   **Sensitivity**

Sensitivity Table to No of Units Across and Expenses Down

Interval Across	1.00
Interval Down	500.00

4,000.00	19	20	21	22	23	24	25
38,500.00	(500.00)	1,500.00	3,500.00	5,500.00	7,500.00	9,500.00	11,500.00
39,000.00	(1,000.00)	1,000.00	3,000.00	5,000.00	7,000.00	9,000.00	11,000.00
39,500.00	(1,500.00)	500.00	2,500.00	4,500.00	6,500.00	8,500.00	10,500.00
40,000.00	(2,000.00)	-	2,000.00	4,000.00	6,000.00	8,000.00	10,000.00
40,500.00	(2,500.00)	(500.00)	1,500.00	3,500.00	5,500.00	7,500.00	9,500.00
41,000.00	(3,000.00)	(1,000.00)	1,000.00	3,000.00	5,000.00	7,000.00	9,000.00
41,500.00	(3,500.00)	(1,500.00)	500.00	2,500.00	4,500.00	6,500.00	8,500.00

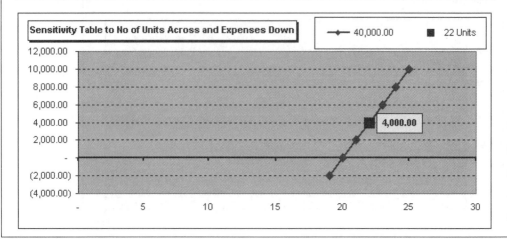

Sensitivity Table to No of Units Across and Expenses Down — 40,000.00 — 22 Units

margin becomes negative. The problem is to understand the level of risk involved based on the two key factors of occupancy and expenses.

The stages in layering a simulation on to the model are:

- Decide on the probability distributions, their attributes and possible inter-relationships.
- Use random numbers to generate large numbers of possible scenarios.
- Draw a scatter chart of the data output.
- Count results in bins (ranges).
- Calculate the descriptive statistics of the distribution.
- Draw a histogram of the results.

In this case, there appears to be no historic pattern of occupancy and therefore a uniform distribution is used between the high and low figures. This can be generated in Excel using a RANDBETWEEN function. The expenses appear to have a mean of 40,000 and to vary by 1000 a month. This appears, on past experience, to be a normal distribution which can be modelled using the function RAND. The workings for the data are at the bottom of the sheet in Figure 5.10.

The revenue is a random number between 20 and 25 multiplied by the rental per month.

```
=RANDBETWEEN($D$6,$E$6)
```

Column D generates a random number between 0 and 1 using RAND and the costs are derived using the NORMINV function (see Figure 5.11). This takes the arguments of probability, mean and standard deviation. The last two are inputs and the probability is the random number. The margin is therefore the revenue minus the costs. This is repeated 100 times down the page to gain a sample of 100 scenarios.

The next stage is to draw a scatter chart of the results using an XY scatter

Norminv function

Figure 5.11

	F115	▼	fx	=-NORMINV(E115,$C$8,$D$8)		
	A	B	C	D	E	F	G
112							
113		Simulation	Random	Revenue	Random	Costs	Margin
114							
115		1	22	44,000.00	0.79	(40,806.75)	3,193.25
116		2	24	48,000.00	0.12	(38,819.42)	9,180.58
117		3	24	48,000.00	0.59	(40,233.92)	7,766.08
118		4	25	50,000.00	0.69	(40,493.64)	9,506.36
119		5	20	40,000.00	0.27	(39,372.37)	627.63
120		6	25	50,000.00	0.75	(40,673.55)	9,326.45

chart with a linear trend line through the data. This shows the relationship between increased occupancy and increased margin (see Figure 5.12). At each level of occupancy there is a spread of values reflecting the standard deviation of the costs.

The scatter chart only provides an idea of the results. The FREQUENCY

Figure 15.12	Scatter chart

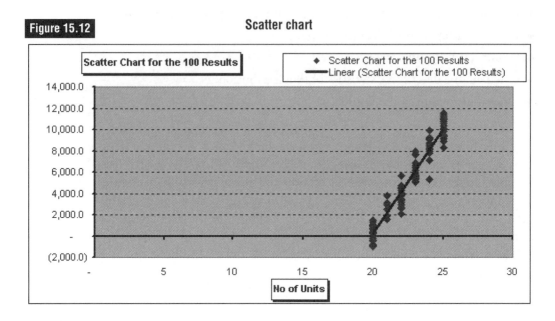

Figure 5.13	Frequency

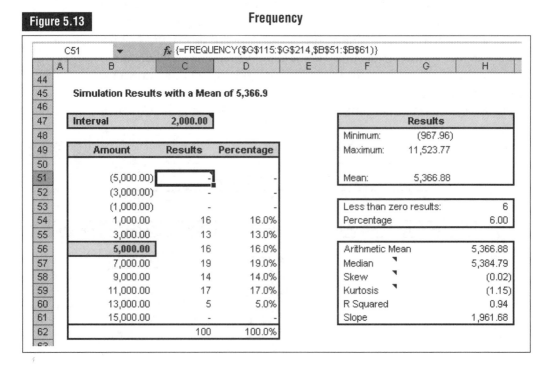

C51   fx {=FREQUENCY($G$115:$G$214,$B$51:$B$61)}

Simulation Results with a Mean of 5,366.9

Interval	2,000.00				Results	
				Minimum:	(967.96)	
Amount	Results	Percentage		Maximum:	11,523.77	
(5,000.00)	-	-		Mean:	5,366.88	
(3,000.00)	-	-				
(1,000.00)	-	-		Less than zero results:	6	
1,000.00	16	16.0%		Percentage	6.00	
3,000.00	13	13.0%				
5,000.00	16	16.0%		Arithmetic Mean	5,366.88	
7,000.00	19	19.0%		Median	5,384.79	
9,000.00	14	14.0%		Skew	(0.02)	
11,000.00	17	17.0%		Kurtosis	(1.15)	
13,000.00	5	5.0%		R Squared	0.94	
15,000.00	-	-		Slope	1,961.68	
	100	100.0%				

function allows counting into bins. This shows a peak of margin between 5000 and 7000 which is higher than the single point answer (see Figure 5.13). This is because the input was 22 and the average of 20 to 25 is 22.50.

Other statistics are also available in Excel using functions shown in Table 5.1.

The counted results can then be plotted with the bins as the x-axis and the number of results as the y-axis.

The histogram shows the results of the FREQUENCY function (see Figure 5.14). Based on the inputs for occupancy and costs, the margin may not be as firm as 4000 as there are a number of results at around zero. The histogram demonstrates that the overall margin should be higher; however, percentiles would also show the range of values.

The percentile takes the data array and the K value as its arguments. Figures 5.15 and 5.16 show that 50 per cent of the values fall below 4257.96.

```
=PERCENTILE($G$115:$G$214,K47)
```

The simulation model provides far more information than the single-point model about how the variables behave and therefore the inherent risk.

Table 5.1

Function	Result
MIN	Minimum number in an array
MAX	Maximum number in an array
COUNTIF	Count if a condition is true – in this case less than zero to count the trials with no margin
AVERAGE	Arithmetic mean
MEDIAN	Middle result in an array
SKEW	Skew characterizes the degree of asymmetry of a distribution around its mean. Positive skew indicates a distribution with an asymmetric tail extending toward more positive values. Negative skew indicates a distribution with an asymmetric tail extending toward more negative values
KURT	Kurtosis of the distribution. Positive kurtosis indicates a relatively peaked distribution. Negative kurtosis indicates a relatively flat distribution.
SLOPE	Slope of the data using a linear trend line ($y = mx + b$)
RSQ	r^2 is the measure of fit between the linear regression line and the data. The r^2 value can be interpreted as the proportion of the variance in y attributable to the variance in x.

Figure 5.14

Histogram of results

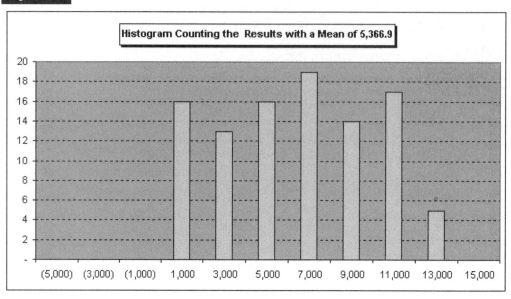

Histogram Counting the Results with a Mean of 5,366.9

Figure 5.15

Percentiles

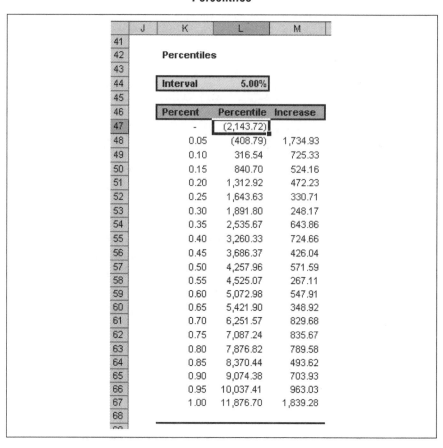

	J	K	L	M
41				
42		**Percentiles**		
43				
44		**Interval**	**5.00%**	
45				
46		**Percent**	**Percentile**	**Increase**
47		-	(2,143.72)	
48		0.05	(408.79)	1,734.93
49		0.10	316.54	725.33
50		0.15	840.70	524.16
51		0.20	1,312.92	472.23
52		0.25	1,643.63	330.71
53		0.30	1,891.80	248.17
54		0.35	2,535.67	643.86
55		0.40	3,260.33	724.66
56		0.45	3,686.37	426.04
57		0.50	4,257.96	571.59
58		0.55	4,525.07	267.11
59		0.60	5,072.98	547.91
60		0.65	5,421.90	348.92
61		0.70	6,251.57	829.68
62		0.75	7,087.24	835.67
63		0.80	7,876.82	789.58
64		0.85	8,370.44	493.62
65		0.90	9,074.38	703.93
66		0.95	10,037.41	963.03
67		1.00	11,876.70	1,839.28
68				

Percentiles chart

Figure 5.16

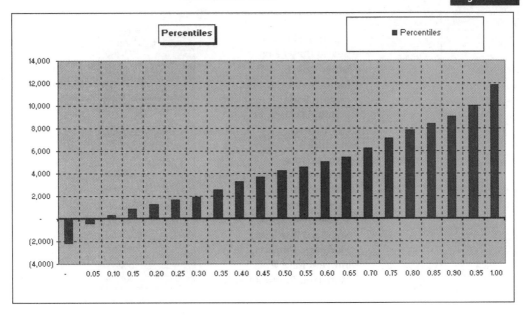

Increasing the standard deviation of the costs will increase the range of possible outcomes. Similarly, increasing the lowest occupancy to 22 will reduce the range of revenue and therefore the spread of results.

REAL ESTATE EXAMPLE

This example revisits the real estate model in Chapter 3 to examine the factors voids and rental per month. The method uses a mean and a standard deviation for these two factors on the Simulation sheet which drive the inputs on the Model sheet. The random number generation is in Visual Basic code since models become slower with more and more calculations. Here, the number of iterations is 1000 and it is sometimes easier to generate the data in code and then transfer it to Excel. The stages are:

- the model generates the numbers for a particular scenario;
- it transfers them to the Model sheet;
- it recalculates and then stores the numbers in an array;
- it loops 1000 times and then pastes the results in a two-dimensional range J5:Q1005 on the Simulation sheet;
- it produces a scatter chart, frequency table, statistics, percentiles and a histogram.

Figure 5.17   **Real estate inputs**

Purchase Price	100,000.00
Stamp Duty / Tax	1.00
Other Costs	0.75
Reburbishment Costs	2.00
Letting Fees	1.18
Building Insurance	0.30
Gas Safety	0.05
Inventory	0.06
Maintenance	0.50
Assumed Rental per Month	666.67
Standard Deviation	50.00
Capital Growth	4.00
Voids %	10.00
Standard Deviation	4.00
Mortgage Period (yrs)	10.00
Interest Rate %	5.51
Mortgage Percentage %	50.00

The inputs use the Base Case scenario on the Model sheet with the standard deviation for the monthly rental at 50 and 10 per cent for the percentage voids. The income after capital growth is 2600.49 and the net yield percentage 4.84 for this initial case. The simulation layer therefore seeks to show the possible spread in the answers when the ranges of inputs are taken into account.

The code below declares the values and sets highs and lows for each of the factors. It starts a For Next loop, derives the values based on random numbers and the normal probability distribution, and transfers the values for calculation to the Model sheet. When it gets to the end of the loops, the code has built an array or grid of variables that is 1000 cells down by seven across. Seven items of data are saved per scenario and these are then pasted on to the sheet at the end.

```
Sub Simulation()

Dim Result(1000, 7) 'Set up an array variable
1000 down by 7 across
Dim RandomFactorA, RandomFactorB, Count,
ExistingValue1, ExistingValue2
Dim FactorA, FactorAHigh, FactorALow, FactorAStd,
FactorB, FactorBHigh, FactorBLow, FactorBStd

ExistingValue1 = Range("model!d15") 'Remember
existing values
```

```
ExistingValue2 = Range("model!d17")

Range("Simulation_Results") = ""        'Zero
existing results
Randomize
Application.Calculation = xlSemiautomatic   'Turn
off calculation of tables

Range("model!d15") = Range("simulation!c15")
Range("model!d18") = Range("simulation!c18")

Range("simulation!B75") =
(Int((Range("model!i10") * 10))) / 10 ' set
centre of frequency table

FactorA = Range("simulation!c15")    'Rental
FactorB = Range("simulation!c18")    'Voids

FactorAHigh = FactorA + Range("simulation!c16")
'Range and StDev for A
FactorALow = FactorA - Range("simulation!c16")
FactorAStd = (FactorAHigh - FactorALow) / 4

FactorBHigh = FactorB + Range("simulation!c19")
'Range and StDev for B
FactorBLow = FactorB - Range("simulation!c19")
FactorBStd = (FactorBHigh - FactorBLow) / 4

For Count = 1 To 1000          'START OF LOOP
    RandomFactorA = Rnd 'Find factor for A for
    this trial
    Range("model!d15") =
    Application.NormInv(RandomFactorA, FactorA,
    FactorAStd)
    randomfactorb = Rnd 'Find factor for B for
    this trial
    Range("model!d17") =
    Application.NormInv(randomfactorb, FactorB,
    FactorBStd)
    Result(Count, 0) = RandomFactorA
    'Random factor A
    Result(Count, 1) = Range("model!d15")
    'Rental per month
```

```
                    Result(Count, 2) = randomfactorb
                    'Random factor B
                    Result(Count, 3) = Range("model!d17")
                    'Voids
                    Result(Count, 4) = Range("model!I29")
                    'Gross margin
                    Result(Count, 5) = Range("model!c36")    'Net
                    margin with capital growth
                    Result(Count, 6) = Range("model!d34")
                    'Gross yield
                    Result(Count, 7) = Range("model!d36")    'Net
                    yield
                    Range("Simulation!f7") = Count
            Next Count                          'END OF LOOP

            Application.Calculation = xlAutomatic
            Range("Simulation_Results") = Result      'Paste
            results
            Range("model!d15") = ExistingValue1       'Put back
            existing inputs
            Range("model!d17") = ExistingValue2

            End Sub
```

The information saved is as shown in Figure 5.18.

The model then uses some of the code from the previous example to draw scatter charts and histograms (see Figure 5.19). As the percentage of voids rise, the overall yield declines. With 1000 trials there are still a number of data points outside the main concentration and running the model for more trials would increase the accuracy based on the Central Limit theorem.

The table uses the FREQUENCY and other statistical functions to summarize and describe the distribution of results (see Figures 5.20 and 5.21).

Figure 5.18	Simulation results

Simulation Results

Factor A	Rental	Factor B	Int Rate	Net Rental Income	Total Income	Yield %	Yield %
0.4784	665.32	0.0449	6.61	(1,143.20)	2,856.80	(2.13)	5.31
0.5549	670.12	0.8341	11.94	(1,518.28)	2,481.72	(2.82)	4.62
0.2564	650.31	0.1478	7.91	(1,413.01)	2,586.99	(2.63)	4.81
0.1859	644.34	0.3721	9.35	(1,590.25)	2,409.75	(2.96)	4.48
0.5934	672.96	0.4969	9.98	(1,330.29)	2,669.71	(2.47)	4.97
0.2540	650.12	0.0714	7.07	(1,349.59)	2,650.41	(2.51)	4.93
0.0410	623.18	0.8042	11.71	(1,997.30)	2,002.70	(3.72)	3.73
0.6858	678.77	0.9645	13.61	(1,563.03)	2,436.97	(2.91)	4.53

The majority of returns cluster between 4.4 and 5.8 per cent as shown in the left-hand table in Figure 5.20. The right-hand table in Figure 5.20 summarizes the input data for the monthly rental and the voids percentage, and then lists the mean and other statistics for the output distribution.

Both the quartiles and percentiles are calculated so that you can see how many results provided low returns (see Figures 5.22 and 5.23). In this case, 25 per cent of the trials resulted in returns below 4.4 per cent and an income

Scatter chart

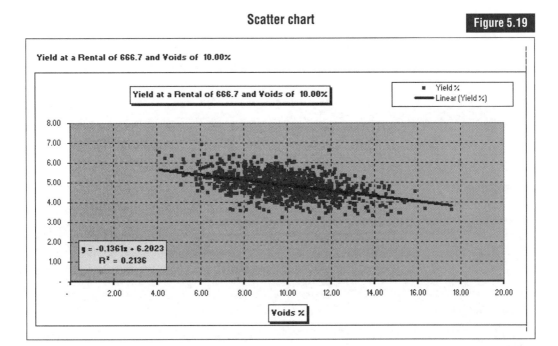

Figure 5.19

Frequency results

Figure 5.20

Frequency Results: Yield at a Rental of 666.7 and Voids of 10.00%

Interval		0.50

Amount	No of Results	Percentage
2.300	▼	-
2.800	-	
3.300	2	0.2%
3.800	43	4.3%
4.300	122	12.2%
4.800	290	29.0%
5.300	306	30.6%
5.800	187	18.7%
6.300	40	4.0%
6.800	9	0.9%
7.300	1	0.1%
	1,000	100.0%

	Rental	Voids %
Minimum:	585.27	4.13
Maximum:	770.26	17.59
Range:	184.99	13.47
Mean:	666.78	9.8713

Yield	
Less than zero no of trials:	-

Arithmetic Mean	4.859
Median ▼	4.853
Skew ▼	0.011
Kurtosis ▼	(0.012)
R Squared	0.214
Slope	(0.136)

Figure 5.21 Histogram

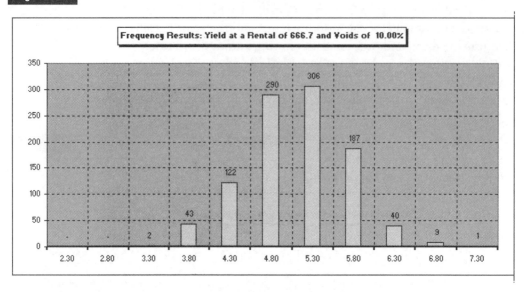

Frequency Results: Yield at a Rental of 666.7 and Voids of 10.00%

Figure 5.22 Frequency tables

Quartiles	Yield %	Count	Total Income	Count
0	3.158	1	1,697.59	1
1	4.477	249	2,406.65	249
2	4.853	250	2,608.71	250
3	5.278	250	2,837.00	250
4	6.929	250	3,724.47	250
Total Results		1,000		1,000
Range	3.771		2,026.882	
Mean		4.86		2,611.58
Median		4.85		2,608.71
Skew		0.011		0.011
Kurtosis		(0.012)		(0.012)
Standard Deviation		0.29		319.46
Coefficient of Variation		0.060		0.122

of 2406.65. Again the simulation model provides more management information about the possible spread of answers. Several sets of scenarios could be run with differing distribution inputs to see the effect of flexing each of the variables.

Quartiles chart

Figure 5.23

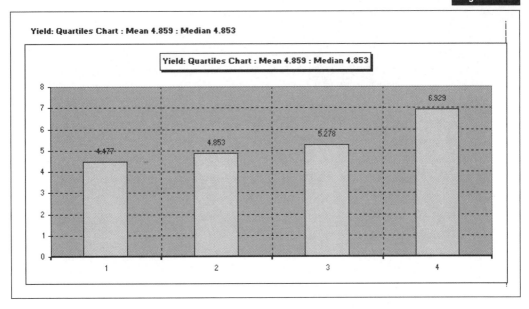

Yield: Quartiles Chart : Mean 4.859 : Median 4.853

SUMMARY

Simulation methods add another layer to financial models allowing a range of inputs based on probability distributions. Running the model through a series of randomly-generated possible scenarios provides an automated 'what if?' analysis. It should be stressed that the outputs are entirely dependent on the input distributions and therefore the model is a probability and not a certainty model. In the real world, there are always events that have not been foreseen by the modeller, which can affect the simulation outputs. Nevertheless, this form of modelling adds another dimension to the information produced by financial models.

6

Financial analysis

File: FT4_06.xls

INTRODUCTION

Financial analysis seeks to outline the main areas of risk highlighted by an organization's set of accounts. Recent company failures, such as Enron, and the consequent tightening of corporate governance as defined by the Sarbanes-Oxley Act in the USA mean that it is important to highlight possible areas of weakness and read the reported data correctly. Since calculating ratios or deriving cash flows with a pocket calculator is time consuming, a risk model can be an important tool for understanding the accounts.

Performance measurement in the form of 'what gets measured gets managed' can be summarized as:

- economy – how well the company buys in the factors of production (labour, materials, knowledge);
- efficiency – how well the company turns the 'raw material' in to goods and services for sale;
- effectiveness – how well the company rewards the key stakeholders including shareholders;
- environment – the company's responsibilities in the wider world;
- ethics – ethical goals such as corporate governance.

Analysis framework

Figure 6.1

Historic analysis
Balance sheet
Income statement
Cash flow
Trends
Competitors
Management strategy

Current position		On-going
Environment		Security
Industry		Settlement exposure
Products	→	Realizable values
Market		
Management		
Profits and cash		

Future		Going concern
Competitiveness		Forecasts
Products		Future cash flows
Management depth	→	Future loan cover
Forecasts		Unexpected events
Cash flow		

Figure 6.1 categorizes the banking analysis. First, the historic position outlines the quality of past decision making and the ability of the management to make and implement strategic decisions leading to an increase in the value of the company. Measures of success will vary by industry: for example, the value added by employees can be important in a service company whereas sales per square metre can indicate increased efficiency in a supermarket chain. For most companies, there are significant indicators of past success.

Past performance is not a guarantee of future success and in assessing loans or financial commitment, analysis needs to switch to the current and forecast position. There are factors within and extra to the organization's control in driving it forward and therefore analysis needs to include some assessment of future performance.

This chapter reviews the analysis from a risk perspective and Figure 6.2 demonstrates the main sources of risk.

- process – limitations of financial statements;
- environment – factors beyond the organization's control;
- industry – competitiveness of the industry and reliability in producing returns;
- financial factors – operating cycle, profitability and financial structure;
- cash flow produced by the interlocking financial factors;
- management competence and depth.

Figure 6.2

Risk framework

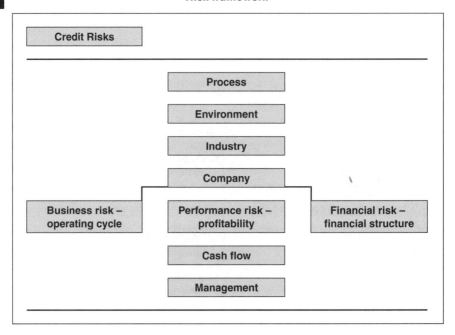

PROCESS

The starting point is the annual report, which in the UK is drawn up based on the following four fundamental principles:

- prudence means that doubtful revenues are not included while potential liabilities and losses are provided for;
- consistency requires similar treatment from one accounting period to the next;
- going concern assumes that the business will continue to operate;
- matching or accruals means that costs should be matched as far as possible to applicable revenue in the same accounting period.

The above principles are augmented by financial reporting standards and conventions which seek to produce similarity in the way that organizations report their results. Internationally, the USA uses a system of financial accounting standards and policies which result in Generally Accepted Accounting Principles (GAAP). Despite the rules on reporting, there are limitations to the financial information so that reports from different companies are not always strictly comparable. For example, there are a number of methods for enhancing earnings which usually involve shifting cost from the income statement to the balance sheet. This could be achieved by adopting a longer depreciation period for fixed assets, capitalization of interest or research and development expenses. The intention here is not to provide a listing of the limitation of accounts but merely to point out that there is a risk in taking the figures as absolute values.

Other distortions could be created by the choice of year end or changes in the composition of group operations. Highly acquisitive companies are difficult to analyze since the figures are not comparable across year ends. Similarly changing year ends reduces the comparability of the figures to the point where trend analysis becomes more difficult.

ENVIRONMENT

The STEEPV model was outlined in Chapter 4 and is applicable here. Any analysis should begin with an assessment of the non-financial factors. These are factors beyond the organization's influence and any analysis should include an understanding of the forces operating on the environment such as the following:

- Economic – economic cycles, interest and exchange rates, inflation both domestic and foreign. In the global economy, economic risks are always present whether an organization is an exporter or domestic service supplier.

■ Demographics and demand in different age groups – Western Europe is an ageing population and this affects the demand for a wide range of products from care homes to nappies.

■ Social – trends that have a medium- and long-term effect on demand.

■ Technology – each industry is affected differently: some may benefit while others may not be able to change rapidly enough to remain competitive. For example, Psion pioneered the personal digital assistant (PDA) market but has recently withdrawn due to increased competition and falling prices.

■ Government changes can change competitiveness. For example, the government reduced the attractiveness of UK finance leases following the Finance Act (No. 2) 1997 by curtailing the tax depreciation benefits relative to operating leases and fixed-term rentals. Changes in the way that government acquires goods and services can also change the landscape such as with the private financing initiatives for the acquisitions of schools and hospitals.

■ Ecology – this factor has assumed more importance with the rise of lobby groups and non-governmental organizations such as Greenpeace. Companies are judged on their 'green' credentials and those such as Shell and Norsk Hydro have been forced to change their policies.

If an environment appears to be stable, then predictions can be made on the basis of the past, but there can be unexpected changes (see Figure 6.3). Where there appears to be dynamic change, then projections of the future are likely to be useful in determining the key success factors and their sensitivity. Where change is both dynamic and complex, then the management ability assumes importance due to the requirement for a market-driven response to change.

Figure 6.3			Response to the environment

	Gauge opinions and make predictions based on the past	Simulation and sensitivity model building
Stable	Gauge opinions and make predictions based on the past	Simulation and sensitivity model building
Dynamic	Focus on future projections. Examine management depth and competence	Simulation and sensitivity models coupled with assessment of quality and depth of management
	Simple	Complex

INDUSTRY

The Michael Porter 'five forces' model (see Figure 6.4) provides a framework for understanding a company's competitive position within an industry. As part of the qualitative analysis, an assessment is made of each of these factors and the impact on competition. Since the management and financial strategy should be coordinated it follows that the industry characteristics influence the type of strategy adopted. The purpose is to try and achieve a 'sustainable competitive advantage' over the short and medium term. In analysis terms this should mean a non volatile cash flow and the ability to meet debts comfortably as they arise.

In the European airline industry, the threat of potential entrants is kept to a minimum by the high capital requirements and the difficulty of accessing new landing slots. National full-cost airlines typically have control over the hub and spoke networks used for intercontinental travel and appear to use their economies of scale to keep out competitors. There are few substitutes to using aircraft travel over longer distances but other forms of travel such as car and rail, most notably the Channel Tunnel, can offer equal benefits. The power of suppliers is great especially in the market for large jets. Lower down there is a duopoly between Boeing and Airbus Industrie which limits airlines' ability to choose. The power of buyers has been increased through deregulation and the rise of low-cost carriers based on the South Western Airlines model in the USA. The 'no frills' package has been developed in Europe by Ryanair and easyJet to such an extent that currently the market capitalization of Ryanair is approximately twice that of British Airways. Therefore the market has become more competitive and the airlines in Europe have a lesser grip leading to reduced profits and prospects.

An alternative method would be to analyze the sources of value and one model uses value chains to assess how a business unit adds value (see Figure 6.5). The key activities are inbound logistics, operations, outbound logistics, marketing and sales, and after service. These areas are supported by the infrastructure, human resources management, technology development

Porter five forces

Figure 6.4

Industry profitability is determined by:	Threat of new entrants	
Bargaining power of suppliers	Rivalry among competitors	Bargaining power of buyers
	Threat of substitutes	

Figure 6.5

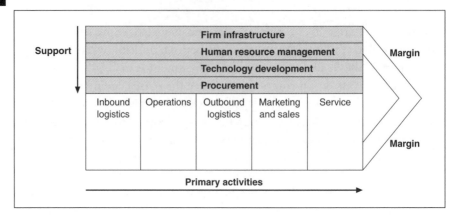

Value chain

and procurement. Business units can be compared to a peer group to assess the degree of success in these areas. The qualitative analysis leads to the modelling and an assessment of risk in the financial reports, and this initial review should provide questions for further considerations when the accounts are standardized as schedules.

FINANCIAL STATEMENTS

After consideration of the macro and industrial context, the model provides a standard method for reviewing companies and identifying trends. The basic question is whether risk is increasing or decreasing in the company. Trade credit tends to be fairly short term while bank loans usually entail a commitment over several years. Bear in mind also the time it takes after the year end to publish accounts. The model spreads the accounts into standard schedules and produces ratios to assist with isolating weaknesses and identifying trends:

- ratios vary widely between different sectors such as retailers, manufacturers and service companies;
- trends need to be considered against the environment and industry sector;
- the absolute numbers are not relevant;
- ratios are backward looking and it usually takes companies some months to report and file accounts;
- analysis against a peer group or sector can highlight areas where the company is more or less efficient.

Most institutions have their own rules about how to treat intangibles or assets under constructions and the spread format introduces a clear and concise method of combining the reported statements together with their notes. The three main areas of risk are:

- operating efficiency – the operating cycle;
- performance – profitability;
- financial – financial structure and leverage.

In reviewing the above three risk sources, the model needs to address

- sales growth and its impact on working capital and cash;
- working capital and the availability of resources;
- cash flow performance, in particular the trading cash flow;
- profitability and the distribution of cost;
- return on capital for shareholders as their return for the risk of investing in the company;
- requirement for capital expenditure to fuel further growth in forecast periods;
- gearing and the proportion of the company funded by outside debt;
- debt repayment ability.

The model conforms to the structure shown in Figure 6.6 and is based on

Model structure

Figure 6.6

Menu	Menu system
	Select sheets
	Basic inputs

Enter income statement and balance sheet	Enter data
	Income Statement
	Balance Sheet

Values updated on income statement and balance sheet	Historic accounting statements updated
	Ratios
	Cash flow
	Free_Cash_Flows

Forecast	Enter performance drivers
	View historic and forecast accounting statements
	Forecast
	FIncome
	FBalance
	FCash flow
	FRatios
	Growth formulas

the standard Systematic application template. The income statement and balance sheet are input schedules and these provide the information for the cash flow and ratio schedules. The forecast sheet uses key performance drivers to redraw the forecast schedules and these act as a basis for the next chapter. Here the emphasis switches to loan cover, sustainable growth and bankruptcy prediction models.

PROFIT AND LOSS

The structure of the profit and loss or income statement follows traditional lines (see Figure 6.7). This is simplified for ease of understanding, but more lines could be added to subdivide the categories to display an increased level of detail.

The input cells in Excel are marked blue and the totals are in bold green on the screen. The latter cells only add up the cells above, which all adhere to the cash flow rule. Cash received is positive, while cash outflows are entered as negative numbers. Numbers are formatted so that zeros display as a '-' to make the schedule easier to understand.

Excel does not allow you to 'drill down' to the answers from one schedule to another. It can be a problem understanding the source of the cell results. The model uses a numbering system, for example 'P' for profit and loss or 'B' for balance sheet, when referring to this data in the calculation schedules. The format for the numbering is:

```
="P"&TEXT(ROW(A10),"00")
```

Figure 6.7	Income statement

No	Item USD'000,000		Dec-98	Dec-99	Dec-00	Dec-01
P10	Sales		7,789.0	17,617.0	35,908.0	39,090.0
P11	Cost of Goods Sold		(6,807.0)	(18,559.0)	(28,020.0)	(30,937.0)
P12	**Gross Margin**		982.0	(942.0)	7,888.0	8,153.0
P13	Depreciation	Manufacturer	-	-	-	-
P14		Amortisation/Other	-	-	-	-
P15	Sales, General &Administration Overheads		-	-	-	-
P16	**Net Operating Profit (NOP)**		982.0	(942.0)	7,888.0	8,153.0
P17	Interest Expense		(450.0)	(692.0)	(966.0)	(970.0)
P18	Interest Income		-	-	-	-
P19	Other Financial Income		46.0	44.0	242.0	385.0
P20	**Profit after Financial Items**		578.0	(1,590.0)	7,164.0	7,568.0
P21	Exceptional Expense		-	-	-	-
P22	**Profit before Tax**		578.0	(1,590.0)	7,164.0	7,568.0
P23	Tax		(393.0)	(877.0)	(2,965.0)	(3,025.0)
P24	**Net Profit after Tax (NPAT)**		185.0	(2,467.0)	4,199.0	4,543.0
P25	Minority Interest		(42.0)	(258.0)	(186.0)	(390.0)
P26	Dividends		-	(42.0)	(72.0)	(65.0)
P27	**Retained Profit for the Year**		143.0	(2,767.0)	3,941.0	4,088.0

Table 6.1

Label	Alternative
Gross Profit	Gross Margin
Net Operating Profit	Earnings or Profit before Interest and Tax (EBIT, PBIT)
Profit after Financial Items	
Profit before Tax	Earnings before Tax
Net Profit after Tax	Earnings or Profit after Tax (EAT, PAT)
Retained Earnings	Retained Profit

This uses the function ROW to return the row number and the function TEXT to change the number to text formatted with two digits.

The levels of profit are clearly marked and Table 6.1 shows the alternative descriptions.

For completeness, the common size analysis is calculated on the right-hand side (see Figure 6.8). This acts as a first step to ratios and shows each of the cost and profit lines as a percentage of sales. Figure 6.8 shows the declining gross margin and profits coupled with an increasing dividend payout ratio.

Income statement – percentages

Figure 6.8

No	Item USD'000,000	Dec-98	Dec-99	Dec-00	Dec-01	Dec-02
P10	Sales	100.0	100.0	100.0	100.0	100.0
P11	Cost of Goods Sold	87.4	105.3	78.0	79.1	90.0
P12	**Gross Margin**	**12.6**	**5.3**	**22.0**	**20.9**	**10.0**
P13	Depreciation Manufacturer	-	-	-	-	-
P14	Amortisation/Other	-	-	-	-	-
P15	Sales, General &Administration Overheads	-	-	-	-	-
P16	**Net Operating Profit (NOP)**	**12.6**	**5.3**	**22.0**	**20.9**	**10.0**
P17	Interest Expense	5.8	3.9	2.7	2.5	4.4
P18	Interest Income	-	-	-	-	-
P19	Other Financial Income	0.6	0.2	0.7	1.0	1.2
P20	**Profit after Financial Items**	**7.4**	**9.0**	**20.0**	**19.4**	**6.8**
P21	Exceptional Expense	-	-	-	-	-
P22	**Profit before Tax**	**7.4**	**9.0**	**20.0**	**19.4**	**6.8**
P23	Tax	5.0	5.0	8.3	7.7	2.6
P24	**Net Profit after Tax (NPAT)**	**2.4**	**14.0**	**11.7**	**11.6**	**4.2**
P25	Minority Interest	0.5	1.5	0.5	1.0	0.1
P26	Dividends	-	0.2	0.2	0.2	0.3
P27	**Retained Profit for the Year**	**1.8**	**15.7**	**11.0**	**10.5**	**3.9**

BALANCE SHEET

The balance sheet shows the book value of assets and liabilities of the company at each year end. The format corresponds to international notation and is split into current and fixed assets followed by current liabilities,

Figure 6.9	Assets					

Assets

No	Assets USD'000,000	Dec-98	Dec-99	Dec-00	Dec-01
B10	Cash and Deposits	155.0	1,727.0	876.0	761.0
B11	Marketable Securities/Invesments	54.0	-	-	-
B12	Trade Debtors (Receivables)	1,241.0	5,309.0	5,746.0	6,815.0
B13	Inventory	-	-	-	-
B14	Sundry Current Assets	424.0	3,733.0	3,702.0	2,179.0
B15	**Current Assets**	**1,874.0**	**10,769.0**	**10,324.0**	**9,755.0**
B16	Land and Buildings	-	-	-	-
B17	Plant and Machinery	7,569.0	26,843.0	33,728.0	44,627.0
B18	Depreciation	(855.0)	(2,275.0)	(5,110.0)	(7,204.0)
B19	**Net Property, Plant and Equipment**	**6,714.0**	**24,568.0**	**28,618.0**	**37,423.0**
B20	Other Investments	1,126.0	4,470.0	4,822.0	5,131.0
B21	Intangibles/Goodwill	13,882.0	47,285.0	47,308.0	46,594.0
B22	**Non Current and Fixed Assets**	**21,722.0**	**76,323.0**	**80,748.0**	**89,148.0**
B23					
B24	**Total Assets**	**23,596.0**	**87,092.0**	**91,072.0**	**98,903.0**

Figure 6.10	Liabilities					

Liabilities

No	Assets USD'000,000	Dec-98	Dec-99	Dec-00	Dec-01
B28	Short Term Bank Loans	11.0	4,757.0	5,015.0	7,646.0
B29	Trade Creditors (Payables)	470.0	1,771.0	6,909.0	6,022.0
B30	Other Creditors	119.0	-	-	-
B31	Other Current Liabilities	1,474.0	9,652.0	5,825.0	4,005.0
B32	**Current Liabilities**	**2,074.0**	**16,180.0**	**17,749.0**	**17,673.0**
B33	Long Term Bank Loans	7,413.0	16,448.0	13,128.0	17,696.0
B34	**Long Term Liabilities**	**7,413.0**	**16,448.0**	**13,128.0**	**17,696.0**
B35	Tax/Deferred Taxation	308.0	5,523.0	6,898.0	5,533.0
B36	**Long Term Liabilities and Provisions**	**7,721.0**	**21,971.0**	**20,026.0**	**23,229.0**
B37	Ordinary Shares (Common Stock)	15,540.0	50,201.0	52,136.0	52,906.0
B38	Profit and Loss Reserve (Retained Earnings)	(1,739.0)	(4,960.0)	(1,438.0)	2,503.0
B39	**Shareholders' Funds**	**13,801.0**	**45,241.0**	**50,698.0**	**55,409.0**
B40	Minorities/Deferred Accounts	-	3,700.0	2,599.0	2,592.0
B41	**Total Liabilities and Equity**	**23,596.0**	**87,092.0**	**91,072.0**	**98,903.0**

CheckSum:	No Errors	-	-	-	-

Market Data

	Dec-98	Dec-99	Dec-00	Dec-01
Number of Shares Issued & Outstanding	981.616	2,776.759	2,849.744	2,887.960
Current Share Price	20.00	45.00	50.00	19.00

long-term debt and shareholders' funds, which is split into shares and retained profit and loss. The number of categories is again limited but could be expanded, for example to include other share categories.

The total assets are given for each year and there is again a percentage split (see Figure 6.9). This is an input sheet and therefore no 'work' is done here. Rather the data is standardized for further analysis in the cash flow and ratios sheets. The schedule includes a 'CheckSum' to check that assets equal liabilities (see Figure 6.10). If they do not, then cell E43 displays a warning message:

```
=IF(SUM(I43:M43)<>0,"Errors","No Errors")
```

Together the income statement and balance sheet constitute the basic inputs to the model. In this form, you can look along the rows and try to pick out trends. The common size views assist with a cursory view of trends, but eventually you need to look more closely by calculating ratios and discerning trends.

OPERATING EFFICIENCY

The three areas of risk determine the quality and quantity generated by the organization. The decisions of what and how much to produce are underpinned by the management. In turn, the efficiency in the business cycle (see Figure 6.11) underlines the control exerted by the management in the use of resources.

Cash is used to purchase raw materials, which move through the production process into finished goods. The company delivers the goods, invoices its clients and has to wait for the customer to pay. It is a measure of

Operating cycle

Figure 6.11

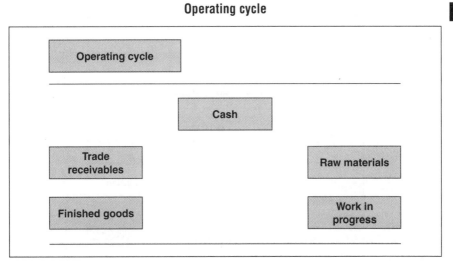

management ability as to how fast it can 'turn' this cycle. If it cannot sell its finished goods, then they will remain in a warehouse and have to be funded from cash in the operating cycle, bank finance or new equity. More borrowings will increase the company's costs and reduce profits through an increased interest burden. This is termed 'business risk'.

Liquidity is the ability of management to turn operating assets into cash. Here it is necessary to question the valuation of the current assets. Questions could relate to the saleability of the stock or the composition of the debtors where cash can safely be expected. For example, a leasing company could fail to terminate slow payers and thereby delay booking a loss due to a client's insolvency. The effect would overstate debtors and profits by including non-viable debts.

Solvency requires that the organization can meet cash demands as they fall due. Bankers require cash payment both of capital and interest. Here the accounts should demonstrate the margin of safety should sales decline. Stocks are of particular interest, especially in industries such as retailing where the number of days stock could hide other more fundamental problems.

The balance sheet structure is shown in Figure 6.12. The model calculates ratios such as:

- Stock days – this is the number of stock days on hand. A rising number of stock days could demonstrate the company's inability to shift old or out-of-date stock. This could be further subdivided into raw materials, work in progress and finished goods.

- Creditor days – this is the number of days taken to pay creditors. A high or rising ratio could indicate that the company was overtrading and using supplier cash.

- Debtor days indicate the accounts receivable days or collection period. The attitude towards credit policy and collection can illustrate the management's abilities or problems with sub-standard or returned products.

- Funding gap or cash conversion cycle. This is the debtor days plus stock

Figure 6.12   **Balance sheet structure**

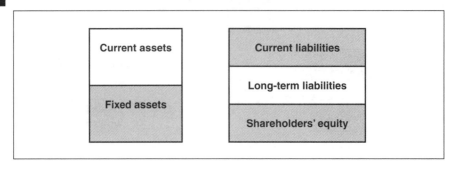

days minus creditor days. A longer cycle means more risk since the company has to wait longer to turn debtors and stock back into cash.

- Working capital turnover. This is sales/(stocks + debtors − creditors) and represents the number of times in a year that the company turns the working capital. Again different companies and industries require differing levels for efficient operation. The ratio may also indicate overtrading where the ratio is high and growing quickly. The level of growth may be too high for the financial resources of the company. In the short term, overtrading may be a source of low-cost financing but in the longer term the risk of insolvency increases. Other symptoms are:
  - decreasing liquidity;
  - high stock turnover;
  - increasing interest costs;
  - high working capital turnover;
  - reduced capital expenditure or increased investment in intangibles.

The model uses functions to determine if last year is better than the two previous years ('Better'), ahead of one year ('OK') or worse than both years ('Worse'). This directs the user at the lines than need investigation or further attention. The cell formula in cell M11 on the ratios sheet is:

```
=IF(K11=0,"N/A",IF(J11=0,"N/A",IF(AND(L11>K11,
L11>J11),"Better",IF(OR(L11>K11,L11>J11),"OK",
"Worse"))))
```

Gearing and inventory together with the funding gap use opposite logic. If the number of days or the gap increases, this means that the company has to find more resources to fund the cycle. The funding gap increases in the two previous periods and so the cell formula returns 'Worse'.

In each formula, the possibility of an error caused by a zero number is handled by an IF statement. This is Ratios cell L11:

```
=IF(Income!M10<>0,(Income!M24/Income!M10)*100,0)
```

An alternative would be to use ISERROR to force zero if Excel cannot calculate a valid answer. The answer is multiplied by 100 since the application standardizes on numbers rather than a mixture of numbers and percentages.

```
=IF(ISERROR(Income!M24/Income!M10),0,(Income!M24/
Income!M10)*100)
```

Figure 6.13 shows an improved position in receivables, where the number of days is declining, and a worsening position for creditors. Working capital turnover is increasing due to the reduced sales, debtors and creditors. Overall the operating efficiency is increasing against a background of falling sales.

Figure 6.13   **Ratios**

Line	Item	USD'000,000	Reference	Dec-01	Dec-02
	Core Ratios				
R11	Return on Sales (NPAT/Sales %)		P24/P10	11.62	4.17
R12	Asset Turnover (Sales / Total Assets)		P10/B24	0.40	0.34
R13	Asset Leverage (Total Assets/Equity)		B24/B39	1.78	1.79
R14	Return on Equity (NPAT/Equity %)		P24/B39	8.20	2.53
	Profitability				
R18	Gross Profit / Sales (%)		P12/P10	20.86	9.99
R19	Net Operating Profit / Sales (%)		P16/P10	20.86	9.99
R20	Profit before Tax / Sales (%)		P22/P10	19.36	6.80
R21	Return on Capital Employed (ROCE)		P16/B39+B33	11.15	3.99
R22	Return on Invested Capital (ROIC)		P16*(1-T)/B28+33+39	14.13	5.49
R23	Return on Assets (ROA)		P16/B24	8.24	3.38
	Operating Efficiency				
R27	Inventory Days		B13/P11	-	-
R28	Trade Receivables (Debtor) Days		B12/P10	63.63	55.07
R29	Creditors Days		B29/P11	71.05	55.84
R30	Funding Gap Debtors+Inventory-Creditors	R25+R26-R27		(7.41)	(0.76)
R31	Working Capital Turnover		P10/B12.13-B29	49.29	75.82
	Financial Structure				
R35	Current Ratio		B15/B32	0.55	1.00
R36	Quick Ratio (Acid Test)		B15-B13/B32	0.55	1.00
R37	Working Capital (Thousands)		B15-B32	(7,918)	(5)
R38	Gross Gearing (%)		B28+B33/B39	45.74	53.22
R39	Net Gearing (%)		B28+B33-B10-11/B39	44.36	50.77
R40	Solvency (Times Interest Earned)		P16/P17	8.41	2.29
R41	Total Equity/Total Assets		B39/B24	56.02	55.75

PROFITABILITY

Profitability is supposed to be the goal of companies to reward the share-holders for risking their investment in the company. Financial reporting standards set out the general rules, but there are always different interpretations of the rules by operating officers. Furthermore, there are several profit and return measures which may provide differing results. If a company is profitable, then one would expect to see the returns revealed in cash flow, but this is not always the case. Therefore, profitability should not be reviewed to the exclusion of operating efficiency, financial structure and cash flow.

Where you have profits, but no cash flow, then you may need to examine the accounting methods and standards. For example, the company in the model has increased sharply the amounts in intangible assets to the point where this is almost as great as the shareholders' funds. This could hide costs that are being 'parked' in the balance sheet in order to bolster profits.

The ratios in this section are:

- gross profit/sales as the percentage gross margin;
- net operating profit/sales as a percentage return on trading;
- profit before tax/sales as the profit margin after interest costs;
- return on capital employed (ROCE) as net operating profit divided by long-term debt plus shareholders' funds;
- return on invested capital (ROIC) as net operating profit multiplied by (1 – tax) divided by long- and short-term debt plus shareholders' funds;
- return on assets as the net operating profit divided by total assets.

Figure 6.14 show a volatile position with returns worse in the last period for all ratios. The income statement profit ratios have all halved and balance sheet measures such as the return on assets have sunk to levels lower than the cost of capital.

Figure 6.14	Profitability					
Item USD'000,000	Dec-98	Dec-99	Dec-00	Dec-01	Dec-02	Action
Gross Profit / Sales (%)	12.61	(5.35)	21.97	20.86	9.99	Worse
Net Operating Profit / Sales (%)	12.61	(5.35)	21.97	20.86	9.99	Worse
Profit before Tax / Sales (%)	7.42	(9.03)	19.95	19.36	6.80	Worse
Return on Capital Employed (ROCE)	4.63	(1.53)	12.36	11.15	3.99	Worse
Return on Invested Capital (ROIC)	7.77	(0.64)	16.20	14.13	5.49	Worse
Return on Assets (ROA)	4.16	(1.08)	8.66	8.24	3.38	Worse

FINANCIAL STRUCTURE

Financial risk is concerned with the structure of the balance sheet together with the sources of finance to the company. Bankers are concerned with the liabilities taken on by companies and their ability to service debt. Prospects are often more volatile than originally anticipated and therefore the model needs to provide information about the financial strength. The company needs to manage debt and equity efficiently in order to reduce the cost of capital but also not take on obligations which cannot be paid back. In general terms, the cost of capital falls with an increasing debt percentage on the balance sheet but the financial risk increases due to the interest burden. The ratios calculated by the model are:

- Current ratio – basic measure of liquidity as the ratio of current assets to liabilities. The working capital requirement varies across industries so the absolute value is less important than the trend.

- Quick ratio – this excludes stock from the current ratio. The rationale is that stock is often difficult to sell at book prices and may not be as realizable in the short term.

- Working capital as current assets minus current liabilities.

- Gross gearing (leverage) as short- plus long-term debt divided by shareholders' funds.

- Net gearing (leverage) as gross gearing debt less cash and marketable securities.

- Solvency or time interest earned measures the number of times profit before interest and tax covers the interest payment.

- Total equity/total assets is a measure of financial strength or who owns the company. Companies with a high ratio are financially more resilient.

Figure 6.15 shows increasing gearing and reduced solvency as returns only cover the interest payment twice over. The findings are in line with operating efficiency and profitability, both of which have declined in the last year.

| Figure 6.15 | | | | Financial structure | | | |

Item USD'000,000	Dec-98	Dec-99	Dec-00	Dec-01	Dec-02	Action
Current Ratio	0.90	0.67	0.58	0.55	1.00	Better
Quick Ratio (Acid Test)	0.90	0.67	0.58	0.55	1.00	Better
Working Capital (Thousands)	(200)	(5,411)	(7,425)	(7,918)	(5)	Better
Gross Gearing (%)	53.79	46.87	35.79	45.74	53.22	Worse
Net Gearing (%)	52.28	43.05	34.06	44.36	50.77	Worse
Solvency (Times Interest Earned)	2.18	(1.36)	8.17	8.41	2.29	Worse
Total Equity/Total Assets	58.49	51.95	55.67	56.02	55.75	OK

CORE RATIOS

One method of calculating ratios from key areas is to use Du Pont or core ratios and calculate the components of the return on equity. Return on equity defines the return the shareholders receive from the enterprise. As a shortcut, the method also provides a ratio from each of the risk areas discussed above.

The return on equity is net profit after tax/shareholders' equity and this can be subdivided into:

Return on Sales	(NPAT/Sales)	Profitability	P24/P10
Asset Turnover	(Sales/Total Assets)	Operating Efficiency	P10/B24
Asset Leverage	(Total Assets/Equity)	Financial Structure	B23/B39

These three ratios, when multiplied together, equal the return on equity.

$$NPAT/Equity = Sales/Total\ assets * Total\ assets/Equity * NPAT/Sales$$

The ratios in this section (see Figure 6.16) are multiplied out to show the composition of the return on equity (see Figure 6.17). This has declined over the period and underlines the worsening performance. Faced with the weaker areas, the analysis can then proceed to review these areas in more detail.

The ratios demonstrate the levers that management can use to extract performance from the business:

- earnings from each $1 of sales – profit margin (income statement)
- sales for each $1 of assets – asset turnover (asset side of balance sheet)
- equity used to finance each $1 of assets – financial or asset leverage (liabilities side of balance sheet).

Core ratios

Figure 6.16

Item USD'000,000	Dec-98	Dec-99	Dec-00	Dec-01	Dec-02	Action
Return on Sales (NPAT/Sales %)	2.38	(14.00)	11.69	11.62	4.17	Worse
Asset Turnover (Sales / Total Assets)	0.33	0.20	0.39	0.40	0.34	Worse
Asset Leverage (Total Assets/Equity)	1.71	1.93	1.80	1.78	1.79	OK
Return on Equity (NPAT/Equity %)	1.34	(5.45)	8.28	8.20	2.53	Worse

Return on equity on the right-hand scale with the components on the left

Figure 6.17

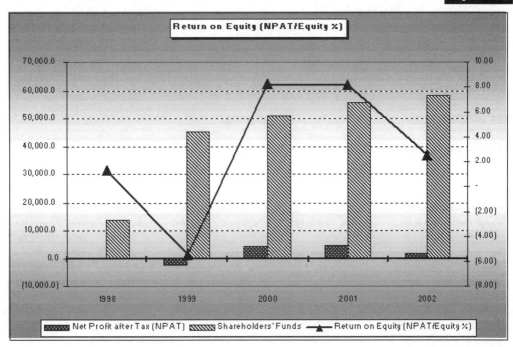

Return on equity is often considered to be the most important return measure, but it has limitations:

- The return on equity (ROE) is historic and may not be a good indicator for the future.

- The calculation does not include a measure of the risk profile of the industry and company. More risk should demand a greater return to shareholders.

- The ROE is an accounting measure and is based on book values. The value of equity may be better presented by the market value of debt and the market value of equity (enterprise value).

Asset turnover depends on the sector and the assets needed in the business. Knowledge-based companies invest in people and information as major assets in developing competitive advantage as opposed to high levels of plant and equipment. These values are not recorded on the balance sheet.

Asset leverage depends on the uncertainty of cash flows. In a risky or volatile business, such as pharmaceuticals, shareholders are normally expected to fund research and development. There may be pressure to advance revenues and capitalize costs which can distort the asset leverage.

MARKET RATIOS

The model includes a number of market ratios (see Figure 6.18). The market capitalization is reducing due to a reduced share price. The earnings per share has declined and the P/E ratio increases due to the reduction in share price. The dividend per share has increased reflecting management's desire to maintain the dividends despite falling profits. The market to book

| Figure 6.18 | Market ratios |

Item USD'000,000	Dec-98	Dec-99	Dec-00	Dec-01	Dec-02	Action
Number of Shares Issued & Outstanding	982	2,777	2,850	2,888	2,933	
Current Share Price	20.00	45.00	50.00	19.00	13.00	
Market Capitalisation	19,632	124,954	142,487	54,871	38,129	Worse
Earnings per Share	0.19	(0.89)	1.47	1.57	0.50	Worse
P / E Ratio	106.12	(50.65)	33.93	12.08	26.01	OK
Dividends per Share	-	0.02	0.03	0.02	0.04	Better
Dividend Cover	-	(64.88)	55.74	63.89	12.83	Worse
Market Price / Book	1.42	2.76	2.81	0.99	0.66	Worse
Enterprise Value (EV)	27,056	146,159	160,630	80,213	68,957	Worse
EV / EBITDA	-	(155.16)	20.36	9.84	19.62	OK

ratio is below one and therefore the stock market does not rate the prospects for the company or have faith in the management.

TREND ANALYSIS

The Historic_Mgt_Analysis sheet provides a dynamic chart for reviewing all the rows in the income statement, balance sheet and ratios. It can often 'see' the trends when faced with the schedules of numbers produced by Excel. On the basis that different audiences needs varying levels of detail, the chart allows you to look at individual lines.

Figure 6.19 shows the return on assets where the components are:

- combo box with the labels as inputs and cell J13 as the link;
- OFFSET function looking at the block of data below and using the cell link as the row number;
- chart of the single series.

Figure 6.20 provides a relative result where the first year is a factor of 100 and the next years the percentage movement. Thus factor 80 would be a 20 per cent reduction.

Dynamic chart

Figure 6.19

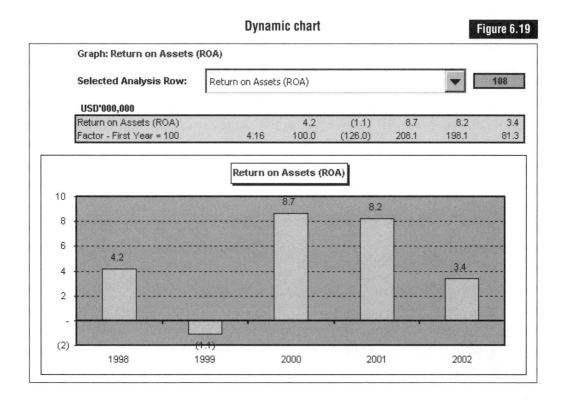

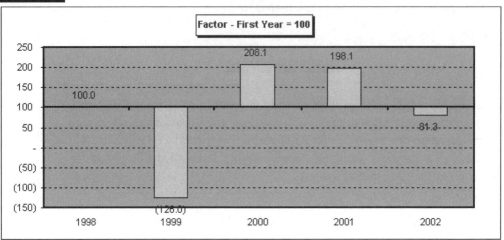

Factor chart

CASH FLOW

The ratio analysis shows a worsening financial position so the next stage is to examine the cash flow produced by operations and consumed by the company. Since cash flow should not be affected by accounting standards and conventions, this analysis may reveal more about the financial prospects. Similarly, as bankers require a steady and non-volatile cash flow to repay debts, cash flow analysis should provide further information on financial health.

The model includes a sheet called Cashflow which reconciles the income statement and balance sheet back to change in cash.

> Starting cash balance
> + Cash generated from operations and other sources
> − Cash used to fund operations, investment, research, etc.
> = Ending cash balance.

The model uses a layout which calculates the trading cash or net operating cash flow (NOCF) and then the uses of the cash together with the new capital introduced into the business to reconcile back to bank. The key objective is to split the cash generated through trading operations, one-off sources of cash, uses of cash and new capital introduced into the business. Provided the model is correct the remaining balance should reconcile back to the change in cash on the balance sheet.

The important lines are:

- EBITDA – net operating profit adding back non-cash items such as depreciation of fixed assets and amortization of goodwill as a simplistic proxy for cash flow;

- net operating cash flow – trading cash produced from the trading of the company;
- cash flow before financing – cash before new capital.

Figure 6.21 illustrates the derivation of the lines in the cash flow. This is particularly useful where the information is derived from the change in balance

Cash flow method

Figure 6.21

Item	Comment
Net Operating Profit (NOP)	Income Statement
Depreciation / Amortisation	Non cash items
Earnings before Interest, Tax, Depreciation and Amortisation (EBITDA)	
Operating Items	
(+)/- Current Assets	Inc = negative, Dec = positive
+/(-) Current Liabilities	Inc = Positive, Dec = negative
Net Operating Cash Flow (NOCF)	EBITDA + change in working capital
Returns on Investment and Servicing of Finance	
Interest Received	Income statement
Interest Paid	Income statement
Dividends	Income statement
Net Cash Outflow from Returns on Investments and Servicing of Finance	
Taxation	
Taxes Paid	Income statement
Deferred Tax	Change in balance sheet
Net Cash Outflow for Taxation	
Investing Activities	
Expenditure on Property, Plant and Equipment	Change in balance sheet + depreciation in P&L
Expenditure on Investments & Intangibles	Change in balance sheet
Marketable Securities	Change in balance sheet
Net Cash Outflow for Capital Expenditure and Financial Investment	
Exceptional and Minority Items	
Exceptional Income and Expense	Income statement and balance sheet (if applicable)
Net Cash Outflow from Exceptional and Minority Items	
Reconciliation	
Reconciliation Figure	Difference between RE on P&L and balance sheet
Total Cash (Outflow)/Inflow before Financing	Addition
Financing	
Share Capital and Reserves	Change in balance sheet
Short Term Debt and Provisions	Change in balance sheet
Long Term Debt and Provisions	Change in balance sheet
Net Cash Inflow/(Outflow) from Financing	
Increase / (Decrease) in Cash	Addition

Figure 6.22	Cash flow

Line	Item USD'000,000	Reference	Dec-02
C10	**Net Operating Profit (NOP)**		3,514.0
C11	Depreciation / Amortisation	P13.14	-
C12	**Earnings before Interest, Tax, Depreciation and Amortisation (EBITDA)**		3,514.0
C14	**Operating Items**		
C15	(+)/- Current Assets	B12.14	1,205.0
C16	+/(-) Current Liabilities	B29.31	(1,607.0)
C17	**Net Operating Cash Flow (NOCF)**		3,112.0
C19	**Returns on Investment and Servicing of Finance**		
C20	Interest Received	P18	-
C21	Interest Paid	P17	(1,533.0)
C22	Dividends	P26	(117.0)
C23	**Net Cash Outflow from Returns on Investments and Servicing of Finance**		**(1,650.0)**
C25	**Taxation**		
C26	Taxes Paid	P23	(927.0)
C27	Deferred Tax	B35	1,102.0
C28	**Net Cash Outflow for Taxation**		175.0
C30	**Investing Activities**		
C31	Expenditure on Property, Plant and Equipmen B19+P13+P14		(1,386.0)
C32	Expenditure on Investments, LT Assets & Int: B20.21+P19		(3,763.0)
C33	Marketable Securities	B11	-
C34	**Net Cash Outflow for Capital Expenditure and Financial Investment**		**(5,149.0)**
C36	**Exceptional and Minority Items**		
C37	Exceptional Income and Expense	P21+P25+B40	(2,456.0)
C38	**Net Cash Outflow from Exceptional and Minority Items**		**(2,456.0)**
C40	**Reconciliation**		
C41	Reconciliation Figure		(285.0)
C42	**Total Cash (Outflow)/Inflow before Financing**		**(6,253.0)**
C44	**Financing**		
C45	Share Capital and Reserves	B37	1,422.0
C46	Short Term Debt and Provisions	B28	(6,856.0)
C47	Long Term Debt and Provisions	B33	12,342.0
C48	**Net Cash Inflow/(Outflow) from Financing**		6,908.0
C50	**Increase / (Decrease) in Cash**		**655.0**
C52	**Reconciliation of Net Cash Flow to Bank**		
C53	Cash	B10	655.0
C54			
C55	CheckSum: No Errors		-

from the beginning to the end of the year in the balance sheet and the amounts passed through the income statement.

The method is summarized in Figure 6.21 where the statement starts with the net operating profit and adds back non-cash items resulting in earnings before interest, tax, depreciation and amortization (EBITDA). The changes in working capital are subtracted to form the net operating cash flow. An increase in current assets results in a reduction of cash while an increase in current liabilities results in an increase of cash.

The net operating cash flow is usually the first line of a reported cash flow statement and the lines above are shown as a note. Below the net operating cash flow, there are categories for returns on investment and servicing of finance, taxation, investing activities, exceptional and minority items.

The reconciliation items catch any differences between the retained earnings in the income statement and the amount actually added to the reserves in the balance sheet. These could consist of:

- prior year P&L adjustment;
- shares issued or repurchased;
- preference shares issued;
- goodwill written off or written back;
- foreign exchange translation;
- revaluation for the year;
- transfer to/from reserves.

The balance at the bottom should agree with the change in cash and there is a CheckSum to ensure that any errors are reported visually on the schedule (see Figure 6.22).

Net operating cash flow (NOCF)

Figure 6.23 illustrates the variability in the underlying cash flow over the four periods. The operating cash flow has declined in the last three periods.

NOCF

Figure 6.23

Line	Item	USD'000,000	Dec-99	Dec-00	Dec-01	Dec-02
C10	**Net Operating Profit (NOP)**		(942.0)	7,888.0	8,153.0	3,514.0
C11	Depreciation / Amortisation		-	-	-	-
C12	**EBITDA**		(942.0)	7,888.0	8,153.0	3,514.0
C14	**Operating Items**					
C15	(+)/- Current Assets		(7,377.0)	(406.0)	454.0	1,205.0
C16	+/(-) Current Liabilities		9,360.0	1,311.0	(2,707.0)	(1,607.0)
C17	**Net Operating Cash Flow (NOCF)**		**1,041.0**	**8,793.0**	**5,900.0**	**3,112.0**

Figure 6.24   **Cash ratios**

Item USD'000,000	Dec-98	Dec-99	Dec-00	Dec-01	Dec-02	Action
EBITDA / Sales (%)	-	(5.35)	21.97	20.86	9.99	Worse
Net Operating Cash Flow/Sales		5.91	24.49	15.09	8.85	Worse
Cash Flow before Financing/Sales		(266.05)	0.77	(20.68)	(17.77)	Worse

The ratios schedule contains cash flow ratios at the bottom calculated by dividing different cash measures back into sales (see Figure 6.24). These again show a reduction in cash flow. Sales are used since this number should not be varied by international accounting conventions but there are still variances on when revenues are recognized.

- EBITDA/sales (%)
- net operating cash flow/sales
- cash flow before financing/sales.

Free cash flow

Free cash flow has a number of definitions and Figure 6.25 shows the difficulty of defining the elements that should be included or excluded. In simple terms, free cash flow is the cash flow available to pay debt providers and equity holders. It is defined here as:

> net operating profit (NOP)
>   + depreciation/amortization/non-cash items
> earnings before interest, tax, depreciation and amortization (EBITDA)
>   +/– changes in net working assets
> net operating cash flow (NOCF)
>   – expenditure on property, plant and equipment, investment and proceeds of sale
>   – net cash outflow for taxation.
> operating free cash flow.

There is a schedule in the model called Free_Cash_Flows, which uses information from the cash flow schedule to derive free cash flow. This schedule includes expenditure on investments and shows a cash outflow when capital expenditure and investments are taken into account (see Figure 6.25).

Free cash flow

Figure 6.25

Reference	USD'000,00	Dec-00	Dec-01	Dec-02
Free Cash Flow				
Operating Profit (NOP)	C10	7,888.0	8,153.0	3,514.0
Depreciation / Amortisation / Non-cash Items	C11	-	-	-
Earnings before Interest, Tax, Depreciation and Amortisation (E	**FCF11.12**	**7,888.0**	**8,153.0**	**3,514.0**
Changes in Net Working Assets	C15.16	905.0	(2,253.0)	(402.0)
Net Operating Cash Flow (NOCF)	**FCF13.14**	**8,793.0**	**5,900.0**	**3,112.0**
Expenditure on Property, Plant and Equipment /Proceeds of Sale	C31.32	(4,183.0)	(8,015.0)	(5,149.0)
Net Cash Outflow for Taxation	C28	(1,590.0)	(4,390.0)	175.0
Operating Free Cashflow	**FCF15.17**	**3,020.0**	**(6,505.0)**	**(1,862.0)**

FORECASTS

The financial analysis model has concentrated on the historic results whereas this section sets out the forecast method used in the file. Bankers need to forecast cash flows in order to ascertain the ability to repay future debts. Whilst statistical methods such as exponential smoothing or harmonic means could be applied, this method focuses on the key determinants of value creation.

The objective is to provide values for key drivers such as sales growth or capital expenditure and then to redraw the financial statements to provide both a historic and forecast perspective. This provides an income statement, balance sheet together with a cash flow, and ratios. The exact layouts are used for the forecast and historic schedules in order to minimize the errors. Similarly, management analysis can be enhanced with charts to show the anticipated changes.

The completed model should assist in answering management questions, for example:

- Does the company possess sufficient internal resources to fund the antici-pated growth?
- Will the company's financial position strengthen or weaken?
- Is the risk of insolvency likely to increase?

Key drivers

This approach is sometimes called percent of sales forecasting. It involves:

- calculating profit and loss items as a percentage of sales;

- calculating balance sheet items as a percentage of sales;
- drawing the profit and loss;
- drawing the balance sheet;
- using cash or short-term overdraft as the 'plug' to make the balance sheet add up.

Figure 6.26 is an extract from the forecast sheet showing drivers and the historic percentages.

Since most variables on the income statement are assumed to have a linear relationship to sales, the only items with links to the balance sheet are interest payments and receipts together with depreciation. These require information from the income statement and balance sheet as detailed in Figure 6.27. New equity, capital expenditure and investments are actual amounts rather than percentages. This matrix could be made more complex with more drivers and amounts rather than sales percentages.

Sales growth is usually the most important variable since it drives the company forward. The growth rate in cell G12 is based on this formula. In all cases, the model will display zero if there are no sales in the previous period, and it will suppress mathematical errors.

```
=IF(F11=0,0,(G11-F11)/F11)
```

Columns K to O are inputs for the five years of the forecast and the user simply reviews the previous five-year period and after investigation can select a percentage for each of the variables. It is a good idea to establish a 'Base

---

Figure 6.26 **Key drivers**

Line	Item	USD* Reference	Dec-98	Dec-99	Dec-00	Dec-01	Dec-02
			Actual	Actual	Actual	Actual	Actual
	Forecast						
F11	Initial sales	P10	7,789.0	17,617.0	35,908.0	39,090.0	35,179.0
F12	Sales growth	Change P10		126.2%	103.8%	8.9%	(10.0%)
F13	Costs of goods sold/Sales	P11/P10	87.4%	105.3%	78.0%	79.1%	90.0%
F14	Depreciation rate	P13.P14/B19	-	-	-	-	-
F15	SG&A/Sales	P15/P10	-	-	-	-	-
F16	Interest paid on debt	P17/B28+B33	6.1%	3.3%	5.3%	3.8%	5.0%
F17	Interest earned on cash	P18.19/B10.11	22.0%	2.5%	27.6%	50.6%	29.1%
F18	Exceptionals/Sales	P21/F11	-	-	-	-	-
F19	Marginal tax rate	P23/P22	68.0%	(55.2%)	41.4%	40.0%	38.7%
F20	Dividend payout ratio	P26/P24	-	(1.7%)	1.7%	1.4%	8.0%
F21	Fixed assets increase	B19		17,854	4,050	8,805	1,386
F22	Intangibles increase	B21		33,403	23	(714)	3,943
F23	Current assets/Sales	B11.14/F11	22.1%	51.3%	26.3%	23.0%	22.1%
F24	Current liabilities/Sales	B32-B28/F11	26.5%	64.8%	35.5%	25.7%	23.9%
F25	Debt/Sales	B33+B28/F11	95.3%	120.4%	50.5%	64.8%	87.6%
F26	Deferred tax/Sales	B35/F11	4.0%	31.4%	19.2%	14.2%	18.9%
F27	New Equity	B37		34,661	1,935	770	1,422
F28	Current Share Price		20.00	45.00	50.00	19.00	13.00

Variables

Figure 6.27

Item	Reference	
Forecast		
Initial sales	P10	Use last year as the base
Sales growth	Change P10	Sales growth
Costs of goods sold/Sales	P11/P10	
Depreciation rate	P13.P14/B19	Depreciation on previous year's fixed asset in balance sheet
SG&A/Sales	P15/P10	
Interest paid on debt	P17/B28+B33	Interest paid on debt in balance sheet
Interest earned on cash	P18.19/B10.11	Interest received on marketable securities in balance sheet
Exceptionals/Sales	P21/F11	
Marginal tax rate	P23/P22	Tax paid / Profit before tax
Dividend payout ratio	P26/P24	Dividends / Profit after tax
Net fixed assets/Sales	B19/F11	
Intangibles/Sales	B20.21/F11	
Current assets/Sales	B12.14/F11	
Current liabilities/Sales	B32-B28/F11	
Debt/Sales	B33+B28/F11	
Deferred tax/Sales	B35/F11	
New Equity	B37	Actual amount

Case' and save it as a scenario using Tools, Scenarios, Add. It is likely that you would want to test various views of the future and scenarios are a good way of recording the 'audit trail'. For example, the case in the model is optimistic as it anticipates growth and a reduced cost of sales. Using figures for the previous year will not produce such a positive outcome.

The percentages are all shown as input cells in Figure 6.28. You can then develop the answers by changing individual years. There is no rule that sales growth or depreciation has to be the same each year although for simplicity the inputs have been restricted to the first two years.

The model provides the user with immediate feedback as each variable is changed. You do not want to have to select the forecast statement to see the answer every time you change an input cell. Below the main table, there is a table of results showing the net operating profit, shareholders' funds, net operating cash flow and the return on equity (see Figure 6.29).

Figures 6.30 to 6.32 show a construction of the financial statements by line.

Deriving financial statements

The model produces the income statement (see Figure 6.33) and balance sheet by applying the ratio percentages to the enhanced sales. These are

Figure 6.28

Forecast variables

Line	Item	Dec-02	Dec-03	Dec-04	Dec-05
		Actual	Forecast	Forecast	Forecast
	Forecast				
F11	Initial sales	35,179.0	37,641.5	40,276.4	43,095.8
F12	Sales growth	(10.0%)	7.0%	7.0%	7.0%
F13	Costs of goods sold/Sales	90.0%	85.0%	85.0%	85.0%
F14	Depreciation rate	-	5.0%	5.0%	5.0%
F15	SG&A/Sales	-	0.0%	0.0%	0.0%
F16	Interest paid on debt	5.0%	5.0%	5.0%	5.0%
F17	Interest earned on cash	29.1%	5.0%	5.0%	5.0%
F18	Exceptionals/Sales	-	0.0%	0.0%	0.0%
F19	Marginal tax rate	38.7%	35.0%	35.0%	35.0%
F20	Dividend payout ratio	8.0%	8.0%	8.0%	8.0%
F21	Fixed assets increase	1,386	2,000	2,000	2,000
F22	Intangibles increase	3,943	4,000	4,000	4,000
F23	Current assets/Sales	22.1%	25.0%	25.0%	25.0%
F24	Current liabilities/Sales	23.9%	24.0%	24.0%	24.0%
F25	Debt/Sales	87.6%	85.0%	85.0%	85.0%
F26	Deferred tax/Sales	18.9%	19.0%	19.0%	19.0%
F27	New Equity	1,422	-	-	-
F28	Current Share Price	13.00	13.00	13.00	13.00

Figure 6.29

Results

Line	Item	Dec-02	Dec-03	Dec-04	Dec-05
F17	Interest earned on cash	29.1%	5.0%	5.0%	5.0%
F18	Exceptionals/Sales	-	0.0%	0.0%	0.0%
F19	Marginal tax rate	38.7%	35.0%	35.0%	35.0%
F20	Dividend payout ratio	8.0%	8.0%	8.0%	8.0%
F21	Fixed assets increase	1,386	2,000	2,000	2,000
F22	Intangibles increase	3,943	4,000	4,000	4,000
F23	Current assets/Sales	22.1%	25.0%	25.0%	25.0%
F24	Current liabilities/Sales	23.9%	24.0%	24.0%	24.0%
F25	Debt/Sales	87.6%	85.0%	85.0%	85.0%
F26	Deferred tax/Sales	18.9%	19.0%	19.0%	19.0%
F27	New Equity	1,422	-	-	-
F28	Current Share Price	13.00	13.00	13.00	13.00
	Results				
F32	Net Operating Profit (NOP)	3,514	3,706	4,098	4,518
F33	Shareholders' Funds	57,930	59,572	61,347	63,310
F34	Net Operating Cash Flow (N	3,112	4,639	6,015	6,436
F35	Return on Equity (NPAT/Equ	2.5	2.9	3.1	3.3

Income statement

Figure 6.30

No	Item	USD'000,000	Description
P10	Sales		Calculate using sales growth
P11	Cost of Goods Sold		Calculate using gross profit margin
P12	**Gross Margin**		
P13	Depreciation	Manufacturer	Use Deprn. / (average) FA ratio
P14		Amortisation/Other	
P15	Sales, General &Administration Overheads		SGA / Sales
P16	**Net Operating Profit (NOP)**		
P17	Interest Expense		Use interest % on (average) debt
P18	Interest Income		
P19	Other Financial Income		
P20	**Profit after Financial Items**		
P21	Exceptional Expense		
P22	**Profit before Tax**		
P23	Tax		Use tax payout ratio
P24	**Net Profit after Tax (NPAT)**		
P25	Minority Interest		Retain at same rate
P26	Dividends		Use dividend payout ratio
P27	**Retained Profit for the Year**		

Assets

Figure 6.31

No	Assets	USD'000,000	Description
B10	Cash and Deposits		
B11	Marketable Securities		Balance
B12	Trade Debtors (Receivables)		Current assets / Sales
B13	Inventory		Current assets / Sales
B14	Sundry Current Assets		Current assets / Sales
B15	**Current Assets**		
B16	Land and Buildings		Actual increase / (decrease)
B17	Plant and Machinery		Actual increase / (decrease)
B18	Depreciation		Balance + P&L Deprn
B19	**Net Property, Plant and Equipment**		
B20	Other Investments		Actual increase / (decrease)
B21	Intangibles/Goodwill		Actual increase / (decrease)
B22	**Non Current and Fixed Assets**		
B23			
B24	**Total Assets**		

Figure 6.32   **Liabilities**

No	Liabilities USD'000,000	Description
B28	Short Term Bank Loans	
B29	Trade Creditors (Payables)	Current liabilities / Sales
B30	Other Creditors	Current liabilities / Sales
B31	Other Current Liabilities	Current liabilities / Sales
B32	**Current Liabilities**	
B33	Long Term Bank Loans	Debt / Sales
B34	**Long Term Liabilities**	
B35	Tax/Deferred Taxation	Deferred tax / Sales
B36	**Long Term Liabilities and Provisions**	
B37	Ordinary Shares (Common Stock)	Balance + New equity
B38	Profit and Loss Reserve (Retained Earnings)	Balance + retained earnings
B39	**Shareholders' Funds**	
B40	Minority Interests	Balance
B41	**Total Liabilities and Equity**	

Figure 6.33   **Income statement**

No	Item USD'000,000	Dec-02	Dec-03	Dec-04
		Actual	Forecast	Forecast
P10	Sales	35,179.0	37,641.5	40,276.4
P11	Cost of Goods Sold	(31,665.0)	(31,995.3)	(34,235.0)
P12	**Gross Margin**	**3,514.0**	**5,646.2**	**6,041.5**
P13	Depreciation Manufacturer	-	(1,940.5)	(1,943.4)
P14	Amortisation/Other	-	-	-
P15	Sales, General &Administration Overheads	-	-	-
P16	**Net Operating Profit (NOP)**	**3,514.0**	**3,705.8**	**4,098.0**
P17	Interest Expense	(1,533.0)	(1,501.9)	(1,599.8)
P18	Interest Income	-	70.8	-
P19	Other Financial Income	412.0	412.0	412.0
P20	**Profit after Financial Items**	**2,393.0**	**2,686.7**	**2,910.3**
P21	Exceptional Expense	-	-	-
P22	**Profit before Tax**	**2,393.0**	**2,686.7**	**2,910.3**
P23	Tax	(927.0)	(940.3)	(1,018.6)
P24	**Net Profit after Tax (NPAT)**	**1,466.0**	**1,746.3**	**1,891.7**
P25	Minority Interest	35.0	35.0	35.0
P26	Dividends	(117.0)	(139.7)	(151.3)
P27	**Retained Profit for the Year**	**1,384.0**	**1,641.6**	**1,775.3**

called FIncome and FBalance and follow exactly the framework of the historic sheets. The past results are repeated together with the future values.

Colour coding in the form of shaded cells is also used to highlight the forecast. The method used to create the sheets was:

- copy the historic sheet using Edit, Move, Create a Copy;

- change the name to 'F' (e.g. FIncome);
- code the labels in columns B to G to look up the historic sheet (this means that if you change anything on the Income sheet it will update on the forecast);
- insert the formulas in the historic cells to look up the values in the historic sheet;
- insert the formulas by multiplying out from the Forecast sheet;
- check the results including the signs (negative or positive).

The formulas use the forecast sheet to derive the new values as with the detail for column N below. In rows 17 and 18, the logic checks if cash is positive or negative and only applies funding interest on negative balances. The cash rules are followed and costs are all negative. (See Figure 6.34.)

The balance sheet follows the same pattern using the drivers from the Forecasting sheet. Where necessary, the model apportions the forecast percentage between different rows. The current assets percentage is 40 per cent and this is split between debtors, inventory and sundry current assets in rows 12 to 14.

```
=(Forecast!K$11*Forecast!K$23)*(M12/SUM
(M$12:M$14))
```

Cash and short-term debt are used to balance the assets and liabilities as the model's 'plug' (see Figures 6.34 and 6.35). The model includes workings at row 47 on the forecast balance sheet, which compare the assets without cash to the liabilities without short-term debt. If the assets are greater than liabilities, the model assumes there is a requirement for loans. In the event that liabilities are greater than assets, the model adds the balance to cash.

Assets

Figure 6.34

No	Assets	USD'000,000	Dec-02	Dec-03	Dec-04	Dec-05
			Actual	Forecast	Forecast	Forecast
B10	Cash and Deposits		1,416.0	-	107.6	920.6
B11	Marketable Securities/Invesments		-	-	-	-
B12	Trade Debtors (Receivables)		5,308.0	6,412.9	6,861.8	7,342.2
B13	Inventory		-	-	-	-
B14	Sundry Current Assets		2,481.0	2,997.5	3,207.3	3,431.8
B15	**Current Assets**		**9,205.0**	**9,410.4**	**10,176.7**	**11,694.5**
B16	Land and Buildings		-	-	-	-
B17	Plant and Machinery		48,661.0	50,661.0	52,661.0	54,661.0
B18	Depreciation		(9,852.0)	(11,792.5)	(13,735.9)	(15,682.1)
B19	**Net Property, Plant and Equipment**		**38,809.0**	**38,868.6**	**38,925.1**	**38,978.9**
B20	Other Investments		5,363.0	5,363.0	5,363.0	5,363.0
B21	Intangibles/Goodwill		50,537.0	54,537.0	58,537.0	62,537.0
B22	**Non Current and Fixed Assets**		**94,709.0**	**98,768.6**	**102,825.1**	**106,878.9**
B23						
B24	**Total Assets**		**103,914.0**	**108,178.9**	**113,001.8**	**118,573.4**

Figure 6.35   **Liabilities**

No	Assets USD'000,000	Dec-02	Dec-03	Dec-04	Dec-05
B28	Short Term Bank Loans	790.0	325.1	-	-
B29	Trade Creditors (Payables)	4,844.0	5,197.2	5,561.0	5,950.3
B30	Other Creditors	-	-	-	-
B31	Other Current Liabilities	3,576.0	3,836.8	4,105.3	4,392.7
B32	**Current Liabilities**	**9,210.0**	**9,359.1**	**9,666.3**	**10,343.0**
B33	Long Term Bank Loans	30,038.0	31,995.3	34,235.0	36,631.4
B34	**Long Term Liabilities**	**30,038.0**	**31,995.3**	**34,235.0**	**36,631.4**
B35	Tax/Deferred Taxation	6,635.0	7,151.9	7,652.5	8,188.2
B36	**Long Term Liabilities and Provisions**	**36,673.0**	**39,147.2**	**41,887.5**	**44,819.6**
B37	Ordinary Shares (Common Stock)	54,328.0	54,328.0	54,328.0	54,328.0
B38	Profit and Loss Reserve (Retained Earnings)	3,602.0	5,243.6	7,019.0	8,981.8
B39	**Shareholders' Funds**	**57,930.0**	**59,571.6**	**61,347.0**	**63,309.8**
B40	Minorities/Deferred Accounts	101.0	101.0	101.0	101.0
B41	**Total Liabilities and Equity**	**103,914.0**	**108,178.9**	**113,001.8**	**118,573.4**
	CheckSum: No Errors	-	-	-	-

The balance sheet self-checks and there are no errors at the bottom in row 43 (see Figure 6.35). If there are errors of addition, an error message is displayed.

With the completed financial statements, you can review the figures for obvious logic and formula errors and then examine the trends in the figures. The sales growth has to be financed and therefore you would expect to see changes in the structure of the balance sheet:

- fixed assets – new and replacement assets;
- requirement for new debt and consequent changes in gearing;
- debtors + inventory – creditors = funding gap;
- discretionary funding = new loans and equity.

New funding requirement, expressed simply in this model as cash, is either positive or negative and makes the balance sheet assets equal liabilities. These are the cash workings in N10, which represents liabilities and equity and all the asset rows except cash:

```
=N41-SUM(N20:N21)-SUM(N16:N18)-SUM(N11:N14)
```

The second stage of the forecast is to copy forward to cash flow and ratios information to new worksheets. You can then update the cell formulas to point at FIncome and FBalance. Since the logic on the cash flow worked with the historic sheet, it must also work when using data from the forecast (see Figure 6.36).

The formula in cell N15, change in current assets, calculates the

Forecast cash flow

Figure 6.36

Line	Item USD'000,000	Reference	Dec-02	Dec-03	Dec-04
			Actual	Forecast	Forecast
C10	**Net Operating Profit (NOP)**		3,514.0	3,705.8	4,098.0
C11	Depreciation / Amortisation	P13.14	-	1,940.5	1,943.4
C12	**Earnings before Interest, Tax, Depreciation and Amortisation (EBITD**		3,514.0	5,646.2	6,041.5
C14	**Operating Items**				
C15	(+)/- Current Assets	B12.14	1,205.0	(1,621.4)	(658.7)
C16	+/(-) Current Liabilities	B29.31	(1,607.0)	614.0	632.4
C17	**Net Operating Cash Flow (NOCF)**		3,112.0	4,638.8	6,015.1
C19	**Returns on Investment and Servicing of Finance**				
C20	Interest Received	P18	-	70.8	-
C21	Interest Paid	P17	(1,533.0)	(1,501.9)	(1,599.8)
C22	Dividends	P26	(117.0)	(139.7)	(151.3)
C23	**Net Cash Outflow from Returns on Investments and Servicing of Fin**		(1,650.0)	(1,570.8)	(1,751.1)
C24	**Taxation**				
C25	Taxes Paid	P23	(927.0)	(940.3)	(1,018.6)
C26	Deferred Tax	B35	1,102.0	516.9	500.6
C27	**Net Cash Outflow for Taxation**		175.0	(423.4)	(518.0)
C29	**Investing Activities**				
C30	Expenditure on Property, Plant and Equipme	B19+P13+P14	(1,386.0)	(2,000.0)	(2,000.0)
C31	Expenditure on Investments, LT Assets & Int	B20.21+P19	(3,763.0)	(3,588.0)	(3,588.0)
C32	Marketable Securities	B11	-	-	-
C33	**Net Cash Outflow for Capital Expenditure and Financial Investment**		(5,149.0)	(5,588.0)	(5,588.0)
C35	**Exceptional and Minority Items**				
C36	Exceptional Income and Expense	P21+P25+B40	(2,456.0)	35.0	35.0
C37	**Net Cash Outflow from Exceptional and Minority Items**		(2,456.0)	35.0	35.0
C39	**Reconciliation**				
C40	Reconciliation Figure	0	(285.0)	-	-
C41	**Total Cash (Outflow)/Inflow before Financing**		(6,253.0)	(2,908.4)	(1,806.9)
C43	**Financing**				
C44	Share Capital and Reserves	B37	1,422.0	-	-
C45	Short Term Debt and Provisions	B28	(6,856.0)	(464.9)	(325.1)
C46	Long Term Debt and Provisions	B33	12,342.0	1,957.3	2,239.7
C47	**Net Cash Inflow/(Outflow) from Financing**		6,908.0	1,492.4	1,914.5
C49	**Increase / (Decrease) in Cash**		655.0	(1,416.0)	107.6

difference between the two balance sheet dates:

```
=SUM(FBalance!M12:FBalance!M14)-
SUM(FBalance!N12:FBalance!N14)
```

The other cells all follow exactly the logic in the Cashflow sheet. The advantage is now a longer period to view:

- EBITDA;
- net operating cash flow (NOCF);
- cash flow before financing;
- cash movement.

175

The ratios are forecast using the same method in FRatios, by copying forward and then using `Edit, Replace` to update the cells and then copy to the right (see Figure 6.37).

The text on the right refers to the last two years actual and the first year of the forecast to provide some information on the direction of the ratios. If the forecast is better than the last two years, the cell displays 'Better' and if there is an improvement over one of two years, displays 'OK'. If the ratio has deteriorated, the cell reads 'Worse'. The formula in cell R11 reads:

```
=IF(P11=0,"N/A",IF(O11=0,"N/A",IF(AND(Q11>P11,
Q11>O11),"Better",IF(OR(Q11>P11,Q11>O11),"OK",
"Worse"))))
```

Figure 6.37 **Forecast ratios**

Line	Item USD'000,000	Reference	Dec-02	Dec-03	Dec-04
			Actual	Forecast	Forecast
	Core Ratios				
R11	Return on Sales (NPAT/Sales %)	P24/P10	4.17	4.64	4.70
R12	Asset Turnover (Sales / Total Assets)	P10/B24	0.34	0.35	0.36
R13	Asset Leverage (Total Assets/Equity)	B24/B39	1.79	1.82	1.84
R14	Return on Equity (NPAT/Equity %)	P24/B39	2.53	2.93	3.08
	Profitability				
R18	Gross Profit / Sales (%)	P12/P10	9.99	15.00	15.00
R19	Net Operating Profit / Sales (%)	P16/P10	9.99	9.84	10.17
R20	Profit before Tax / Sales (%)	P22/P10	6.80	7.14	7.23
R21	Return on Capital Employed (ROCE)	P16/B39+B33	3.99	4.05	4.29
R22	Return on Invested Capital (ROIC)	P16*(1-T)/B28+33+39	5.49	5.44	5.79
R23	Return on Assets (ROA)	P16/B24	3.38	3.43	3.63
	Operating Efficiency				
R27	Inventory Days	B13/P11	-	-	-
R28	Trade Receivables (Debtor) Days	B12/P10	55.07	62.18	62.18
R29	Creditors Days	B29/P11	55.84	59.29	59.29
R30	Funding Gap Debtors+Inventory-Creditors	R25+R26-R27	(0.76)	2.90	2.90
R31	Working Capital Turnover	P10/B12.13-B29	75.82	30.96	30.96
	Financial Structure				
R35	Current Ratio	B15/B32	1.00	1.01	1.05
R36	Quick Ratio (Acid Test)	B15-B13/B32	1.00	1.01	1.05
R37	Working Capital (Thousands)	B15-B32	(5)	51	510
R38	Gross Gearing (%)	B28+B33/B39	53.22	54.25	55.81
R39	Net Gearing (%)	B28+B33-B10-11/B39	50.77	54.25	55.63
R40	Solvency (Times Interest Earned)	P16/P17	2.29	2.47	2.56
R41	Total Equity/Total Assets	B39/B24	55.75	55.07	54.29

FINANCIAL ANALYSIS

The qualitative analysis shows an improving financial position with solid cash flow over the forecast period. Such a scenario may or may not be achievable by the management team, but were it to achieve these figures then cash flow and return ratios certainly improve as per the summary shown in Figure 6.38.

Two more schedules in the application assist with analysis: they are called Management_Summary and Management_Analysis. The first looks up important lines in the other schedules and puts together the summary of the income statement, balance sheet, cash flow and ratios. The tests on the right try to assist with pinpointing the rows for management attention in the first year of the forecast.

The Management_Analysis looks up each line from the four forecast schedules in rows 79 to 224 and uses a control and an OFFSET function to form a dynamic graph. This enables you to analyze a line on three graphs:

- line graph with three series, historic, forecast and historic trend line, extrapolated by five years;

Management summary

Figure 6.38

Line	Item	Reference	Dec-02	Dec-03	Dec-04	Dec-05
			Actual	Forecast	Forecast	Forecast
MS10	Sales	P10	35,179.0	37,641.5	40,276.4	43,095.8
MS11	Sales growth	F12	(10.0%)	7.0%	7.0%	7.0%
MS12	Gross Margin	P12	3,514.0	5,646.2	6,041.5	6,464.4
MS13	Net Operating Profit (NOP)	P16	3,514.0	3,705.8	4,098.0	4,518.1
MS14	Net Profit after Tax (NPAT)	P24	1,466.0	1,746.3	1,891.7	2,095.4
MS16	Current Assets	B15	9,205.0	9,410.4	10,176.7	11,694.5
MS17	Non Current and Fixed Assets	B22	94,709.0	98,768.6	102,825.1	106,878.9
MS18	Current Liabilities	B32	9,210.0	9,359.1	9,666.3	10,343.0
MS19	Long Term Liabilities and Provisions	B36	36,673.0	39,147.2	41,887.5	44,819.6
MS20	Shareholders' Funds	B39	57,930.0	59,571.6	61,347.0	63,309.8
MS22	Net Operating Cash Flow (NOCF)	C17	3,112.0	4,638.8	6,015.1	6,436.2
MS23	Total Cash (Outflow)/Inflow before Financ	C42	(6,253.0)	(2,908.4)	(1,806.9)	(1,583.5)
MS24	Increase / (Decrease) in Cash	C50	655.0	(1,416.0)	107.6	813.0
MS26	Return on Sales (NPAT/Sales %)	P24/P10	4.17	4.64	4.70	4.86
MS27	Asset Turnover (Sales / Total Assets)	P10/B24	0.34	0.35	0.36	0.36
MS28	Asset Leverage (Total Assets/Equity)	B24/B39	1.79	1.82	1.84	1.87
MS29	Return on Equity (NPAT/Equity %)	P24/B39	2.53	2.93	3.08	3.31

- block graph of the historic and forecast figures;
- block graph of the factors where the first period is equal to 100.

An example of the historic and forecast net operating cash flow is shown in Figure 6.39. This method illustrates clearly the reduction in cash flow in the most recent period. The forecast is rising according to expectations and this merits further investigation.

The advantage of this method is that you can view each line, because none of the lines is hard coded and you can see immediately the link between the past and the future. You can change the inputs on the Forecast sheet to see the result on the ratios or cash flow. In this example, net operating cash flow is variable and therefore the next stage would be to review the operating cycle ratios, such as debtor or creditor days, and then the requirement for new funding and the borrowing ratios.

The second set of block graphs (see Figure 6.40) contains one series, but the individual points are formatted differently. The pattern on the forecast was produced by selecting the individual data point, right clicking it, and then formatting patterns.

The forecast has shown a favourable position, but the company would exhibit worse prospects if the same pattern as for the previous year were to be repeated. The sales decline and the cost of goods sold remains high. This

Figure 6.39 **Dynamic graph**

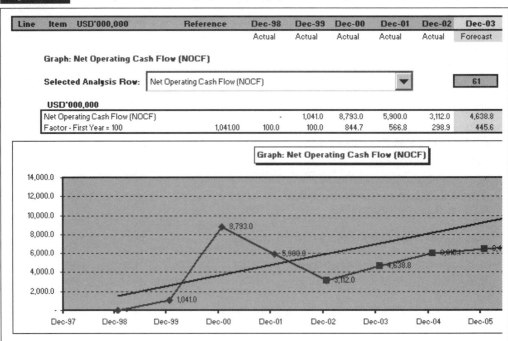

Block graphs

Figure 6.40

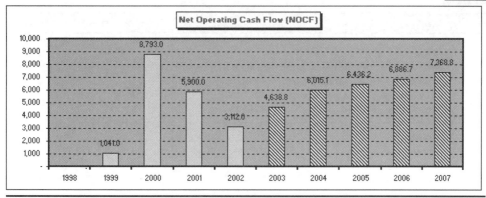

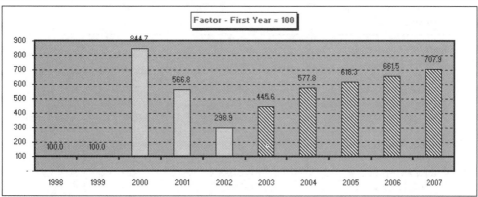

Revised forecast

Figure 6.41

Line	Item	Dec-02	Dec-03	Dec-04	Dec-05
		Actual	Forecast	Forecast	Forecast
	Forecast				
F11	Initial sales	35,179.0	**31,661.1**	**28,495.0**	**25,645.5**
F12	Sales growth	(10.0%)	**-10.0%**	**-10.0%**	**-10.0%**
F13	Costs of goods sold/Sales	90.0%	**90.0%**	**90.0%**	**90.0%**
F14	Depreciation rate	-	**0.0%**	**0.0%**	**0.0%**
F15	SG&A/Sales	-	**0.0%**	**0.0%**	**0.0%**
F16	Interest paid on debt	5.0%	**5.0%**	**5.0%**	**5.0%**
F17	Interest earned on cash	29.1%	**29.1%**	**29.1%**	**29.1%**
F18	Exceptionals/Sales	-	**0.0%**	**0.0%**	**0.0%**
F19	Marginal tax rate	38.7%	**38.7%**	**38.7%**	**38.7%**
F20	Dividend payout ratio	8.0%	**8.0%**	**8.0%**	**8.0%**
F21	Fixed assets increase	1,386	**1,386**	**1,386**	**1,386**
F22	Intangibles increase	3,943	**3,943**	**3,943**	**3,943**
F23	Current assets/Sales	22.1%	**22.1%**	**22.1%**	**22.1%**
F24	Current liabilities/Sales	23.9%	**23.9%**	**23.9%**	**23.9%**
F25	Debt/Sales	87.6%	**87.6%**	**87.6%**	**87.6%**
F26	Deferred tax/Sales	18.9%	**18.9%**	**18.9%**	**18.9%**
F27	New Equity	1,422	-	-	-
F28	Current Share Price	13.00	**13.00**	**13.00**	**13.00**

Figure 6.42		Revised ratios			

Line	Item USD'000,000	Reference	Dec-02	Dec-03	Dec-04
			Actual	Forecast	Forecast
	Core Ratios				
R11	Return on Sales (NPAT/Sales %)	P24/P10	4.17	4.82	4.04
R12	Asset Turnover (Sales / Total Assets)	P10/B24	0.34	0.30	0.26
R13	Asset Leverage (Total Assets/Equity)	B24/B39	1.79	1.80	1.85
R14	Return on Equity (NPAT/Equity %)	P24/B39	2.53	2.57	1.90
	Profitability				
R18	Gross Profit / Sales (%)	P12/P10	9.99	9.99	9.99
R19	Net Operating Profit / Sales (%)	P16/P10	9.99	9.99	9.99
R20	Profit before Tax / Sales (%)	P22/P10	6.80	7.87	6.59
R21	Return on Capital Employed (ROCE)	P16/B39+B33	3.99	3.63	3.33
R22	Return on Invested Capital (ROIC)	P16*(1-T)/B28+33+39	5.49	4.70	3.97
R23	Return on Assets (ROA)	P16/B24	3.38	2.95	2.55
	Operating Efficiency				
R27	Inventory Days	B13/P11	-	-	-
R28	Trade Receivables (Debtor) Days	B12/P10	55.07	55.07	55.07
R29	Creditors Days	B29/P11	55.84	55.84	55.84
R30	Funding Gap Debtors+Inventory-Creditors	R25+R26-R27	(0.76)	(0.76)	(0.76)
R31	Working Capital Turnover	P10/B12.13-B29	75.82	75.82	75.82
	Financial Structure				
R35	Current Ratio	B15/B32	1.00	0.51	0.30
R36	Quick Ratio (Acid Test)	B15-B13/B32	1.00	0.51	0.30
R37	Working Capital (Thousands)	B15-B32	(5)	(6,850)	(14,457)
R38	Gross Gearing (%)	B28+B33/B39	53.22	57.31	64.36
R39	Net Gearing (%)	B28+B33-B10-11/B39	50.77	57.31	64.36
R40	Solvency (Times Interest Earned)	P16/P17	2.29	2.12	2.06
R41	Total Equity/Total Assets	B39/B24	55.75	55.46	54.14
	Cashflow Ratios				
R45	EBITDA / Sales (%)	C12/P10	9.99	9.99	9.99
R46	Net Operating Cash Flow/Sales	C17/P10	8.85	9.79	9.79
R47	Cash Flow before Financing/Sales	C42/P10	(17.77)	(14.58)	(17.16)

squeezes profits and cash flow and cash is still expended on capital expenditure and investments. Debt increases to fund the outgoings (see Figure 6.41).

The accounts become weaker in the key areas of operating efficiency, profitability and financial structure as borrowings rise and solvency ratios fall (see Figures 6.42 and 6.43). Profitability remains static at the previous period's levels, but the return on capital and asset falls. This would be an unacceptable position for bankers and shareholders.

Revised net operating cash flow

Figure 6.43

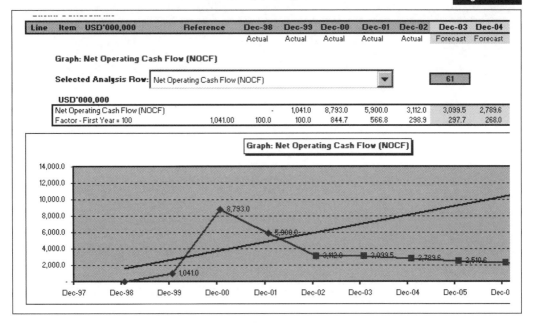

Line	Item	USD'000,000	Reference	Dec-98	Dec-99	Dec-00	Dec-01	Dec-02	Dec-03	Dec-04
				Actual	Actual	Actual	Actual	Actual	Forecast	Forecast
	Graph: Net Operating Cash Flow (NOCF)									
	Selected Analysis Row:	Net Operating Cash Flow (NOCF) ▼							61	
	USD'000,000									
	Net Operating Cash Flow (NOCF)			-	1,041.0	8,793.0	5,900.0	3,112.0	3,099.5	2,789.6
	Factor - First Year = 100		1,041.00	100.0	100.0	844.7	566.8	298.9	297.7	268.0

Graph: Net Operating Cash Flow (NOCF)

SUMMARY

The financial analysis model can be built up from the templates for the income statement and balance sheet. Ratios and cash flows are derived to examine the key areas of risk which affect the operating cash flow. The model supports other non-financial data about a company and should show the risk inherent as evidenced in the accounts.

Forecasts are useful for understanding the performance or key drivers producing value. In particular, forecasts can reveal the requirement for capital expenditure or new debt. Alternatively, they can be used to check client forecasts. The model has shown that the example cash flows are volatile and that the trading position is worsening. Using a different forecast illustrates the uncertainty of future trading and the next stage is to introduce methods for examining loan cover and models for bankruptcy analysis.

Credit risk

File: FT4_07.xls

The previous chapter reviewed a financial analysis model in terms of the sources of risk inherent in the financial statements and forecasts. This chapter extends the model to include credit risk models to show the ability of a company to repay debt or to remain solvent during a forecast period. The existing forecast model provides forecast cash flow and ratios schedules. However, the analysis needs to reveal any inherent weaknesses with the company. If a bank grants credit and the client becomes insolvent and is unable to repay, the potential losses usually outweigh the potential margin many times. Therefore it would improve the analysis if the model could look for signs of weakness.

There are many reasons for financial weakness, but here are some of the main ones:

- cyclical decline in demand and failure to react to a changing environment;
- weak management with a lack of a coherent strategy or conflict at board level;
- lack of centralized financial control and direction;
- poor acquisitions or lack of integration strategy;
- inappropriate product, market strategy or an inward-looking product mentality;
- wrong financial policy, poor working capital management or a failure to control overheads;
- problems with new projects or products.

Risk increases with each of the above and a marked deterioration in ratios is often evident. The signs could be:

- liquidity – reduced working capital, reduced creditor days and increased stock and debtor days;
- profitability – reduced profits and return on assets and capital: reduced profits will mean a falling interest cover;
- financial structure – increased loans and gearing, which will lead to increased interest charges and lower profits in the future;
- cash flow – reduced cash flow perhaps augmented by one-off sales of assets or subsidiaries to reduce debts;
- market – falling share price, earnings per share and market to book ratio.

Figure 7.1   **Cash flow**

Item	Reference	Dec-99	Dec-00	Dec-01	Dec-02	Dec-03	Dec-04
Free Cash Flow							
Operating Profit (NOP)		(942.0)	7,888.0	8,153.0	3,514.0	3,705.8	4,098.0
Depreciation / Amortisation / Non-cash		-	-	-	-	1,940.5	1,943.4
EBITDA		**(942.0)**	**7,888.0**	**8,153.0**	**3,514.0**	**5,646.2**	**6,041.5**
Changes in Net Working Assets		1,983.0	905.0	(2,253.0)	(402.0)	(1,007.4)	(26.3)
Net Operating Cash Flow (NOCF)		**1,041.0**	**8,793.0**	**5,900.0**	**3,112.0**	**4,638.8**	**6,015.1**
Expenditure on Property, Plant etc		(54,557.0)	(4,183.0)	(8,015.0)	(5,149.0)	(5,588.0)	(5,588.0)
Net Cash Outflow for Taxation		4,338.0	(1,590.0)	(4,390.0)	175.0	(423.4)	(518.0)
Operating Free Cashflow		**(49,178.0)**	**3,020.0**	**(6,505.0)**	**(1,862.0)**	**(1,372.6)**	**(90.8)**

CASH FLOW

For any lender the levels of cash flow confirm the cash available to meet further commitments (seem Figure 7.1). The Loan Cover sheet sets out the categories:

- earnings before interest, taxation, depreciation and amortization (EBITDA) as the net operating profit plus the non-cash items such as depreciation and amortization;

- net operating cash flow (NOCF) as the EBITDA less changes in working capital such as debtors, creditors, stock, prepayments and accruals – this is the primary cash from trading operations;

- operating free cash flow as the net operating cash flow less expenditure on fixed assets and investments and taxation.

There are several definitions of free cash flow to define the cash available to specific stakeholder groups. This is the cash available to pay dividends to shareholders and interest and principal to debt providers. An alternative definition would deduct dividends to form the cash flow available to debt providers. Nevertheless, the method provides a meaningful measure of cash flow.

COVER RATIOS

The Loan Cover sheet includes a calculator for estimating the amount of cash required on a new loan. An annual rental is calculated based on a period, nominal interest rate, capital value and terminal or future value. The model computes the annual rental and then the level of cover created by the different cash flow lines. This is simply the cash that has to be found rather than loan amortization plus interest. For example, solvency ratios concentrate on the times interest is earned rather than cash whereas this is an estimate of cash covers.

Here a loan of 10 million is derived over a five-year period at a rate of 10 per cent nominal (see Figure 7.2). This is a time value of money problem and can be solved using the PMT function. Cell E18 calculates the annual payment using the function. There is an IF condition to ensure that all entries are present before a rental is calculated.

```
=IF(SUM(E12:E15)<>0,PMT(E13,E12,
-ABS(E14),E15,D71),0)
```

The annual rental can then be used to derive covers against the cash flow lines. The cash flow is volatile and whilst the covers increase against operating profit and EBITDA, the cover at the NOCF level is declining. The level is also lower in the forecast period based on the forecast in the previous chapter. When capital expenditure, investments and taxation are taken into account, the covers are negative since the trading cash is being absorbed by investment (see Figure 7.3). If the cash flow is negative, the proposed loan can only be covered by new loans or share capital. In the example, net loans have increased by 6 billion dollars in the last year and share capital by 1.4 billion.

Loan Cover — Figure 7.2

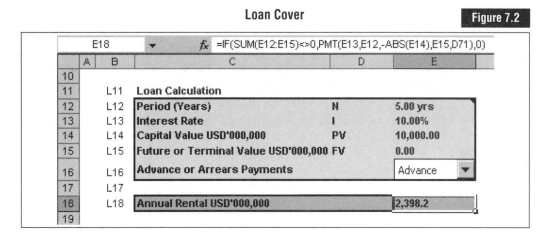

Times Cover — Figure 7.3

Item	Reference	Dec-99	Dec-00	Dec-01	Dec-02	Dec-03	Dec-04
Free Cash Flow							
Operating Profit (NOP) : Times Cover		(0.39)	3.29	3.40	1.47	1.55	1.71
EBITDA : Times Cover		(0.39)	3.29	3.40	1.47	2.35	2.52
Net Operating Cash Flow (NOCF) : Times Cover		0.43	3.67	2.46	1.30	1.93	2.51
Operating Free Cashflow : Times Cover		(20.51)	1.26	(2.71)	(0.78)	(0.57)	(0.04)

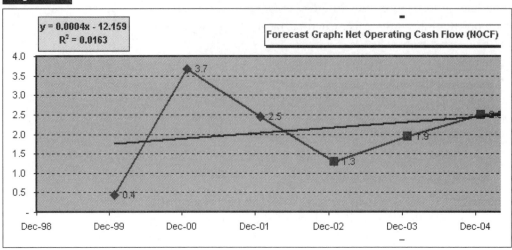

Figure 7.4

Net operating cash flow times cover

The dynamic chart (see Figure 7.4) shows clearly the variance in the net operating cash flow and the risk to any lender in advancing more funds to the company. The forecast appears to rise and therefore an analyst can question the reality of the projection and the management's ability to deliver the cash flow.

Sensitivity

With the initial model in place, one key area of risk is the sales growth. The forecast shows a 7 per cent growth, but one could question what happens to the covers if the sales growth is lower or higher. Sales growth is important since it drives costs and investment.

There is a sheet called Loan Cover Sensitivity which looks up information from a data table at the bottom of the Forecast sheet (see Figure 7.5). You

Figure 7.5

Loan Cover Sensitivity

	4.0%	5.0%	6.0%	7.00%	8.0%
Operating Profit (NOP)	3,705.8	3,547.5	3,600.2	3,653.0	3,705.8	3,758.5
Depreciation / Amortisation / Non-cash Items	1,940.5	1,940.5	1,940.5	1,940.5	1,940.5	1,940.5
EBITDA	5,646.2	5,487.9	5,540.7	5,593.5	5,646.2	5,699.0
Changes in Net Working Assets	(1,007.4)	(996.9)	(1,000.4)	(1,003.9)	(1,007.4)	(1,010.9)
Net Operating Cash Flow (NOCF)	4,638.8	4,491.1	4,540.3	4,589.6	4,638.8	4,688.1
Expenditure on Property, Plant and Equipment	(5,588.0)	(5,588.0)	(5,588.0)	(5,588.0)	(5,588.0)	(5,588.0)
Net Cash Outflow for Taxation	(790.1)	(783.3)	(776.1)	(767.2)	(790.1)	(811.4)
Operating Free Cashflow	(1,372.6)	(1,665.5)	(1,567.9)	(1,470.3)	(1,372.6)	(1,275.0)
Cash Flow - Minimum Values						
Operating Profit (NOP) : Times Cover	1.55	1.48	1.50	1.52	1.55	1.57
EBITDA : Times Cover	2.35	2.29	2.31	2.33	2.35	2.38
Net Operating Cash Flow (NOCF) : Times Cover	1.93	1.87	1.89	1.91	1.93	1.95
Operating Free Cashflow : Times Cover	(0.57)	(0.69)	(0.65)	(0.61)	(0.57)	(0.53)

Data table

Figure 7.6

	A	B	C	I	J	K	L	M	N
8		Line	Item	Dec-02	Dec-03	Dec-04	Dec-05	Dec-06	Dec-07
20									
21		L21	**Free Cash Flow**						
22		L22	Operating Profit (NOP)	3,514.0	18,762.4	20,208.6	21,756.4	23,412.9	25,185.7
23		L23	Depreciation / Amortisation / Non-cash Item	-	1,940.5	1,943.4	1,946.3	1,948.9	1,951.5
24		L24	**Earnings before Interest, Tax, Depre**	**3,514.0**	**20,702.8**	**22,152.1**	**23,702.7**	**25,361.9**	**27,137.2**
25		L25	Changes in Net Working Assets	(402.0)	(1,007.4)	(26.3)	(28.2)	(30.2)	(32.3)
26		L26	**Net Operating Cash Flow (NOCF)**	**3,112.0**	**19,695.4**	**22,125.7**	**23,674.5**	**25,331.7**	**27,104.9**
27		L27	Expenditure on Property, Plant and Equipmer	(5,149.0)	(5,588.0)	(5,588.0)	(5,588.0)	(5,588.0)	(5,588.0)
28		L28	Net Cash Outflow for Taxation	175.0	(5,693.3)	(6,308.5)	(6,956.8)	(7,661.6)	(8,427.4)
29		L29	**Operating Free Cashflow**	**(1,862.0)**	**8,414.2**	**10,229.2**	**11,129.8**	**12,082.1**	**13,089.5**

cannot look up information on a data table on another sheet and therefore the solution is to locate the table in workings on the forecast sheet and then look up the information on a reporting sheet.

The left column uses the function, MIN, to find the minimum along the forecast columns. Cell H41 obtains the minimum on the loan cover sheet since you want to know the low point in the forecast period. The function below returns 18,762.4 (see Figure 7.6).

```
=MIN(Loan_Cover!J22:N22)
```

The data table is set up to use the sales growth on the forecast grid at cell Forecast!K12 as the input. The sales growth is along the top of the table and the elements down the left-hand side. This means that you can obtain the results for each of the cash flow lines and covers for differing levels of sales growth. With only one variable, you only need an input for the row input cell (see Figure 7.7).

On the Loan Cover Sensitivity sheet, you can see the results with a chart for each of the key lines (see Figure 7.8). This fits with the modularity of the model with a separate report for management purposes.

Data table entry

Figure 7.7

	4.0%	5.0%	6.0%	7.00%	8.0%	9.0%	10.0%
18,762.4	18,181.9	18,375.4	18,568.9	**18,762.4**	18,955.9	19,149.4	19,342.8
1,940.5	1,940.5	1,940.5	1,940.5	**1,940.5**	1,940.5	1,940.5	1,940.5
20,702.8	20,122.4	20,315.9	20,509.4	**20,702.8**	20,896.3	21,089.8	21,283.3
(1,007.4)					(1,010.9)	(1,014.5)	(1,018.0)
19,695.4					19,885.4	20,075.4	20,265.3
(5,588.0)					(5,588.0)	(5,588.0)	(5,588.0)
(8,427.4)					(8,795.3)	(9,173.3)	(9,561.8)
8,414.2					8,603.3	8,792.3	8,981.4
7.82					7.90	7.99	8.07
8.63					8.71	8.79	8.87
8.21					8.29	8.37	8.45
3.51	3.27	3.35	3.43	**3.51**	3.59	3.67	3.75

Table dialog: Row input cell: k12   Column input cell: OK   Cancel

Figure 7.8

Sensitivity chart

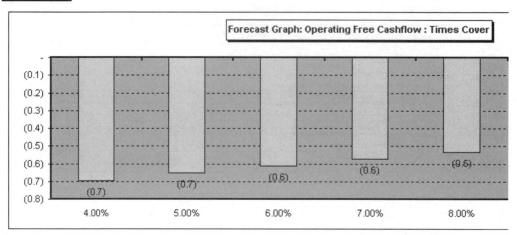

Forecast Graph: Operating Free Cashflow : Times Cover

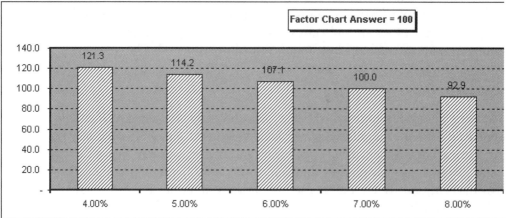

Factor Chart Answer = 100

SUSTAINABILITY

Two areas of financial analysis can be difficult to ascertain from the figures: growth and decline. Figure 7.9 is the classic 1972 Greiner model showing the crises of growth for a young company. Organizations typically grow and pass through a number of stages with periods of rapid and slower growth. Particularly small companies are undercapitalized and show signs of over-trading. Mature companies become inefficient and start to decline. For these reasons, models of management competence often focus on these stages in company evolution as exhibiting a greater risk of insolvency.

The models in this section on the Growth sheet demonstrate methods for highlighting overtrading where a company's retained profits and existing resources are not sufficient to fund the actual growth percentages. There are a number which seek to show ratios of available resources and the degree of overtrading.

The model below seeks to show the ability to grow without restraining resources(see Figure 7.10). If there is capacity in fixed assets then a 1 per

Greiner growth model

Figure 7.9

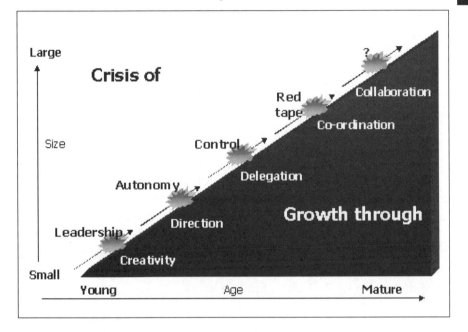

Growth model (1)

Figure 7.10

Item	USD'000,000 Reference	Dec-98	Dec-99	Dec-00	Dec-01	Dec-02
		Actual	Actual	Actual	Actual	Actual
Sales	P10	7,789.0	17,617.0	35,908.0	39,090.0	35,179.0
G = Sales Growth %	F12	-	126.18	103.83	8.86	(10.01)
Profit after Tax	P22	578.0	(1,590.0)	7,164.0	7,568.0	2,393.0
Profit after Tax before Depreciation	P22-P13-P14	578.0	(1,590.0)	7,164.0	7,568.0	2,393.0
Dividend	P26	-	(42.0)	(72.0)	(65.0)	(117.0)
Dividend Percentage	P26/P24	-	(0.02)	0.02	0.01	0.08
Net Working Assets	B12.14-B29.31	(398.0)	(2,381.0)	(3,286.0)	(1,033.0)	(631.0)
Fixed Assets	B19	6,714.0	24,568.0	28,618.0	37,423.0	38,809.0
Liabilities/Equity	B28+B33/B39	0.54	0.47	0.36	0.46	0.53
Profit or (Loss) for the Financial Year	P27	143.0	(2,767.0)	3,941.0	4,088.0	1,384.0
Current Assets	B15	1,874.0	10,769.0	10,324.0	9,755.0	9,205.0
Sustainable Growth	G12+G13	**(0.59)**	**2.18**	**(0.68)**	**(0.88)**	**(0.78)**
Sustainable Growth % (1)		**10.07**	**(6.85)**	**38.88**	**25.97**	**6.34**
Variance Actual-Equilibrium		-	**133.03**	**64.94**	**(17.11)**	**(16.34)**
Sales Growth with same Liabilities/Equity Ratio		**22.50**	**(2.08)**	**(1.38)**	**(1.55)**	**(0.84)**

cent growth in sales will need a 1 per cent increase in net working assets. This is given by the first formula on line 22:

$$g = (PATBD - D)/NWA - (PATBD - D)$$

where:

g	sustainable growth
$PATBD$	profit after tax before depreciation
D	dividend
NWA	net working assets.

The assumptions may be slightly unrealistic since a company also needs to invest in fixed assets as it grows. The formula can therefore be extended to include both net working and fixed assets.

$$g = (PATBD - D)/[(NWA + FA) - (PATBD - D)]$$

If growth is in excess of the formula, then the company would have the choice of raising extra debt, issuing more shares or reducing the dividend payout. This model shows a sustainable growth below the equilibrium in the last two years after rapid growth in the first two periods. This is also reflected by the relatively unchanged turnover in the last periods.

The last model in this section attempts to ascertain the rate of sales growth that can be achieved while maintaining the same ratio of external liabilities to equity(see Figure 7.11). The formula is:

$$g = [(PAT/S) * (1 - (Dividend/PAT)) * (1 + (Liabilities/Equity))]/$$
$$[((FA + CA)/S) - (PAT/S) * (1 - (Dividend/PAT))$$
$$* (1 + (Liabilities/Equity))]$$

where:

PAT	profit after tax
S	sales
FA	fixed assets
CA	current assets.

Figure 7.11		Growth model (2)					
Item USD'000,000	Reference	Dec-98	Dec-99	Dec-00	Dec-01	Dec-02
R = Retained Earnings / Sales	F19/F10	1.84	(15.71)	10.98	10.46	3.93
T=TotalAssets/Sales	G17+G20/G10	1.10	2.01	1.08	1.21	1.36
Growth from Retained Earnings (R/T)	G29/G30	**1.67**	**(7.83)**	**10.12**	**8.67**	**2.88**
Sustainable Growth RE/Opening OF (2)	B39/B24	-	**(17.88)**	**9.28**	**8.96**	**2.65**
Variance Actual-Equilibrium		-	**144.05**	**94.54**	**(0.10)**	**(12.65)**

The sustainable rate keeping the liabilities/equity percentage constant is −0.84 per cent in the last year. The liabilities/equity ratio is 0.53 and this will remain the same with this growth rate.

The second model is based on two formulas:

$R = Retained\ earnings/Sales$

$T = Total\ assets/Sales$

$g = R/T$

This formula is then simplified as:

$Retained\ earnings/Opening\ owners'\ funds$

Growth in excess of this rate will require extra equity or will cause a weakening of the balance sheet.

The next model (PRAT) derives the sustainable growth by multiplying out the drivers detailed below:

- profit margin (*P*) as net operating profit/sales
- retained earnings (*R*) as retained earnings/sales
- asset turnover (*A*) as sales/total assets
- asset equity (*T*) as total assets/shareholders' equity.

The sustainable growth is lower in the final periods as the balance sheet has weakened (see Figure 7.12). The reduction is from 7 per cent to 2 per cent reflecting the same findings as the earlier models.

The last model of equilibrium growth uses the formula:

$g = [R * T] * return\ on\ assets$

$R = retained\ earnings$

$T = asset\ equity$

Again this formula shows a declining equilibrium growth. Figure 7.13

PRAT formula Figure 7.12

Item	USD'000,000 Reference	Dec-98	Dec-99	Dec-00	Dec-01	Dec-02
Profit Margin (P)	P24/P10	0.02	(0.14)	0.12	0.12	0.04
Retained Earnings (R)	P27/P10	0.02	(0.16)	0.11	0.10	0.04
Asset Turnover (A)	R12	0.33	0.20	0.39	0.40	0.34
Asset Equity (T)	B24/B39	1.71	1.93	1.80	1.78	1.79
Sustainable Growth (PRAT) (3)		0.25	8.56	9.09	8.57	1.00
Variance Actual-Equilibrium		-	117.61	94.74	0.29	(11.00)
Return on Assets	R23	4.16	(1.08)	8.66	8.24	3.38
Retention * Leverage R*T	G37*G39	0.03	(0.30)	0.20	0.19	0.07
Equilibrium Growth = (RT * ROA) (4)	G43*G44	1.31	3.27	17.08	15.39	2.39
Variance Actual-Equilibrium		-	122.91	86.75	(6.53)	(12.39)

Figure 7.13   Growth model summary

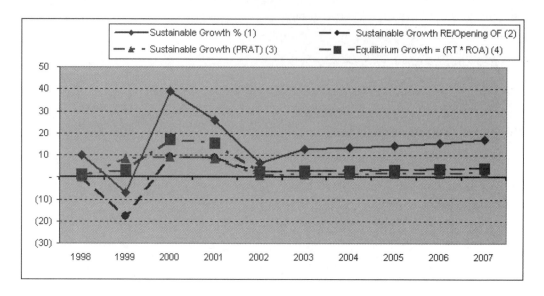

summarizes the findings from the four methods where the high growth in the early periods was higher than could be sustained through retained earnings. The growth in the last two periods has been more restrained and below the maximums indicated by the model.

BEAVER'S MODEL

There are several ratio models for predicting bankruptcy and Beaver's early work reviewed single ratios as important indicators of failure. He identified trends in three key ratios for predicting default (see Figure 7.14):

- operating free cash flow/total debt
- net profit after tax/total debt
- total debt/total assets.

Figure 7.14   Beaver's model

Item	USD'000,000 Reference	Dec-98	Dec-99	Dec-00	Dec-01	Dec-02
		Actual	Actual	Actual	Actual	Actual
Beaver Model						
Cash flow / total debt	LC29/B28+B33	-	(2.32)	0.17	(0.26)	(0.06)
Net income / total debt	P24/B28+B33	0.02	(0.12)	0.23	0.18	0.05
Total debt / total assets	B28+B33/B24	0.31	0.24	0.20	0.26	0.30

Bathory model

Figure 7.15

Item	USD'000,000	Reference	Dec-98	Dec-99	Dec-00	Dec-01	Dec-02
Bathory's Model							
X1 - Gross cash flow / current debt	0.20	P24+P13.14/B28+B33	0.025	(0.116)	0.231	0.179	0.048
X2 - Pretax profit / capital employed	0.20	P16/B33+B39	0.046	(0.015)	0.124	0.112	0.040
X3 - Equity / current liabilities	0.20	B39/B32	6.654	2.796	2.856	3.135	6.290
X4 - Tangible net worth / total liabilities	0.20	B39-B21/B41	(0.003)	(0.023)	0.037	0.089	0.071
X5 - Working capital / total assets	0.20	R36/B24	(0.008)	(0.062)	(0.082)	(0.080)	(0.000)
Formula = 0.2 * X1 + 0.2 * X2 + 0.2 * X3 + 0.3 * X4 0.2 * X5			**1.343**	**0.516**	**0.633**	**0.687**	**1.290**

BATHORY MODEL

Whilst single ratios provide part of the answer, it may be unsafe to depend on them. Writers have studied combinations of ratios which provide some guidance on the tendency towards insolvency. The Bathory model does not try to weight a series of ratios, but instead picks ratios associated with company failure and multiplies them out equally (see Figure 7.15). The factors are:

- X1 – Gross cash flow/Current debt;
- X2 – Pre-tax profit/Capital employed;
- X3 – Equity/Current liabilities;
- X4 – Tangible net worth/Total liabilities;
- X5 – Working capital/Total assets.

Gross cash flow is the profit after tax plus depreciation and amortization. Debt includes all sources of debt including leasing and hire purchase. Capital employed is composed of shareholders' funds and loans over one year. Equity means the shareholders' funds while tangible net worth is the shareholders' funds less intangible assets.

The result here is unconvincing as the score appears to rise whereas all the indicators so far have pointed to a weaker financial situation. On closer examination, the main contender is X3 which rises due to a reduction in current liabilities. It appears that credit is being squeezed and this leads to an increase in the ratio and the overall score. Given that there are equal weights, this would seem an unscientific method of determining weakness.

Z SCORES

Altman and other have attempted to find statistical answers to why some companies go bust and others survive. The technique is known as multi-discriminant analysis which uses a sample of companies and then splits them into failed and survivor companies. Studies take a number of ratios and then determine combinations of ratios and weightings which result in a score that predicts failure.

Altman started with 22 ratios and classified them into five ratio groups:

- liquidity
- profitability
- leverage
- solvency
- activity.

The original data sample consisted of 66 firms, half of which had filed for bankruptcy under Chapter 11 of the US bankruptcy code. All businesses in the database were manufacturers, and small firms with assets of less than $1 million turnover were eliminated. The Z-score calculates five ratios:

- $X1$ = Working capital/Total assets.
- $X2$ = Retained earnings/Total assets. This is a measure of cumulative profitability that should increase with the firm's age as well as earning power. Studies have shown failure rates to be closely related to the age of the business especially for mature companies.
- $X3$ = Earnings before income taxes/Total assets. This is a measure of operating efficiency separated from any leverage effects. It recognizes operating earnings as a key to long-term viability.
- $X4$ = Market value of equity/Book value of debt. This ratio adds a market dimension and academic studies of stock markets suggest that security price changes may foreshadow upcoming problems.
- $X5$ = Sales/Total assets. This is a standard turnover measure of activity.

The formula calculates a weighted score:

$$1.2 * X1 + 1.4 * X2 + 3.3 * X3 + 0.6 * X4 + 0.999 * X5$$

These ratios are then multiplied by the predetermined weight factors above, and the results are added together. The final number (Z score) normally yields a number between −4 and +8. Financially-sound companies show Z scores above 2.99, while those scoring below 1.81 are in fiscal danger, maybe even heading toward bankruptcy. Scores that fall between these ends indicate potential trouble. In Altman's initial study of 66 bankrupt companies, Z scores for 95 per cent of these companies pointed to trouble or imminent bankruptcy.

Although the numbers that go into calculating the Z score (and a company's financial soundness) are influenced by external macro factors, it

Public Z scores

Figure 7.16

Item	USD'000,000 Reference		Dec-98	Dec-99	Dec-00	Dec-01	Dec-02
Z-Score							
Working capital / total assets			(0.008)	(0.062)	(0.082)	(0.080)	(0.000)
Retained earnings / total assets			(0.074)	(0.057)	(0.016)	0.025	0.035
EBIT / total assets			0.042	(0.011)	0.087	0.082	0.034
Market value equity / total liabilities			2.644	5.893	7.854	2.165	1.237
Sales / total assets			0.330	0.202	0.394	0.395	0.339
Z Score: If Publicly Held							
1.2 * Working capital / total assets	2.9	1.200	(0.010)	(0.075)	(0.098)	(0.096)	(0.000)
1.4 * Retained earnings / total assets	1.81	1.400	(0.103)	(0.080)	(0.022)	0.035	0.049
3.3 * EBIT / total assets		3.300	0.137	(0.036)	0.286	0.272	0.112
0.6 * Market value equity / total liabilities		0.600	1.587	3.536	4.712	1.299	0.742
0.999 * Sales / total assets		0.999	0.330	0.202	0.394	0.395	0.338
Public Z Score Sum	Slope	(104.369)	**1.940**	**3.548**	**5.272**	**1.905**	**1.240**
% Differerence in Z Score:				82.832	48.601	(63.858)	(34.902)
Probability of failure: >2.9=Unlikely, 1.81-2.9=Not Sure, <1.81=Very High			Not Sure	Unlikely	Unlikely	Not Sure	High

provides a useful quick analysis of where an organization stands, and a tool for analyzing the variances in a company's financial stability over time. In the example, below the deteriorating financial position is clearly visible in the Z score which ends the period at 1.24 within the range for high probability of failure (see Figure 7.16).

The model uses the SUMPRODUCT function to multiply the factors by the ratios and then adds them to form the score. The probability of failure uses IF statements between the limits of 2.9 and 1.81. The results are 1 for unlikely, −1 for not sure and zero for high, and the colours are set using square brackets as per the custom number format below.

```
[Black]"Unlikely";[Red]"Not
Sure";[Black]"High"?_-;_-@_-
```

Using the sample, Altman gained the results shown in Table 7.1 over five years. The model appeared to provide success of up to 72 per cent over two years.

Altman's results

Table 7.1

Years prior to bankruptcy	N	Hits	Misses	Percentage correct
1	33	31	2	95
2	32	23	9	72
3	29	14	15	48
4	28	8	20	29
5	25	9	16	36

Privately held firms

If a firm's stocks and shares are not publicly traded, the X4 term (Market value of equity/Book value of debt) cannot be calculated. To correct for this problem, the Z score can be re-estimated using book values of equity. This provides the following score:

$$Z \ score = 0.717 * X1 + 0.847 * X2 + 3.107 * X3$$
$$+ 0.420 * X4 + 0.998 * X5$$

The upper limit is set at 2.9 and the lower limit at 1.23 with the uncertain zone in the middle.

Merchandising and service firms

The X5 (Sales/Total assets) ratio is believed to vary significantly by industry. It is likely to be higher for merchandising and service firms than for manufacturers, since the former are typically less capital intensive. Consequently, non-manufacturers would have significantly higher asset turnovers and Z scores. The model is thus likely to under-predict certain sorts of bankruptcy. To correct for this potential defect, Altman used a correction that eliminates the X5 ratio:

$$Z \ score = 6.56 * X1 + 3.26 * X2 + 6.72 * X3 + 1.05 * X4$$

The upper limit is set at 2.6 and the lower limit at 1.11 with the uncertain zone in the middle. Figure 7.17 displays the results for this example with

| Figure 7.17 | | Private and service scores | | | | | | |

Item	USD'000,000	Reference		Dec-98	Dec-99	Dec-00	Dec-01	Dec-02
Z Score: If Privately Held								
0.717 * Working capital / total assets	2.9		0.717	(0.006)	(0.045)	(0.058)	(0.057)	(0.000)
0.847 * Retained earnings / total assets	1.23		0.847	(0.062)	(0.048)	(0.013)	0.021	0.029
3.107 * EBIT / total assets			3.107	0.129	(0.034)	0.269	0.256	0.105
0.042 * Market value equity / total liabilities			0.042	0.111	0.247	0.330	0.091	0.052
0.998 * Sales / total assets			0.998	0.329	0.202	0.393	0.394	0.338
Private Z Score Sum		Slope	760.623	**0.501**	**0.323**	**0.921**	**0.706**	**0.524**
% Differerence in Z Score:					(35.57)	185.04	(23.36)	(25.70)
Probability of failure: >2.9=Unlikely, 1.23-2.9=Not Sure, <1.23=High				High	High	High	High	High
Z Score: If Small Firms & Service & Retail & Wholesale								
6.56 * Working capital / total assets	2.6		6.560	(0.056)	(0.408)	(0.535)	(0.525)	(0.000)
3.26 * Retained earnings / total assets	1.11		3.260	(0.240)	(0.186)	(0.051)	0.083	0.113
6.72 * EBIT / total assets			6.720	0.280	(0.073)	0.582	0.554	0.227
1.05 * Sales / total assets			1.050	0.347	0.212	0.414	0.415	0.355
Small Firm Z Score Sum		Slope	792.597	**0.330**	**(0.454)**	**0.410**	**0.526**	**0.695**
% Differerence in Z Score:					(237.26)	(190.34)	28.44	32.14
Probability of failure: >2.6=Unlikely, 1.11-2.6=Not Sure, <1.11=High				High	High	High	High	High

bankruptcy predicted in all periods. The example is, however, a public company so the results are for illustration only.

SPRINGATE ANALYSIS

This model was developed in 1978 by Gordon L. V. Springate, following procedures developed by Altman. Springate used step-wise multiple discriminate analysis to select four out of 19 popular financial ratios that best distinguished between sound businesses and those that actually failed. The Springate model uses this formula:

$$Z = 1.03A + 3.07B + 0.66C + 0.4D$$

where:

    A = Working capital/total assets
    B = Net profit before interest and taxes/total assets
    C = Net profit before taxes/current liabilities
    D = Sales/total assets.

If $Z < 0.862$ then the firm is classified as 'failed' (see Figure 7.18).

This model achieved an accuracy rate of 92.5 per cent using the 40 companies tested by Springate and can be used in conjunction with other models. Companies achieving low scores may not go bust within the time period and the analysis merely suggests those companies exhibiting risk characteristics.

Springate model

Figure 7.18

Item	USD'000,000	Reference	Dec-98	Dec-99	Dec-00	Dec-01	Dec-02
Springate							
Working capital / total assets			(0.008)	(0.062)	(0.082)	(0.080)	(0.000)
Net profit before interest and taxes / total assets			0.044	(0.010)	0.089	0.086	0.038
Net profit before taxes / current liabilities			0.496	(0.056)	0.458	0.483	0.426
Sales / total assets			0.330	0.202	0.394	0.395	0.339
1.03 * Working capital / total assets		1.030	(0.009)	(0.064)	(0.084)	(0.082)	(0.000)
3.07 * Net profit before interest and taxes / total assets		3.070	0.134	(0.032)	0.274	0.265	0.116
0.66 * Net profit before taxes / current liabilities		0.660	0.327	(0.037)	0.302	0.319	0.281
0.4 * Sales / total assets		0.400	0.132	0.081	0.158	0.158	0.135
Sum	Slope	622.632	**0.584**	**(0.051)**	**0.650**	**0.660**	**0.533**
% Differerence in Score:				(108.79)	(1,365.64)	1.45	(19.23)
Probability of failure: <0.862=High		0.862	High	High	High	High	High

LOGIT ANALYSIS

The Altman model has been widely used but despite the positive results of his study, Altman's model has some weaknesses for commercial use:

- the model assumes variables in the sample data to be normally distributed;
- beyond two years prior to failure, it has a poorer predictive ability than a random chance model of 50 per cent;
- it is based on small samples so may not be representative;
- it does not eliminate all the problems relating to accounting ratios and book values;
- it is based on US industrial companies.

The Logit model attempts to correct the problem of abnormal distribution. The output from the model is a probability (in terms of a percentage) of bankruptcy (see Figure 7.19). This could be considered a measure of the effectiveness of management since effective management would not allow a company to drift towards bankruptcy.

Application of the Logit model requires four steps:

- calculation of a series of seven financial ratios;
- Each ratio is multiplied by a coefficient unique to that ratio (coefficient either positive or negative);
- resulting values are summed together (y);
- probability of bankruptcy for a firm is calculated as the inverse of $(1 + e^y)$.

Figure 7.19			Logit model				

Item	USD'000,000 Reference		Dec-98	Dec-99	Dec-00	Dec-01	Dec-02
Logit Analysis							
Average inventories / sales			0.159	0.186	0.154	0.161	0.172
Average receivables / average Inventories			-	-	-	-	-
Cash + marketable securities / total assets			0.009	0.020	0.010	0.008	0.014
Quick assets / current liabilities			0.904	0.666	0.582	0.552	0.999
Income from continuing operations / (total assets - current liab)			0.048	(0.013)	0.111	0.105	0.041
Long-term debt / (total assets - current liab)			0.344	0.232	0.179	0.218	0.317
Sales / (net working capital + fixed assets)			1.196	0.920	1.694	1.325	0.907
Constant		0.239	0.239	0.239	0.239	0.239	0.239
-0.108 * Average inventories / sales		(0.108)	(0.017)	(0.020)	(0.017)	(0.017)	(0.019)
-1.583 * Average receivables / average Inventories		(1.583)	-	-	-	-	-
-10.78 * Cash + marketable securities / total assets		(10.780)	(0.095)	(0.214)	(0.104)	(0.083)	(0.147)
3.074 * Quick assets / current liabilities		3.074	2.778	2.046	1.788	1.697	3.072
0.486 * Income from continuing operations / (total assets - (		0.486	0.023	(0.006)	0.054	0.051	0.020
-4.35 * Long-term debt / (total assets - current liab)		(4.350)	(1.498)	(1.009)	(0.779)	(0.948)	(1.380)
0.11 * Sales / (net working capital + fixed assets)		0.110	0.132	0.101	0.186	0.146	0.100
Y = Sum of Ratios and Constant	Slope	507.172	**1.560**	**1.137**	**1.368**	**1.084**	**1.886**
Probability of Bankruptcy			**90.3%**	**83.6%**	**87.6%**	**82.5%**	**93.7%**

Table 7.2

Financial ratio	Coefficient
Constant	+0.23883
Average inventories/sales	−0.108
Average receivables/average inventories	−1.583
(Cash + marketable securities)/total assets	−10.78
Quick assets/current liabilities	+3.074
Income from continuing operations/ (total assets − current liabilities)	+0.486
Long-term debt/(total assets − current liabilities)	−4.35
Sales/(net working capital + fixed assets)	+0.11
y =	Sum of (coefficient ∗ ratio)
Probability of bankruptcy =	$1/(1 + e^y)$

The model uses the ratios above and multiplies them out by the factors shown in Table 7.2.

The formula in cell H98 =1/(1+\$G\$89^H97). The evaluation using the formula auditing tool (found in Excel XP) is as in Figure 7.20 repeating the formula $(1 + e^y)$.

Explanatory variables with a negative coefficient increase the probability of bankruptcy because they reduce e^y toward zero, with the result that the bankruptcy probability function approaches 1/1, or 100 per cent. Likewise, independent variables with a positive coefficient decrease the probability of bankruptcy. The example above shows an increasing probability of bankruptcy, from 82.5 per cent to 93.7 per cent (see Figure 7.19).

Evaluate H98

Figure 7.20

Evaluate Formula

Reference: Failure_Prediction!\$H\$98 =

Evaluation: 1/(1+0.23883^*1.56014550127834*)

To show the result of the underlined expression, click Evaluate. The most recent result appears italicized.

Evaluate | Step In | Step Out | Close

H-FACTOR MODEL

Fulmer used step-wise multiple discriminate analysis to evaluate 40 financial ratios applied to a sample of 60 companies: 30 failed and 30 were successful. The average asset size of these firms was $455,000. Fulmer reported a 98 per cent accuracy rate in classifying the test companies one year prior to failure and an 81 per cent accuracy rate more than one year prior to bankruptcy.

The H-factor model takes the following form:

$$H = 5.528\,(V1) + 0.212\,(V2) + 0.073\,(V3) + 1.270\,(V4)$$
$$- 0.120\,(V5) + 2.335\,(V6) + 0.575\,(V7)$$
$$+ 1.083\,(V8) + 0.894\,(V9) - 6.075$$

where:

$V1$ = Retained earnings/total assets
$V2$ = Sales/total assets
$V3$ = EBIT/equity
$V4$ = Cash flow/total debt
$V5$ = Total debt/total assets
$V6$ = Current liabilities/total assets
$V7$ = Log tangible total assets
$V8$ = Working capital/total debt

Figure 7.21		Fulmer H-Factor					

Fulmer H-Factor

Item	USD'000,000	Reference	Dec-98	Dec-99	Dec-00	Dec-01	Dec-02
Fulmer H-Factor							
Retained earnings / total assets			(0.074)	(0.057)	(0.016)	0.025	0.035
Sales / total assets			0.330	0.202	0.394	0.395	0.339
EBIT / equity			0.063	(0.019)	0.151	0.154	0.065
Cash flow / total debt			-	0.063	0.670	0.333	0.104
Total debt / total assets			0.314	0.189	0.144	0.179	0.289
Current liabilities / total assets			0.088	0.186	0.195	0.179	0.089
Log tangible total assets			3.827	4.390	4.457	4.573	4.589
Working capital / total debt			(0.027)	(0.329)	(0.566)	(0.447)	(0.000)
Log EBIT / interest			0.339	-	0.912	0.925	0.360
5.528 * Retained earnings / total assets	5.528		(0.407)	(0.315)	(0.087)	0.140	0.192
0.212 * Sales / total assets	0.212		0.070	0.043	0.084	0.084	0.072
0.073 * EBIT / equity	0.073		0.005	(0.001)	0.011	0.011	0.005
1.27 * Cash flow / total debt	1.270		-	0.080	0.851	0.423	0.132
-0.12 * Total debt / total assets	(0.120)		(0.038)	(0.023)	(0.017)	(0.021)	(0.035)
2.335 * Current liabilities / total assets	2.335		0.205	0.434	0.455	0.417	0.207
0.575 * Log tangible total assets	0.575		2.201	2.524	2.563	2.630	2.639
1.083 * Working capital / total debt	1.083		(0.029)	(0.356)	(0.613)	(0.485)	(0.000)
0.894 * Log EBIT / interest	0.894		0.303	-	0.815	0.827	0.322
Constant	(6.075)		(6.075)	(6.075)	(6.075)	(6.075)	(6.075)
Sum	Slope	502.828	**(3.766)**	**(3.689)**	**(2.014)**	**(2.049)**	**(2.543)**
Classification			Failed	Failed	Failed	Failed	Failed

$V9$ = Log EBIT/Interest
Constant = 6.075.

The model multiplies out the factors and adds up the score (see Figure 7.21). If the score is less than zero, the company is classed as failed. Again, this company is classed as failed using this analysis since it has a negative score.

RATINGS AGENCY

One widely used measure of a firm's default risk is its bond rating, which is assigned by an independent ratings agency. The ratings process begins when a company requests a rating from a bond ratings agency. Information is collated from public and company sources and the agency analyzes the information to ascertain the company's ability to service and repay the debt. The rating will provide a score of financial strength. Firms that are profitable and have low debt ratios with strong cash flow are more likely to be rated higher than indebted companies with marginal profitability.

This model is introduced on the FRatios_Debt sheet. It produces a score for each year but the scores should be treated as a guide in conjunction with other methods:

- the medians are not intended to be hurdles or scores that have to be achieved to attain a specific rating score;
- caution should be exercised when using the ratio medians for comparisons with specific company or industry data because of major differences in method of ratio computation, importance of industry or business risk, and the impact of mergers and acquisitions;
- since company ratings are designed to be valid over the entire business cycle, ratios of a particular firm at any point in the cycle may not appear to be in line with its assigned debt ratings;
- particular caution should be used when making cross-border comparisons, due to major differences in accounting principles, financial practices and business environments.

Table 7.3 sets out the characteristics for each category. The financial ratios used to measure default risk are:

1. EBIT interest coverage = [earnings from continuing operations before interest and taxes]/[gross interest incurred before subtracting (1) capitalized interest and (2) interest income]
2. EBITDA interest coverage = [earnings from continuing operations

Table 7.3

Ratings

Rating	Comment
AAA	Issues rated AAA are judged to be of the best quality and offer the highest safety for timely payment of interest and principal.
AA	High safety for timely payment of interest and principal.
A	Adequate safety for timely payment of interest and principal. More susceptible to changes in circumstances and economic conditions than debts in higher-rated categories.
BBB	Moderate safety for timely payment of interest and principal. Lacking in certain protective elements. Changes in circumstances are more likely to lead to weakened capacity to pay interest and principal than debts in higher-rated categories.
BB	Inadequate safety for timely payment of interest and principal. Future cannot be considered as well-assured.
B	High risk associated with timely payment of interest and principal. Adverse business or economic conditions would lead to lack of ability on the part of the issuer to pay interest or principal.
CCC	Very high risk of default. Factors present make them vulnerable to default. Timely payment of interest and principal possible only if favourable circumstances continue.
D	Payment of interest and/or repayment of principal are in arrears. Already in default.

before interest, taxes, depreciation and amortization]/[gross interest incurred before subtracting (1) capitalized interest and (2) interest income]

3. Funds from operations/total debt = [net income from continuing operations + depreciation, amortization, deferred income taxes and other non-cash items]/[long-term debt + current maturities, commercial paper and other short-term borrowings]

4. Free operating cash flow/total debt = [funds from operations – capital expenditures, – (+) increase (decrease) in working capital (excluding changes in cash, marketable securities and short-term debt)]/[long-term debt + current maturities, commercial paper and other short-term borrowings]

5. Return on capital = EBIT/[average of beginning of year and end of year capital, including short-term debt, current maturities, long-term debt, non-current deferred taxes and equity]

Median scores

Table 7.4

	AAA	AA	A	BBB	BB	B	CCC
1 EBIT int. cov. (x)	21.4	10.1	6.1	3.7	2.1	0.8	0.1
2 EBITDA int. cov. (x)	26.5	12.9	9.1	5.8	3.4	1.8	1.3
3 Free oper. cash flow/Total debt (%)	84.2	25.2	15.0	8.5	2.6	(3.2)	(12.9)
4 FFO/Total debt (%)	128.8	55.4	43.2	30.8	18.8	7.8	1.6
5 Return on capital (%)	34.9	21.7	19.4	13.6	11.6	6.6	1.0
6 Operating income/Sales (%)	27.0	22.1	18.6	15.4	15.9	11.9	11.9
7 Long-term debt/Capital (%)	13.3	28.2	33.9	42.5	57.2	69.7	68.8
8 Total debt/Capital (incl. STD) (%)	22.9	37.7	42.5	48.2	62.6	74.8	87.7
Companies	8	29	136	218	273	281	22

6. Operating income/sales = [sales – cost of goods manufactured (before depreciation and amortization), selling, general and administrative, and research and development costs]/sales

7. Long-term debt/capital = long-term debt/[long-term debt + shareholders' equity (including preferred stock) + minority interest]

8. Total debt/capital = [long-term debt + current maturities, commercial paper and other short-term borrowings]/[(long-term debt + current maturities, commercial paper and other short-term borrowings) + shareholders' equity (including preferred stock) + minority interest]

The medians scores used for each of the rating classes are shown in Table 7.4.

Figure 7.22 shows the calculation of the rating for EBIT coverage. The ratio is calculated as 2.29 in the final historic year. The next line then compares each ratio against the listing and converts it back into a rating.

This is the code in cell M123 which uses the MATCH function along the listing of EBIT coverage for each rating. The value of 2.29 is closest to the

EBIT interest coverage

Figure 7.22

Item	USD'000,000	Reference	Dec-98	Dec-99	Dec-00	Dec-01	Dec-02
EBIT Interest Coverage X							
1	EBIT	P16	982.0	(942.0)	7,888.0	8,153.0	3,514.0
	Interest	P17	(450.0)	(692.0)	(966.0)	(970.0)	(1,533.0)
	1. EBIT/Interest		2.18	(1.36)	8.17	8.41	2.29
	Ratio EBIT/Interest		BB	Default	A	A	BB

fifth value 2.1 and therefore the function returns 5.

```
=IF(M17>$I137,0,IF(M17<$O137,7,MATCH(M17,$I137:
$O137,-1)))+1
```

In cell M18 this can be used as an OFFSET value along the list of ratings letters, which in this case is BB. This process is repeated for each ratio and the values are averaged as a score (see Figure 7.23). For December 2002, this

Figure 7.23   **Ratings calculation**

		Dec-98	Dec-99	Dec-00	Dec-01	Dec-02
1	EBIT Interest Coverage X	5	8	3	3	5
2	EBITDA Interest Coverage X	6	8	4	4	6
3	Funds Flow Operations/Total Debt %	5	7	2	2	5
4	Free Operating Cash Flow/Total Debt %		8	6	8	8
5	Return on Capital %	7	8	6	6	7
6	Operating Income/Sales %	6	8	3	3	8
7	Long Term Debt/Capital %	4	2	2	2	3
8	Total Debt/Capital %	2	2	2	2	2
	Average	5.00	6.38	3.50	3.75	5.50
	Offset Roundup	5	7	4	4	6
	Rating	BB	CCC	BBB	BBB	B

Figure 7.24   **EBITDA/Interest chart**

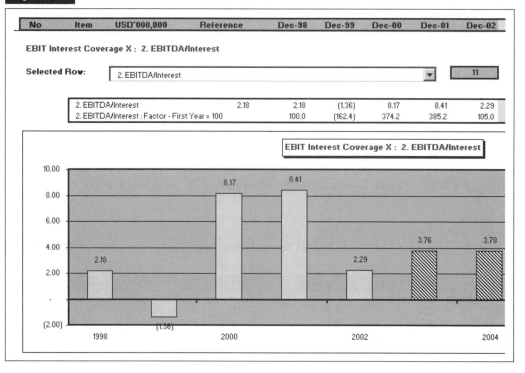

No	Item	USD'000,000	Reference	Dec-98	Dec-99	Dec-00	Dec-01	Dec-02

EBIT Interest Coverage X : 2. EBITDA/Interest

Selected Row: 2. EBITDA/Interest   11

2. EBITDA/Interest	2.18	2.18	(1.36)	8.17	8.41	2.29
2. EBITDA/Interest : Factor - First Year = 100		100.0	(162.4)	374.2	385.2	105.0

EBIT Interest Coverage X : 2. EBITDA/Interest

8.17   8.41   3.76   3.78   2.18   2.29   (1.36)

1998   2000   2002   2004

is 5.50, which is rounded up using the ROUNDUP function with zero decimal places:

```
=ROUNDUP(M131,0)
```

Again this score can be read using the list of ratings with an OFFSET function where cell M132 has the value 6. The result is a B rating:

```
=OFFSET($H$136,0,M132)
```

Again, Figure 7.23 provides a trend over time and the score above is declining from a BBB in December 1999 to a B in December 2002. This confirms the same results trend as the default models earlier in this chapter. At the bottom, there is a dynamic chart allowing review of any line. Figure 7.24 is the EBITDA/Interest coverage. The chart shows clearly the volatility and the declining financial strength.

SUMMARY

This chapter has reviewed credit risks and introduced methods for extending financial analysis to understand more fully an organization's solvency risk and ability to repay debts. The methods have included cash flow sensitivity, sustainability and growth measures, insolvency models such as Z scores or Logit analysis and finally bond ratings. The modular approach demonstrates again how a basic model can be extended with further blocks to improve the quality of management information. The model now yields extra information since the example company shows declining financial strength and this is reinforced by the findings of sustainability and bankruptcy models.

REFERENCES

Altman, E. I., 1968, 'Financial Ratios, Discriminant Analysis, and the Prediction of Corporate Bankruptcy', *Journal of Finance*, 23.

Altman, E. I., Haldeman, R. and Narayanan, P., 1977, 'ZETA Analysis: A New Model to Identify Bankruptcy Risk of Corporation', *Journal of Banking and Finance*, 29–55.

Altman, E.I., 1983, *Corporate Financial Distress and Bankruptcy: A Complete Guide to Predicting, Avoiding and Dealing with Bankruptcy* (John Wiley).

Altman, E.I., 1993, *Corporate Financial Distress and Bankruptcy: A Complete Guide to Predicting and Avoiding Distress* (Wiley and Sons, New York).

Bathory, A.,1987, *The Analysis of Credit* (McGraw Hill).

Beaver, W., 1966, 'Financial Ratios as Predictors of Failure', *Journal of Accounting Research, Supplement on Empirical Research in Accounting*, 71–111.

Fulmer, John G. Jr., Moon, James E., Gavin, Thomas A., Erwin, Michael J., 1984, 'A Bankruptcy Classification Model For Small Firms', *Journal of Commercial Bank Lending* (July): 25–37.

Greiner, L., 1972, 'Evolution and Revolution as Organizations Grow,' *Harvard Business Review*.

Zavgren, C., 1983, 'The Prediction of Corporate Failure: The State of the Art', *Journal of Accounting Literature*, 2, 1–37.

Valuation

File: FT4_08.xls

INTRODUCTION

Financial analysis models can be extended to form valuation models using cash flow methods. This chapter introduces a free cash flow company valuation model as a buyout model with options. The transaction value is funded by a mixture of cash and debt, and the company is forecast to grow over a ten-year period to an exit point. The objective is to understand and develop the net present value (NPV) or valuation for the equity investors and the whole firm. Value is derived from the free cash flows over the forecast period and the compounded value of the firm on expiry. The internal rate of return (IRR) to the firm and investors is also important in determining the acceptability of the proposal. The lower the cost of capital, the higher the eventual valuation.

Figure 8.1 shows the necessary tasks. The model must calculate the future cash flows to equity and to the organization, which will vary based on sales growth costs, interest rates and capital expenditure requirements. A suitable discount rate is required, which reflects the weighted cost of the sources of capital and a terminal value as a value of the organization in ten years. A completed model is structured with these components:

- inputs or control section for the initial transaction, funding rates, future growth rates, costs, capital expenditure, cost of capital and exit route;
- cash flow to equity and to the organization over ten years to build up the profit and loss and cash statements with terminal values;

Free cash flow model   Figure 8.1

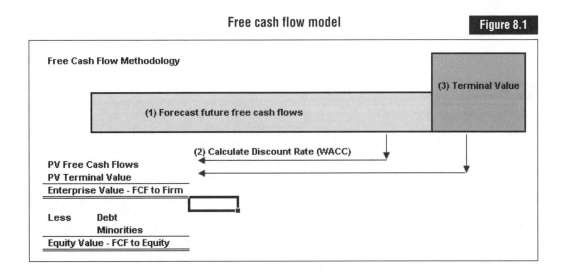

- capital structure sheet for calculation of the debt/equity ratio, cost of equity, after-tax cost of debt and weighted average cost of capital;
- results such as the NPV and IRR to equity and to the firm, and a decision on their acceptability;
- sensitivity of the answer to equity injection against the firm's beta or the exit multiple built up with sensitivity tables, conditional formatting and dynamic charts;
- management summary of key inputs and results.

INPUTS

The first inputs are for the cost of the transaction and the breakdown of funding (see Figure 8.2). Here 20 per cent is equity and the remaining 80 per cent debt. There is space for up to three funding facilities together with preference shares. Debt will increase the interest burden and depress cash flow, but an efficient equity injection will increase returns for the investors. The model should therefore show how returns to the organization and equity investors flex as the percentage of equity investment increases.

Figure 8.3 sets out the interest cost for each facility and the repayment percentages per annum. The percentages are added on the right-hand side

Figure 8.2		**Cost**		
	(1) Transaction Cost			
C006	Current Share Price	20.0	Equity Injection	1000.0
C007	Number of Shares Outstanding	200.0	Preferred Shares	-
C008	Current Debt Outstanding	1,000.0	Facility 1	2,000.0
C009	Other Costs (Banker, Legal etc.)	-	Facility 2	2,000.0
C010			Facility 3	-
C011	Total Cost	5,000.0	Total	5,000.0

Figure 8.3   **Deal financing**

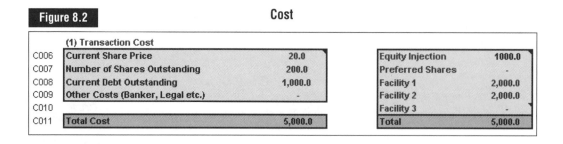

		A	B	C	D	E	F	G
12								
13				Source		Int. Rate	1	2
14				(2) Deal Financing				
15	C015			Preferred Shares		0.00%		
16	C016			Debt: Facility 1		10.00%	20.00%	20.00%
17	C017			Debt: Facility 2		8.00%	10.00%	10.00%
18	C018			Debt: Facility 3		0.00%	0.00%	0.00%
19	C019			Interest Rate on Debt Remaining in Terminal Year		10.00%		

and error checked with the formula below to ensure that they add up to 100 per cent or less:

```
=IF(OR($Q$16>1,$Q$17>1,Q18>1),"ERROR: Check the
loan repayment schedule","No errors")
```

The model has an option of using an exit multiple or a growth model calculation to derive the terminal value. The interest rate on debt remaining in the terminal year is used in the calculation of interest in the final year. If the debt outstanding is zero, as in the inputs above, then the value is not used.

Figure 8.4 shows the income statement variables together with the growth rates over the ten-year period. The revenue starts at 10,000 and grows at 10 per cent per annum. Similarly, capital spending commences at 500 and grows by 5 per cent per annum. Cost of goods sold is a calculated cell using the formula:

1 – (EBIT + Depreciation)/Revenues

The current risk-free rate, tax rate and risk premium are needed in the cost of capital calculations.

The section is mainly control driven by scroll bars and combo boxes (see Figure 8.5). Sliding the scroll bars changes the organization's beta and exit multiple using cell links in the workings area below the printed schedule (see Figure 8.6). Using a control means that cells E38 and E41 can be formulas and the same formulas can be used in the Sensitivity tables. Since these are direct references this ensures that the tables remain synchronized without resorting to macros.

The model includes both single discount rate and periodic discount rate calculations. An NPV is simpler to derive with a single rate and both answers are given (see Figure 8.7). The exit formula is either an exit multiple of cash flow or a derivation of the perpetuity model.

The Sensitivity tables are set up to return multiple values. Rather than creating a table just to look at a single value, the combo box returns an index

Income statement

Figure 8.4

	Source	Int. Rate	1	2	3	4	5
	(3) Income Statement						
C022	Revenues	10,000.0		COGS as % of Revenue			85.00%
C023	Current Earnings before Interest and Tax (EBIT)	1,000.0		Current Capital Spending			500.0
C024	Current Interest Cost	200.0		Interest Rate on Debt Currently			10.00%
C025	Current Depreciation	500.0					
	(4) Future Growth						
C028	Revenues	10.00%	5.00%	5.00%	5.00%	5.00%	5.00%
C029	Depreciation Growth	5.00%	5.00%	5.00%	5.00%	5.00%	5.00%
C030	Capital Spending Growth	5.00%	5.00%	5.00%	5.00%	5.00%	5.00%
C031	Working Capital as % of Revenue	15.00%	15.00%	15.00%	15.00%	15.00%	15.00%
C032	Cost of Goods Sold as % of Revenues	85.00%	85.00%	85.00%	85.00%	85.00%	85.00%

Figure 8.5　　　　　　　　**Background and exit information**

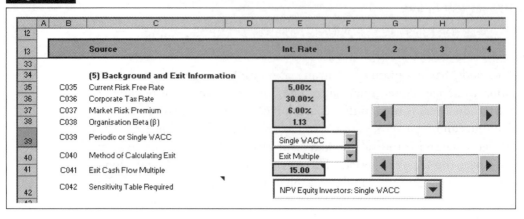

Figure 8.6　　　　　　　　　**Format scroll bar control**

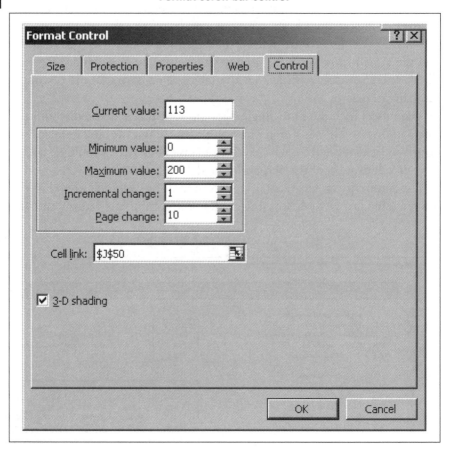

Control workings

Figure 8.7

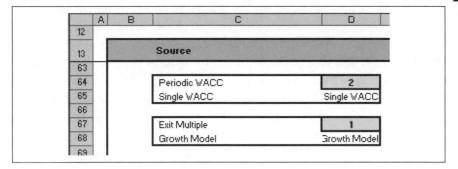

number which can be used to make the tables more flexible. This means that the tables can include any one of the following options:

- present value of cash flow to equity investors;
- present value of cash flow to all investors;
- valuation for equity investors;
- valuation for all investors;
- IRR for equity investors;
- IRR for all investors;
- decision for equity investors;
- decision for all investors.

The text in the combo box is a text string, for example:

```
=Capital_Structure!$F$35&"
"&Capital_Structure!$C$36 (Valuation Equity
Investors: Periodic WACC)
```

The control area contains all the entries for the cash flow and other sheets. The cash flow and capital structure sheets build up the cash flows using these inputs to a valuation and return result.

CASH FLOW

The cash flow schedule includes line numbers and references to show the source of the figures. This is achieved by formulas, for example row eight:

```
Cell B8="P"&TEXT(ROW(A8),"000")
Cell D8=$B$8&"*(1+"&Inputs!$B$28&")"
```

Each line uses dynamic references and this means that references will remain synchronized even if lines are inserted or deleted. The statement builds up the earnings before interest and tax and charges interest on each of the facilities against earnings. The income is taxed and depreciation added back to form cash from operations. To achieve cash due to equity, capital expenditure, the change in working capital and capital repayments are subtracted. The final cash flow due to the organization reduces the cash flow to equity by preference dividend, after-tax interest and principal repayments.

Lines 26 and 30 of Figure 8.8 show the cash flow to equity and the firm. The terminal value is also required as the end cash flow. This is the forecast valuation at the end of the forecast period. The choices are an exit multiple or a perpetuity model calculation. Option one is an exit multiple, which takes the final equity cash flow and multiplies it by the exit multiple input in the control area.

```
=IF(Inputs!D67=1,Cash_Flow!P26*Inputs!E41,$P$26/
(Capital_Structure!$P$20-Inputs!$O$28))
```

Figure 8.8

Cash flow layout

	B	C	D
			Reference
	P008	Revenues	P008 * (1+C028)
	P009	Cost of Goods Sold (COGS)	P008 * C032
	P010	Depreciation	P018 * (1+C029)
	P011	**Earnings before Interest and Tax (EBIT)**	
	P012	Interest: Facility 1	S008 * C016
	P013	Interest: Facility 2	S009 * C017
	P014	Interest: Facility 3	S010 * C018
	P015	**Taxable Income**	
	P016	- Taxes	P015 * C036
	P017	Net Income	Sum
	P018	+ Depreciation	P018 * (1+C029)
	P019	**Cash Flow from Operations**	
	P020	- Capital Expenditure	P020 * (1+C030)
	P021	- Working Capital Charge	Δ P008 * C031
	P022	- Preference Dividend	C015 * C007
	P023	- Principal Repayment: Facility 1	C016 * C008
	P024	- Principal Repayment: Facility 2	C017 * C009
	P025	- Principal Repayment: Facility 3	C018 * C010
	P026	**Cash Flow to Equity**	
	P027	+ Preference Dividend	P022
	P028	+ Interest (1-Tax)	P012.P014 * (1-C036)
	P029	+ Principal Repayment	P023.P025
	P030	**Cash Flow to Firm**	
	P031	Terminal Value of Equity	P026/(S020-C028)
	P032	Terminal Value of Firm	P031+S008.S010

Completed cash flow

Figure 8.9

	B	C	E	F	G
5					
6			**Current**	**1**	**2**
7					
8	P008	Revenues	10,000.00	11,000.00	11,550.00
9	P009	Cost of Goods Sold (COGS)	(8,500.00)	(9,350.00)	(9,817.50)
10	P010	Depreciation	(500.00)	(525.00)	(551.25)
11	P011	**Earnings before Interest and Tax (EBIT)**	**1,000.00**	**1,125.00**	**1,181.25**
12	P012	Interest: Facility 1	(200.00)	(200.00)	(160.00)
13	P013	Interest: Facility 2	-	(160.00)	(144.00)
14	P014	Interest: Facility 3	-	-	-
15	P015	**Taxable Income**	**800.00**	**765.00**	**877.25**
16	P016	- Taxes	(240.00)	(229.50)	(263.18)
17	P017	Net Income	560.00	535.50	614.08
18	P018	+ Depreciation	500.00	525.00	551.25
19	P019	**Cash Flow from Operations**	**1,060.00**	**1,060.50**	**1,165.33**
20	P020	- Capital Expenditure	(500.00)	(525.00)	(551.25)
21	P021	- Working Capital Charge	(136.36)	(150.00)	(82.50)
22	P022	- Preference Dividend	-	-	-
23	P023	- Principal Repayment: Facility 1	-	(400.00)	(400.00)
24	P024	- Principal Repayment: Facility 2	-	(200.00)	(200.00)
25	P025	- Principal Repayment: Facility 3	-	-	-
26	P026	**Cash Flow to Equity**	**423.64**	**(214.50)**	**(68.43)**
27	P027	+ Preference Dividend	-	-	-
28	P028	+ Interest (1-Tax)	140.00	252.00	212.80
29	P029	+ Principal Repayment	-	600.00	600.00
30	P030	**Cash Flow to Firm**	**563.64**	**637.50**	**744.38**
31	P031	Terminal Value of Equity			
32	P032	Terminal Value of Firm			

The second option uses the perpetuity model with the formula:

Final cash flow/(Cost of equity – Revenue growth rate)

For example: $1154.77/(10.77\% - 5\%) = 1154.77/5.77\% = 20,013.34$.

Figure 8.9 shows all the cash flows necessary for the valuation with the flexibility to choose the method of calculating the terminal value. There are no inputs on this sheet and all the variables are contained on the Inputs sheet.

CAPITAL STRUCTURE

The schedule needs to calculate a discount rate that reflects the cost of each source of capital and weights the final cost by the market weighting of each source of capital. The first lines of the schedule calculate the percentages of debt, equity and preferred shares (see Figure 8.10). In year one after the acquisition, debt is four times equity or alternatively debt is 80 per cent of the combined capital.

The cost of equity is based on the Capital Asset Pricing Model (CAPM) using the formula:

$$Cost\ of\ equity = Risk\ free\ rate + \beta * Risk\ premium$$

Beta is a measure of risk plotted as the volatility of the share against the market, which here was input as 1.13. The market is one and therefore this share appears more risky than the market. The other variables are also on the Input sheet. The beta needs to be un-levered to strip out the effect of the historic debt burden and then re-levered using the forecast debt to equity ratio. The formulas are:

$$Un\text{-}levered\ \beta\ or\ Asset\ \beta = \beta/(1 + (1 - Tax) * Debt/Equity)$$

Figure 8.10			Capital structure		

	A	B	C	D	E	F
5						
6					Current	1
7						
8		S008	Debt: Facility 1	S008 - P023	1,000.00	2,000.00
9		S009	Debt: Facility 2	S009 - P024	-	2,000.00
10		S010	Debt: Facility 3	S010 - P025	-	-
11		S011	Preferred Shares	C007	-	-
12		S012	Equity Injection	S012 - P017	4,000.00	1,000.00
13		S013	Debt / Equity (D/E)	S008.S010/S012	25.00%	400.00%
14		S014	D / (D+E+Preferred)	S008.S010/S008.S012	20.00%	80.00%
15		S015	Preferred / (D+E+Preferred)	S011/S008.S012	0.00%	0.00%
16						
17		S017	Asset Beta (β)	(S018/(1+(1-C036)*S013))		0.96
18		S018	Organisation Beta (β)	S017*(1+(1-C036)*S013)	1.13	3.65
19						
20		S020	Cost of Equity	C035+S018*C037	11.78%	26.93%
21		S021	Interest rate	(S008*C016+S009*C017+S010*C 018)/S008.S010)	10.00%	9.00%
22		S022	**WACC**	**S020*(1-S014-S015)+S021*(1- C036)*S014+S015*C015**	**10.82%**	**10.43%**
23						
24		S024	Cumulative Cost of Equity	S024*(1+S020)		1.2693
25		S025	Cumulative WACC	S025*(1+S022)		1.1043
26						
27		S027	Cash Flow to Equity	P026	(1,000.00)	(214.50)
28		S028	Cash Flow to Firm	P030	(5,000.00)	637.50
29						
30		S030	Cumulative Valuation - Equity	S027/S024		(169.00)
31		S031	Cumulative Valuation - Firm	S028/S025		577.31

Re-levered or Equity $\beta = \beta * (1 + (1 - Tax) * Debt/Equity)$

In the example above, the initial beta is 1.13 which reduces to 0.96 as an asset beta. With the effect of the high forecast debt/equity ratio, the beta rises to 3.65. The cost of equity is therefore:

$$\text{Cost of equity} = \text{Risk free rate} + \beta * \text{Risk premium}$$
$$= 5\% + 3.65 * 6\%$$
$$= 26.9\%$$

The cost of debt depends on the balances outstanding and the formula below weights the interest rate against the balance in each of the three facilities. Since the company is paying tax, the cost of debt used in the final cost of capital calculation will be multiplied by $(1 - Tax)$ as an after-tax rate.

Cell F21 = (F8*Inputs!$E16 + F9*Inputs!$E17 + F10*Inputs!$E18)/ SUM(F8:F10)

The weighted average cost of capital uses the market weights of each source and multiplies them out by the individual costs. The cost of capital changes in each period as the capital structure changes with the repayment of loans.

Cell F22 = F20*(1-F14-F15) + F21*(1-Inputs!$E36)*F14 + F15* Inputs!$E15

In order to compute a present value based on the periodic, it is necessary to compound the discount rate in rows 24 and 25 (see Figure 8.11). The number increases progressively as a compound figure to year ten. Rows 27 and 28 bring forward the cash flows from the previous schedule. The present value for the period is therefore the cash flow divided by the compounded discount rate. The periodic values can simply be added to form the total in the last column. The final results are in Figure 8.12.

Present value calculations

Figure 8.11

	F	G	H	I
23				
24	=(1+F20)	=F24*(1+G20)	=G24*(1+H20)	=H24*(1+I20)
25	=(1+F22)	=F25*(1+G22)	=G25*(1+H22)	=H25*(1+I22)
26				
27	=Cash_Flow!F26	=Cash_Flow!G26	=Cash_Flow!H26	=Cash_Flow!I26
28	=Cash_Flow!F30	=Cash_Flow!G30	=Cash_Flow!H30	=Cash_Flow!I30
29				
30	=F27/F24	=G27/G24	=H27/H24	=I27/I24
31	=F28/F25	=G28/G25	=H28/H25	=I28/I25

Figure 8.12

Final present values

	B	C	D	N	O	P
5						Units $'000,000
6				9	10	Term Year
23						
24	S024	Cumulative Cost of Equity	S024*(1+S020)	3.4673	3.8440	
25	S025	Cumulative WACC	S025*(1+S022)	2.4661	2.7311	
26						
27	S027	Cash Flow to Equity	P026	825.01	18,210.13	20,130.95
28	S028	Cash Flow to Firm	P030	1,047.41	18,421.33	
29						
30	S030	Cumulative Valuation - Equity	S027/S024	237.94	4,737.33	5,634.90
31	S031	Cumulative Valuation - Firm	S028/S025	424.72	6,745.09	11,429.71

VALUATION AND RETURNS

The objective of the model is to compute the valuation and returns. There is an alternative using a single cost of capital but this would tend to give an incorrect answer since the capital structure changes markedly during the period. The IRR uses the full cash flows on the schedule and the decision is a simple IF statement, where the valuation needs to be greater than the initial investment:

```
=IF(F36>ABS(G36),"Accept","Decline")
```

Results are shown in Figure 8.13.

The cell formatting uses conditional formatting to emphasize the answer (see Figure 8.14).

Other answers include background information on the cash flows, leverage and beta. The cash flow formulas use simple formulas:

```
=AVERAGE(Cash_Flow!F30:O30)
=MAX(Cash_Flow!F30:O30)
```

Figure 8.13

Results

	B	C	D	E	F	G	H	I	J
33									
34		Results							
35	S035				PV of CF	Investment	Valuation	IRR	Decision
36	S036	Equity Investors: Periodic WACC			5,634.90	(1,000.00)	4,634.90	36.16%	Accept
37	S037	All Investors: Periodic WACC			11,429.71	(5,000.00)	6,429.71	23.93%	Accept
38									
39		Cashflow to Firm							
40	S040	Average FCF			884.5				
41	S041	Maximum FCF in period 10			1,099.8				
42	S042	Minimum FCF in period 1			637.5				
43	S043	Standard Deviation of FCF			143.8				
44									
45		Leverage					Beta		
46	S046	Debt/Equity Ratio before Transaction			25.00%		Beta before LBO		1.13
47	S047	Debt/Equity Ratio after Transaction			400.00%		Beta after LBO		3.85
48	S048	Debt/Equity Ratio in Year 5			22.30%		Beta in Year 5		1.26
49	S049	Debt/Equity Ratio in Year 10			0.00%		Beta in Year 10		0.36

Conditional formatting

Figure 8.14

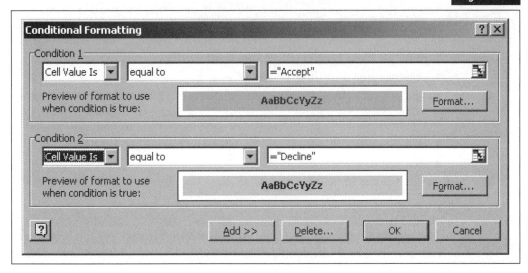

Single rate workings

Figure 8.15

```
=MIN(Cash_Flow!F30:O30)
=STDEV(Cash_Flow!F30:O30)
```

The single discount rate workings use the discount rates from cells E20 and E22, 11.78 per cent and 10.82 per cent respectively (see Figure 8.15). This provides a simple sensitivity table against the rates and the chart is plotted on the Sensitivity_Beta sheet.

SENSITIVITY ANALYSIS

Since the inputs for data tables have to be on the same sheet, all the workings for the two sets of data tables are at the bottom of the Inputs sheet in the workings area. The two tables are:

■ Equity injection across and organization beta (β) down;

■ Equity injection across and exit cash flow multiple down.

This is to provide information on how the answers change as you vary the beta or the exit multiple. Remember that the tables are flexible in that you can choose using the combo box in the Inputs area:

- present value of cash flow to equity investors;
- present value of cash flow to all investors;
- valuation for equity investors;
- valuation for all investors;
- IRR for equity investors;
- IRR for all investors;
- decision for equity investors;
- decision for all investors.

The inputs for the tables are the equity injection in cell 16, the beta in cell E38 and the exit multiple in cell E41 (see Figure 8.16). Note that these cells are updated by spinners and are not input cells. The data table axes are also linked to the spinners in order to keep the tables synchronized.

| **Figure 8.16** | | | | **Sensitivity tables** | | | | |

Valuation Equity Investors: Periodic WACC: Sensitivity Table to Equity Injection Across and Organisation Beta

Spinners

| Interval Across | 100.00 | | | | 3 | | 113 |
| Interval Down | 0.10 | | | | | | 1,000.00 |

4,634.90	700.00	800.00	900.00	**1,000.00**	1,100.00	1,200.00	1,300.00
0.83	5,553.14	5,729.31	5,876.38	6,000.67	6,106.69	6,197.74	6,276.31
0.93	5,053.41	5,231.49	5,381.09	5,508.27	5,617.32	5,711.47	5,793.12
1.03	4,598.13	4,775.77	4,925.87	5,054.10	5,164.59	5,260.38	5,343.82
1.13	4,182.90	4,358.21	4,507.10	**4,634.90**	4,745.45	4,841.67	4,925.78
1.23	3,803.77	3,975.24	4,121.56	4,247.67	4,357.17	4,452.78	4,536.61
1.33	3,457.26	3,623.67	3,766.31	3,889.71	3,997.21	4,091.35	4,174.12
1.43	3,140.24	3,300.66	3,438.73	3,558.59	3,663.31	3,755.26	3,836.28

| Periodic WACC | 1 |
| Single WACC | riodic WACC |

		17,321.55	17,321.55
Exit Multiple	1	1	17,321.55	17,321.55
Growth Model	Exit Multiple	2	20,012.61	20,012.61

Valuation Equity Investors: Periodic WACC: Sensitivity Table to Equity Injection Across and Exit Cash Flow Mu

| Interval Down | 2.00 | | | | Spinner | 15 | |

4,634.90	700.00	800.00	900.00	**1,000.00**	1,100.00	1,200.00	1,300.00
9.00	2,624.88	2,711.08	2,779.05	2,832.43	2,873.89	2,905.41	2,928.53
11.00	3,144.22	3,260.12	3,355.06	3,433.25	3,497.74	3,550.83	3,594.28
13.00	3,663.56	3,809.16	3,931.08	4,034.07	4,121.60	4,196.25	4,260.03
15.00	4,182.90	4,358.21	4,507.10	**4,634.90**	4,745.45	4,841.67	4,925.78
17.00	4,702.23	4,907.25	5,083.12	5,235.72	5,369.31	5,487.10	5,591.53
19.00	5,221.57	5,456.29	5,659.14	5,836.54	5,993.17	6,132.52	6,257.28
21.00	5,740.91	6,005.34	6,235.16	6,437.36	6,617.02	6,777.94	6,923.03

The tables have conditional formatting to generate the exact formatting for the answer and the distinctive stripes for the *x*- and *y*-axis of the answer. The answer should always stay in the middle of the table. Figure 8.17 shows the conditional formatting for the first table which uses both cell value and formula parameters.

There are two sensitivity schedules to bring forward the data from the tables and display charts. You need the charts to be able to assess easily the rate of change in the underlying result. The two schedules are Sensitivity_Beta (see Figure 8.18) and Sensitivity_Exit (see Figure 8.19). Each provides a dynamic chart to plot a single row from the table and insert the answer as a point. The beta represents the risk on the share so as you increase risk the valuation declines due to the increased cost of capital. Figure 8.18 illustrates how the equity value rises with increased investment at a constant beta. The downside is that the rate of return falls as the effect of leverage decreases.

The exit multiple could be the projected sale price at the end of the period and therefore Figure 8.19 shows an increased valuation with a higher multiple. The values range from 2624 to 6923. As an alternative, the second table in Figure 8.19 highlights the cells where the answers are within the input 15 per cent plus or minus of the single point value.

The conditional formatting uses the formulas: = $B$11*(1 – $C$20)

Conditional formatting

Figure 8.17

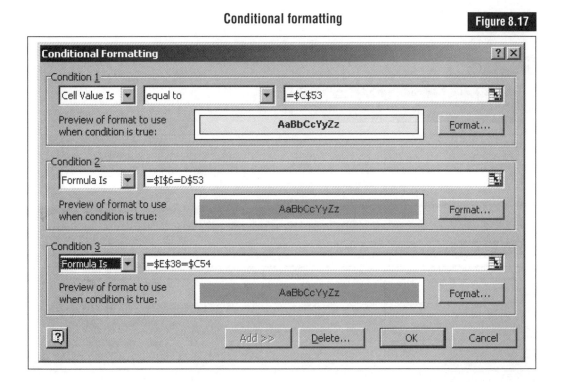

Figure 8.18

Sensitivity to beta

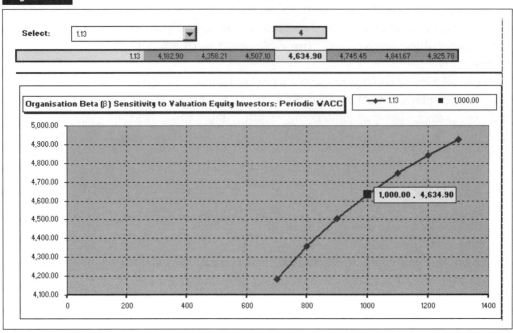

Figure 8.19

Sensitivity to exit multiples

Equity Injection Valuation	1,000.00
Exit Cash Flow Multiple	15.00
Valuation Equity Investors: Periodic WAC	4,634.90

4,634.90	700.00	800.00	900.00	1,000.00	1,100.00	1,200.00	1,300.00
9.00	2,624.88	2,711.08	2,779.05	2,832.43	2,873.89	2,905.41	2,928.53
11.00	3,144.22	3,260.12	3,355.06	3,433.25	3,497.74	3,550.83	3,594.28
13.00	3,663.56	3,809.16	3,931.08	4,034.07	4,121.60	4,196.25	4,260.03
15.00	4,182.90	4,358.21	4,507.10	4,634.90	4,745.45	4,841.67	4,925.78
17.00	4,702.23	4,907.25	5,083.12	5,235.72	5,369.31	5,487.10	5,591.53
19.00	5,221.57	5,456.29	5,659.14	5,836.54	5,993.17	6,132.52	6,257.28
21.00	5,740.91	6,005.34	6,235.16	6,437.36	6,617.02	6,777.94	6,923.03

Shaded Tolerance to 4,635	15.00%

4,634.90	700.00	800.00	900.00	1,000.00	1,100.00	1,200.00	1,300.00
9.00	2,624.88	2,711.08	2,779.05	2,832.43	2,873.89	2,905.41	2,928.53
11.00	3,144.22	3,260.12	3,355.06	3,433.25	3,497.74	3,550.83	3,594.28
13.00	3,663.56	3,809.16	3,931.08	4,034.07	4,121.60	4,196.25	4,260.03
15.00	4,182.90	4,358.21	4,507.10	4,634.90	4,745.45	4,841.67	4,925.78
17.00	4,702.23	4,907.25	5,083.12	5,235.72	5,369.31	5,487.10	5,591.53
19.00	5,221.57	5,456.29	5,659.14	5,836.54	5,993.17	6,132.52	6,257.28
21.00	5,740.91	6,005.34	6,235.16	6,437.36	6,617.02	6,777.94	6,923.03

Conditional formatting

Figure 8.20

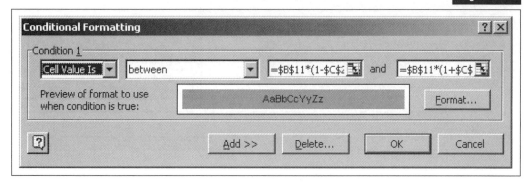

Cash flow exit multiple

Figure 8.21

and = \$B\$11*(1 + \$C\$20) to capture the values (see Figure 8.20). This allows a range of values to be used since the variables are not hard coded.

Figure 8.21 explains how valuation increases with increased equity injection and uses the same format as the beta chart.

MANAGEMENT SUMMARY

The management summary brings together all the findings on a single-page report (see Figure 8.22). This includes a summary of the initial transaction,

Figure 8.22

Summary results

Current Share Price	20.00		Equity Injection	1,000.00
Number of Shares Outstanding	200.00		Preferred Shares	-
Current Debt Outstanding	1,000.00		Facility 1	2,000.00
Other Costs (Banker, Legal etc.)	-		Facility 2	2,000.00
Total Cost	5,000.00		Facility 3	-
			Total	5,000.00

Results

	PV of CF	Investment	Valuation	IRR	Decision
Equity Investors: Periodic WACC	5,634.90	(1,000.00)	4,634.90	36.16%	Accept
All Investors: Periodic WACC	11,429.71	(5,000.00)	6,429.71	23.93%	Accept

Cashflow to Firm

Average FCF	884.54
Maximum FCF in period 10	1,099.78
Minimum FCF in period 1	637.50
Standard Deviation of FCF	143.83

Leverage

Debt/Equity Ratio before Transaction	0.25
Debt/Equity Ratio after Transaction	4.00
Debt/Equity Ratio in Year 5	0.22
Debt/Equity Ratio in Year 10	-

Figure 8.23

Data tables

Valuation Equity Investors: Periodic WACC: Sensitivity Table to Equity Injection Across and Organisation Beta (β) Down

Organisation Beta (β)	1.13						
4,634.90	700.00	800.00	900.00	1,000.00	1,100.00	1,200.00	1,300.00
0.83	5,553.14	5,729.31	5,876.38	6,000.67	6,106.69	6,197.74	6,276.31
0.93	5,053.41	5,231.49	5,381.09	5,508.27	5,617.32	5,711.47	5,793.12
1.03	4,598.13	4,775.77	4,925.87	5,054.10	5,164.59	5,260.38	5,343.82
1.13	4,182.90	4,358.21	4,507.10	4,634.90	4,745.45	4,841.67	4,925.78
1.23	3,803.77	3,975.24	4,121.56	4,247.67	4,357.17	4,452.78	4,536.61
1.33	3,457.26	3,623.67	3,766.31	3,889.71	3,997.21	4,091.35	4,174.12
1.43	3,140.24	3,300.66	3,438.73	3,558.59	3,663.31	3,755.26	3,836.28

Valuation Equity Investors: Periodic WACC: Sensitivity Table to Equity Injection Across and Exit Cash Flow Multiple Down

Exit Cash Flow Multiple	15.00						
4,634.90	700.00	800.00	900.00	1,000.00	1,100.00	1,200.00	1,300.00
9.00	2,624.88	2,711.08	2,779.05	2,832.43	2,873.89	2,905.41	2,928.53
11.00	3,144.22	3,260.12	3,355.06	3,433.25	3,497.74	3,550.83	3,594.28
13.00	3,663.56	3,809.16	3,931.08	4,034.07	4,121.60	4,196.25	4,260.03
15.00	4,182.90	4,358.21	4,507.10	4,634.90	4,745.45	4,841.67	4,925.78
17.00	4,702.23	4,907.25	5,083.12	5,235.72	5,369.31	5,487.10	5,591.53
19.00	5,221.57	5,456.29	5,659.14	5,836.54	5,993.17	6,132.52	6,257.28
21.00	5,740.91	6,005.34	6,235.16	6,437.36	6,617.02	6,777.94	6,923.03

the valuations and return calculations, and the sensitivity tables. This provides all the key findings, without the detail, on a simple report.

The data tables are shown in Figure 8.23.

SUMMARY

This chapter uses a leveraged buyout model to show the key elements in free cash flow models and includes advanced data tables to demonstrate the variability in the answers as a result of changing the beta or the exit multiple. The steps are to include sufficient inputs to calculate a free cash flow to equity and to the company, formulate a method for computing a terminal value, setting out a suitable risk-adjusted discount rate, and then calculating the valuation and the return to investors and the organization. With a single-point answer in place, advanced data tables provide more information on the possible spread of expected results.

Bonds

File: FT4_09.xls

INTRODUCTION

This chapter reviews risk on fixed-income products. Bonds can be valued as the present value of the regular interest payments and the final principal payments discounted at a rate that reflects the risk of default. The level of the interest payments is fixed on issue and therefore an investor is purchasing the right to receive a set of regular coupon or interest payments together with the final return of the principal. The final cash flow includes the final interest payment and the principal. Governments and commercial institutions issue bonds as a form of financing and there are a range of possibilities based on convertability, term and coupon payments.

BOND PRICES

For clarity, these terms are used in the bonds market:

- issue date – original issue date of the bond;
- settlement – pricing or yield date;
- maturity – date when principal and final coupon is due;
- redemption value – par value, usually 100;
- coupon (per cent) – interest rate fixed for the period of the bond;
- coupons per annum – usually paid once (annual) or twice (bi-annual) a year;
- basis – see Table 9.1;
- yield to maturity – inherent interest rate that varies during the period based on markets;
- price – price of bond based on yield to maturity.

An example of bond cash flows showing final coupon and principal repayment is shown in Figure 9.1.

Since the payments are fixed, the price of a bond is inversely linked to the yield to maturity. As yield increases, the price of the bond must decline and vice versa. Bond pricing assumes:

- round periods rather than actual days, as used for other borrowing instruments;
- individual periods are regular;
- pricing is the compound net present value (NPV).

If the pricing is required on the date a coupon is due, then there are no issues

| Figure 9.1 | Bond cash flows showing the final coupon and principal repayment |

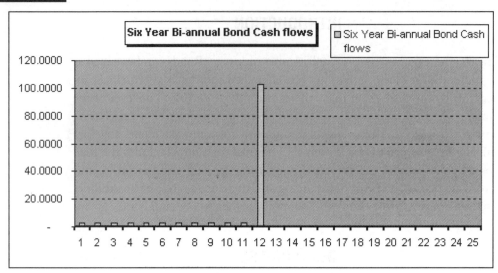

with accrued interest. Between periods, a seller expects to receive the accrued coupon within the period, while the buyer will only pay the present value of the future payments. The convention for quoting prices is:

- clean price – present value of the coupons and principal (dirty price – accrued coupon);

- dirty price – clean price plus the accrued interest (NPV of all cash flows).

Accrued interest on the coupon from the last payment date is payable using simple interest calculations. If there are 30 days from the start of the period and it is assumed there are 360 days in the year, then the interest would be calculated as 30/360 * coupon rate. The first period could be less than the coupon periods depending on the purchase date, but thereafter coupons are payable annually, bi-annually or sometimes quarterly. The dates are the same, for example 15 September and 17 September for a bi-annual bond, and are not based on the exact number of days.

Day and year conventions vary and these are used in the various Excel functions. The methods are the number of days in the month and days in the year (see Table 9.1).

The combinations used in Excel functions are as below:

0   US (NASD) 30/360

1   Actual/actual

2   Actual/360

3   Actual/365

4   European 30/360

Table 9.1

Days	Actual	Actual number of calendar days
	30 (European)	Day 31 is changed to 30
	30 (American)	If the second day is 31 but the first date is not 31
		or 30, then the day is not changed from 31 to 30
Year	365	Assumes 365 days in the year
	360	Assumes 360 days in year
	Actual	Actual including leap years

There are a number of defined bond functions in Excel, which are present in the Analysis Toolpak. Go to Tools, Add-ins and ensure that the add-in is ticked. This is a complete list of security-related functions:

- ACCRINT – accrued interest for a security that pays periodic interest;
- ACCRINTM – accrued interest for a security that pays interest at maturity;
- AMORDEGRC – depreciation for each accounting period by using a depreciation;
- COUPDAYBS – number of days from the beginning of the coupon period to the settlement date;
- COUPDAYS – number of days in the coupon period that contains the settlement date;
- COUPDAYSNC – number of days from the settlement date to the next coupon date;
- COUPNCD – next coupon date after the settlement date;
- COUPNUM – number of coupons payable between the settlement date and maturity date;
- COUPPCD – previous coupon date before the settlement date;
- CUMIPMT – cumulative interest paid between two periods;
- CUMPRINC – cumulative principal paid on a loan between two periods;
- DURATION – annual duration of a security with periodic interest payments;
- MDURATION – Macauley modified duration for a security with an assumed par value of $100;
- ODDFPRICE – price per $100 face value of a security with an odd first period;
- ODDFYIELD – yield of a security with an odd first period;
- ODDLPRICE – price per $100 face value of a security with an odd last period;

- ODDLYIELD – yield of a security with an odd last period;
- PRICE – price per $100 face value of a security that pays periodic interest;
- PRICEDISC – price per $100 face value of a discounted security;
- PRICEMAT – price per $100 face value of a security that pays interest at maturity;
- TBILLEQ – bond-equivalent yield for a US Treasury bill;
- TBILLPRICE – price per $100 face value for a US Treasury bill;
- TBILLYIELD – yield for a US Treasury bill.

The main functions used in the file are:

- PRICE – price of a bond;
- YIELD – yield to maturity;
- DURATION – duration discussed later;
- MDURATION – modified duration.

INTEREST RATES

Bond prices change with rises or falls in the required rate of return. As a bond's credit status falls, the rate investors require to accept the risk of the future cash flows increases and therefore the price of the bond falls. The issue for investors is to assess the sensitivity of the bond to changes in interest rates. The price of the bond is simply the present value of future cash flows discounted at a periodic nominal rate.

This is an example of a bi-annual bond with six years remaining priced at 10 per cent with an annual coupon rate of 6 per cent. Combo boxes offer

Figure 9.2

Inputs

Reference	Six Year Bi-annual Bond
Amount:	1,000.0
Issue date:	1-Jan-00
Settlement:	1-Jan-04
Maturity 6 years:	1-Jan-10
Redemption value:	100.000
Coupon %:	6.000
Yield to maturity:	10.000
Price:	100.000
Coupons per annum:	2: Bi-annual
Basis:	US (NASD) 30/360

selection of the periodicity and payment convention as set out in the previous section (see Figure 9.2).

The resulting cash flows can be discounted at 5 per cent per period to form a price of 82.27 (see Figure 9.3).

Figure 9.4 shows the bond with 12 coupons remaining and the price is

Cash flows

Figure 9.3

	Period	Date	Cashflow	PV
58	Six Year Bi-annual Bond Cash flows	Price:		82.2735
60	Period	Date	Cashflow	PV
61		1-Jan-04	-	
62	1.00	1-Jul-04	3.0000	2.8571
63	2.00	1-Jan-05	3.0000	2.7211
64	3.00	1-Jul-05	3.0000	2.5915
65	4.00	1-Jan-06	3.0000	2.4681
66	5.00	1-Jul-06	3.0000	2.3506
67	6.00	1-Jan-07	3.0000	2.2386
68	7.00	1-Jul-07	3.0000	2.1320
69	8.00	1-Jan-08	3.0000	2.0305
70	9.00	1-Jul-08	3.0000	1.9338
71	10.00	1-Jan-09	3.0000	1.8417
72	11.00	1-Jul-09	3.0000	1.7540
73	12.00	1-Jan-10	103.0000	57.3543

PRICE function

Figure 9.4

Function Arguments   ? ✕

PRICE

Settlement $D$8   = 37987

Maturity $D$9   = 40179

Rate $D$11/100   = 0.06

Yld $D$12/100   = 0.1

Redemption $D$10   = 100

= 82.27349673

Returns the price per $100 face value of a security that pays periodic interest.

Settlement is the security's settlement date, expressed as a serial date number.

Formula result =   82.2735

Help on this function   OK   Cancel

Figure 9.5

Sensitivity

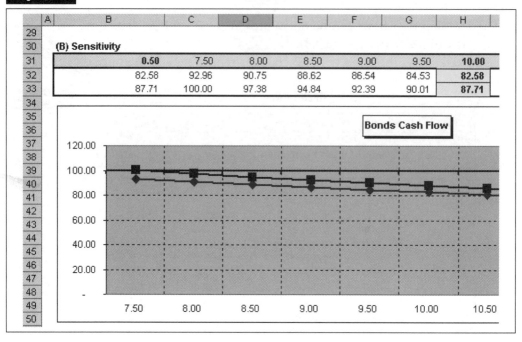

		0.50	7.50	8.00	8.50	9.00	9.50	10.00
		82.58	92.96	90.75	88.62	86.54	84.53	82.58
		87.71	100.00	97.38	94.84	92.39	90.01	87.71

calculated by adding the periodic discounted cash flows. An alternative would be to use the PRICE Excel function.

The bond price responds inversely to changes in yield. As the yield increases, so the price of the bond falls as shown by Figure 9.5 – a table of two bonds on the Cash Flow sheet. This example shows a five- and ten-year bond with the same coupon rate.

YIELD

Yield to maturity

The bond calculator includes various measures of yield. If you know the yield of a bond, you can calculate the market price; if you know the price, then you can compute the yield. There are a number of derivations and they are usually referred to as:

- yield to maturity (YTM);
- yield;
- redemption yield;
- gross redemption yield (GRY).

The yield is an iterative formula, which like the internal rate of return (IRR), assumes that all cash flows can be reinvested at the same rate. This is a failing with internal rates of return; nevertheless this is a simple concept and most investors understand the implied return on an investment.

The yield measures are in the Model sheet with the summary answers as shown in Figure 9.6. All the examples are saved as scenarios using Tools, Scenarios, New and can be accessed using the combo box control to the right of the sheet.

The model calculates the clean price as 82.27 – the present value of the coupons and principal. There are no coupons accrued and therefore the dirty price is the same as the clean price. The yield workings are shown in Figure 9.7.

Current yield

This is a simple measure and is calculated as:

Current yield = Coupon rate/(Clean price/100)

In this case, it is 6%/(82.27/100) = 7.2927%. The method ignores the time value of money and therefore it cannot be used for comparing different maturity dates and coupon periods.

Bond calculator

Figure 9.6

Reference		Summary	
Amount:	1,000.0	Clean price	82.2735
Issue date:	1-Jan-00	Coupon days 0 dys	0.0000
Settlement:	1-Jan-04	Dirty price	82.2735
Maturity 6 years:	1-Jan-10	Yield to maturity	10.0000
Redemption value:	100.000	Duration	5.0178 yrs
Coupon %:	6.000	Modified duration	4.7789 yrs
Yield to maturity:	10.000	Bi-annual convexity	27.8041
Price:	100.000	Change per 0.5%	(2.3547)
Coupons per annum:	2: Bi-annual	Revised price (3) 10.50%	80.3362
Basis:	US (NASD) 30/360		

Reference: Six Year Bi-annual Bond

Workings

Figure 9.7

(A) Price

Coupon amount	3.0000	Coupon divided by 2 payments per annum
Clean price	82.2735	Present value of coupons and principal
Coupon days	0 days	Days in this coupon period
Accrued interest at 6%	0.0000	Simple interest based on number of days in coupon period
Dirty price	82.2735	Clean price plus accrued interest
Price amount	82,273	Nominal value multiplied by amount

(B) Yield

Current yield	7.2927	Coupon/Price
Adjusted coupon yield	10.8829	[Coupon + ((Redemption-Clean)/Years to Maturity)] / [Clean]
Yield to maturity	10.0000	Calculated yield
Periodic interest rate	5.0000	

Figure 9.8

YIELD function

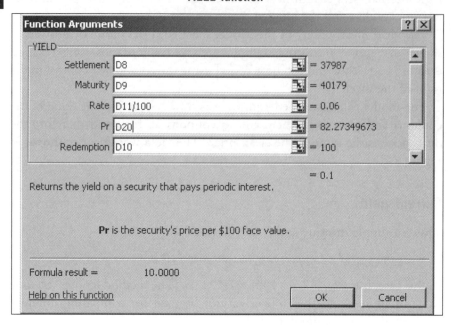

Function Arguments		? X
YIELD		
Settlement	D8	= 37987
Maturity	D9	= 40179
Rate	D11/100	= 0.06
Pr	D20	= 82.27349673
Redemption	D10	= 100

= 0.1

Returns the yield on a security that pays periodic interest.

Pr is the security's price per $100 face value.

Formula result =   10.0000

Help on this function   OK   Cancel

Simple yield to maturity

The simple yield to maturity again does not consider time value of money:

[Coupon + ((Redemption − Clean)/Years to maturity)]/[Clean/100]

The example is paying annual 6 per cent coupons and is priced at 82.27 with the simple yield computed as 10.88 per cent.

Yield to maturity

The yield to maturity function uses the settlement and maturity dates, the rate and number of payments per annum, the redemption value and the payment convention, to return the annual yield (see Figure 9.8).

DURATION AND MATURITY

There are four measures of sensitivity that are commonly used to measure risk in a bond. These are:

- simple maturity
- duration
- modified duration
- convexity.

Simple maturity

Simple maturity is the time left on the bond. Since risk increases with time then a long-dated bond is more risky that one which is due to mature sooner. Since the principal is paid back on expiry, bonds are dissimilar to loans where a portion of the principal is paid with each instalment. Figure 9.9 shows two zero coupon bonds: the first is five years and the second ten years. The series plots the changes to the price as interest rates rise. The interest rise has a greater impact on the bond with the longer maturity.

Duration

The maturity of a bond is not a suitable indicator of risk since the cash flows occur during the period to and at maturity. A bond with a longer maturity is more risky due to the possibility of adverse yield changes over a longer period. Duration attempts to provide a weighted measure of maturity in the formula:

$$Duration = \frac{\sum PV \, of \, cashflow * Period \, no}{Price}$$

This is the value-weighted average of the timing of the included cash flows. The cash flow schedule multiples out the present value cash flow by its

Zero coupons

Figure 9.9

8.50	9.00	9.50	10.00	10.50	11.00	11.50	12.00	12.50
66.50	64.99	63.52	62.09	60.70	59.35	58.03	56.74	55.49
44.23	42.24	40.35	38.55	36.84	35.22	33.67	32.20	30.79
4.41	2.90	1.43	-	(1.39)	(2.75)	(4.07)	(5.35)	(6.60)
5.67	3.69	1.80	-	(1.71)	(3.34)	(4.88)	(6.36)	(7.76)

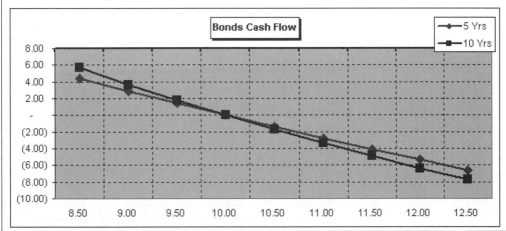

weighting and then adds them at the bottom of the schedule (see Figure 9.10). There is also a function for duration as in cell D31:

```
=DURATION(D8,D9,D11/100,IF(D12=0,D28,D12)/100,C13
4,F139)
=DURATION(Settlement,Maturity,Coupon,Yield,
Frequency,Basis)
```

If the bond carries no coupon, as in a zero coupon bond, then the duration will always be its maturity. Duration can be applied to any groups of cash flows and is useful when linked to the concept of immunization. If yields fall then the following occurs:

- earnings on reinvesting coupons will fall;
- the price of the bond rises if held to maturity.

At some point between the date and maturity, the loss of interest returns and the capital gains from a higher bond price balance or cancel each other out

Figure 9.10

Duration cash flows

	Period	Date	Cashflow	PV	Weighting	Duration
59						
60	**Period**	**Date**	**Cashflow**	**PV**	**Weighting**	**Duration**
61		1-Jan-04	-			
62	1.00	1-Jul-04	3.0000	2.8571	0.0347	0.0347
63	2.00	1-Jan-05	3.0000	2.7211	0.0331	0.0661
64	3.00	1-Jul-05	3.0000	2.5915	0.0315	0.0945
65	4.00	1-Jan-06	3.0000	2.4681	0.0300	0.1200
66	5.00	1-Jul-06	3.0000	2.3506	0.0286	0.1429
67	6.00	1-Jan-07	3.0000	2.2386	0.0272	0.1633
68	7.00	1-Jul-07	3.0000	2.1320	0.0259	0.1814
69	8.00	1-Jan-08	3.0000	2.0305	0.0247	0.1974
70	9.00	1-Jul-08	3.0000	1.9338	0.0235	0.2115
71	10.00	1-Jan-09	3.0000	1.8417	0.0224	0.2239
72	11.00	1-Jul-09	3.0000	1.7540	0.0213	0.2345
73	12.00	1-Jan-10	103.0000	57.3543	0.6971	8.3654
74	13.00	-	-	-	-	-
75	14.00	-	-	-	-	-
76	15.00	-	-	-	-	-
77	16.00	-	-	-	-	-
78	17.00	-	-	-	-	-
79	18.00	-	-	-	-	-
80	19.00	-	-	-	-	-
81	20.00	-	-	-	-	-
82	21.00	-	-	-	-	-
83	22.00	-	-	-	-	-
84	23.00	-	-	-	-	-
85	24.00	-	-	-	-	-
86	25.00	-	-	-	-	-
87			136.0000	82.2735	1.0000	10.0356

if an investor devises an immunized portfolio where:

- present value of assets equal the present value of liabilities;
- duration of assets is equal to the duration of liabilities.

Modified duration

The model also includes a calculation of modified duration which is a more accurate measure of the link between interest rates and bond prices. This is defined as:

$$D = -\frac{1}{P} \cdot \frac{\Delta P}{\Delta Y}$$

where:

P = bond price
ΔP = change in price
ΔY = change in the yield to maturity.

```
=MDURATION(D8,D9,D11/100,IF(D12=0,D28,D12)/100,C1
34,F139)
```

Sensitivity selection

Figure 9.11

		4.78	8.50	9.00	9.50	10.00	10.50	11.00	11.50
15	1-Jul-02	5.78	5.74	5.70	5.66	5.63	5.59	5.55
16	1-Jan-03	5.48	5.45	5.42	5.38	5.35	5.31	5.28
17	1-Jul-03	5.17	5.14	5.12	5.09	5.06	5.03	5.00
18	1-Jan-04	4.85	4.83	4.80	4.78	4.75	4.73	4.70
19	1-Jul-04	4.52	4.50	4.48	4.46	4.44	4.42	4.39
20	1-Jan-05	4.18	4.16	4.14	4.12	4.10	4.09	4.07
21	1-Jul-05	3.82	3.80	3.79	3.77	3.76	3.74	3.73

Figure contents:

Schedule   Menu

v1.0 1-Jan-2003

Select a variable and date : Modified duration ▼   14
1-Jan-04 ▼   4

Yield to maturity	10.00
Settlement:	1-Jan-04
Modified duration	4.78

Sensitivity table to Modified duration: Yield across Settlement date down

| Date: 1-01-2004 | | 4.85 | 4.83 | 4.80 | 4.78 | 4.75 | 4.73 | 4.70 |
| Change per 0.5% | | 0.02 | 0.02 | 0.02 | 0.02 | 0.02 | 0.02 | |

```
=MDURATION(Settlement,Maturity,Coupon,Yield,
  Frequency,Basis)
```

This is equivalent to:

```
=((1/(1+Yield to Maturity/100/Pmts per Year))*
  Duration)
```

Duration varies with yield and time and the model has a Sensitivity sheet for reviewing the effect of these two variables on a number of answers. This is a dynamic table enabling the selection of multiple lines, which updates the charts (see Figure 9.11).

The selection for the combo box is the range D18 to D55 on the Model sheet (see Figure 9.12). Making the data table dynamic increases the potential range of information. The second combo box selects a row from

Combo box selection

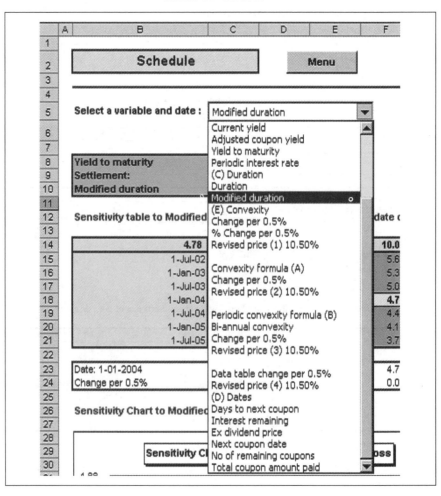

the two-dimensional data table for the chart. Since the variables are located on the Model sheet, the actual data table is contained in workings and looked up on the Sensitivity sheet. The cell at the top left of the table uses an OFFSET function to return the value for the row selected by the combo box.

```
=OFFSET(D18,Sensitivity!G5,0)
```

The table in Figure 9.13 shows duration and therefore risk declining as the time moves towards maturity. Duration also increases as the yield declines. The chart in Figure 9.13 plots the middle series of the table as an XY scatter and draws the answer as a single point with a data label. Duration assumes that the relationship between the bond price and yield to maturity is linear whereas the true relationship is not linear. The strict relationship is only true over small changes in yield or price. In practice, the line is slightly curved as shown in Figure 9.13 since the slope changes as you move along it.

Sensitivity to duration

Figure 9.13

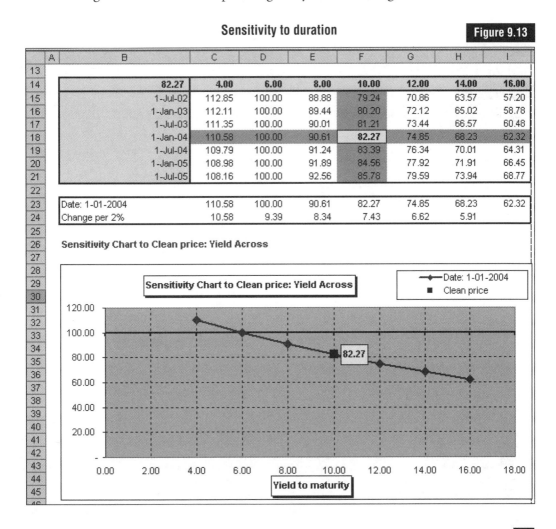

CONVEXITY

Duration and modified duration do not fully explain the link between prices and yield, and convexity provides a solution to predicting prices. The actual change depends on the amount of curvature and this is known as convexity. The Model sheet contains three formulas of calculating convexity and the sensitivity is explored on a second sheet called Convexity.

Formula 1

The first formula is an approximation to be used for small changes since it still assumes a linear relationship. The formula calculates the price movement based on a 1 per cent yield change. The coupon rate is the periodic rate rather than the annual rate. This is the formula for a 1 per cent change:

$$1 - Duration * Price * [1/(1 + Periodic\ coupon\ rate)] * 0.01$$

```
Cell D34=-$D$31*$D$20*(1/(1+(($D$28/$C$134)/
100)))*C120/100
```

Figure 9.14　　　　　　　　　　　　**Convexity**

	B	C	D	E	F	G	H	I
30	**(C) Duration**							
31	Duration		5.0178 yrs		Maturity: 6.00 years			
32	Modified duration		4.7789 yrs		Duration / [1+(Yield / No of Coupons)] = Slope of series			
33	**(E) Convexity**							
34	Change per 2%		(7.8635)		Duration * Price * [1/1+Int] * 2.00%			
35	% Change per 2%		(9.5577)		Change*(Par/Price)			
36	Revised price (1) 12.00%		74.4100		Price+Change			
37								
38	Change per 2%		(7.8635)		Percentage change			
39	% Change per 2%		(9.5577)		Modified duration * Δ yield			
40	Revised price (2) 12.00%		74.4100		Price+Change			
41								
42	Convexity formula (A)		27.8041		Formula: [(ΔP ₊₁ /P) + (ΔP ₋₁ /P)] * 10^8			
43	Change per 2%		(9.0017)		Variance to simple formula: 0.5561			
44	Revised price (3) 12.00%		74.8675		Price+Change			
45								
46	Periodic convexity formula (B)		111.2165		PV convexity cash flow			
47	Bi-annual convexity		27.8041		Periodic = annual /(N periods ^ N periods)			
48	Change per 2%		(9.0017)		Variance to simple formula: 0.5561			
49	Revised price (4) 12.00%		74.8675		Price+Change			
50								
51	Data table change per 2%		(8.9770)		Variance to simple formula: 0.5807			
52	Revised price (5) 12.00%		74.8878		Actual Price　74.8485　　(0.0902)			
53	**(D) Dates**							
54	Days to next coupon		182 days		Days remaining in this coupon period			
55	Interest remaining		(3.0333)		Interest still to be accrued in period			
56	Ex dividend price		79.2402		Clean price minus interest remaining in period			
57	Next coupon date		1-Jul-04		Next coupon date (Bi-annual)			
58	No of remaining coupons		12		Number until maturity			
59	Total coupon amount paid		24.0330		Coupon amounts paid since issue date			

This is derived as −7.8635 or 9.55 per cent for an increase to a 12 per cent yield. The answer is revised price (1) which is 74.41 (see Figure 9.14).

Formula 2

The modified duration can also be used for calculating the price change per 1 per cent of yield using the formula:

−Dirty price * Change in yield * Modified duration

This results in the same answer for the 12 per cent yield. Again this assumes a linear relationship and will become progressively inaccurate.

Formula 3

The first convexity formula is:

$$C = 10^8 \left[\frac{\Delta P_{d+1}}{P_d} + \frac{\Delta P_{d-1}}{P_d} \right]$$

This involves calculating the price change for plus and minus 100 basis points using a data table in workings on the right-hand side (see Figure 9.15). Convexity is calculated as:

```
Cell D43=(((N35/D20)+(P35/D20))*10^8)
```

The formula for a change in price is then:

$$\Delta\, Price = -Modified\ duration * \Delta Yield + \frac{Convexity}{2} * \Delta Yield^2$$

```
Cell D43=(-$D$32*($C$124/100)+0.5*D42*
($C$124/100)^2)*100
```

The final result due to the curvature is 74.8485 rather than 74.4100 by the simpler linear formula.

Convexity working

Figure 9.15

L	M	N	O	P	Q
31					
32	**Convexity Workings**				
33		9.99	10.00	10.01	12.00
34	82.2735	82.3128	82.2735	82.2342	74.84847
35	Change	0.0393		(0.0393)	(7.3857)
36	%	0.0478		(0.0478)	(8.9770)
37	(4) Variances				
38	Data table to convexity			0.0203	
39	Data table to simple formula			0.4778	
40	Convexity to simple formula			0.4575	
41					

Formula 4

The model also includes the full convexity formulas in the cash flow on the model sheet (see Figure 9.16) build up as a schedule using the formula below:

$$Convexity = \frac{1}{P} \cdot \frac{\Delta^2 P}{(\Delta y)^2} = \frac{1}{(1+y)^2} \cdot \sum_{t=1}^{r} t \cdot (t+1) \cdot \frac{C_t}{(1+y)^t} / P$$

The weightings column is the present value in column E of Figure 9.16 divided by the sum of the cash flows in cell E91. The duration is the period number multiplied by the weighting. The convexity for the period is:

Figure 9.16		Convexity workings					

A	B	C	D	E	F	G	H
62	Six Year Bi-annual Bond Cash flows						
63							
64	**Period**	**Date**	**Cashflow**	**PV**	**Weighting**	**Duration**	**Convexity**
65		1-Jan-04	-				
66	1.00	1-Jul-04	3.0000	2.8571	0.0347	0.0347	0.0629
67	2.00	1-Jan-05	3.0000	2.7211	0.0331	0.0661	0.1800
68	3.00	1-Jul-05	3.0000	2.5915	0.0315	0.0945	0.3428
69	4.00	1-Jan-06	3.0000	2.4681	0.0300	0.1200	0.5442
70	5.00	1-Jul-06	3.0000	2.3506	0.0286	0.1429	0.7774
71	6.00	1-Jan-07	3.0000	2.2386	0.0272	0.1633	1.0366
72	7.00	1-Jul-07	3.0000	2.1320	0.0259	0.1814	1.3163
73	8.00	1-Jan-08	3.0000	2.0305	0.0247	0.1974	1.6118
74	9.00	1-Jul-08	3.0000	1.9338	0.0235	0.2115	1.9188
75	10.00	1-Jan-09	3.0000	1.8417	0.0224	0.2239	2.2335
76	11.00	1-Jul-09	3.0000	1.7540	0.0213	0.2345	2.5526
77	12.00	1-Jan-10	103.0000	57.3543	0.6971	8.3654	98.6397
78	13.00	-	-	-	-	-	-
79	14.00	-	-	-	-	-	-
80	15.00	-	-	-	-	-	-
81	16.00	-	-	-	-	-	-
82	17.00	-	-	-	-	-	-
83	18.00	-	-	-	-	-	-
84	19.00	-	-	-	-	-	-
85	20.00	-	-	-	-	-	-
86	21.00	-	-	-	-	-	-
87	22.00	-	-	-	-	-	-
88	23.00	-	-	-	-	-	-
89	24.00	-	-	-	-	-	-
90	25.00	-	-	-	-	-	-
91			136.0000	82.2735	1.0000	10.0356	111.2165
92							
93					Price:		82.2735
94					Annual Convexity		27.8041
95					Change per 2%		(9.0017)

Convexity results

Figure 9.17

	B	C	D	E	F	G	H
41							
42	Convexity formula (A)		27.8041		Formula: [(ΔP $_{+1}$ /P) + (ΔP $_{-1}$ /P)] * 10^8		
43	% Change per 2%		(9.0017)		Variance to simple formula: 0.5561		
44	Revised price (3) 12.00%		74.8675		Price+Change		
45							
46	Periodic convexity formula (B)		111.2165		PV convexity cash flow		
47	Bi-annual convexity		27.8041		Periodic = annual /(N periods ^N periods)		
48	% Change per 2%		(9.0017)		Variance to simple formula: 0.5561		
49	Revised price (4) 12.00%		74.8675		Price+Change		
50							
51	Data table change per 2%		(8.9770)		Variance to simple formula: 0.5807		
52	Revised price (5) 12.00%		74.8878		Actual Price	74.8485	(0.0902)

```
Period+Next Period*Weighting*(1/1+Periodic
Yield)^2
Cell H66=B66*B67*F66*(1/(1+($D$28/Pmt_Year/
100) )^2)
```

At the bottom of the schedule the periodic convexity results are added:

```
Cell H91 ==SUM(H66:H90)
```

The annual rate is the sum divided by (payments per year ^ payments per year). The convexity is 27.80 and with this factor the change in the bond price can be derived with:

$$\Delta Price = -Modified\ duration * \Delta Yield + \frac{Convexity}{2} * \Delta Yield^2$$

The value is 74.8675 (see Figure 9.17). The schedule also includes data table workings for comparison to the calculated values and this is 74.8878 (see Figure 9.17).

COMPARISON

The Convexity sheet calculates the bond price at each of the yield to maturities on the left using a PRICE function.

```
=PRICE(Model!$D$8,Model!$D$9,Model!$D$11/100,B10/
  100,Model!$D$10,Model!$C$138,Model!$F$143)
=PRICE(Settlement,Maturity,Coupon,Yield,
  Redemption,Frequency,Basis)
```

Column F of Figure 9.18 repeats formula 2 (−dirty price * change in

Figure 9.18   **Summary table**

	A	B	C	D	E	F	G	H	I	J	K
4											
5		**Convexity: Predicted and Actual**									
6											
7		**Interval**	**1.00**								
8											
9		**Yield to maturity**	**Change in yield**	**Actual change %**	**Clean price**	**-D"Δ in yield %**	**Revised price (2) 12.00%**	**Difference (2)**	**Periodic convexity formula (B)**	**Revised price (4) 12.00%**	**Difference (4)**
10		2.00	(8.0000)	48.9060	122.5102	38.2310	113.7275	8.7827	47.1283	121.0476	1.4625
11		3.00	(7.0000)	41.4323	116.3613	33.4521	109.7957	6.5655	40.2641	115.4002	0.9611
12		4.00	(6.0000)	34.3997	110.5753	28.6732	105.8640	4.7114	33.6780	109.9816	0.5938
13		5.00	(5.0000)	27.7798	105.1289	23.8944	101.9322	3.1967	27.3699	104.7917	0.3372
14		6.00	(4.0000)	21.5458	100.0000	19.1155	98.0005	1.9995	21.3398	99.8305	0.1695
15		7.00	(3.0000)	15.6731	95.1683	14.3366	94.0687	1.0996	15.5878	95.0981	0.0702
16		8.00	(2.0000)	10.1387	90.6149	9.5577	90.1370	0.4779	10.1138	90.5945	0.0204
17		9.00	(1.0000)	4.9209	86.3221	4.7789	86.2052	0.1169	4.9179	86.3196	0.0025
18		**10.00**	-	0.0000	82.2735	-	82.2735	0.0000	-	82.2735	0.0000
19		11.00	1.0000	(4.6428)	78.4537	(4.7789)	78.3417	0.1120	(4.6399)	78.4561	(0.0024)
20		12.00	2.0000	(9.0248)	74.8485	(9.5577)	74.4100	0.4385	(9.0017)	74.8675	(0.0190)
21		13.00	3.0000	(13.1622)	71.4445	(14.3366)	70.4783	0.9662	(13.0854)	71.5077	(0.0632)
22		14.00	4.0000	(17.0702)	68.2293	(19.1155)	66.5465	1.6827	(16.8912)	68.3765	(0.1473)
23		15.00	5.0000	(20.7628)	65.1912	(23.8944)	62.6148	2.5765	(20.4189)	65.4742	(0.2829)
24		16.00	6.0000	(24.2531)	62.3196	(28.6732)	58.6830	3.6366	(23.6685)	62.8006	(0.4810)
25		17.00	7.0000	(27.5536)	59.6042	(33.4521)	54.7513	4.8530	(26.6401)	60.3557	(0.7515)
26		18.00	8.0000	(30.6756)	57.0356	(38.2310)	50.8195	6.2161	(29.3337)	58.1397	(1.1040)

Figure 9.19   **Convexity chart**

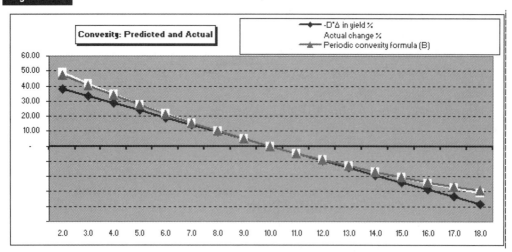

yield * modified duration) as the duration multiplied by the change in yield to obtain the percentage change. This can then be multiplied out against the existing price. Column I uses formula 4 to obtain the percentages and these are added in column J. You can see that the differences are small when close to the current yield to maturity but due to convexity, become more pronounced as you move further from the existing price.

Percentage differences to actual prices

Figure 9.20

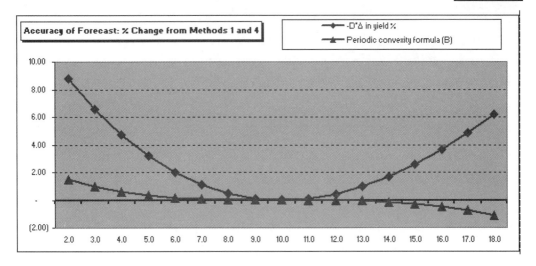

Two further charts illustrate the table (see Figures 9.19 and 9.20). Figure 9.19 plots the actual and predicted changes in amounts from formulas 2 and 4. The convexity formula rather than the duration-based formula is more accurate in tracking the actual price changes. The periodic convexity follows the actual change closely.

Figure 9.20 plots the percentage differences against the predicted actual prices. The duration-based formula becomes progressively less accurate away from the current yield of 10 per cent. By contrast, formula 4, based on the convexity cash flows, remains more accurate further from the current yield.

SUMMARY

Bond mathematics provides a method of assessing risk in fixed income products. The requirements include assessing price, yield and risk. Since the value of a bond varies inversely with the yield, this chapter has provided methods of assessing the sensitivity of a bond's value to changes in interest rates. The main methods are duration and convexity, which provide a standardized measure of risk in the product. Using these measures, it is possible to assess the sensitivity to interest rate changes which will affect the value of the bond cash flows.

Options

File: FT4_10.xls

INTRODUCTION

This chapter introduces options models and maps the pricing and pay-offs whereby the holders can use these instruments to reduce downside risk upon payment of premiums. The models show how downside risk is removed and how combinations of options can deal with varying expectations of future volatility in the markets. The usual definitions are as follows.

- An *option* provides an opportunity to buy or sell a specified quantity of an underlying asset at or before an expiry date at a strike or exercise price.
- A *call option* is a contract giving its holder the right (but not the obligation) to buy at a fixed price at any time on or before a given date. The premium is paid at the beginning and if at expiration, the asset value is less than the strike price, then the option is worthless and the holder would decide not to exercise the option. If it is greater, the holder would exercise the option and purchase at the exercise price. The variance between the asset price and the exercise price would constitute a profit less the initial price for the option.
- A *put option* is a contract giving its holder the right (but not the obligation) to sell at a fixed price at any time on or before a given date. The holder pays the premium. On expiry, if the price of the asset is greater than the strike price, the option would not be exercised. If the price is less than the strike price, the put option would be exercised and stock sold at the strike price. The difference between the strike price and the expiry market value of the asset would represent a profit on the transaction.

American options use the above definitions whereas European options can only be exercised on the expiry date. Since you can allow an option to lapse if it is worthless, options can be useful in covering possible downside risk. Since there are two sides to the bargain, the pricing reflects perceptions of risk and uncertainty in the underlying asset. The pricing of options is determined by:

- volatility of variance in the price of the underlying asset since the uncertainty has to be priced into the contract;
- initial value of the underlying asset;
- strike price at expiry;
- time to expiry since risk usually increases with time;
- risk less interest rate for the period of the option.

Table 10.1 shows the effects on call and put values of various variables.

Table 10.1

Variable	Effect on call value	Effect on put value
Increase in volatility	Increase	Increase
Increase in asset price	Increase	Decrease
Increase in strike price	Decrease	Increase
Increase in time to expiry	Increase	Increase
Increase in risk-free rate	Increase	Decrease

OPTIONS

The sheet called Call_Put_Option demonstrates the workings of an option. The scenario called Example 1 contains the example shown in Figure 10.1. The option is the right to buy shares at 5.00 over a period ending in June. The underlying price at the time of writing the contracts is 5.00 and the price of the option is 0.78. This fixes the maximum loss at 0.78 since this is a right and not an obligation to buy. Likewise, the maximum loss on the put options is limited to 0.38. The possible courses of action are:

- the price rises – sell the option in the market or exercise the option on expiry;

Figure 10.1   Options inputs

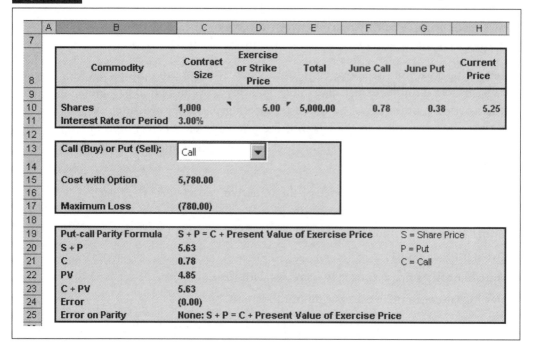

■ the price falls – allow the option to lapse as it is worthless.

The inputs section checks the pricing of the call and put options since the pricing should, in theory, equate to call put parity through this formula:

Spot price + Put = Call + Present value of exercise price

Call option table and pay-off diagrams

Figure 10.2

	Interval for Graph and Table	0.20	Cost with option	Adopt	Cost without Option		Profit / (Loss)
28	Expiry Security Price	4.00	4,780.00	4,780.00	4,000.00		(780.00)
29		4.20	4,980.00	4,980.00	4,200.00		(780.00)
30		4.40	5,180.00	5,180.00	4,400.00		(780.00)
31		4.60	5,380.00	5,380.00	4,600.00		(780.00)
32		4.80	5,580.00	5,580.00	4,800.00		(780.00)
33		5.00	5,780.00	5,780.00	5,000.00		(780.00)
34		5.20	5,980.00	5,780.00	5,200.00		(580.00)
35		5.40	6,180.00	5,780.00	5,400.00		(380.00)
36		5.60	6,380.00	5,780.00	5,600.00		(180.00)
37		5.80	6,580.00	5,780.00	5,800.00		20.00
38		6.00	6,780.00	5,780.00	6,000.00		220.00
39		6.20	6,980.00	5,780.00	6,200.00		420.00
40		6.40	7,180.00	5,780.00	6,400.00		620.00
41		6.60	7,380.00	5,780.00	6,600.00		820.00
42		6.80	7,580.00	5,780.00	6,800.00		1,020.00
43		7.00	7,780.00	5,780.00	7,000.00		1,220.00

Pay-off chart

Figure 10.3

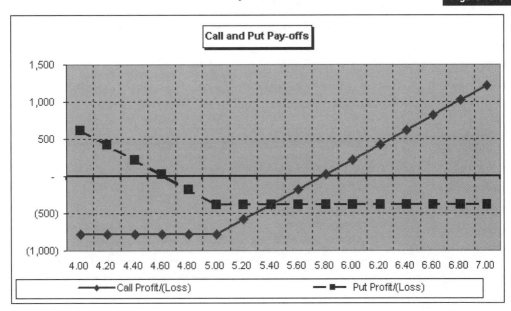

Figure 10.4

Put option

	Interval for Graph and Table	0.20	Cost with option	Adopt	Cost without Option	Profit / (Loss)
28	Expiry Security Price	4.00	4,620.00	4,620.00	4,000.00	620.00
29		4.20	4,620.00	4,620.00	4,200.00	420.00
30		4.40	4,620.00	4,620.00	4,400.00	220.00
31		4.60	4,620.00	4,620.00	4,600.00	20.00
32		4.80	4,620.00	4,620.00	4,800.00	(180.00)
33		5.00	4,620.00	4,620.00	5,000.00	(380.00)
34		5.20	4,620.00	4,620.00	5,200.00	(380.00)
35		5.40	4,620.00	4,620.00	5,400.00	(380.00)
36		5.60	4,620.00	4,620.00	5,600.00	(380.00)
37		5.80	4,620.00	4,620.00	5,800.00	(380.00)
38		6.00	4,620.00	4,620.00	6,000.00	(380.00)
39		6.20	4,620.00	4,620.00	6,200.00	(380.00)
40		6.40	4,620.00	4,620.00	6,400.00	(380.00)
41		6.60	4,620.00	4,620.00	6,600.00	(380.00)
42		6.80	4,620.00	4,620.00	6,800.00	(380.00)
43		7.00	4,620.00	4,620.00	7,000.00	(380.00)

Figure 10.5

Workings

Workings - Graph

	Call	Adopt	Call Profit/(Loss)	Put	Adopt	Put Profit/(Loss)
28	4,780.00	4,780.00	(780.00)	4,620.00	4,620.00	620.00
29	4,980.00	4,980.00	(780.00)	4,620.00	4,620.00	420.00
30	5,180.00	5,180.00	(780.00)	4,620.00	4,620.00	220.00
31	5,380.00	5,380.00	(780.00)	4,620.00	4,620.00	20.00
32	5,580.00	5,580.00	(780.00)	4,620.00	4,620.00	(180.00)
33	5,780.00	5,780.00	(780.00)	4,620.00	4,620.00	(380.00)
34	5,980.00	5,780.00	(580.00)	4,620.00	4,620.00	(380.00)
35	6,180.00	5,780.00	(380.00)	4,620.00	4,620.00	(380.00)
36	6,380.00	5,780.00	(180.00)	4,620.00	4,620.00	(380.00)
37	6,580.00	5,780.00	20.00	4,620.00	4,620.00	(380.00)
38	6,780.00	5,780.00	220.00	4,620.00	4,620.00	(380.00)
39	6,980.00	5,780.00	420.00	4,620.00	4,620.00	(380.00)
40	7,180.00	5,780.00	620.00	4,620.00	4,620.00	(380.00)
41	7,380.00	5,780.00	820.00	4,620.00	4,620.00	(380.00)
42	7,580.00	5,780.00	1,020.00	4,620.00	4,620.00	(380.00)
43	7,780.00	5,780.00	1,220.00	4,620.00	4,620.00	(380.00)

The present value is calculated in the model using the basic formula $1/(1 + Interest\ rate)$ using the periodic interest rate entered in cell C11. Plotting the pay-offs for a call and a put are clearer in Excel and this schedule contains tables and charts (see Figures 10.1, 10.2 and 10,3).

If the share price was below the strike price of 5.00 plus the cost of the option of 0.78, Figure 10.2 shows losses and the options would not be exercised. The maximum loss is fixed at 0.78 per unit. Above 5.78, the profits increase since the strike plus premium price remains at 5.78.

The reverse is true for the put option where the losses increase as the price rises. The break even is 5.00 less the price of the option of 0.38 per unit (see Figure 10.4).

The chart is driven by the workings area on the right, which calculates both series simultaneously (see Figure 10.5). The code uses simple IF statements to decide whether to adopt the result or not. This means, for example, that the call option will adopt the 5.78 figure.

OPTIONS EXAMPLE

This Options_Example sheet allows you to choose a call or a put and view the net pay-offs at different strike prices. The data inputs are shown in Figure 10.6.

The controls allow you to select a call or a put and to select the option to be drawn in the chart at the bottom of the schedule. This is the code in cell

Inputs and prices

Figure 10.6

		(A) Call Options				(B) Put Options			Units $0
		Strike Price	Premium (points)			Strike Price	Premium (points)		
Price less 3.0	100.00	3.50			100.00	0.60			
Price less 2.0	101.00	2.80			101.00	0.85			
Price less 1.0	102.00	2.15			102.00	1.20			
At-the-money	103.00	1.50			103.00	1.50			
Price plus 1.0	104.00	1.20			104.00	2.20			
Price plus 2.0	105.00	0.85			105.00	2.80			
Price plus 3.0	106.00	0.70			106.00	3.65			

C25, which contains a first IF statement using cell C75 (the result cell from the Call/Put control).

```
=IF($C$75=1,IF($B25>C$22,$B25-C$22-C$23,-
C$23),IF($B25<C$22,C$22-$B25-C$23,-C$23))
```

With the call, if the market price is greater than the contract price it calculates a profit, otherwise the loss is the maximum, which is the option premium. With a put option, the opposite is true and a margin is available if the market price is below the contract price.

Below the inputs, there is a table showing the results from a put option on market prices between 95.00 and 110.00 (see Figure 10.7). There are workings for the chart on the right-hand side and column K displays the results

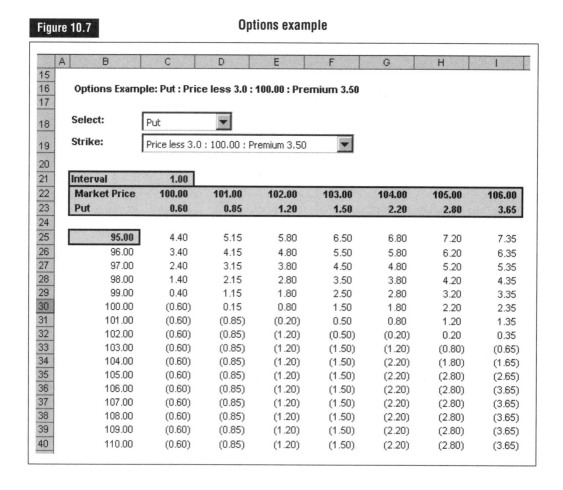

Figure 10.7   Options example

	A	B	C	D	E	F	G	H	I
15									
16		Options Example: Put : Price less 3.0 : 100.00 : Premium 3.50							
17									
18		Select:	Put						
19		Strike:	Price less 3.0 : 100.00 : Premium 3.50						
20									
21		Interval	1.00						
22		Market Price	100.00	101.00	102.00	103.00	104.00	105.00	106.00
23		Put	0.60	0.85	1.20	1.50	2.20	2.80	3.65
24									
25		95.00	4.40	5.15	5.80	6.50	6.80	7.20	7.35
26		96.00	3.40	4.15	4.80	5.50	5.80	6.20	6.35
27		97.00	2.40	3.15	3.80	4.50	4.80	5.20	5.35
28		98.00	1.40	2.15	2.80	3.50	3.80	4.20	4.35
29		99.00	0.40	1.15	1.80	2.50	2.80	3.20	3.35
30		100.00	(0.60)	0.15	0.80	1.50	1.80	2.20	2.35
31		101.00	(0.60)	(0.85)	(0.20)	0.50	0.80	1.20	1.35
32		102.00	(0.60)	(0.85)	(1.20)	(0.50)	(0.20)	0.20	0.35
33		103.00	(0.60)	(0.85)	(1.20)	(1.50)	(1.20)	(0.80)	(0.65)
34		104.00	(0.60)	(0.85)	(1.20)	(1.50)	(2.20)	(1.80)	(1.65)
35		105.00	(0.60)	(0.85)	(1.20)	(1.50)	(2.20)	(2.80)	(2.65)
36		106.00	(0.60)	(0.85)	(1.20)	(1.50)	(2.20)	(2.80)	(3.65)
37		107.00	(0.60)	(0.85)	(1.20)	(1.50)	(2.20)	(2.80)	(3.65)
38		108.00	(0.60)	(0.85)	(1.20)	(1.50)	(2.20)	(2.80)	(3.65)
39		109.00	(0.60)	(0.85)	(1.20)	(1.50)	(2.20)	(2.80)	(3.65)
40		110.00	(0.60)	(0.85)	(1.20)	(1.50)	(2.20)	(2.80)	(3.65)

from the 'do nothing' alternative. At the strike price of 103.00, the only loss is the premium, but below this figure, the losses mount.

The chart plots several of the price lines to illustrate the trade off on the put option (see Figure 10.8). The losses are limited to the premium paid for the put.

The chart is reversed with a call option where there are gains below the mid-price of 103.00 (see Figure 10.9). This method of charting pay-off diagrams makes it easier to understand the profit and losses under different prices. It is also another method of auditing the model to ensure that it produces plausible values.

Put options chart

Figure 10.8

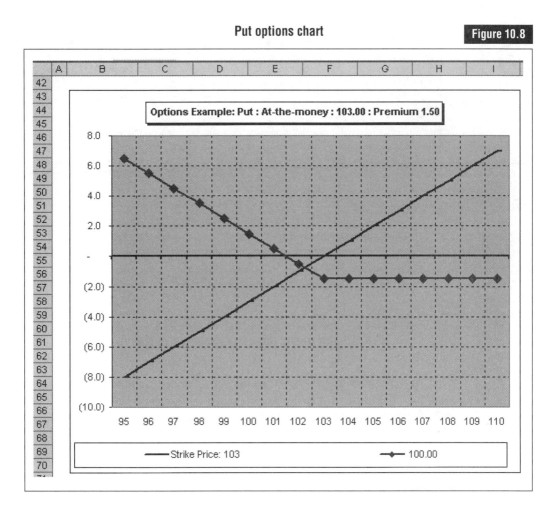

Options Example: Put : At-the-money : 103.00 : Premium 1.50

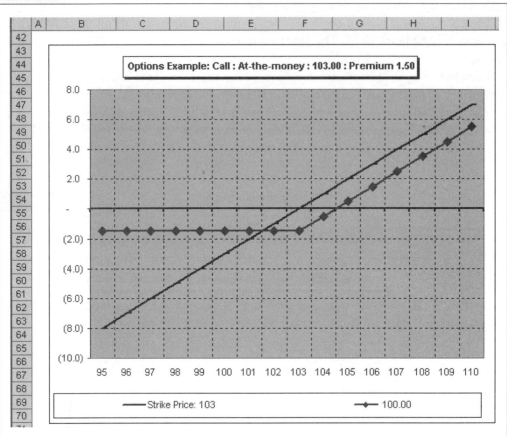

Figure 10.9

Call option chart

OPTIONS HEDGING STRATEGY

The strategy sheet allows the investigation of options strategies since there are inputs for up to two strike prices of:

- buy call
- buy put
- sell/write call
- sell/write put.

The spreadsheet uses a series of eight blocks of workings on the right which collect data from the inputs area (see Figure 10.10). This is to allow strategies such as so-called butterflies with options purchased at different rates.

In each case, the workings use the number of options, the price and premium paid, if received, to work out if the options is in or out of the money (see Figure 10.11). This decides whether the option is worth exercising or not and then the block derives the amount, and removes the premium to leave the net pay-off for the underlying expiry price.

Strategy inputs

Figure 10.10

	A	B	C	D	E	F	G	H	I	J	K
4											
5			Number	Price	Premium				Strike	Call	Put
6		Buy Call	1	103.00	1.50						
7			1	105.00	0.85		Price less 0.0		100.00	3.50	0.60
8		Buy Put	0	-	-		Price less 0.0		101.00	2.80	0.85
9			0	-	-		Price less 0.0		102.00	2.15	1.20
10		Write Call	1	104.00	1.20		At-the-money		103.00	1.50	1.50
11			1	104.00	1.20		Price plus 0.0		104.00	1.20	2.20
12		Write Put	0	-	-		Price plus 0.0		105.00	0.85	2.80
13			0	-	-		Price plus 0.0		106.00	0.70	3.65
14		Interval		1.00							Units $0

Workings

Figure 10.11

	L	M	N	O	P
11					
12				No	1.00
13				Price	103.00
14		(1) Buy Call		Premium	1.50
15					
16		In/Out	Buyer	Premium	Net Put
17					
18		N	-	(1.50)	(1.50)
19		N	-	(1.50)	(1.50)
20		N	-	(1.50)	(1.50)
21		N	-	(1.50)	(1.50)
22		N	-	(1.50)	(1.50)
23		N	-	(1.50)	(1.50)
24		N	-	(1.50)	(1.50)
25		N	-	(1.50)	(1.50)
26		N	-	(1.50)	(1.50)
27		Y	1.00	(1.50)	(0.50)
28		Y	2.00	(1.50)	0.50
29		Y	3.00	(1.50)	1.50
30		Y	4.00	(1.50)	2.50
31		Y	5.00	(1.50)	3.50
32		Y	6.00	(1.50)	4.50
33		Y	7.00	(1.50)	5.50
34					
35					0.25
36					2.38

Figure 10.12

Buy and write a call

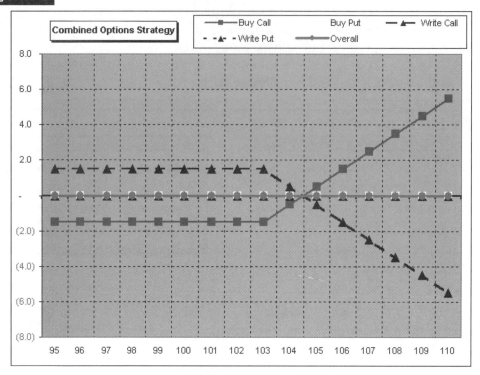

Figure 10.13

Buy and write a put

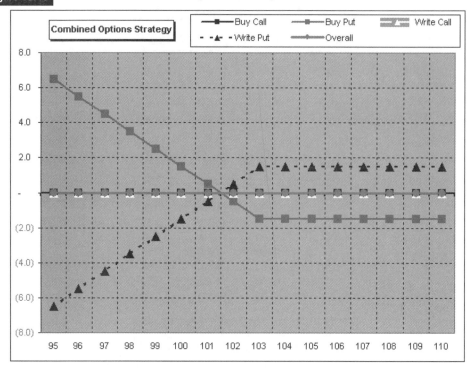

The calculations can be checked to show the net sum from writing and buying a put or a call. Figures 10.12 and 10.13 show the charts from both methods with a zero pay-off since both options are at the same price of 103.0. The net position series runs along the x-axis. Using the grid, the next section considers option strategies in stable and volatile environments.

Neutral – sell straddle

Each of the following strategies are saved as scenarios to the model to allow easy loading of the values. The expectation with a sell straddle is for a stable environment where prices are likely to fluctuate in a very narrow range (see Figure 10.14). A call option and a put option are sold with the same strike price since the expected is not likely to move. There is a profit if the market stays within a narrow range but losses on both sides if there is greater fluctuation.

The lower point will be the strike minus the value of two premiums received and the upper point will be the strike plus the two premiums received. There is, of course, unlimited downside risk if the market rises or falls outside the band.

Sell straddle

Figure 10.14

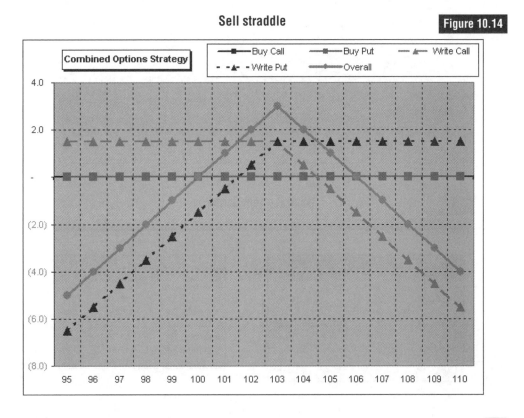

Neutral – sell strangle

Prices here are expected to fluctuate in a broader range (see Figure 10.15). A put option is sold with a strike price at the money and a call option is sold with the higher strike price. The breakeven will be the lower strike minus the two premiums received and the upper point will be the higher strike plus the two premiums received. Again, the downside risk is unlimited outside the bands chosen.

 Figure 10.15

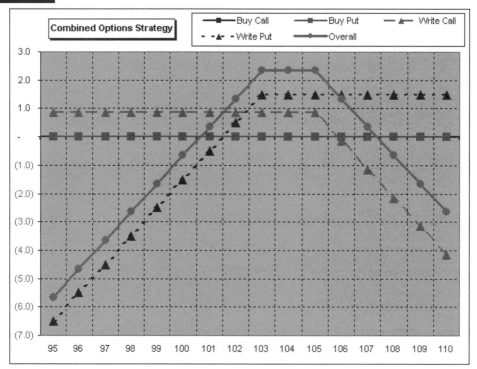

Sell strangle

Figure 10.16   **Neutral – long butterfly**

	A	B	C	D	E	F	G	H	I	J	K
4											
5			Number	Price	Premium				Strike	Call	Put
6		Buy Call	1	100.00	3.50						
7			1	106.00	0.70		Price less 0.0		100.00	3.50	0.60
8		Buy Put	0	-	-		Price less 0.0		101.00	2.80	0.85
9			0	-	-		Price less 0.0		102.00	2.15	1.20
10		Write Call	1	103.00	1.50		At-the-money		103.00	1.50	1.50
11			1	103.00	1.50		Price plus 0.0		104.00	1.20	2.20
12		Write Put	0	-	-		Price plus 0.0		105.00	0.85	2.80
13			0	-	-		Price plus 0.0		106.00	0.70	3.65
14		Interval		1.00							Units $0

Neutral – long butterfly

Here investors are moderately certain that prices will not fluctuate much outside the current band (see Figures 10.16 and 10.17). Investors think that the market will not be volatile during the term, but wants to cap the downside risk. A call option with low strike is bought, two call options with medium strike are sold, and a call option with high strike is bought. The upside potential is limited to the difference between the lower and middle strikes minus the net debit of establishing the spread. The downside risk is limited to the initial net debit of establishing the spread.

Volatile – buy straddle

Investors expect prices to be very volatile and want to be protected against extreme movements (see Figure 10.18). The position will lose if prices do not fluctuate outside the narrow range. A call option and put option are bought with the same strike price, usually at-the-money. There is upside potential at expiry away from the strike prices and the lower point is the

Neutral – long butterfly chart **Figure 10.17**

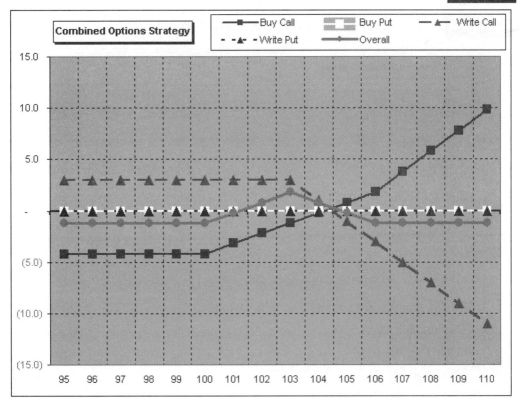

Figure 10.18

Volatile – buy straddle

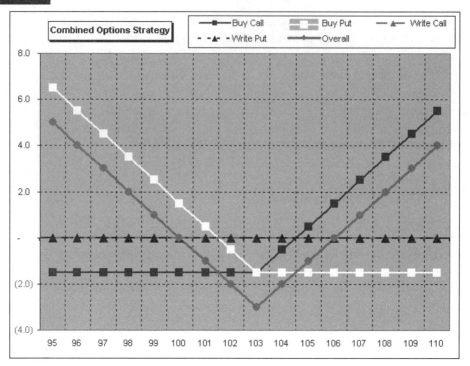

Figure 10.19

Volatile – buy strangle

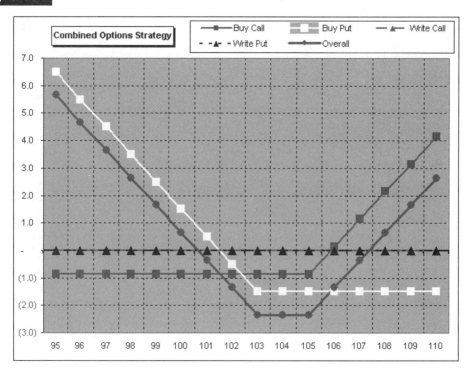

strike minus the two premiums paid while the upper position is the strike plus the two premiums. The downside is limited to the total of the two premiums paid.

Volatile – buy strangle

Prices are expected to be volatile and the investor therefore purchases a put option with low strike price (103 as shown in Figure 10.19) and a call option is bought with at a higher strike price (105 as shown in

Volatile – short butterfly inputs

Figure 10.20

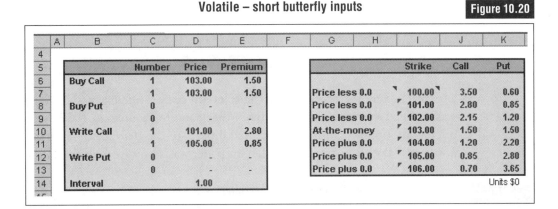

		Number	Price	Premium				Strike	Call	Put
Buy Call		1	103.00	1.50						
		1	103.00	1.50	Price less 0.0		100.00	3.50	0.60
Buy Put		0	-	-	Price less 0.0		101.00	2.80	0.85
		0	-	-	Price less 0.0		102.00	2.15	1.20
Write Call		1	101.00	2.80	At-the-money		103.00	1.50	1.50
		1	105.00	0.85	Price plus 0.0		104.00	1.20	2.20
Write Put		0	-	-	Price plus 0.0		105.00	0.85	2.80
		0	-	-	Price plus 0.0		106.00	0.70	3.65
Interval			1.00						Units $0

Volatile – short butterfly chart

Figure 10.21

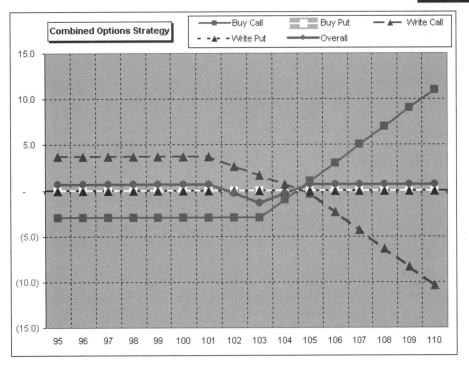

Figure 10.19). The upside potential is unlimited if the market falls or rises greatly. The downside is limited to the two premiums paid.

Volatile – short butterfly

Investors here expect prices to be moderately volatile (see Figures 10.20 and 10.21). A call option is sold with a low strike price, two call options are bought with a medium strike price, and a call option is sold with a higher strike price. The upside is limited to initial credit received while the downside is limited to the difference between the lower and middle strikes minus the initial spread credit.

BLACK–SCHOLES

The Black–Scholes schedule uses the standard option pricing model which was outlined in the paper written by F. Black and M. Scholes in 1973, 'The pricing of options and corporate liabilities' in the *Journal of Political Economy* (May/June, pp. 637–54). This paper was a breakthrough since the

Figure 10.22	Black–Scholes workings

	A	B	C	D
115		Days in current year		=DATE(YEAR(D5),12,31)-DATE(YEAR(D5)-1,12,31)
116		T		=T
117		r (Int)		=Int
118		S		=S
119		P		=P
120		X		=X
121				
122		**(1) Call Option**		
123		d_1		=(LN(P/X)+(Int+0.5*S^2)*T)/(S*SQRT(T))
124		d_2		=D123-SQRT(T)*S
125		N(d_1)		=NORMSDIST(D123)
126		N(d_2)		=NORMSDIST(D124)
127		Call price		=IF(S<0,0,IF(ISERROR(P*D125-X*EXP(-Int*T)*D126),0,P*D125-X*EXP(-Int*T)*D126))
128				
129		**(2) Put Option**		
130		-d_1		=-D123
131		-d_2		=-D124
132		N(-d_1)		=NORMSDIST(D130)
133		N(-d_2)		=NORMSDIST(D131)
134		Put price		=IF(S<0,0,IF(ISERROR(-(P*D132-X*EXP(-Int*T)*D133)),0,-(P*D132-X*EXP(-Int*T)*D133)))
135				
136		**(3) Check Put-call**		
137		Formula		
138		P + Put		=P+I10
139		Call Price		=I8
140		PV of X		=X/(1+Int)^(T)
141		C + PV		=D140+D139
142		Variance		=D138-D141
143		Error on Parity		=IF(ROUND(D138-D141,1)=0,"None",D138-D141)
144				

model appeared to price risk correctly and used a limited number of observable quantities such as:

- maturity date (*T*)
- domestic interest rate (*Int*)
- volatility of the share price as measured by standard deviation (*S*)
- current stock price (*P*)
- exercise price (*X*).

The main assumptions for the model are:

- Relative price rises in the future are independent of changes in the current price.
- Interest rates and volatility remain constant during the period and assume that future volatility equals past volatility in prices. This may not be true since volatility reduces as you near the maturity date.

Black–Scholes inputs

Figure 10.23

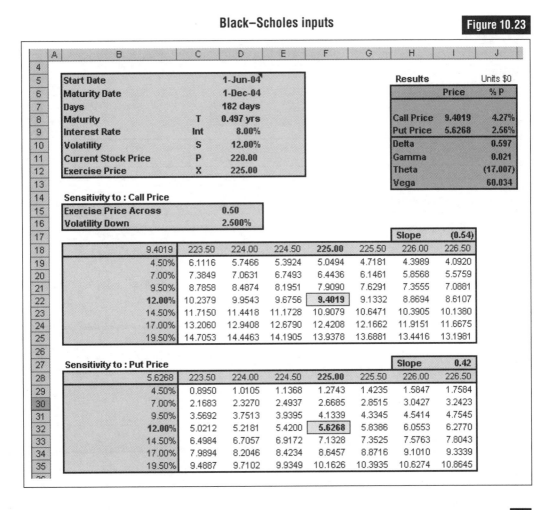

- The probability distribution of relative price changes is lognormal, which means that there is a smaller probability of significant deviations from the mean.

- There are no transaction costs to distort the pricing patterns.

The workings for a call and put options are located at the bottom of the Black–Scholes schedule (see Figure 10.22). To make the workings more understandable, the cells have been named as in cells C115 to C120 and this shows how the formula is built up.

The inputs for the example are as shown in Figure 10.23, saved as a scenario called Example 1. The workings for the pricing are at the base of the schedule and summarized on the right.

The results from the workings are repeated as a management summary at the top and there are two Sensitivity tables, one each for calls and puts (see Figure 10.24). The two axes are the exercise price across and the volatility down, and the answers are highlighted by conditional formatting. An

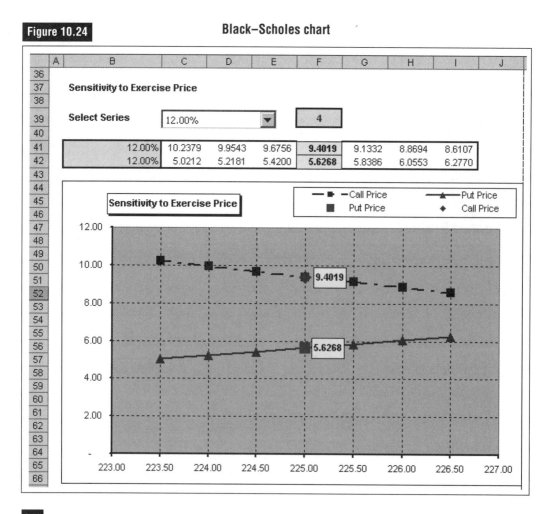

Figure 10.24   **Black–Scholes chart**

update table macro is linked to the button at the top and this code copies down the share price and volatility to the inputs on each table.

The chart at the bottom gives a representation of the two options in the centre of the tables. The selection is linked to a pull-down control and an OFFSET function to find the data. This is an XY scatter chart with lines, and the put and call options are plotted as individual series.

There are two important advantages with using the Black–Scholes formula to value the option and this information can be useful in formulating hedging strategies.

- There is no requirement to forecast the price on expiry.

- You can deduct mathematically the price sensitivities since as a call increases:
  - the exercise price decreases;
  - the time to expiry increases;
  - the stock price increases;
  - the interest rate increases;
  - the volatility increases.

These sensitivities are sometimes known as the 'Greeks' and these formulas are modelled in the workings together with notes on their derivation (see Figures 10.25 and 10.26).

Greeks workings

Figure 10.25

	A	B	C	D	E
146		**(4) Delta**			Change in price when underlying price changes
147		N(d1)		=D126	
149		**(5) Gamma**			Rate at which delta changes
150		Ln(P/X)		=LN(P/X)	Gamma highest when option at the money and
151		Adjusted return		=(Int-S^2/2)*T	reduces away from the price
152		Time adjusted volatility		=S*T^0.5	
153		d2		=(D150+D151)/D152	Writer is always negative gamma
154		d1		=D152+D153	
155		Coefficient		=(2*PI())^-0.5	
156		(d1^2/2)		=D154^2/2	
157		Exp-(d1^2/2)		=EXP(-D156)	
158		N'(d1)		=D155*D157	
159		=N'(d1)/(P*Time_Adj_Volatility)		=D158/(P*D152)	
161		**(6) Theta**			
162		d1 at 0% Interest		=(LN(P/X)+(0.5*S^2)*T	Minimum when share price equals exercise price
163		r*Call-r*P*Delta-0.5*(S^2)*(P^2)*Gamma		=Int*I8-(Int)*P*D147-0.5	="For every 1/100 of a year premium moves by "&"
165		**(7) Vega**			
166		N'd1		=NORMDIST(D124,0,1	Sensitivity of an option to a change in volatility
167		P*Sqrt(T)*N'd1		=P*SQRT(T)*D166	Most senstive when at the money

Figure 10.26   **Greeks results**

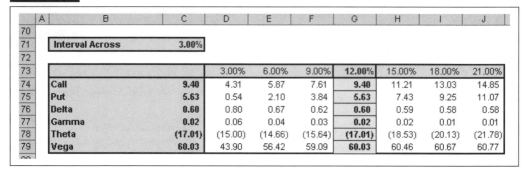

	A	B	C	D	E	F	G	H	I
145									
146		**(4) Delta**				Change in price when underlying price changes			
147		N(d1)		0.5975					
148									
149		**(5) Gamma**				Rate at which delta changes			
150		Ln(P/X)		(0.0225)		Gamma highest when option at the money and			
151		Adjusted return		0.0362		reduces away from the price			
152		Time adjusted volatility		0.0846					
153		d2		0.1622		Writer is always negative gamma			
154		d1		0.2469					
155		Coefficient		0.3989					
156		(d1^2/2)		0.0305					
157		Exp-(d1^2/2)		0.9700					
158		N'(d1)		0.3870					
159		=N'(d1)/(P*Time_Adj_Volatility)		0.0208					
160									
161		**(6) Theta**							
162		d1 at 0% Interest		(0.2233)		Minimum when share price equals exercise price			
163		r*Call-r*P*Delta-0.5*(S^2)*(P^2)*Gamma		(17.0073)		For every 1/100 of a year premium moves by -17.007			
164									
165		**(7) Vega**							
166		N'd1		0.3870		Sensitivity of an option to a change in volatility			
167		P*Sqrt(T)*N'd1		60.0338		Most senstive when at the money			

Figure 10.27   **Sensitivity of Greeks to volatility**

	A	B	C	D	E	F	G	H	I	J
70										
71		**Interval Across**	**3.00%**							
72										
73				3.00%	6.00%	9.00%	**12.00%**	15.00%	18.00%	21.00%
74		Call	**9.40**	4.31	5.87	7.61	**9.40**	11.21	13.03	14.85
75		Put	**5.63**	0.54	2.10	3.84	**5.63**	7.43	9.25	11.07
76		Delta	**0.60**	0.80	0.67	0.62	**0.60**	0.59	0.58	0.58
77		Gamma	**0.02**	0.06	0.04	0.03	**0.02**	0.02	0.01	0.01
78		Theta	**(17.01)**	(15.00)	(14.66)	(15.64)	**(17.01)**	(18.53)	(20.13)	(21.78)
79		Vega	**60.03**	43.90	56.42	59.09	**60.03**	60.46	60.67	60.77

The definitions of the factors are:

- delta measures how much the option's price will change when there is a change in the price of the underlying asset;

- gamma measures the rate at which the delta changes – a high gamma value means that a moderate change in the underlying price results in a larger change in delta;

- theta measures the change in value over time;

- vega is the change in the option value which results from increased volatility and this is always a positive value. Increases in volatility increase the value of options since it is the risk or volatility that contributes to the price.

Delta volatility chart

Figure 10.28

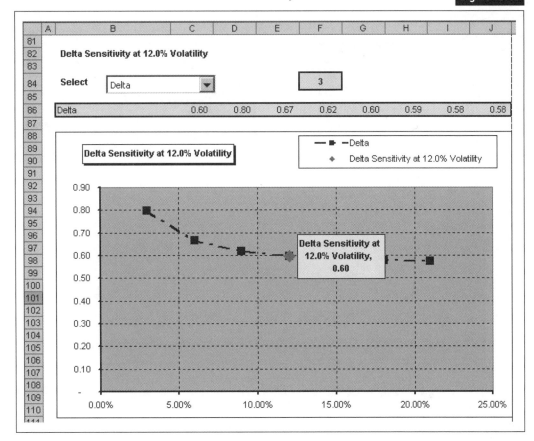

In order to show the sensitivity, there is a table of each of the values plotted against volatility (see Figure 10.27).

The chart includes a combo box for selecting multiple lines from the Sensitivity table (see Figure 10.28).

SIMULATION OPTIONS PRICING

This is an alternative to the Black–Scholes, which although time-consuming will produce a similar result. The Simulation sheet is set to run 1000 scenarios using an input volatility value and standard deviation. The rest of the data is looked up from the Black–Scholes sheet. The volatility is randomized within the standard deviation limits, entered on the Black–Scholes sheet and recalculated. The model recalculates 1000 times and notes the volatility, call and put results for each scenario. These are then pasted as a table on the right (see Figure 10.29). The application then updates the scatter graph and a histogram together with the workings for the call and put. Finally, the

Figure 10.29　　　　　　　Simulation options pricing

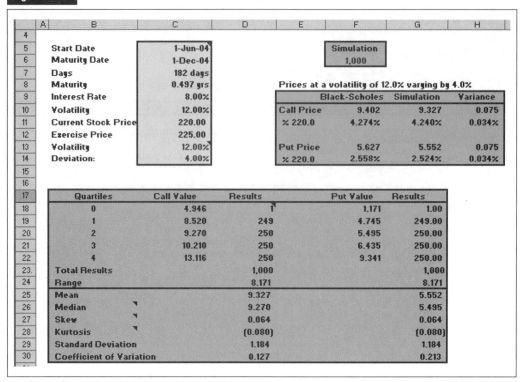

	A	B	C	D	E	F	G	H
4								
5		Start Date	1-Jun-04			Simulation		
6		Maturity Date	1-Dec-04			1,000		
7		Days	182 days					
8		Maturity	0.497 yrs		Prices at a volatility of 12.0% varying by 4.0%			
9		Interest Rate	8.00%			Black-Scholes	Simulation	Variance
10		Volatility	12.00%		Call Price	9.402	9.327	0.075
11		Current Stock Price	220.00		% 220.0	4.274%	4.240%	0.034%
12		Exercise Price	225.00					
13		Volatility	12.00%		Put Price	5.627	5.552	0.075
14		Deviation:	4.00%		% 220.0	2.558%	2.524%	0.034%
15								
16								
17		Quartiles	Call Value	Results		Put Value	Results	
18		0	4.946	1		1.171	1.00	
19		1	8.520	249		4.745	249.00	
20		2	9.270	250		5.495	250.00	
21		3	10.210	250		6.435	250.00	
22		4	13.116	250		9.341	250.00	
23		Total Results		1,000			1,000	
24		Range		8.171			8.171	
25		Mean		9.327			5.552	
26		Median		9.270			5.495	
27		Skew		0.064			0.064	
28		Kurtosis		(0.080)			(0.080)	
29		Standard Deviation		1.184			1.184	
30		Coefficient of Variation		0.127			0.213	

Figure 10.30　　　　　　　Simulation results

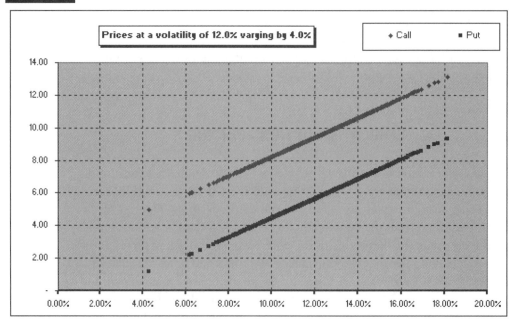

results are compared against the Black–Scholes formula pricing in the summary table and the variances noted.

The results are reasonably close between the two methods. If you were to run the model for 2000 or 3000 attempts, then the margin of error between the two methods would reduce further.

The variance between the two is 0.075. The difference will vary each time you rerun the simulation. The results from the table on the right of Figure 10.29 are plotted on the scatter chart and there are two parallel series for the call and one for the put (see Figure 10.30).

The call results show the number and percentage in each of the frequency bins. The simulation macro updates the mid-point and you can vary the interval manually. The call price is the arithmetic mean in the table on the right of Figure 10.31. The other statistics of median, skew and kurtosis are also calculated using the `MEDIAN`, `SKEW` and `KURTOSIS` functions.

The histogram shown in Figure 10.32 provides an illustration of the range of values with the majority of values clustered around the mean. The quartiles chart demonstrates the high and low values and the borders between each 25 per cent band.

There is also a box plot as an alternative form of chart to display a box for each series consisting of a minimum, first quartile, media, third quartile and maximum (see Figure 10.33). This can be helpful in displaying the shape and characteristics of a distribution.

The method is as follows:

- Set up the data exactly in the order in Figure 10.33.

Frequency results

Figure 10.31

(A) Call: Simulation Frequency Results with an Interval of 0.500

Interval	0.50

Amount	No of Results	Percentage
6.900	17	1.7%
7.400	30	3.0%
7.900	62	6.3%
8.400	114	11.6%
8.900	135	13.7%
9.400	192	19.5%
9.900	129	13.1%
10.400	130	13.2%
10.900	98	9.9%
11.400	52	5.3%
11.900	27	2.7%
	986	100.0%

	Factor	% P
Minimum:	0.0001	2.2480%
Maximum:	0.9989	5.9620%
Mean:	0.4795	4.2396%

Minimum Volatility:	0.0430
Maximum Volatility:	0.1815

Less than zero NPV % of trials:	-

Arithmetic Mean	9.327
Median	9.270
Skew	0.064
Kurtosis	(0.080)
R Squared	1.000
Slope	59.889

Figure 10.32   **Call simulation histogram**

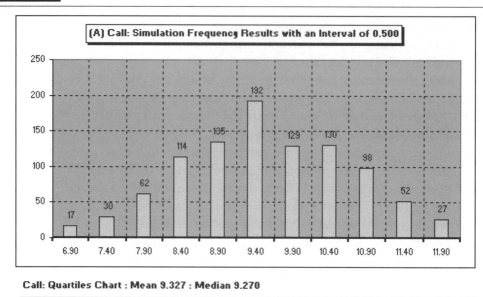

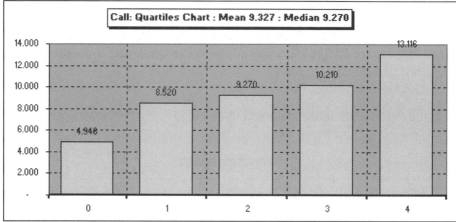

- Highlight the whole table, including figures and series labels.
- Click on the Chart Wizard.
- Select a Line Chart.
- At Step 2 plot by Rows (the default is Columns), then press Finish.
- Select each of the data series in turn.
- Use Format Data Series to remove each of the connecting lines.
- Select any of the data series and go to Format Data Series.
- Select the Options tab and switch on the checkboxes for High-Low lines and Up-Down bars.

Box plots and data

Figure 10.33

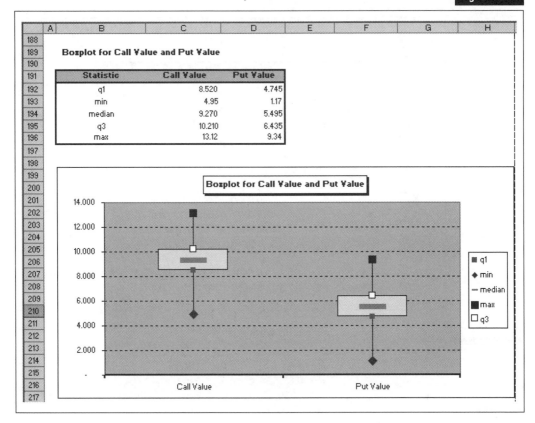

BINOMIAL MODEL

The binomial model is an alternative to the Black–Scholes model for options pricing and is based on the fact that asset prices can move up or down at the end of a time period (see Figures 10.34 and 10.35). This is the view that prices follow binomial paths and there is a probability of moving in one direction or another. The model checks the calculations against the Black–Scholes model.

The formulas for the call and put options are:

```
Call =IF(B98<=$E$12,COMBIN($E$12,$B98) *
$C$19^$B98 * $C$20^($E$12-$B98) * MAX($E$7 *
$C$15^$B98 * $C$16^($E$12-$B98)-$E$10,0),0)

Call = Previous Result + Combin(N, Period) * Q up
^ Period * Q down ^ (N - Period) * Max(Strike *
Up ^ Period * Down ^(N - Period) - Exercise, 0)
```

Figure 10.34

Binomial inputs

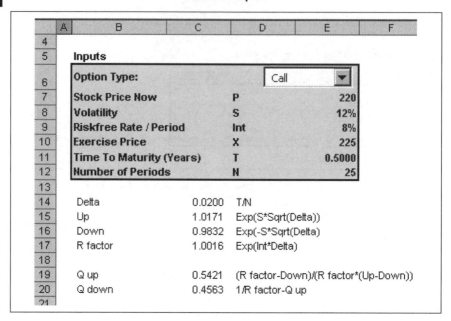

	A	B	C	D	E	F
4						
5		**Inputs**				
6		**Option Type:**			Call ▼	
7		**Stock Price Now**		P	220	
8		**Volatility**		S	12%	
9		**Riskfree Rate / Period**		Int	8%	
10		**Exercise Price**		X	225	
11		**Time To Maturity (Years)**		T	0.5000	
12		**Number of Periods**		N	25	
13						
14		Delta	0.0200	T/N		
15		Up	1.0171	Exp(S*Sqrt(Delta))		
16		Down	0.9832	Exp(-S*Sqrt(Delta)		
17		R factor	1.0016	Exp(Int*Delta)		
18						
19		Q up	0.5421	(R factor-Down)/(R factor*(Up-Down))		
20		Q down	0.4563	1/R factor-Q up		
21						

Figure 10.35

Factor workings

Delta	=E11/E12	T/N
Up	=EXP(E8*SQRT(C14))	Exp(S*Sqrt(Delta))
Down	=EXP(-E8*SQRT(C14))	Exp(-S*Sqrt(Delta))
R factor	=EXP(E9*C14)	Exp(Int*Delta)
Q up	=(C17-C16)/(C17*(C15-C16)	(R factor-Down)/(R factor*(Up-Down))
Q down	=1/C17-C19	1/R factor-Q up

```
Put =IF(B98<=$E$12,COMBIN($E$12,$B98) *
$C$19^$B98 * $C$20^($E$12-$B98) * MAX($E$10-
$C$15^$B98 * $C$16^($E$12-$B98) * $E$7,0),0)

Put = Previous Result + Combin(N, Period) * Q up
^Period * Q down ^ (N - Period) * Max(Exercise -
Up ^ Period * Down ^(N - Period) * Strike, 0)
```

The function COMBIN is used to return the number of combinations for a given number of items. Here the function determines the total possible number of groups from the period number and the total number of periods. The COMBIN formulas are as follows:

$$\binom{n}{k} = \frac{P_{k,n}}{k!} = \frac{n!}{k!(n-k)!}$$

where:

$$P_{k,n} = \frac{n!}{(n-k)!}$$

The schedule sets out the cumulative results for the number of steps in the binomial lattice. The maximum number of steps is 25 and using IF statements, the model will accept a lesser number (see Figure 10.36).

The Black–Scholes results are calculated on the schedule shown in Figure 10.37. The formulas used are the same as before.

Figure 10.38 shows how the binomial option moves closer to the Black–Scholes result. With fewer steps the binomial model will converge more quickly on the Black–Scholes result.

Figure 10.39 plots the differences between the options and the Black–Scholes model and in this example the difference reduces to 0.01 by the last period.

Call and put schedule

Figure 10.36

			Black Scholes	Variance			Black Scholes	Variance
	Period	**Call**				**Put**		
98	1	0	9.4217	(9.4217)		0.0000	5.6260	(5.6260)
99	2	0	9.4217	(9.4217)		0.0001	5.6260	(5.6259)
100	3	0	9.4217	(9.4217)		0.0009	5.6260	(5.6251)
101	4	0	9.4217	(9.4217)		0.0055	5.6260	(5.6205)
102	5	0	9.4217	(9.4217)		0.0262	5.6260	(5.5998)
103	6	0	9.4217	(9.4217)		0.0995	5.6260	(5.5264)
104	7	0	9.4217	(9.4217)		0.3062	5.6260	(5.3197)
105	8	0	9.4217	(9.4217)		0.7767	5.6260	(4.8492)
106	9	0	9.4217	(9.4217)		1.6421	5.6260	(3.9839)
107	10	0	9.4217	(9.4217)		2.9125	5.6260	(2.7134)
108	11	0	9.4217	(9.4217)		4.3434	5.6260	(1.2826)
109	12	0	9.4217	(9.4217)		5.4272	5.6260	(0.1988)
110	13	0	9.4217	(9.4217)		5.6099	5.6260	(0.0161)
111	14	0.9777	9.4217	(8.4439)		5.6099	5.6260	(0.0161)
112	15	2.8781	9.4217	(6.5435)		5.6099	5.6260	(0.0161)
113	16	5.0945	9.4217	(4.3271)		5.6099	5.6260	(0.0161)
114	17	7.0123	9.4217	(2.4093)		5.6099	5.6260	(0.0161)
115	18	8.3110	9.4217	(1.1106)		5.6099	5.6260	(0.0161)
116	19	9.0089	9.4217	(0.4127)		5.6099	5.6260	(0.0161)
117	20	9.3054	9.4217	(0.1162)		5.6099	5.6260	(0.0161)
118	21	9.4032	9.4217	(0.0184)		5.6099	5.6260	(0.0161)
119	22	9.4275	9.4217	0.0058		5.6099	5.6260	(0.0161)
120	23	9.4317	9.4217	0.0101		5.6099	5.6260	(0.0161)
121	24	9.4322	9.4217	0.0106		5.6099	5.6260	(0.0161)
122	25	9.4322	9.4217	0.0106		5.6099	5.6260	(0.0161)

Figure 10.37

Black–Scholes calculations

	A	B	C	D	E	F	
22							
23		**Black Scholes Calculations**					
24		Call					
25		d1	0.2490	(LN(S/X)+(r+0.5*SV^2)*T)/(sigma*SQRT(T))			
26		d2	0.1641	d_1-SV*SQRT(T)			
27		N(d1)	0.5983	Formula NormSDist(d1)			
28		N(d2)	0.5652	Formula NormSDist(d2)			
29		Call	9.4217	P*N(d1)-X*exp(-r*T)*N(d2)			
30							
31		Put					
32		-d1	(0.2490)				
33		-d2	(0.1641)				
34		N(-d1)	0.4017	Formula NormSDist(-d1)			
35		N(-d2)	0.4348	Formula NormSDist(-d2)			
36		Put	5.6260	P*N(-d1)-X*exp(-r*T)*N(-d2)			

Figure 10.38   Comparison of binomial and Black–Scholes call option

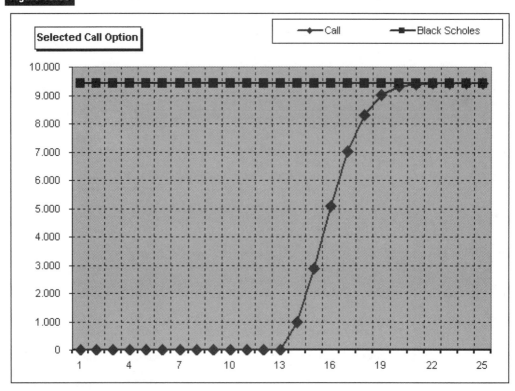

Variance chart

Figure 10.39

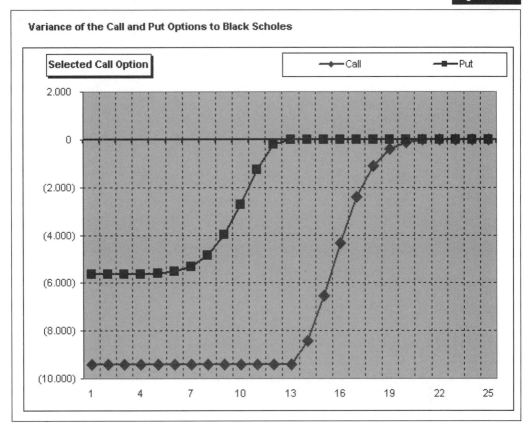

Variance of the Call and Put Options to Black Scholes

SUMMARY

Options products seek to manage the risk of price change in underlying assets and this chapter has presented some examples of options pay-offs, trading strategies and pricing using the Black–Scholes and binomial models. The trading strategies and pricing are based on the variables of the underlying and expiry prices, a risk-free rate, the length time and the volatility in the price of the underlying asset.

Real options

File: FT4_11.xls

INTRODUCTION

This chapter reviews further methods of adding risk to project appraisal and by extension to company valuation. The traditional view of investment analysis is that payback and accounting return are deficient when compared to time value of money methods such as net present value (NPV). You produce a set of pre- and post-tax free cash flows for a project and then discount them to a present value at a rate which reflects the cost of capital and any implied project risk. If a project yields a positive NPV then you may decide to proceed; otherwise the project fails on value grounds. A positive result adds value to the company whereas a negative result destroys value. This approach may assist with cash-saving projects but may be inflexible when applied to technology or other industries where operational flexibility is required. The traditional NPV method is thought to be deficient since the cash flows appear fixed from inception without any possibility of variance. In reality, management has the ability to terminate a failing project by incurring extra costs or salvaging work to date. Alternatively, the market prospects may rise allowing the choice of continuation or expansion to capitalize on new market opportunities. As a third alternative, a delay could be useful to gather more information or wait for competitive response.

When a company undertakes a capital project, it possesses a series of options to grow or contract. The flexibility has a value and the model in this chapter uses options theory to calculate a variance and a value for the option. Uncertainty and volatility are generally accepted to have increased in the past decade and this methodology enhances the NPV rule by incorporating the risk and uncertainty. A company with an opportunity to invest holds a financial call option since it has the right, but not the obligation, to make the investment in return for an uncertain stream of cash flows. The 'now or never' NPV rule is therefore replaced by a series of options which may or may not be exercised. By committing to an investment a company effectively destroys the option and dispenses with the possibility of waiting. The lost option value represents an opportunity cost which should be included as part of the investment. Instead of an NPV greater than or equal to zero, the present value of the expected cash flows should exceed the initial cost of the investment by an amount equal to the value of retaining the open option. See Figure 11.1.

The opportunity cost is highly sensitive to change in economic conditions and options theory uses a Black–Scholes model for pricing in volatility or uncertainty. Risk is present in the receipt of future cash flows and changes could have an impact on the decision to invest. A delay could allow more information or market knowledge to become available. Only when the option has been exercised does it become irreversible. If the option value increases, so does the benefit of investing, while a decline means that the project can be abandoned with the cost capped at the value of the preliminary or sunk work. This chapter introduces a project model and then calcu-

Figure 11.1

Call option pay-off diagram

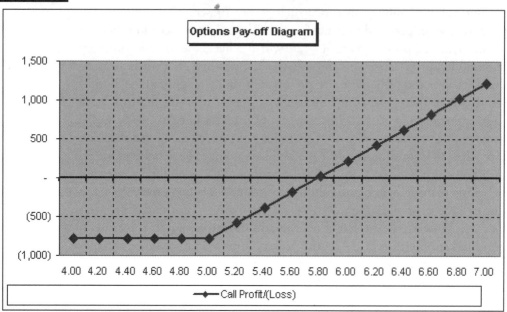

Figure 11.2

Project inputs

Scenario Name:	Case 1
Prepared by:	Product Management
Product Code:	MJD-123
Manager:	Matthew Miles
Start Date:	01-Jan-03
Initial Investment:	2,000,000.00
Initial Sales Price per Unit:	50.00
Annual Price Change:	(10.00%)
Initial Cost per Unit:	40.00
Annual Cost Improvement:	20%
Project Life:	10.00 yrs
Residual Value:	0.00
Working Capital as % of Sales:	10.0000%
Selling and Administration Costs	300,000.00
Cost of Funds:	12.0000%

lates the value of options to undertake alternative actions comprising delay, abandonment and expansion.

PROJECT

The basic model uses a non-tax project based on the inputs shown in Figure 11.2. The project lasts ten years and there are sales and costs per unit of output with annual price and cost variances. The volume is set at 50,000 per annum for ten years in the Case 1 scenario.

Financial statements

Figure 11.3

	A	B	C	D	E	F	G	H
22								
23						Year 0	1	2	3
24						Jan-03	Dec-03	Dec-04	Dec-05
25									
26		Sales Volume				50,000	50,000	50,000
27		Price per Unit				50.00	45.00	40.50
28									
29		Sales Revenue				2,500,000	2,250,000	2,025,000
30									
31		Annual Cost per Unit				40.00	32.00	25.60
32		Manufacturing Cost				(2,000,000)	(1,600,000)	(1,280,000)
33									
34									
35		**Profit and Loss Account**						
36		Sales Revenue				2,500,000	2,250,000	2,025,000
37		Cost of Sales				(2,000,000)	(1,600,000)	(1,280,000)
38		Contribution				500,000	650,000	745,000
39		Selling and Administration Costs				(300,000)	(300,000)	(300,000)
40		Recovery of Development Costs				(200,000)	(200,000)	(200,000)
41		**Profit/(Loss)**				-	150,000	245,000
42									
43									
44		**Balance Sheet**						
45		Fixed Asset			2,000,000	2,000,000	2,000,000	2,000,000
46		Depreciation			-	(200,000)	(400,000)	(600,000)
47		Net Fixed Assets			2,000,000	1,800,000	1,600,000	1,400,000
48									
49		Cash			(2,000,000)	(2,050,000)	(1,675,000)	(1,207,500)
50									
51		**Total Assets**			-	(250,000)	(75,000)	192,500
52									
53		Working Capital - (Liability)/Asset				(250,000)	(225,000)	(202,500)
54									
55		Shareholders Funds			-	-	150,000	395,000
56									
57		**Total Liabilities**			-	(250,000)	(75,000)	192,500

The schedule builds up a manufacturing account, income statement, balance and cash flow, and calculates an NPV at the input cost of capital of 12 per cent. The cash flow is dependent on the volume and sale price per unit against the declining cost price. The model displays the present value and addresses other management tests in a summary box at the top of the schedule (see Figure 11.3). Following the design method, you can see changes in the answers immediately you amend the inputs.

The management tests show that this project passes all the tests (see Figure 11.4). The workings at the side use MATCH and IF statements to work out if the periodic cash flows or profits are below the input minimums. The first statement checks if the value is below the minimum; the second row puts in a '1' if it is below the required level; and the third uses a MATCH function to look for '1' along the line so it can report the period number in which the rule failed.

```
=IF(G41<$I$11,G41,0)
=IF(S41=0,0,IF(S41<$I$11,1,0))
=IF(SUM(R42:AA42)=0,0,MATCH(1,R42:AA42,0))
```

There are two further scenarios in the model and these provide changed inputs and results. One is more pessimistic and the other more optimistic. A further sheet called Scenarios contains the scenarios report with probabilities as an expected net present value (ENPV) – see Figure 11.5. The user assigns a probability to each of the scenarios and then the model multiples out the answer. Thus, 50,831.72 is 254,158 * 0.20.

The data table suppresses impossible values by ensuring that all values add up to one. Case 3 is not used and the sensitivity uses Case 1 as the x-axis and Case 2 as the y-axis. The formula at the top-left of the data table is:

```
=IF(AND(D7>=0,D6>=0,D6+D7+D8=1),E10,0)
```

The formulas ensure that all the inputs add up to one and that the X and Y inputs are positive or equal to zero. The answer is in the middle of the table using 0.20 of Case 1, 0.40 of Case 2 and 0.40 of Case 3. The three scenarios

Figure 11.4

Management summary

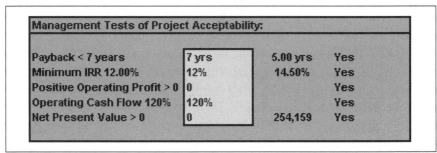

Expected net present value

Figure 11.5

	Scenario	NPV	Probability	Result	
	Case 1	254,158.59	0.20	50,831.72	
	Case 2	(976,206.27)	0.40	(390,482.51)	
	Case 3	2,570,613.63	0.40	1,028,245.45	
	Expected Net Present Value (ENPV)		1.00	688,594.66	

Sensitivity Table to Case 1 Across and Case 2 Down

Interval Across	0.05
Interval Down	0.05

688,594.66	0.05	0.10	0.15	0.20
0.25	-	-	-	-
0.30	-	-	-	-
0.35	-	-	-	-
0.40	-	-	-	688,594.7
0.45	-	-	627,076.4	-
0.50	-	565,558.2	-	-
0.55	504,039.9	-	-	-

are the best estimates of the future and further risk techniques such as data tables, standard deviation and simulation could be applied. However, the emphasis here is on extending the model to find a value for possibilities other than committing the 2,000,000 in its entirety on inception.

OPTION TO DELAY

The first section introduced flexibility into the investment process by introducing the possibility of delay, expansion or abandonment. The sheet called 'Delay' uses a Black–Scholes model with inputs from the Project sheet. The extra inputs are the risk-free rate and the volatility. The latter could be gained from a Monte Carlo simulation or previous projects, but for simplicity this is an input to this model (see Figure 11.6).

The number of years, present value (PV) of future cash flows and the initial investment are looked up from Case 1 on the Project sheet. The inputs are:

■ years – life of the project;

■ risk-free rate – rate such as a ten-year government bond currently at around 5 per cent;

Figure 11.6

Delay inputs

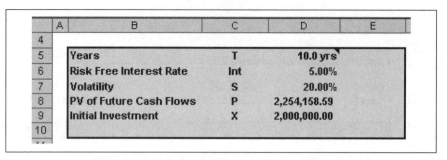

	A	B	C	D	E
4					
5		Years	T	10.0 yrs	
6		Risk Free Interest Rate	Int	5.00%	
7		Volatility	S	20.00%	
8		PV of Future Cash Flows	P	2,254,158.59	
9		Initial Investment	X	2,000,000.00	
10					

Figure 11.7

Option calculation

	A	B	C	D	E	F	G	H
56								
57		**Definitions and Calculations**						
58		Variance		0.0400				
59		Annualised yield		10.00%				
60		d_1		(0.2852)	(LN(S/X)+(Int-Yield+Variance/2)*T)/(sigma*SQRT(T))			
61		$N(d_1)$		0.3877	Formula NormSDist(d_1)			
62		d_2		(0.9176)	d_1-(sigma*SQRT(T))			
63		$N(d_2)$		0.1794	Formula NormSDist(d_2)			
64								
65		Call price		103,918.61	(EXP((0-Yield)*T))*P*N(d1)-X*(EXP((0-Int)*T))*N(d2)			

Figure 11.8

NORMSDIST function

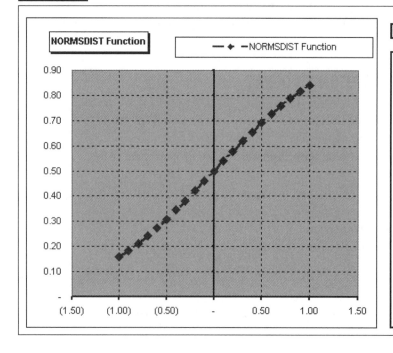

NORMSDIST Function	
Interval	**0.10**
(1.00)	0.16
(0.90)	0.18
(0.80)	0.21
(0.70)	0.24
(0.60)	0.27
(0.50)	0.31
(0.40)	0.34
(0.30)	0.38
(0.20)	0.42
(0.10)	0.46
-	0.50
0.10	0.54
0.20	0.58
0.30	0.62
0.40	0.66
0.50	0.69
0.60	0.73
0.70	0.76
0.80	0.79
0.90	0.82
1.00	0.84

- volatility – forecast future variance in cash flows;
- present value of future cash flows before subtracting initial investment;
- initial investment as the cost of the project on inception.

This project achieves a positive NPV but there may still be advantages in delaying the investment. The rule in the first section was that the NPV should be greater than the option value of the delay. A delay could allow more market research, better use of technology or gaining more information on competitive response.

The workings at the bottom of the schedule (see Figure 11.7) calculate the terms d1 and d2 and use the function NORMSDIST to return the standard normal cumulative distribution function. This distribution has a mean of 0 (zero) and a standard deviation of one, as shown in Figure 11.8 generated by the function.

The value of the option is 103,918 and this can be compared against the NPV – the variance is positive. There is also a data table showing the sensitivity to the present value of cash flows and the volatility displaying the change in the option price (see Figure 11.9). A dynamic chart also provides the possibility of reviewing individual lines in the table.

The table uses two types of conditional formatting to form an XY cross at the answer together with particular formatting for the answer (see Figure 11.10). $D$8 is the input for the present value of the cash flows and $D$7 is the input for volatility used by the data table.

It is also interesting to know how the value of the option changes over time to understand at what point in the ten-year cycle the option ceases to have value. The present value calculation on the Project sheet uses a lookup for period zero against a table of NPVs for year zero, one, two, etc. This means that a data table can be constructed using the offset value as the input. Line 124 contains the delay option which rises in value and then declines towards the expiry date (see Figure 11.11). Calculating a price in this

Sensitivity to cash flows and volatility

Figure 11.9

Sensitivity: Call Option							
PV of Future Cash Flows Across 50,000.00							Units $0
Volatility Down	5.000%						
						Slope	0.14
103,918.6063	2,104,158.6	2,154,158.6	2,204,158.6	2,254,158.6	2,304,158.6	2,354,158.6	2,404,158.6
5.00%	101.2	167.8	270.2	423.0	644.8	959.1	1,393.8
10.00%	10,641.3	12,670.2	14,964.9	17,542.0	20,417.3	23,605.5	27,120.0
15.00%	41,579.9	46,117.4	50,943.5	56,060.6	61,470.2	67,173.3	73,170.0
20.00%	83,646.6	90,152.2	96,910.4	103,918.6	111,173.9	118,673.2	126,413.1
25.00%	130,532.6	138,574.7	146,830.0	155,294.6	163,964.3	172,835.0	181,902.9
30.00%	179,130.8	188,425.0	197,898.6	207,547.5	217,367.5	227,354.5	237,504.7
35.00%	227,774.6	238,127.3	248,631.8	259,284.1	270,080.2	281,016.4	292,089.2

Figure 11.10   **Conditional formatting**

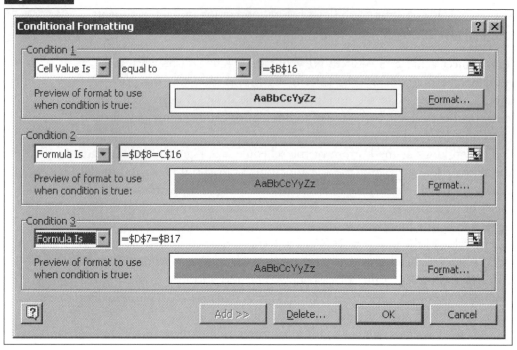

Figure 11.11   **Change in option prices**

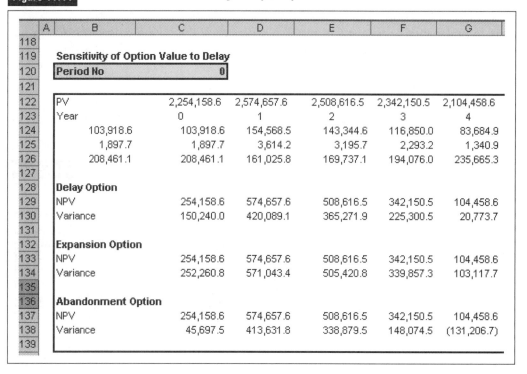

manner assumes that the behaviour of the cash flows does not change over time. This may be ultimately unrealistic but it at least creates a benchmark.

OPTION TO ABANDON

Investment means that an option has been exercised but there are still possibilities to abandon or expand. If the value of the project is greater than abandonment then you continue; otherwise you consider exercising the option. This takes the form of a put option (see Figure 11.12).

The Abandon sheet calculated the value of this option in the first year. The inputs here change since the liquidation or salvage value is needed as opposed to an initial investment (see Figure 11.13).

The number of years and the present value are brought forward from the Project sheet. The extra inputs are the number of years remaining and the percentage salvage value of the original investment. The calculation therefore provides a value immediately after inception and assumes a constant salvage value of 50 per cent. See Figures 11.14 and 11.15.

There are workings to calculate the option value against falling salvage values in future years. The PV in cell D8 depends on the number of years remaining and uses this offset to look along the row of present values on the Project sheet. This is illustrated in Figure 11.11.

Put option

Figure 11.12

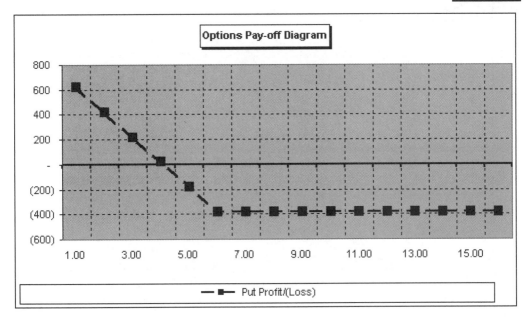

Figure 11.13

Abandon sheet inputs

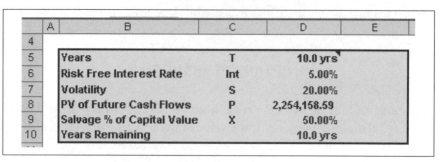

	A	B	C	D	E
4					
5		Years	T	10.0 yrs	
6		Risk Free Interest Rate	Int	5.00%	
7		Volatility	S	20.00%	
8		PV of Future Cash Flows	P	2,254,158.59	
9		Salvage % of Capital Value	X	50.00%	
10		Years Remaining		10.0 yrs	

Figure 11.14

Abandonment Sensitivity

Sensitivity: Put Option

| PV of Future Cash Flows Across | 100,000 | | | | | Units $0 |
| Volatility Down | 5.00% | | | | | |

						Slope	(0.0777)
87,239.2603	1,954,158.6	2,054,158.6	2,154,158.6	**2,254,158.6**	2,354,158.6	2,454,158.6	2,554,158.6
5.00%	7,511.5	3,998.7	2,043.4	1,006.8	480.3	222.7	100.7
10.00%	38,688.0	30,617.9	24,119.9	18,926.5	14,802.2	11,544.5	8,983.3
15.00%	75,781.6	66,274.9	57,947.4	50,663.2	44,298.3	38,741.0	33,891.6
20.00%	113,975.4	104,185.2	95,302.0	**87,239.3**	79,918.2	73,267.2	67,221.7
25.00%	151,950.8	142,369.8	133,509.7	125,308.4	117,710.0	110,663.5	104,122.5
30.00%	189,114.7	179,981.3	171,435.3	163,429.2	155,920.2	148,869.5	142,241.8
35.00%	225,109.2	216,544.6	208,467.0	200,838.4	193,624.9	186,795.6	180,322.8

Figure 11.15

Sensitivity chart

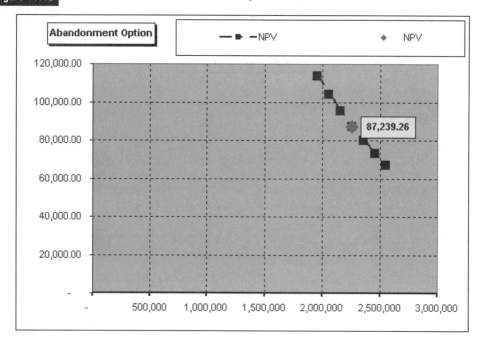

```
=OFFSET(Project!C122,0,10-Abandon!D10)
```

The workings table at the bottom of the schedule uses a salvage value from input percentages and the number of years remaining to generate a grid of values (see Figure 11.16). The values in bold are possible values and other values should be ignored. The value 87,239 represents ten years outstanding and the initial salvage value.

The net result is a table of present values remaining in each year and the put option associated with it (see Figure 11.17). The salvage values can be adjusted and this will work through the tables and update the option values. The value declines as the present value and salvage values decrease in the latter stages of the project.

Workings

Figure 11.16

	A	B	C	D	E	F	G	H
105								
106		Workings - Flexible Period						
107				87,239	10	9	8	7
108			10.00	50.0%	1,000,000	**87,239**	54,766	46,547	43,161
109			9.00	45.0%	900,000	63,130	**37,526**	30,874	27,797
110			8.00	40.0%	800,000	43,019	23,957	**18,935**	16,420
111			7.00	35.0%	700,000	27,048	13,915	10,456	**8,638**
112			6.00	30.0%	600,000	15,209	7,090	4,991	3,866
113			5.00	25.0%	500,000	7,266	2,985	1,927	1,367
114			4.00	20.0%	400,000	2,693	935	535	334
115			3.00	15.0%	300,000	645	176	84	43
116			2.00	10.0%	200,000	64	12	4	2
117			1.00	5.0%	100,000	1	0	0	0
118			-	-	-	-	-	-	-

Abandonment summary

Figure 11.17

	A	B	C	D	E	F	G
68							
69		Change in Value of Abandonment Option based on Period Number					
70							
71		Year	NPV	Salvage	Value	Option	Variance
72		0	254,158.6	**50.00%**	1,000,000.0	87,239.3	166,919.3
73		1	574,657.6	**45.00%**	900,000.0	37,526.0	537,131.6
74		2	508,616.5	**40.00%**	800,000.0	18,934.7	489,681.8
75		3	342,150.5	**35.00%**	700,000.0	8,637.8	333,512.8
76		4	104,458.6	**30.00%**	600,000.0	3,332.8	101,125.7
77		5	(182,281.4)	**25.00%**	500,000.0	970.5	(183,251.9)
78		6	(501,422.7)	**20.00%**	400,000.0	170.4	(501,593.1)
79		7	(840,670.1)	**15.00%**	300,000.0	10.6	(840,680.7)
80		8	(1,191,148.4)	**10.00%**	200,000.0	0.0	(1,191,148.5)
81		9	(1,546,667.3)	**5.00%**	100,000.0	0.0	(1,546,667.3)
82							

OPTION TO EXPAND

Expansion is the last of the possibilities since management may have the flexibility to increase the investment and thereby improve the overall NPV (see Figure 11.18). This is dependent on an initial investment in the project and therefore there is a cut-off at the expiry of the project life. Also it depends on the competitive position and the ability to retain control over future cash flows. The pay-off diagram is similar to the option to delay with characteristics of a call option.

The inputs are:

- years – this is looked up from the Project sheet;
- interest rate – the risk-free rate;
- volatility – volatility of future cash flows which could be different to the other options;
- expansion potential – this is expressed as a percentage of the present value of cash flows;
- investment required – this is a percentage of the initial investment, here 2,000,000;
- cost of delay – this is the cost of waiting until the new investment starts to provide positive benefits.

The sensitivity table (see Figure 11.19) shows the variance of the percentage expansion against the volatility using the inputs of cells D8 (expansion) and D7 (volatility). As the expansion percentage rises, with the investment remaining static, the value of the option increases. With greater volatility, the value also rises.

Figure 11.20 shows the single series of 20 per cent volatility rising from 5 to 35 per cent expansion in the initial present value.

The workings at the base of the schedule repeat the methodology of the abandonment schedule (see Figure 11.21). The x-axis of the table represents the number of years outstanding and the y-axis the expansion amounts

Expansion option

	A	B	C	D	E
4					
5		Years	T	10.0 yrs	
6		Interest Rate	Int	5.00%	
7		Volatility	S	20.00%	
8		Expansion Potential	P	20.00%	
9		Investment Required	X	10.00%	
10		Cost of Delay %		5.00%	

Expansion sensitivity

Figure 11.19

Sensitivity: Call Option

Expansion Potential Across	5.00%						Units $0
Volatility Down	**5.00%**						
						Slope	1,204,048.6
157,366.6116	5.00%	10.00%	15.00%	20.00%	25.00%	30.00%	35.00%
5.00%	0.5	18,051.3	83,779.2	152,137.1	220,497.9	288,858.8	357,219.6
10.00%	393.4	25,051.1	84,770.7	152,228.8	220,506.8	288,859.7	357,219.7
15.00%	2,333.8	32,644.5	88,747.0	153,633.9	220,981.0	289,026.0	357,281.4
20.00%	5,539.8	40,276.6	94,807.9	**157,366.6**	223,133.9	290,259.7	357,998.5
25.00%	9,421.7	47,791.8	101,897.3	162,951.9	227,290.2	293,303.0	360,226.6
30.00%	13,617.9	55,110.7	109,427.5	169,683.4	233,015.1	298,082.2	364,194.0
35.00%	17,920.7	62,179.6	117,071.4	177,032.6	239,769.3	304,170.4	369,636.7

Sensitivity chart

Figure 11.20

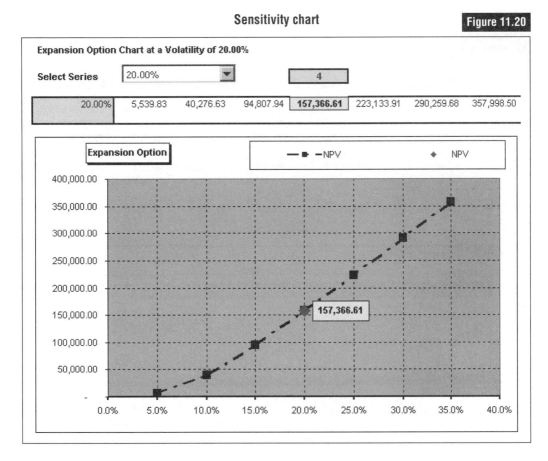

Expansion Option Chart at a Volatility of 20.00%

Select Series   20.00% ▼   4

| 20.00% | 5,539.83 | 40,276.63 | 94,807.94 | **157,366.61** | 223,133.91 | 290,259.68 | 357,998.50 |

assigned to each of the years. Again the possible combinations are represented in bold type.

Figure 11.22 shows the present values for expansion against the option value with a chart of the option. The option loses value during the life of the project as the benefits from expansion decline.

Figure 11.21

Expansion table

	A	B	C	D	E	F	G	H
105								
106		**Workings - Flexible Period**						
107				157,367	10	9	8	7
108		10	20.0%	450,832	**157,367**	164,445	171,877	179,704
109		9	18.0%	405,749	131,787	**137,384**	143,229	149,350
110		8	16.0%	360,665	106,900	111,044	**115,321**	119,747
111		7	14.0%	315,582	83,015	85,767	88,538	**91,321**
112		6	12.0%	270,499	60,585	62,067	63,461	64,739
113		5	10.0%	225,416	40,277	40,701	40,960	41,009
114		4	8.0%	180,333	23,030	22,736	22,258	21,553
115		3	6.0%	135,250	10,049	9,505	8,838	8,031
116		2	4.0%	90,166	2,468	2,136	1,782	1,413
117		1	2.0%	45,083	109	74	46	25
118		-	-	-	-	-	-	-

Figure 11.22

Expansion summary

Year	NPV	Expansion	Value	Option	Variance
0	254,158.6	**20.00%**	450,831.7	157,366.6	293,465.1
1	574,657.6	**18.00%**	405,748.5	137,383.8	268,364.8
2	508,616.5	**16.00%**	360,665.4	115,321.4	245,343.9
3	342,150.5	**14.00%**	315,582.2	91,321.3	224,260.9
4	104,458.6	**12.00%**	270,499.0	65,866.9	204,632.2
5	(182,281.4)	**10.00%**	225,415.9	40,231.5	185,184.4
6	(501,422.7)	**8.00%**	180,332.7	17,439.6	162,893.1
7	(840,670.1)	**6.00%**	135,249.5	3,143.3	132,106.2
8	(1,191,148.4)	**4.00%**	90,166.3	24.5	90,141.8
9	(1,546,667.3)	**2.00%**	45,083.2	0.0	45,083.2

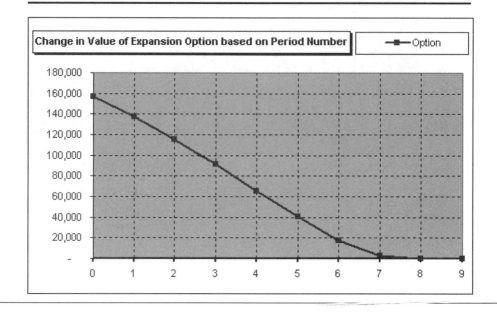

Change in Value of Expansion Option based on Period Number ■— Option

SUMMARY

This chapter uses a ten-year project model with three initial scenarios based on the expected Case 1 and two alternative pessimistic and optimistic views. Given that management has operational flexibility, the chapter develops an options model for reviewing other choices such as expansion, delay or abandonment. The basic methodology follows the Black–Scholes model. Delay and expansion possess characteristics similar to call options while abandonment is similar to a put option. The chapter also provides some sensitivity tables to show how the values flex with changing present value and volatility. Gaining further information on the value of different options can provide more insight and alleviate some of the deficiencies of the rigid NPV rule. As part of a decision process, the method provides more information for management.

Equities

File: FT4_12.xls

INTRODUCTION

Portfolios of stocks possess varying levels of risk and return and this chapter models the possible future returns over the next 12 months based on historic data. Different stocks possess different characteristics of risk and return and portfolio risk can easily be modelled. Excel is used to generate 1000 future scenarios and these are incorporated into the monthly returns over the next year.

Modern portfolio theory is based on the 1952 work of Harry Markowitz, whose doctoral thesis suggested a new method of assessing stock performance. He looked at the performance of a portfolio of assets based on the combination of its components' risk and return rather than fundamental analysis of stocks. Whilst it was assumed that diversification was better than investing in single stocks, previously there was no underlying theory to back this up. Portfolio theory provides the mathematical basis and shows how you can combine risky assets into portfolios, which then contain less overall risk due to the effect of diversification.

With any stock, you can calculate the expected return at the end of a time period. Since the assets are risky, you cannot be sure about the return on these assets. By using the past to project into the future, investors can determine the likelihood of a certain return. The expected return on a risky asset is based on the probabilities attached to all possible rates of return for the asset. With a 50–50 chance of a favourable outcome, the expected return on a portfolio with one asset returning 30 per cent and the other 10 per cent is its weighted average of 20 per cent. Figure 12.1 shows a normal distribution with the percentage results contained by one, two and three standard deviations.

In many problems involving probabilities, the probabilities of all possible outcomes are assumed to have a bell-shaped normal distribution as in Figure 12.1. The mean is the top of the distribution and the area under the normal curve is the probability of realizing a return between the extreme points on the curve. This probability is equal to one.

The historical annual volatility or the degree of variation from the expected return is measured by the standard deviation. Assuming a normal distribution, we can say with a 68.26 per cent certainty that the actual one-year return will be somewhere between a low of the expected return less one standard deviation and a high of the expected return plus one standard deviation. You can calculate similar results for two and three standard deviations. The actual return of a less volatile stock, say, one with a standard deviation of 10 per cent will move within a narrower range of possible returns than a stock with a standard deviation of 15 per cent.

Figure 12.1   **Normal distribution of outcomes**

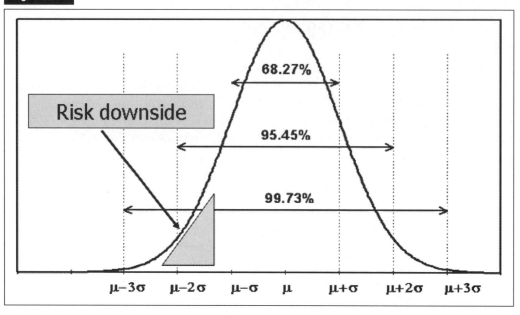

Diversification involves a trade off between risk and return. If you were certain of a stock's future value, then you would buy only that asset yielding the maximum return under those conditions, and no trade off would be necessary. The theory makes some assumptions about the way investors behave regarding risk. Although some investors can take more risk than others, investors are assumed to be risk averse rather than risk seeking. Risk averse means that where assets promise the same return, you would choose the assets with the least downside risk. In order for you to accept higher risk, you would want to be compensated with the potential for earning a higher return and vice versa. Table 12.1 and Figure 12.2 show the US experience from 1926 to 1994 where stocks, bonds and bills show different rates of risk defined by standard deviation and average return.

The general assumptions for the portfolio model are:

■ each possible investment has a probability distribution of expected returns over time;

Table 12.1   **US experience (1926–94)**

Measure	Small companies	Large companies	Government bonds	Treasury bills
Return	12%	10%	5%	4%
Standard deviation	35%	20%	9%	3%

US stock returns

Figure 12.2

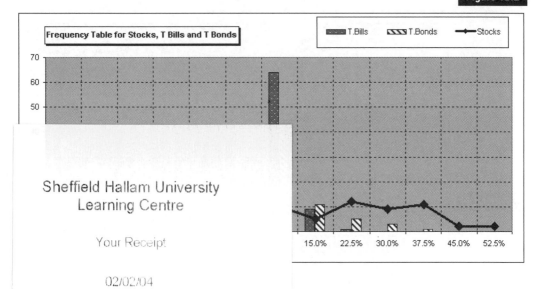

returns for increased risk;

ted returns (standard devi-

king investment decisions;

given risk level.

here would be no point in
same direction and would
this is unlikely to be the case
different weights, the theory
th different characteristics of
if there is no other portfolio
same or lower risk. It there-
e a portfolio ceases to be effi-
d the 'best' portfolio and the
neration and Solver within
ck portfolio.

or five stocks over a five-year
ges and show the gain or loss
lata points in all.
rsification would not yield

Figure 12.3

Stock returns

Period	Date	Stock 1	Stock 2	Stock 3	Stock 4	Stock 5
1	30-Jun-98	0.02889	0.00732	(0.03863)	(0.03993)	0.05202
2	30-Jul-98	(0.05080)	0.11197	(0.00401)	(0.06690)	0.03297
3	30-Aug-98	0.05070	0.09415	0.04840	0.09302	(0.02660)
4	30-Sep-98	(0.30295)	(0.37391)	(0.14231)	(0.16666)	(0.24590)
5	30-Oct-98	(0.06538)	0.04254	(0.03586)	(0.10639)	(0.13768)
6	30-Nov-98	0.19342	-	(0.04189)	0.03809	0.06723
7	30-Dec-98	-	(0.02250)	0.06798	0.05275	0.07087
8	30-Jan-99	0.01034	0.02301	0.11362	(0.05011)	0.00735
9	28-Feb-99	-	(0.04081)	0.07347	0.05961	(0.09489)
10	30-Mar-99	0.06826	0.49768	0.06084	0.00867	0.02419
11	30-Apr-99	0.01917	(0.00947)	0.14695	(0.07297)	0.00787
12	30-May-99	0.03135	0.08143	0.02969	0.04167	0.09375

Figure 12.4

Correlation matrix

Correlation

	1	2	3	4	5
1	1.00000	0.49444	0.23646	0.57353	0.71299
2	0.49444	1.00000	0.18573	0.31712	0.53990
3	0.23646	0.18573	1.00000	0.37459	0.30987
4	0.57353	0.31712	0.37459	1.00000	0.50848
5	0.71299	0.53990	0.30987	0.50848	1.00000

benefits with perfectly correlated assets. A correlation matrix (see Figure 12.4) shows the relationship between the stocks using the function CORREL.

```
=CORREL($D$9:$D$68,E$9:E$68)
```

RETURNS SUMMARY

The Returns sheet summarizes the data and includes a table for generating future scenarios. The scenario number uses the RANDBETWEEN function to generate a number between one and 60. This is a uniform distribution since the possibility of any of the outcomes is equal. The random number is used as a row number in the table on the Data sheet to look up a return and then multiplies the result to the cumulative amount in the previous row. The starting point is one so the gains and losses are percentages.

```
C7 formula =RANDBETWEEN(Data!$B$9,Data!$B$68)
D7 formula =D6*(1+OFFSET(Data!$B$8,$C7,2))
```

The formula uses a two-dimensional OFFSET formula to start at the top left-hand corner of the table and go down by the number of rows generated by the RANDBETWEEN function and across to the column containing Stock 1 (see Figure 12.5). By pressing F9 and recalculating, further scenarios can be generated based on the historic data. Each month adds a new gain or

Scenario table
Figure 12.5

Month	Scenario	Stock 1	Stock 2	Stock 3	Stock 4	Stock 5
0		1.00000	1.00000	1.00000	1.00000	1.00000
1	40	1.05365	1.20584	1.08565	1.06229	1.02174
2	10	1.12557	1.80596	1.15170	1.07150	1.04646
3	12	1.16086	1.95303	1.18590	1.11615	1.14456
4	8	1.17287	1.99797	1.32064	1.06023	1.15298
5	36	1.21100	1.93055	1.36482	1.06750	1.15298
6	46	1.21776	2.02996	1.39400	1.12940	1.14548
7	24	1.24764	1.74531	1.58839	1.15296	1.22012
8	7	1.24764	1.70605	1.69637	1.21377	1.30658
9	38	1.10351	1.49696	1.62117	1.20170	1.21697
10	5	1.03135	1.56064	1.56304	1.07386	1.04942
11	8	1.04202	1.59656	1.74064	1.02005	1.05714
12	40	1.09793	1.92519	1.88972	1.08359	1.08012
Periodic		0.00782	0.05610	0.05447	0.00671	0.00644
Nominal Return		0.09379	0.67323	0.65361	0.08055	0.07732
Effective Return		0.09793	0.92519	0.88972	0.08359	0.08012

Effective interest rates
Figure 12.6

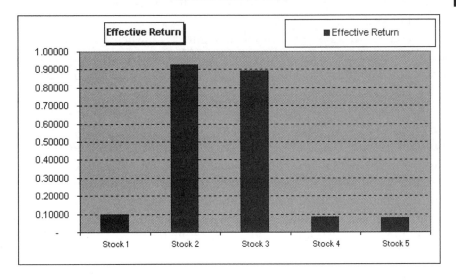

loss to the previous cumulative amount. This is the uniform distribution where any result is equally likely.

At the bottom, the inherent interest rates are calculated using the RATE and EFFECT functions. The periodic rate is calculated by the number of periods per annum (12) to form the nominal rate.

```
D20 formula =RATE($B18,0,D6,-D18,0)
D22 formula
=IF(ISERROR(EFFECT(D21,$B18)),0,EFFECT(D21,$B18))
```

Scenario chart

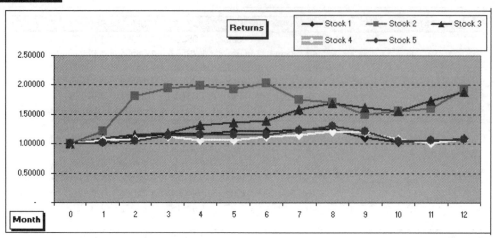

The RATE function is equivalent to this calculation: $[1.0793/1.000]^{[1/12]}$. The EFFECT function provides the effective (annual equivalent) based on the number of compounding periods in the year (see Figure 12.6). The formula is $[(1 + Nominal/C)^{C}] - 1$, where C is the number of compounding periods per annum.

You can see the range of outcomes in Figure 12.7, where two of the stocks have virtually doubled over the 12-month period. This of course will change every time you press F9. However, the range of outcomes will be based on the average and standard deviation of the historic returns.

The second part of the schedule summarizes the historic data. This uses a FREQUENCY array function to count the number of results in the bins between −20 per cent and +20 per cent. To further describe the distributions, the minimum, maximum, median, skew, kurtosis, mean standard deviations and range are shown (see Figure 12.8). The distributions offer different characteristics of mean and standard deviation with stocks 1 and 2 with the highest mean, and stock 2 with the highest standard deviation. Stock 2 seems to offer a higher return than the other stocks but only with higher risk expressed by standard deviation.

The formulas are:

```
Maximum              =MAX(Data!D$9:D$68)
Minimum              =MIN(Data!D$9:D$68)
Median               =MEDIAN(Data!D$9:D$68)
Skew                 =SKEW(Data!D$9:D$68)
Kurtosis             =KURT(Data!D$9:D$68)
Mean                 =AVERAGE(Data!D$9:D$68)
Standard deviation=STDEVP(Data!D$9:D$68)
```

Another method of describing the distributions is to draw out the quartiles

Figure 12.8

Frequency table

Intervals	Stock 1	Stock 2	Stock 3	Stock 4	Stock 5
(20.00%)	1	2	1	0	1
(18.00%)	0	0	0	0	0
(16.00%)	0	0	0	1	0
(14.00%)	0	1	1	0	0
(12.00%)	0	1	0	0	3
(10.00%)	1	4	0	1	0
(8.00%)	1	3	2	2	3
(6.00%)	1	1	2	4	3
(4.00%)	5	4	6	5	5
(2.00%)	4	7	7	7	2
-	5	5	6	8	8
2.00%	9	5	6	6	7
4.00%	12	6	9	6	9
6.00%	8	3	6	8	7
8.00%	5	3	4	2	7
10.00%	2	2	3	6	1
12.00%	2	2	4	1	1
14.00%	1	2	1	1	1
16.00%	1	4	1	1	2
18.00%	1	0	0	0	0
20.00%	1	1	1	1	0
Sum	60	56	60	60	60
Maximum	0.19342	0.49768	0.19287	0.19099	0.15578
Minimum	(0.30295)	(0.37391)	(0.31166)	(0.16666)	(0.24590)
Median	0.02563	0.01096	0.00917	0.00900	0.01397
Skew	(1.17252)	0.81352	(1.00200)	0.13572	(0.74248)
Kurtosis	5.90705	4.00196	4.49051	0.41327	1.67589
Mean	0.02129	0.02341	0.01232	0.01063	0.00540
Standard deviation	0.07266	0.13010	0.07618	0.06524	0.07116
Range	0.49636	0.87159	0.50453	0.35765	0.40168

using the same data. This is a convenient way of calculating the minimum, maximum and median together (see Table 12.2 and Figure 12.9).

The chart of the table also illustrates the spread of results effectively: the range on Stock 2 shows up clearly with the lowest minimum and the highest maximum (see Figure 12.10). By contrast, Stock 4 has the lowest range.

Figure 12.10 is a non-standard chart called a box plot and was created with the data in the specific order in Table 12.3.

The instructions are:

■ highlight the whole table, including figures and series labels and then click on the Chart Wizard;

■ select a Line Chart;

Table 12.2

Quartile number	Answer
0	Minimum value
1	First quartile (25th percentile)
2	Median value (50th percentile)
3	Third quartile (75th percentile)
4	Maximum value

Figure 12.9   Quartiles

Quartiles Table

Intervals		Percentile	Stock 1	Stock 2	Stock 3	Stock 4	Stock 5
0		Minimum	(0.30295)	(0.37391)	(0.31166)	(0.16666)	(0.24590)
1		25th	(0.00388)	(0.04138)	(0.02689)	(0.03500)	(0.03005)
2		50th Median	0.02563	0.01096	0.00917	0.00900	0.01397
3		75th	0.05423	0.07371	0.05372	0.05122	0.04630
4		Maximum	0.19342	0.49768	0.19287	0.19099	0.15578
Mean			0.06735	0.13524	0.05722	0.05405	0.04650

Figure 12.10   Quartiles chart

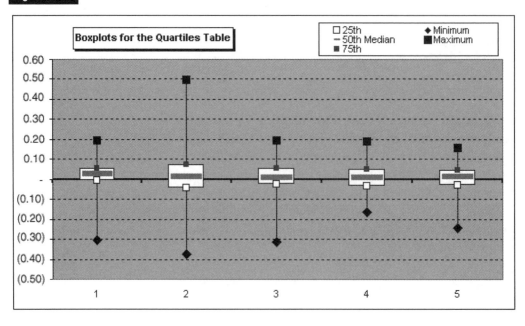

	Stock 1	Stock 2	Stock 3	Stock 4	Stock 5	
25th	(0.00388)	(0.04138)	(0.02689)	(0.03500)	(0.03005)	Table 12.3
Minimum	(0.30295)	(0.37391)	(0.31166)	(0.16666)	(0.24590)	
50th (median)	0.02563	0.01096	0.00917	0.00900	0.01397	
Maximum	0.19342	0.49768	0.19287	0.19099	0.15578	
75th	0.05423	0.07371	0.05372	0.05122	0.04630	

- at Step 2 plot by Rows (the default is Columns), then Finish;
- select each data series in turn and use Format Data Series to remove the connecting lines;
- select any of the data series and Format Data Series; select the Options tab and switch on the checkboxes for High-Low lines and Up-Down bars.

A further chart on the schedule allows you to compare two distributions (see Figures 12.11 and 12.12). This allows you to test the shape of Stocks 2 and 4 with the individual frequencies and the variance between them.

Comparison of two stocks

Figure 12.11

Individual Stock Frequency Comparison: Stock 2 and Stock 4

Stock 2 ▼
Stock 4 ▼

Intervals	Stock 2	Stock 4	Variance
(0.20)	-	-	-
(0.18)	-	-	-
(0.16)	-	1	(1)
(0.14)	1	-	1
(0.12)	1	-	1
(0.10)	4	1	3
(0.08)	3	2	1
(0.06)	1	4	(3)
(0.04)	4	5	(1)
(0.02)	7	7	-
-	5	8	(3)
0.02	5	6	(1)
0.04	6	6	-
0.06	3	8	(5)
0.08	3	2	1
0.10	2	6	(4)
0.12	2	1	1
0.14	2	1	1
0.16	4	1	3
0.18	-	-	-
0.20	1	1	-
Sum	54	60	(6)

Figure 12.12   **Comparison chart**

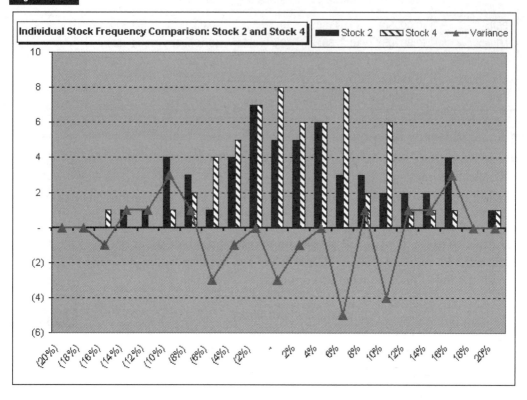

SIMULATION

The Simulation sheet contains 1000 lines of data generated by the Simulation macro. The macro recalculates and, based on the random numbers generated by the RANDBETWEEN function, builds up to a value at the end of 12 months. This value is pasted into the stock returns row and the process repeats 1000 times through a FOR NEXT loop. This assumes that the possibility of any of the previous months happening again is random. The process is repeated 1000 times so that there is sufficient data to provide a theoretical distribution.

The portfolio return (see Figure 12.13) is comprised of the values for that row multiplied by the weightings in row nine on the Portfolio sheet. The SUMPRODUCT function is a convenient method for multiplying out the two arrays.

```
=SUMPRODUCT(Portfolio!$C$9:$G$9,Simulation!C6:G6)
-1
```

Figure 12.13

Simulation Number	Stock 1	Stock 2	Stock 3	Stock 4	Stock 5	Portfolio Return	Shortfall to Simulation Target Return
0001	1.56947	1.06573	1.23475	0.92709	0.88365	0.44284	-
0002	1.58196	2.08344	0.78052	1.32517	1.25780	0.37896	-
0003	0.75801	0.51282	0.82261	0.99317	0.76079	(0.23407)	(0.33407)
0004	1.04803	0.75922	1.18697	0.68118	0.86953	0.06886	(0.03114)
0005	1.60341	1.27073	1.14528	1.17541	0.96830	0.45281	-
0006	1.33897	0.75410	1.24898	0.99370	1.22282	0.28015	-
0007	1.36089	1.18384	1.03399	0.96722	1.16094	0.25568	-
0008	1.54141	1.12101	1.04027	1.10478	1.23224	0.37407	-
0009	1.67916	1.10139	0.86575	1.32606	1.13873	0.41637	-
0010	1.60480	2.40755	1.37063	1.20390	1.62253	0.57606	-
0011	1.72714	1.09307	1.23935	1.25885	1.52425	0.55228	-
0012	1.00597	1.09384	1.31794	0.89826	0.93192	0.09753	(0.00247)
0013	1.23765	0.87952	1.34802	1.27053	1.34264	0.25072	-
0014	1.20472	1.03470	1.79369	1.23291	1.00823	0.36255	-
0015	1.12267	1.12102	1.75588	1.30630	1.00828	0.30315	-

Where the portfolio return falls below the minimum (in this case 10 per cent), this is recorded using an IF function. This is used later to calculate the probability of a loss.

```
=IF(H6<Portfolio!$C$7,Portfolio!$C$7-H6,0)
```

Below is the text of the macro, which recalculates and pastes the data into the sheet. Each time you run the macro a fresh set of data is created in the Simulation sheet:

```
Sub Simulation()
Dim Original_Answer

Original_Answer = Range("Returns!d18:h18")
Range("Simulation_Results") = "" 'Zero previous
results

Randomize
Application.Calculation = xlSemiautomatic
Application.ScreenUpdating = False

For r = 1 To 1000 'START OF LOOP
    RandomFactor = Rnd
    Calculate
    Sheets("Returns").Select
    Range("d18:h18").Select
    Selection.Copy

    Sheets("Simulation").Select
```

```
        Range("C5").Select
        ActiveCell.Offset(r, 0).Select

        Selection.PasteSpecial Paste:=xlPasteValues,
        Operation:=xlNone, SkipBlanks:= False,
        Transpose:=False

        Application.CutCopyMode = False
        Range("a2").Select

        Sheets("Data").Select
        Range("A2").Select
        Application.ScreenUpdating = True
        Range("data!h5") = r
        Application.ScreenUpdating = False
    Next r                        'END OF LOOP

    Sheets("Returns").Select
    Application.CutCopyMode = False
    Range("a2").Select
    Application.ScreenUpdating = True
    Application.Calculation = xlAutomatic

    End Sub
```

PORTFOLIO

The Portfolio sheet uses the Simulation sheet data to construct optimum portfolios with the Solver add-in. This allows you to maximize, minimize or target a particular cell value by changing multiple cells subject to a number of rules or constraints. On the schedule there are inputs for the required return, risk-free rate, a minimum return (for working out the possibility of loss) and weighting for each of the five stocks (see Figure 12.14). The sum of the weightings must be equal to one.

The statistics are calculated as follows:

- Mean   =AVERAGE(Simulation!H$6:H$1005)
- Standard deviation   =STDEVP(Simulation!H$6:H$1005)
- Possibility of loss   =PERCENTRANK(Simulation! I$6:I$1005,0)
- Downside risk   =-AVERAGE(Simulation!I6:I1005)
- Sharpe ratio   =(H13-C6)/H14

Figure 12.14

	Stock 1	Stock 2	Stock 3	Stock 4	Stock 5	Portfolio
Required Return	25.00%					
Risk Free Rate (Rf)	5.00%					
Market Rate (Rm)	12.00%					
Market Standard Deviation	10.00%					
Simulation Target Return	10.00%					
Weights	0.65655	0.05140	0.28235	0.00969	-	1.00000
Mean	1.28464	1.32736	1.15959	1.12716	1.06086	
Standard Deviation	0.30584	0.58834	0.31627	0.24166	0.26028	
Portfolio Return						0.25000
Standard Deviation						0.25289
Probability of Loss						0.27600
Downside Risk						0.04287
Sharpe Ratio						0.79087

The mean is the weighted average return on the portfolio. The standard deviation uses the function for a population with the following formula:

$$\sqrt{\frac{n \sum x^2 - \left(\sum x^2\right)}{n^2}}$$

The possibility of loss uses the function PERCENTRANK to derive the percentage of results below zero and therefore constituting a loss. Similarly the downside risk is the percentage of observations which fall below the minimum input of 10 per cent.

The Sharpe ratio of the portfolio is a composite measure for evaluating performance. It seeks to measure total risk by including the standard deviation of returns. The measure provides the risk premium earned per unit of total risk. It follows therefore that a high score indicates a more efficient portfolio in terms of risk and reward:

$$\frac{\mu - r}{\sigma}$$

where

$\mu =$ mean return on the portfolio
$r =$ risk-free rate
$\sigma =$ standard deviation of the portfolio.

The standard deviation, possibility of loss, downside risk and Sharpe ratio are all portfolio measures that could be used to define a portfolio with certain characteristics. You could minimize the first three or maximize the Sharpe ratio. The model attempts to maximize the Sharpe ratio by changing

Figure 12.15   **Solver dialog box**

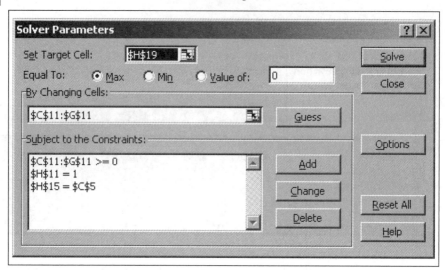

the weights afforded to each stock with the provisos that the minimum return has to be met and that the weights cannot be less than zero or add up to more than 100 per cent. This is the manual Solver dialog box (see Figure 12.15).

Note that there are sometimes problems with different language versions Solver used in code. The fact that Solver will be required has to be noted as a reference in the Visual Basic Window. If you get an error while running the macro, then check that Excel can find the Solver add-in. Re-click the add-in and the macro should run.

The Solver Parameters box shown in Figure 12.16 produces a single portfolio at a given rate but a chart of several portfolios is required to understand how it 'behaves'. The sheet contains a macro to take required returns in order, perform a Solver analysis, paste the weightings and the answers into a table and then go on to the next expected return. The full text of the SolverTable macro is as follows:

```
Sub SolverTable()
'

Dim Original_Answer, Required_Return
Application.Calculation = xlSemiautomatic

SolverOk SetCell:="$H$19", MaxMinVal:=1,
Valueof:=0, ByChange:="$C$11:$G$11"
SolverSolve userfinish:=True

Original_Answer = Range("portfolio!c11:g11")
```

Solver reference

Figure 12.16

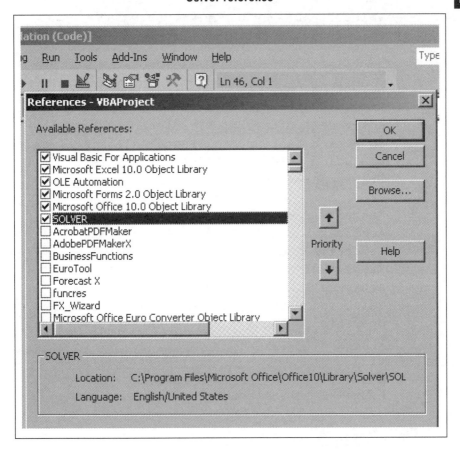

```
Required_Return = Range("c5")
Range("SolverTable") = ""

For r=1 To 7

   Range("c11:g11") = 0

   Range("B21").Select
   ActiveCell.Offset(r, 0).Select
   Selection.Copy
   Range("c5").Select
   Selection.PasteSpecial Paste:=xlPasteValues,
   Operation:=xlNone, SkipBlanks :=False,
   Transpose:=False

   SolverOk SetCell:="$H$19", MaxMinVal:=1,
   Valueof:=0, ByChange:="$C$11:$g$11"
```

```
'SolverOk SetCell:="$H$14", MaxMinVal:=2,
ValueOf:="0", ByChange:="$C$9:$g$9"
SolverSolve userfinish:=True

Range("C11:G11").Select
Selection.Copy
Range("C21").Select
ActiveCell.Offset(r, 0).Select
Selection.PasteSpecial Paste:=xlPasteValues,
Operation:=xlNone, SkipBlanks :=False,
Transpose:=False

Range("H15:H19").Select
Application.CutCopyMode = False
Selection.Copy
Range("H21").Select
ActiveCell.Offset(r, 0).Select
Selection.PasteSpecial Paste:=xlPasteValues,
Operation:=xlNone, SkipBlanks :=False,
Transpose:=True

Application.CutCopyMode = False
Range("B21").Select

Next r

Range("portfolio!c11:g11") = Original_Answer
Range("c5") = Required_Return
Range("a2").Select
Application.Calculation = xlAutomatic

End Sub
```

The result is a table of returns stepping up in pre-determined intervals showing the weighting of stock and the results in terms of standard deviation and the Sharpe ratio. As the required return increases, Stocks 4 and 5 are removed since they do not offer a sufficient return (see Figure 12.17).

Standard deviation increases with return whereas the probability of loss and the downside risk reduce and then start to increase. The Sharpe ratio increases until the required return of 27 per cent and then starts to decline (see Figure 12.18).

The chart is an XY scatter chart with standard deviation as the *x*-axis and the required return as the *y*-axis. This shows the efficient frontier where it

Portfolio weightings

Figure 12.17

Solver TableTarget Portfolio Return	Stock 1	Stock 2	Stock 3	Stock 4	Stock 5
19.00%	0.32455	0.01667	0.28293	0.36405	0.01180
21.00%	0.43160	0.02830	0.28391	0.25619	-
23.00%	0.54408	0.03985	0.28313	0.13294	-
25.00%	0.65655	0.05140	0.28235	0.00969	-
27.00%	0.76155	0.09048	0.14797	-	-
29.00%	0.86590	0.13190	0.00220	-	-
31.00%	0.40643	0.59357	-	-	-

Portfolio results

Figure 12.18

Solver TableTarget Portfolio Return	Portfolio Return	Standard Deviation	Probability of Loss	Downside Risk	Sharpe Ratio
19.00%	0.19000	0.21644	0.34600	0.04682	0.64682
21.00%	0.21000	0.22451	0.31000	0.04399	0.71268
23.00%	0.23000	0.23685	0.29400	0.04290	0.75997
25.00%	0.25000	0.25289	0.27600	0.04287	0.79087
27.00%	0.27000	0.27550	0.27800	0.04548	0.79855
29.00%	0.29000	0.30751	0.28100	0.05044	0.78047
31.00%	0.31000	0.41961	0.32400	0.06974	0.61962
Risk Free Rate (Rf)	0.05000	-			-
Actual Market Rate (Rm)	0.12000	0.10000			0.70000

Efficient frontier

Figure 12.19

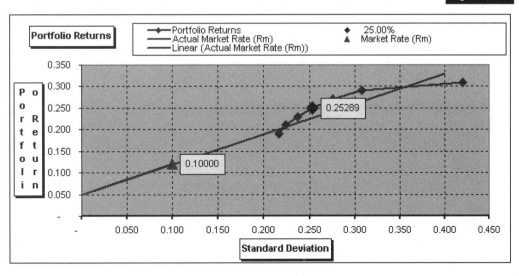

leads to diminishing returns after 27 per cent to demand a greater return (see Figure 12.19). Each extra unit of return costs more in risk. As a check the market line has been calculated using a market rate of 12 per cent and a risk free rate of 5 per cent. Based on a standard deviation of 10 per cent, the Sharpe ratio is 0.70. The market line is drawn on the chart and a forecast linear trend line directed through it. Portfolios at expected returns of 19 per cent and 31 per cent lie below the market line. The optimum portfolio lies between 25 per cent and 27 per cent.

Figure 12.20 shows the composition of each of the portfolios. Stock 1 increases as a percentage of the portfolio until the required return is 29 per cent and is then overtaken by Stock 2 when the higher yield is specified. Stock 5 hardly features since the return is low compared with the other stocks.

A third chart allows you to select one of the measures and check the answer along the line. Figure 12.21 illustrates how the Sharpe ratio starts to decline with the increasing risk inherent in the higher yielding portfolios. This type of chart allows you to test the portfolios graphically and here it emphasizes the viable portfolios up to about 30 per cent after which each unit of return brings decreased portfolio benefits.

Figure 12.20 **Portfolio composition**

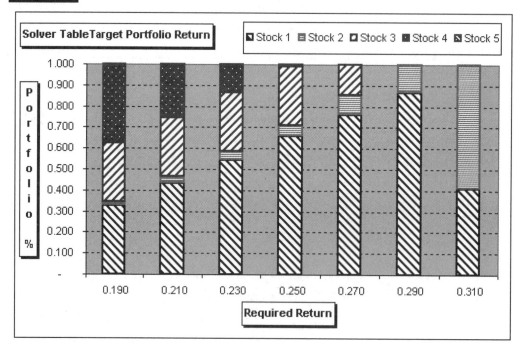

Sharpe ratio

Figure 12.21

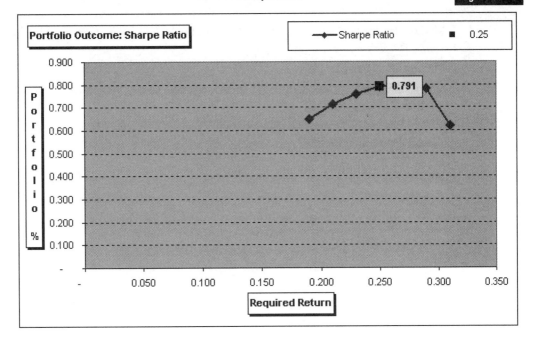

SUMMARY

Portfolio theory shows how you can combine risky assets and use diversification to reduce overall portfolio risk. This model uses simulation to generate a data set of possible portfolios and then analyzes the findings using Solver to build portfolios with the optimum balance of risk and return at required portfolio rates of return. It goes one stage further using macros to build up a table of solved portfolios and draws charts of the portfolios. The Portfolio sheet provides a graphical and tabular answer to finding the optimum portfolios for this set of data. Using these tools, portfolios can be constructed (as in the example in this chapter) with predetermined rates of risk and return.

REFERENCES

Markowitz, Harry M., 1952, 'Portfolio Selection', *Journal of Finance*, March, 77–91.

Markowitz, Harry M., 1991, *Portfolio Selection*, second edition, Blackwell.

Sharpe, William F., 1966, Mutual Fund Performance, *Journal of Business*, 39, no. 1, part 2 (January), 119–38.

Sharpe, William F., 1994, 'The Sharpe Ratio', *Journal of Portfolio Management*, 21, no. 1 (Autumn), 49–59.

Risk adjusted returns

File: FT4_13.xls

INTRODUCTION

The measurement of economic capital provides a common framework for quantifying risk arising from varied sources and also allows the calculation of equity that a bank should hold to support the various levels of risk taking. 'Capital' is defined here as the difference between the value of assets and the value of liabilities. The value of both sides of the equation can change daily and this can impact on the bank's ability to pay its debts. This means that there is a direct relationship between the amount of capital held, the amount of risk capacity generated and the probability of default.

ECONOMIC CAPITAL

Economic capital is said to represent the emerging best practice for measuring and reporting all kinds of risk across a financial organization. It is called 'economic' capital because it measures risk in terms of economic realities rather than potentially misleading regulatory, accounting or book values. The term 'economic capital' is also used since part of the measurement process involves analyzing and converting a risk distribution to the amount of capital that is required to support the risk, in line with the institution's target financial strength or credit rating.

While some risk distributions can be calculated with more certainty than others, market risks tend to be more accessible than operating risks. For example, the approach can be applied in principle to almost all bank risks, and to any business line within the institution. Economic capital therefore provides management with a standardized unit, for comparing and discussing potential profit opportunities and related threats and downsides. Economic capital numbers can also be multiplied by an institution's equity hurdle rate (the minimum acceptable rate of return on equity) to offer a 'cost of risk' number that is comparable to other kinds of bank expense.

In the example shown in Figure 13.1, the bank is 95 per cent leveraged and invests in 1,000 bonds paying 6 per cent and repayable in one period's time. The model calculates the in and outflows. The assets in one year's time should be 1,000 plus 6 per cent, from which the debt and equity holders can be paid. Paying the debt holders for the 950 debt leaves 62.5 which equates to a 25 per cent return. If the default rate rise above zero then the return to shareholders falls since the debt needs to be paid out of a declining income. At 2 per cent default, the return is already −17 per cent.

Figure 13.1		Return on equity			

Equity	(50.00)		Target RO	25.00%	
Debt	(950.00)		Interest	5.00%	
Total	(1,000.00)				
Bond Capital	1,000.00		Coupon	6.00%	
Default Rate	0.00%				

End of Year One					Interval	1.00%
Income Statement		0.00%	1.00%	2.00%	3.00%	4.00%
Assets	1,000.00	1,000.00	1,000.00	1,000.00	1,000.00	1,000.00
Bond Default	-	-	(10.00)	(20.00)	(30.00)	(40.00)
Bond Coupon	60.00	60.00	59.40	58.80	58.20	57.60
Interest on Debt	(997.50)	(997.50)	(997.50)	(997.50)	(997.50)	(997.50)
Total	**62.50**	**62.50**	**51.90**	**41.30**	**30.70**	**20.10**
ROE	**25.00%**	**25.00%**	**3.80%**	**(17.40%)**	**(38.60%)**	**(59.80%)**

The model uses a table to generate the potential losses with increasing default percentages. The interest and capital repayment do not decrease, however there is less income to repay the debt.

Figure 13.2 explains the cell formulas.

Reducing the leverage (see Figure 13.3) reduces the initial return to 10 per cent but the overall losses are also reduced as the default percentage increases. At 4 per cent, the negative return is 11 per cent against 59 per cent, demonstrating the trade-off between risk and return.

The next stage could be to generate a number of scenarios (see Figure 13.4) based on the probability of default and show how the future value of the portfolio could vary. The outcome is a continuous variable as there are an infinite number of outcomes. The representation is a probabil-

Explanation of cell formulas

Figure 13.2

	A	B	C	D	E	F
4						
5		Equity	-50		Target ROE	0.25
6		Debt	-950		Interest	0.05
7		Total	=SUM(C5:C6)			
8						
9		Bond Capital	=-SUM(C5:C6)		Coupon	0.06
10		Default Rate	0			
11						
12		End of Year One				
13		Income Statement		0	=D13+$H$12	=E13+$H$12
14		Assets	=C9	=TABLE(C10,)	=TABLE(C10,)	=TABLE(C10,)
15		Bond Default	=-(C9*C10)	=TABLE(C10,)	=TABLE(C10,)	=TABLE(C10,)
16		Bond Coupon	=(C9-(C9*C10))*F9	=TABLE(C10,)	=TABLE(C10,)	=TABLE(C10,)
17		Interest on Debt	=C6+C6*F6	=TABLE(C10,)	=TABLE(C10,)	=TABLE(C10,)
18		Total	=SUM(C14:C17)	=TABLE(C10,)	=TABLE(C10,)	=TABLE(C10,)
19		ROE	=IF(C5<>0,(C18+C5)/ABS(C5),0)	=TABLE(C10,)	=TABLE(C10,)	=TABLE(C10,)

Reduced leverage

Figure 13.3

Equity	(200.00)		Target RO	25.00%		
Debt	(800.00)		Interest	5.00%		
Total	(1,000.00)					
Bond Capital	1,000.00		Coupon	6.00%		
Default Rate	0.00%					

End of Year One					Interval	1.00%
Income Statement		0.00%	1.00%	2.00%	3.00%	4.00%
Assets	1,000.00	1,000.00	1,000.00	1,000.00	1,000.00	1,000.00
Bond Default	-	-	(10.00)	(20.00)	(30.00)	(40.00)
Bond Coupon	60.00	60.00	59.40	58.80	58.20	57.60
Interest on Debt	(840.00)	(840.00)	(840.00)	(840.00)	(840.00)	(840.00)
Total	220.00	220.00	209.40	198.80	188.20	177.60
ROE	10.00%	10.00%	4.70%	(0.60%)	(5.90%)	(11.20%)

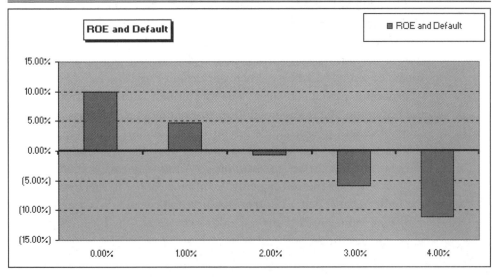

ROE and Default

Figure 13.4

Table scenarios

End of Year One

Income Statement		Standard Deviation	0.50%
Assets	1,000.00	Default Rate	2.00%
Bond Default	-		
Bond Coupon	60.00		
Interest on Debt	(840.00)		
Total	**220.00**		
ROE	**10.00%**		

			ROE 10.00%	Capital 1,060.00
1	0.39	1.86%	17.34%	1,074.69
2	0.01	0.90%	21.13%	1,082.26
3	0.33	1.77%	21.95%	1,083.90
4	0.30	1.74%	15.86%	1,071.71
5	0.08	1.31%	22.45%	1,084.90
6	0.93	2.75%	21.34%	1,082.68
7	0.59	2.11%	22.88%	1,085.77
8	0.32	1.77%	15.49%	1,070.98
9	0.94	2.78%	15.68%	1,071.35
10	0.98	3.03%	23.98%	1,087.97

ity density function, where the *x* axis is the value of the assets and the *y* axis is the probability. With increased capital, the probability of bank default is reduced due to the increased capital base. Economic capital represents this trade-off between initial capital, risks taken and the probability of the bank being forced to default. Economic capital provides the framework for translating risks into a single metric.

The table in Figure 13.4 is based on the RAND function to generate the probability and the NORMINV function to compute the overall default rate. The table returns the return on equity and the total capital after deduction of default. The frequency table and chart (see Figure 13.5) show the spread of results based on a 2 per cent default rate.

Economic capital is the net value that a financial institution must have at the beginning of a trading period to ensure that there is only a small probability of defaulting during the period and producing a loss. The net value is the assets less the liabilities. The small probability is based on the credit rating of the institution, for example an A rating normally equates to about 0.1 per cent over the coming year. Economic capital in this sense represents the buffer against default in that the shareholders and directors must ensure sufficient capital such that the bank can maintain the business profile and target credit rating.

Frequency table

Figure 13.5

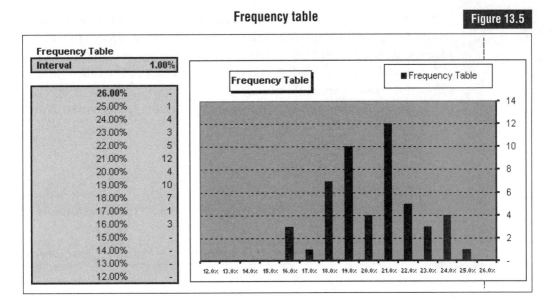

Frequency Table	
Interval	**1.00%**
26.00%	-
25.00%	1
24.00%	4
23.00%	3
22.00%	5
21.00%	12
20.00%	4
19.00%	10
18.00%	7
17.00%	1
16.00%	3
15.00%	-
14.00%	-
13.00%	-
12.00%	-

RISK ADJUSTED RETURN ON CAPITAL (RAROC)

Banks are not only interested in the risk but also the profitability associated with the risk. Risk adjusted performance can be used to assist with business and credit decisions:

- deciding which products are profitable and how they should be priced to be profitable;
- deciding which client relationships yield the highest return;
- deciding whether or not to enter into a transaction and at what price;
- reviewing business units in their use and return on capital in return for the risks undertaken.

Table 13.1 shows the action that management could take to improve profitability or choose between operating units.

Table 13.1

Overcapitalised	Undercapitalised
Reduce capital base	Increase capital base
Buy back shares	Issue shares (ordinary and preference)
Increase dividends	Reduce dividends to shareholders
Increase risks taken	Reduce risks taken
Grow existing units with RAROCs	Cut back on activities with low or negative RAROCs
Buy or build further business activities	Transfer out concentrated risks to others

Common ratios such as return on assets (net operating profit/total assets) or return on equity (earnings after tax/shareholders' funds) do not provide an adequate metric for return since risk is not encapsulated in the measure. The earlier model can be extended to include a further measure called the risk adjusted return on capital (RAROC).

This is calculated as the net risk adjusted profit divided by the economic capital based on market values:

$$RAROC = ENP/EC$$

RAROC treats all transactions as additions to a portfolio and the price is the amount of capital that must be set aside to make the transaction happen. The return equates to the net increase in value. A more complete formula is:

$$RAROC = \frac{(Initial\_Loan * Interest) + Fees - (Debt * Interest) - Operating\_Cost - Losses}{EC}$$

$$RAROC = \frac{(Loan * Interest) + Fees - (Loan - EC) * Interest - Operating\_Cost - Losses}{EC}$$

For a trading position, the RAROC is the net change in the value of the position minus operating costs. The required profitability that must be reached is the hurdle rate multiplied by the economic capital. The equation is:

$$RAROC = \frac{\Delta Value - Operating\_Costs}{Economic\_Capital}$$

Shareholder value added gives an alternative measure of profitability as the amount of value added. This is the amount as per the economic capital equation minus a hurdle return multiplied by economic capital.

$$SVA = (Loan * Interest) + Fees - (Loan - EC)$$
$$* Interest - Operating\_Cost - Losses - Hurdle - EC$$

In this example, the inputs are as shown in Figure 13.6

Figure 13.6		RAROC calculation	

Loan	100.00	Expected Loss	0.060
Interbank Rate	5.50%	Unexpected Loss (Credit Risk)	1.340
Customer Interest Rate	7.00%	Unexpected loss contribution (ULC)	0.232
Operating Costs	1.000	Economic Capital (EC)	1.393
Default Correlation	3.00%		
Loss in Event of Default	30.00%	RAROC	37.09%
Probability of Default	0.20%	Total Return	0.517
Capital Multiplier	6.000	Required Hurdle Return	0.348
Hurdle Rate	25.00%	Shareholder Value Added (SVA)	0.168
		(Total Return - Required Hurdle Return)	

The loan is 100 sold to the client at a rate of 7 per cent against an inter-bank rate of 5.5 per cent. The average default correlation with the rest of the portfolio is 3 per cent and the capital multiplier is 6. The calculation for economic capital is:

> *Expected loss = loan * loss in event of default*
> ** probability = 0.06*
> *Unexpected loss = loan * loss in event of default*
> ** √probability − probability ^2 = 1.34*
> *Unexpected loss contribution (ULC) = √default correlation*
> ** unexpected loss = 0.232*
> *Economic capital = multiplier * ULC = 6 * 0.232 = 1.393*

The RAROC calculation of 37.09 per cent is:

> *(Loan * customer interest rate − (loan − EC)*
> ** interbank rate − operating costs − expected loss)/EC*

The shareholder value added of 0.168 is:

> *(Loan * customer interest rate − (loan − EC)*
> ** interbank rate − operating costs − expected loss) − (hurdle rate * EC)*

Figure 13.7 shows the sensitivity to the customer interest rate and the probability of default. The customer interest rate is plotted across and the probability down. As the customer rate and default correlation fall, the RAROC declines. The chart displays the middle 0.020 series computed above.

Over multiple periods, the RAROC is the expected net profit divided by the economic capital or the internal rate of return of the cash flows. This is more complex since:

- over longer periods, the probability of default increases and therefore increases the required economic capital and debt needed;
- if the default of debt increases, the likelihood of paying all the administration costs therefore declines;
- the outstanding loan can vary accordingly to the amortization profile;
- the security or collateral can change in value thereby increasing or decreasing the potential exposure.

The bank loans the funds at the beginning of the period and to fund this invests some economic capital and raises debt. The net cash flow is equal to the economic capital which has been paid to the customer. During the loan period, the client pays back interest and principal and the bank needs to pay operating costs. The expected receipt is dependent on the probability of

Figure 13.7 **RAROC sensitivity**

Sensitivity Table to Customer Interest Rate Across and Default Correlation Down

| Interval Across | 0.250% |
| Interval Down | 0.0200% |

RAROC ▼   1

Selected: RAROC

0.37	6.25%	6.50%	6.75%	**7.00%**	7.25%	7.50%	7.75%
0.1400%	(19.55%)	1.90%	23.34%	44.79%	66.24%	87.68%	109.13%
0.1600%	(18.42%)	1.65%	21.71%	41.77%	61.84%	81.90%	101.96%
0.1800%	(17.50%)	1.41%	20.33%	39.25%	58.17%	77.08%	96.00%
0.2000%	(16.76%)	1.19%	19.14%	37.09%	55.04%	72.99%	90.93%
0.2200%	(16.13%)	0.98%	18.10%	35.21%	52.33%	69.44%	86.56%
0.2400%	(15.61%)	0.78%	17.17%	33.56%	49.94%	66.33%	82.72%
0.2600%	(15.16%)	0.59%	16.33%	32.08%	47.83%	63.57%	79.32%

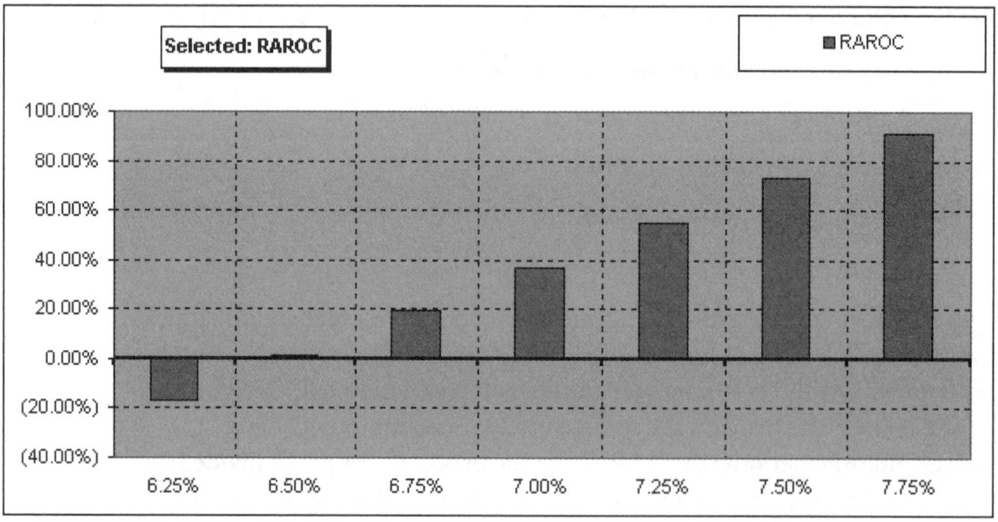

Selected: RAROC   ■ RAROC

default:

$$Cashflow\_In = Loan * (1 + Interest) * (1 - Default\_Probability)$$
$$+ Recovery * Default\_Probability$$
$$Cashflow\_Out = Debt * (1 + Interest) + Operating\_Cost$$

Using these formulas it is possible to construct cash flows for longer periods and find the internal rate of return or RAROC over longer periods. By understanding the capital at risk and the cash flows it is possible to understand the return being made for the risk incurred.

The inputs in Figure 13.8 show a two-year loan using the same figures as the previous schedule. The loss in the event of default rises in the second year as does the probability of default. This implies that the RAROC in the second year will be lower due to the rise in these two factors.

Two year loan

Figure 13.8

Year	1	2
Loan	100.00	
Interbank Rate	5.50%	
Customer Interest Rate	7.00%	
Operating Costs	1.000	1.000
Default Correlation	3.00%	
Loss in Event of Default	30.00%	40.00%
Probability of Default	0.20%	0.25%
Capital Multiplier	6.000	
Hurdle Rate	25.00%	

	1	2
Recovery in the Event of Default	70.000	60.000
Expected Loss	0.060	0.060
Unexpected Loss (Credit Risk)	1.340	1.997
Unexpected loss contribution (ULC)	0.232	0.346
Economic Capital (EC)	1.393	2.076
RAROC	37.09%	26.70%
Total Return	0.517	0.554
Required Hurdle Return	0.348	0.519
Shareholder Value Added (SVA)	0.168	0.035
(Total Return - Required Hurdle Return)		

The cash flows are as in Figure 13.9. The cash on inception is the loan less the economic capital.

The formulas are:

$$Cash\_In\_1 = Loan * Interest * (1 - Prob) + Recovery$$
$$* Prob + Loan\_Year\_2 * (1 - Prob)$$
$$Cash\_Out\_1 = Debt * (1 + Debt\_Interest) + Operating\_Costs$$
$$Cash\_In\_2 = Loan * (1 + Interest) * (1 - Prob) * (1 - Prob\_2)$$
$$+ Recovery * (1 - Prob) * Prob\_2$$
$$Cash\_Out\_2 = Debt\_2 * (1 - Prob) * (1 + Debt\_Interest)$$
$$+ Operating\_Costs * (1 - Prob)$$

Cash flows

Figure 13.9

Cash Flows

	Debt	In	Out	Difference
0		98.61	(100.00)	(1.39)
1	98.61	104.85	(105.03)	(0.18)
2	97.92	106.67	(104.10)	2.57

Internal Rate of Return (RAROC)	29.59%

Figure 13.10	Sensitivity table

Sensitivity Table to Customer Interest Rate Across and Probability of Default Down

Interval Across	0.100%
Interval Down	0.0200%

29.59%	6.70%	6.80%	6.90%	7.00%	7.10%	7.20%	7.30%
0.1400%	12.90%	19.34%	25.86%	32.47%	39.17%	45.95%	52.81%
0.1600%	12.47%	18.70%	25.02%	31.41%	37.87%	44.39%	50.98%
0.1800%	12.06%	18.13%	24.26%	30.45%	36.70%	43.01%	49.37%
0.2000%	11.69%	17.60%	23.57%	29.59%	35.66%	41.77%	47.93%
0.2200%	11.34%	17.11%	22.93%	28.80%	34.70%	40.65%	46.63%
0.2400%	11.01%	16.65%	22.34%	28.07%	33.83%	39.62%	45.44%
0.2600%	10.69%	16.23%	21.79%	27.39%	33.02%	38.67%	44.35%

Internal Rate of Return (RAROC)

■ 0.2000%

The sensitivity table is shown in Figure 13.10.

The RAROC for two years is below the initial answer of 37 per cent. One solution is to use Goal Seek (see Figure 13.11) to solve the customer rate needed to achieve a RAROC of 37 per cent. In this case this is 7.12 per cent using the macro code.

```
Application.Calculation =
xlCalculationSemiautomatic
Range("d35").Goalseek Goal:=Range("i13"),
ChangingCell:=Range("e8")
 Range("a2").Select
Application.Calculation = xlCalculationAutomatic
End Sub
```

Goal seek variables

Figure 13.11

	A	B	C	D	E	F	G	H	I
2		Annual RAROC			Menu				
3									v1.0 1-June-2003
4									
5		Year			1	2		Results	
6		Loan			100.00			IRR (RAROC)	
7		Interbank Rate			5.50%			29.587%	
8		Customer Interest Rate			7.00%				
9		Operating Costs			1.000	1.000			
10		Default Correlation			3.00%			Goalseek	
11		Loss in Event of Default			30.00%	40.00%		Change Customer Rate	
12		Probability of Default			0.20%	0.25%		Target	
13		Capital Multiplier			6.000			RAROC	37.00%
14		Hurdle Rate			25.00%				
15								Goal Seek	
16		Recovery in the Event of Default			70.000	60.000			
17		Expected Loss			0.060	0.060			
18		Unexpected Loss (Credit Risk)			1.340	1.997			
19		Unexpected loss contribution (ULC)			0.232	0.346			
20		Economic Capital (EC)			1.393	2.076			
21									
22		RAROC			37.09%	26.70%			
23									
24		Total Return			0.517	0.554			
25		Required Hurdle Return			0.348	0.519			
26		Shareholder Value Added (SVA)			0.168	0.035			
27		(Total Return - Required Hurdle Return)							
28									
29		Cash Flows							
30			Debt	In	Out	Difference			
31		0		98.61	(100.00)	(1.39)			
32		1	98.61	104.85	(105.03)	(0.18)			
33		2	97.92	106.67	(104.10)	2.57			
34									
35		Internal Rate of Return (RAROC	29.587%						

SUMMARY

Risk adjusted return on capital is a measurement that includes volatility to the calculation of returns. It states the return on capital required to offset losses on the underlying asset should volatility cause its value to decline by two or three standard deviations. This chapter has used an example to show the basic calculations and the effect on returns of changing key variables such as the rate or default probability.

Value at risk

File: FT4_14.xls

INTRODUCTION

Value at risk (VaR) was developed in the early 1990s in response to failures and problems in financial institutions. Initially, the purpose of VaR is to quantify financial risks facing institutions by using standard statistical techniques. It measures the worst expected loss over a given horizon under normal market conditions at a given confidence level. On a $100 million facility, it is unlikely that a bank will lose all its capital and this measure tries to denote the amount that could be lost at a particular confidence interval based on historic experience. Conditions are said to be normal and past volatility is assumed to continue into the future. In addition, quantitative techniques are used so that the models do not capture operational, political, liquidity or personnel risk. However, VaR is now being used to control and manage risk actively rather than just provide information. By making use of VaR tools, institutions obtain more information and can decide how to allocate economic capital and how to evaluate the trade off of risk and return.

VaR is considered by risk managers and regulators because of the promise it holds for improving risk management. The Basle 1995 proposals encouraged banks to develop their own risk measurement systems to assist in calculating capital adequacy. Rather than impose a set of rigid regulations, VaR may be seen as a system of self-regulation. The proposals created incentives since the required amount of risk capital could be reduced compared with banks that followed a standard approach. Similarly, the globalization of capital markets has emphasised the links between institutions and their role in the entire system. In 1994, J. P. Morgan made its RiskMetrics system and data sets available on the Internet and this allowed institutions to develop their own systems or use the growing number of proprietary models.

This chapter first outlines the basic concepts and then works through a simple VaR model in stages.

Definitions

Two more precise definitions of VaR are as follows:

- a forecast of a given percentile, usually in the lower tail, of the distribution of returns on a portfolio over some period; similar in principle to an estimate of the expected return on a portfolio, which is a forecast of the 50th percentile;
- an estimate of the level of loss on a portfolio which is expected to be equalled or exceeded with a given, small probability.

You need to understand both the return and the risk on a portfolio since a higher spread or risk usually means a higher loss at the given probability. If you are told, for example, that there is a 1 in 100 chance of losing *x* dollars over the forecast holding period, then following portfolio theory, this is easy to understand and provides an estimate of the capital at risk. Portfolio theory provides the basic equations and these are modelled in the following sections.

SINGLE ASSET MODEL

This model is on the Single_Asset sheet. In order to measure the VaR for a single asset, the inputs are as shown in Figure 14.1.

The standard deviation is the daily volatility or fluctuation from the mean. If an asset is volatile, there is the opportunity to make large profits or

Figure 14.1 — Inputs

Standard Deviation	0.10000
Horizon Days	5.0 days
Total Period Days	20.0 days
Confidence Level	0.95
VaR Amount	1,000,000.0

Figure 14.2 — Normal distribution

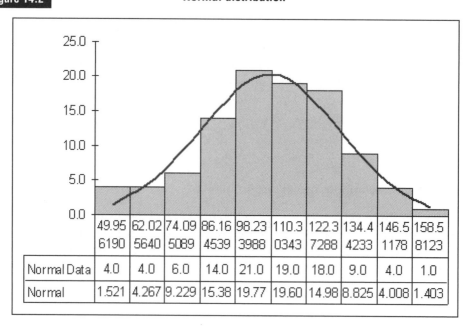

	49.95 6190	62.02 5640	74.09 5089	86.16 4539	98.23 3988	110.3 0343	122.3 7288	134.4 4233	146.5 1178	158.5 8123
Normal Data	4.0	4.0	6.0	14.0	21.0	19.0	18.0	9.0	4.0	1.0
Normal	1.521	4.267	9.229	15.38	19.77	19.60	14.98	8.825	4.008	1.403

large losses against an index. An institution needs to know both its return and also its risk position. The confidence level is 95 per cent and the VaR amount 1,000,000. The model assumes that returns on an asset are normally distributed and follow a classic bell curve (see Figure 14.2). The advantage is that much is known about the attributes of normal distributions.

With a normal distribution, most of the results are clustered around the mean and the standard deviation. Table 14.1 uses the NORMSDIST function to return the probability for a given standard deviation. Thus 0.5 deviations in either direction from the mean encompass 69 per cent of the observations.

Table 14.2 uses a NORMSINV function to return the number of standard deviations for a given probability. This provides a table of the probability or degree of confidence required against the number of standard deviations. Therefore 99 per cent confidence is equivalent to 2.33 standard deviations from the mean.

Table 14.1

Standard deviation	Percentage
0.2500	0.5987
0.5000	0.6915
1.0000	0.8413
1.5000	0.9332
1.6449	0.9500
2.0000	0.9772
2.5000	0.9938
3.0000	0.9987

Table 14.2

Standard deviation	Percentage
0.950	1.6449
0.955	1.6954
0.960	1.7507
0.965	1.8119
0.970	1.8808
0.975	1.9600
0.980	2.0537
0.985	2.1701
0.990	2.3263
0.995	2.5758
0.999	3.0903

Figure 14.3

Single asset VaR

Horizon Standard Deviation	0.05000
No of Standard Deviations	1.64485
Unit VaR	0.08224
Position Limit	12,159,507.4

The horizon standard deviation is derived from the formula:

*Daily standard deviation * Square root (Days/Period days)*
*0.05 * SQRT (5/20) = 0.05*

VaR increases with the time horizon and this is logical since the level of risk usually increases with time. The assumption is that the standard deviation increases with the square root of time, which is based on the random movement of financial asset prices.

The number of standard deviations is derived by the NORMSINV function. The unit VaR is the horizon multiplied by the number of standard deviations (see Figure 14.3).

*0.05 * 1.64485 = 0.08224*
Position limit = VaR amount/Unit VaR = 1,000,000/0.08224

Figure 14.4 shows the VaR percentage, position limit and the variance to the 95 per cent position. The percentage increases at higher confidence levels and therefore the position limit declines.

The chart and combo box allow the VaR percentage, position limit and variance to be plotted (see Figure 14.5). The workings at the bottom

Figure 14.4

Data table

Interval		0.005	
Confidence	**VaR %**	**Position Limit**	**Inc/(Dec)**
	0.0822	12,159,507.4	
0.950	0.0822	12,159,507.4	-
0.955	0.0848	11,797,002.9	(362,504.5)
0.960	0.0875	11,424,443.3	(735,064.1)
0.965	0.0906	11,038,411.7	(1,121,095.7)
0.970	0.0940	10,634,137.7	(1,525,369.7)
0.975	0.0980	10,204,585.6	(1,954,921.8)
0.980	0.1027	9,738,591.4	(2,420,916.0)
0.985	0.1085	9,216,492.2	(2,943,015.2)
0.990	0.1163	8,597,431.1	(3,562,076.3)
0.995	0.1288	7,764,719.6	(4,394,787.8)
0.999	0.1545	6,472,159.6	(5,687,347.8)

Audit trail for chart workings

Figure 14.5

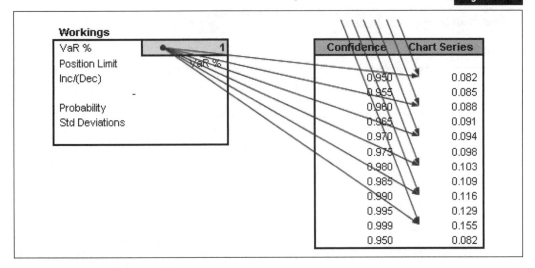

Workings	
VaR %	1
Position Limit	
Inc/(Dec)	
	-
Probability	
Std Deviations	

Confidence	Chart Series
0.950	0.082
0.955	0.085
0.960	0.088
0.965	0.091
0.970	0.094
0.975	0.098
0.980	0.103
0.985	0.109
0.990	0.116
0.995	0.129
0.999	0.155
0.950	0.082

transpose the labels from the table to form the text for the combo box. The chart workings use an OFFSET based on the cell link for the column offset to look up the data.

The chart demonstrates that the position limit declines from 13 million to 6.5 million based on a VaR amount of 1 million (see Figure 14.6). Similarly, the VaR percentages rise on the second chart with increasing confidence levels (see Figure 14.7).

Chart of position limit

Figure 14.6

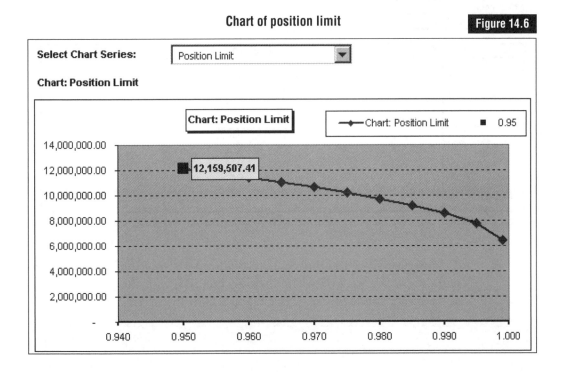

Select Chart Series: Position Limit ▼

Chart: Position Limit

Figure 14.7   **Chart of VaR percentages**

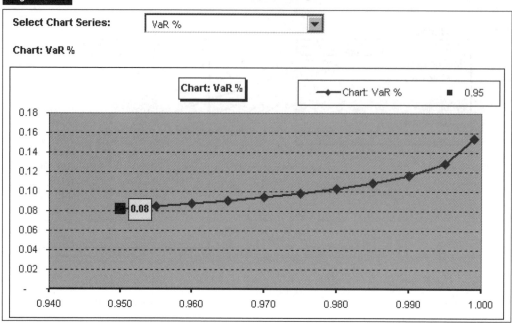

Figure 14.8   **Table of confidence level against horizon days**

VaR % Sensitivity Table to Confidence Level Across and Horizon Days Down

Interval Across	0.01
Interval Down	1.00

0.08	0.92	0.93	0.94	0.95	0.96	0.97	0.98
-	-	-	-	-	-	-	-
1.00	0.031	0.033	0.035	0.037	0.039	0.042	0.046
2.00	0.044	0.047	0.049	0.052	0.055	0.059	0.065
3.00	0.054	0.057	0.060	0.064	0.068	0.073	0.080
4.00	0.063	0.066	0.070	0.074	0.078	0.084	0.092
5.00	0.070	0.074	0.078	0.082	0.088	0.094	0.103
6.00	0.077	0.081	0.085	0.090	0.096	0.103	0.112
7.00	0.083	0.087	0.092	0.097	0.104	0.111	0.121
8.00	0.089	0.093	0.098	0.104	0.111	0.119	0.130
9.00	0.094	0.099	0.104	0.110	0.117	0.126	0.138
10.00	0.099	0.104	0.110	0.116	0.124	0.133	0.145

The sensitivity chart shows the relationship between the number of days and the confidence level where the VaR increases with the number of days and a higher confidence level (see Figure 14.8).

TWO ASSETS

The Two_Assets sheet shows a series of sections leading to a portfolio risk
measure. The calculations are:

- mean and standard deviation
- correlation
- VaR.

Mean and standard deviation

Figures 14.9 and 14.10 show two portfolios both with a mean of 8 per cent.

Two assets   **Figure 14.9**

(A) Volatility

Observation	Portfolio A	Portfolio B	Difference
1	8.25%	6.00%	0.02
2	7.95%	7.00%	0.01
3	7.90%	8.00%	(0.00)
4	8.00%	9.00%	(0.01)
5	7.90%	10.00%	(0.02)
Mean	**8.00%**	**8.00%**	**0.00%**
Standard deviation	**0.146%**	**1.581%**	**(1.435%)**

Two assets chart   **Figure 14.10**

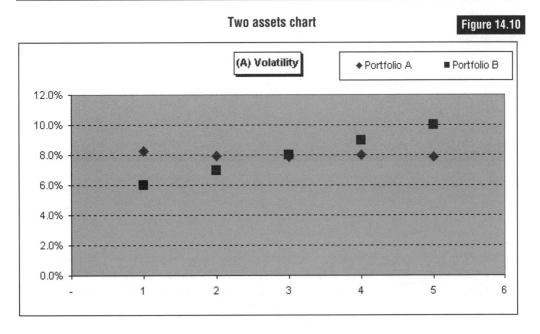

Portfolio A is close to the means on all observations and therefore the standard deviation is also low. If past volatility holds, then the future returns are likely to be close to the mean. Portfolio B has the same mean, but there is a greater variety in the observations and therefore the standard deviation is higher. It follows that a risk adverse investor would chose Portfolio A since the return overall is the same as Portfolio B and the volatility is lower. Thus they could be more sure of returning 8 per cent. Since the risk is higher on Portfolio B it follows that the VaR figure would be higher, in this case at 1.5 per cent.

Figures 14.11 and 14.12 show a mean observation of 5 per cent and then target returns starting below the target and rising above it. Using the standard deviation of 2 per cent, minus two standard deviations means that only 2.28 per cent of future observation will be below 1 per cent. On the other

---

Figure 14.11 **Normal distribution**

(B) Normal Distribution					
Number of Standard Deviations	1.645	(1.000)	-	1.000	1.645
Probability	-95.00%	15.87%	50.00%	84.13%	95.00%
Observation	**1**	**2**	**3**	**4**	**5**
Mean Return	5.00%				
Target Return	1.00%	3.00%	5.00%	7.00%	9.00%
Standard deviation	2.00%				
Number of standard deviations	(2.00)	(1.00)	-	1.00	2.00
Probability below Target Return	2.28%	15.87%	50.00%	84.13%	97.72%

Figure 14.12 **Cumulative distribution**

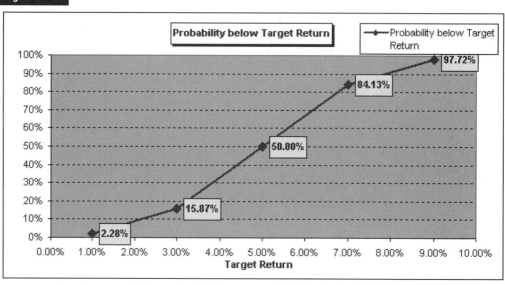

hand, at the mean 50 per cent of observations are likely to be below and 50 per cent above. At the confidence level of 95 per cent 1.64 standard deviations are needs while 2.32 are required for 99 per cent confidence.

The table uses the formula (Target return – Mean return)/Standard deviation to work out the number of standard deviations. The function NORMSDIST is used to compute the probabilities.

Correlation

Portfolio theory suggests that risk can be reduced through diversification. Lower risk means a lower VaR figure and encourages holding a variety of assets, taking risk and minimizing the downside through spreading risk. The diversification assists since all assets in a portfolio are unlikely to rise or fall to extreme values. Traders can reduce their own positions through hedging while contributing to the overall risk of the institution, and correlation shows the effect this has on the overall result.

Figure 14.13 shows a number of assets together with returns. The average returns are the same but correlation plots the degree to which they move together. Correlation values and what they signify are as follows:

- 1 = both sets of values move perfectly together in a positive manner;

Four assets   **Figure 14.13**

(C) Correlation between Assets

Observation	Asset 1	Asset 2	Asset 3	Asset 4
1	8.00%	26.00%	6.00%	20.00%
2	9.00%	21.00%	9.00%	6.00%
3	10.00%	10.00%	10.00%	6.00%
4	11.00%	12.00%	12.00%	20.00%
5	12.00%	9.00%	13.00%	6.00%
6	13.00%	6.00%	13.00%	6.00%
7	14.00%	5.00%	14.00%	20.00%
8	15.00%	3.00%	15.00%	8.00%
Average return	11.50%	11.50%	11.50%	11.50%
Correlation with Company 1		(0.9270)	0.9602	(0.1155)
Standard deviation	2.45%	8.05%	2.98%	7.07%
Required VaR	95.00%			
Number of standard deviations	1.6449			
Volatility or VaR at 5.00%	4.03%	13.25%	4.90%	11.63%

- 0 = no relationship between the data sets;
- −1 = both sets of values move perfectly in a negative linear manner.

In the example shown in Figure 14.13, Asset 2 moves negatively to Asset 1 which implies that when the former is doing well, the latter will perform badly and vice versa. In terms of value, change would have a neutral effect on a portfolio and VaR would be low. This conclusion ignores other factors such as overall market sentiment since steep falls in certain shares or sectors have a consequent effect on the whole market.

Asset 3 is positively correlated and therefore there will be little positive gain from diversification. Both stocks appear to move together and so a change in price for one will be matched by a similar change in the other stock. Asset 4 shows no strong relationship with correlation around zero. There will be some benefit from diversification but this will not be as great as if the correlation were more strongly negative.

The formula for cell D84 uses the function CORREL for correlation:

```
=CORREL(D74:D81,$C$74:$C$81)
```

The formulas for covariance and correlation are:

$$Covariance = [1/No\ of\ observations]$$
$$* Sum[(A - Mean\ A) * (B - Mean\ B)]$$
$$Correlation = Covariance/(Std\ Dev\ A * Std\ Dev\ B)$$

Figure 14.14	Correlation

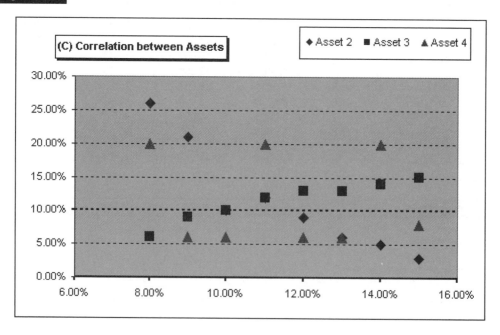

The VaR calculation is the standard deviation multiplied by the number of standard deviations for the confidence level of 95 per cent. Figure 14.14 shows the strong negative correlation on Asset 2 as a declining linear series while the positive correlation for Asset 3 is plotted as rising linear trend.

Portfolio VaR

The VaR for the whole portfolio required the standard deviation for the whole portfolio. Figure 14.15 brings forward the data from the last section for the volatility and correlation coefficients. The weightings for Asset 1 are inputs to show portfolios composed of 50 per cent of Asset 1 and a balance of Assets 2, 3 and 4. The first step is to compute the portfolio standard deviation. The formula is:

$$Variance = (((W\_A)^2)*(SDev\_A)^2 + ((W\_B)^2)*(SDev\_B)^2$$
$$+2*W\_A*SDev\_A*W\_B*SDev\_B*Correlation)$$

where:

W_A	= weighting A
$SDev\_A$	= standard deviation A
W_B	= weighting B

Portfolio VaR

Figure 14.15

(D) Portfolio VaR

	Asset 1	Asset 2	Asset 3	Asset 4
Total Amount	**1,000,000.00**			
Asset 1 Weighting	**50.00%**	**50.00%**	**50.00%**	**50.00%**
Standard Deviation	2.45%			
Second security				
Standard Deviation	2.45%	8.05%	2.98%	7.07%
Individual VaR	4.03%	13.25%	4.90%	11.63%
Weighting	50.00%	50.00%	50.00%	50.00%
Correlation coefficient	1.0000	(0.9270)	0.9602	(0.1155)
Portfolio variance	0.06%	0.09%	0.07%	0.13%
Standard Deviation	2.45%	2.93%	2.69%	3.61%
Number of Standard Deviations	1.6449			
Diversified VaR	4.03%	4.82%	4.42%	5.93%
Amount	40,290.52	48,156.38	44,179.81	59,306.04
Undiversified VaR	4.03%	8.64%	4.46%	7.83%
Amount	40,290.52	86,378.52	44,621.46	78,299.61
Variance	-	(38,222.14)	(441.65)	(18,993.58)

| Figure 14.16 | **Portfolio mix with Assets 1 and 2** |

(E) Data Table: Diversified VaR against Undiversified VaR using Asset 2

Interval Across				10.0%		

	Diversified VaR	Amount	Undiversified VaR	Amount	Variance
	4.82%	48,156.38	8.64%	86,378.52	(38,222.14)
0.0%	13.25%	132,466.52	13.25%	132,466.52	-
10.0%	11.55%	115,495.02	12.32%	123,248.92	(7,753.90)
20.0%	9.86%	98,550.12	11.40%	114,031.32	(15,481.20)
30.0%	8.16%	81,648.38	10.48%	104,813.72	(23,165.34)
40.0%	6.48%	64,823.57	9.56%	95,596.12	(30,772.55)
50.0%	4.82%	48,156.38	8.64%	86,378.52	(38,222.14)
60.0%	3.19%	31,894.89	7.72%	77,160.92	(45,266.03)
70.0%	1.72%	17,228.95	6.79%	67,943.32	(50,714.37)
80.0%	1.26%	12,557.65	5.87%	58,725.72	(46,168.07)
90.0%	2.45%	24,491.99	4.95%	49,508.12	(25,016.13)
100.0%	4.03%	40,290.52	4.03%	40,290.52	-

$SDev\_B$ = standard deviation B
$Correlation$ = correlation between the two assets

The portfolio standard deviation is multiplied by the number of standard deviations required and then by the total amount to derive the portfolio VaR. The undiversified VaR is simply the individual VaR multiplied by their weights. For example in cell D135:

```
=$C$125*D120+D125*D126
=[4.03% * 50%] + [13.25% * 50%] = 8.64%
```

The first column of Figure 14.15 had the same figure of 4.03 per cent since this assumes only Asset 1. The benefits from diversification appear in the next three columns where Asset 2 with the negative correlation obtains a reduced figure, whereas Asset 3 with positive correlation yields little benefit between the diversified and undiversified figures.

Figure 14.16 demonstrates how the risk increases as the more risky Asset 2 appears in the portfolio. The amounts on the left are the percentages of Asset 1. At a split of 20 : 80, diversified VaR increases to 9.86 per cent from 4.82 per cent.

THREE ASSET PORTFOLIO

The formula for standard deviation becomes more complex with more than two assets and it is easier to use matrix methods to multiply out the correlations using the variance–covariance approach. This uses the function

MMULT to multiply matrices as an array. Try the example shown in Figure 14.17. Then to calculate the product using the MMULT function (see Figure 14.18) and enter both arrays and lock them with $ symbols. Copy across and down to form the four squares for the result (see Figure 14.19) and then Control, Shift and Enter at the same time to enter the function.

The Three Asset sheet starts with an example of three assets together with their weightings and standard deviations. The correlation is shown as a matrix such that A : B is 0.6, A : C is 0.5 and B : C is 0.3 (see Figure 14.20). The number of standard deviations relates to the confidence level of 99 per cent.

Matrices A and B

Figure 14.17

A	2	4
	6	8

B	10	12
	14	16

MMULT function

Figure 14.18

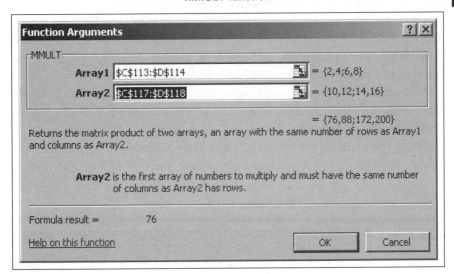

Function Arguments

MMULT

Array1 $C$113:$D$114 = {2,4;6,8}

Array2 $C$117:$D$118 = {10,12;14,16}

= {76,88;172,200}

Returns the matrix product of two arrays, an array with the same number of rows as Array1 and columns as Array2.

Array2 is the first array of numbers to multiply and must have the same number of columns as Array2 has rows.

Formula result =   76

Help on this function   OK   Cancel

MMULT result

Figure 14.19

Result	
76	88
172	200

Figure 14.20	Three Asset input

Value of portfolio	5,000,000		
Confidence level	99.00%		
Asset	A	B	C
Standard deviation	5.00%	2.00%	3.00%
Weighting	45.00%	25.00%	30.00%

No of standard deviations	2.3263

Correlation matrix		A	B	C
	A	1	0.6	0.5
	B	0.6	1	0.3
	C	0.5	0.3	1

The first stage is to multiply the matrices for standard deviation and correlation using MMULT in the cells VC below. The formula is as below with the outer brackets denoting the array function:

$$\{=MMULT(\$D\$21:\$F\$23,\$G\$21:\$I\$23)\}$$

The VC matrix is then multiplied by the standard deviation matrix to form the VCV or Variance–Covariance matrix (see Figure 14.21). The covariance determines the relationship between two data sets.

The third step is to multiply the VCV matrix by the weightings matrix and the answer in this example is 0.1 per cent (see Figure 14.22). Standard deviation is the square root and the VaR the product multiplied by the number of standard deviations, 2.32.

An alternative approach would be to calculate the undiversified VaR and then to include the correlation to calculate the diversified VaR. The undiversified VaR assumes the correlation is equal to one. The first stage is to multiply the matrices for the weightings and the standard deviation as per WV in Figure 14.23. The standard deviation is the sum of the elements and

Figure 14.21	VCV matrix

Portfolio VaR using Matrices		S Deviation (V)			Correlation		
		A	B	C	A	B	C
Variance * correlation	A	5.00%	-	-	1.00	0.60	0.50
	B	-	2.00%	-	0.60	1.00	0.30
	C	-	-	3.00%	0.50	0.30	1.00

		VC			VCV		
		A	B	C	A	B	C
VC * V	A	5.00%	3.00%	2.50%	0.25%	0.06%	0.08%
	B	1.20%	2.00%	0.60%	0.06%	0.04%	0.02%
	C	1.50%	0.90%	3.00%	0.08%	0.02%	0.09%

Portfolio VaR

Figure 14.22

	A	B	C
Weighting * VCV	0.15%	0.04%	0.07%

WVCVW	0.10%
Standard deviation	3.13%
VaR	7.27%
Value at risk	363,526.61

Weightings	
A	0.45
B	0.25
C	0.30

Undiversified VaR

Figure 14.23

Undiversified VaR

	Weightings			Standard Deviation		
	A	B	C	A	B	C
Weightings	0.45	0.25	0.30	5.00%	-	-
				-	2.00%	-
				-	-	3.00%
WV	2.25%	0.50%	0.90%			

Standard Deviation	3.65%
VaR	8.49%
VaR Amount	424,558.33

the VaR is the standard deviation multiplied by 2.32. The VaR is simply the amount multiplied by 7.27 per cent.

To derive the diversified VaR, you multiply the WV matrix by the correlation matrix and this results in the UC matrix. You multiply out the UC matrix by the WV matrix using the function SUMPRODUCT as each matrix has only one axis and the square root of this is the standard deviation. The standard deviation is then multiplied by the confidence and the amount to produce the VaR amount. The figure is the same as that produced by the first method. Again this shows the benefits of diversification since the VaR reduces from 8.49 per cent to 7.27 per cent (see Figure 14.24).

Problems

The normal distribution does not provide all the answers and basic VaR models cannot capture all the facets of market risk. Some of the problems are as follows.

- Markets do not always behave normally. Empirical data suggests that markets deviate consistently from normal distributions. There are more observations clustered around the mean and there are more extreme values possible. This is 'excess kurtosis' and causes problems with predicting values especially over short time horizons.

Figure 14.24   **Diversified VaR**

Diversified VaR

-		A	B	C
Correlation matrix	A	1.00	0.60	0.50
	B	0.60	1.00	0.30
	C	0.50	0.30	1.00

Undiversified * Corr	3.00%	2.12%	2.18%

SumProduct	0.10%
Standard deviation	3.13%
Diversified VaR	7.27%
VaR Amount	363,526.61

- Normal distributions assume randomness and do not take account of the 'herd' mentality. When markets are falling there is often extra pressure to sell and this pushes the market more quickly to extremes.

- Liquidity and operational risks are not included in the calculation.

- Volatility is not constant since the future does not exactly equal the past. Whilst the models suggest that the future will follow average volatility, empirical evidence appears to show periods where volatility changes. This again has an effect on VaR, especially in the area of options pricing where the Black–Scholes formula prices options accordingly to past volatility.

SUMMARY

This chapter summarizes the main elements of value at risk (VaR) as a statistical measure of risk exposure. The measure attempts to provide a figure of potential losses over a time period at a given confidence level using as its basis normal distribution curves. The tool has assumed greater importance as banks try to allocate capital more efficiently and regulators seek to understand the individual and collective risk positions built up by institutions. The model builds up positions with one, two and three assets and shows the use of different methods and array functions in calculating each of the parameters of standard deviation and VaR.

Credit value at risk

Files: FT4_15_01.xls and FT4_15_02.xls

INTRODUCTION

Credit value at risk (VaR) is the application of value at risk methodology to credit portfolios. Institutions traditionally have placed limits on individual clients in an effort to manage overall exposure. Portfolio managers similarly need to know just how much risk is contained in a portfolio of deals. In this context:

- risk can be measured and analyzed through probabilities and distributions;
- uncertainty consists of random events, which cannot easily be measured.

The advances in VaR methodology have shown that it is possible to produce models to quantify risk and assist managers in identifying potential areas of risk. While credit modelling does not replace the intuitive judgement of experienced credit managers, a VaR approach may improve the understanding of marginal credit risk. Credit VaR allows an organization to consolidate credit risk across a company, industry or sector and provides an amended VaR statement based on probabilities due to:

- upgrades in value – improvement in the credit status of the underlying credit;
- downgrades in value – deterioration in the credit rating of the underlying credit;
- default – ultimate failure of the underlying credit.

The above takes into account that credit may deteriorate before ultimate failure. The aims of the method are:

- defining benchmarks for credit risk measurement as a common point of measurement for comparing different sources and measures of risk;
- promoting credit risk transparency and improved risk management tools for improving understanding and market liquidity;
- encouraging a regulatory capital framework that more closely reflects the economic risk associated with credit instruments;
- complementing other elements of credit risk management decisions, for example 'soft' factors.

With more in-depth understanding of a sector and its clients, an institution may be in a better position to predict economic downturns and the subsequent non-performing loans. This concentrates risk and leaves an institution open to cyclical downturns and therefore the ideal situation is to build up specialist knowledge and then diversify risk using financial instruments. VaR methods identify:

- loans that produce the most risk;
- areas where credit derivatives can reduce the overall risk.

Institutions are now faced with taking more complex lending decisions. For example:

- credit spreads have narrowed during the 1990s and banks now retain a greater percentage of their liabilities on their own books without syndication;
- the increase in the number and complexity of financial instruments has created uncertain and market sensitive exposures, which require more 'management' than traditional bonds;
- the increase in high yield 'junk' bonds and emerging markets with globalization is a significant factor;
- the deregulation and proliferation of institutions such as insurance companies offering credit.

Using VaR methodology is therefore a framework for evaluating credit derivatives and other credit transactions on a portfolio basis to provide a monetary value for risk.

PORTFOLIO APPROACH

Credit VaR is a framework for evaluating credit derivatives and other credit transactions on a portfolio basis. This is important for two reasons:

- credit risks for each client across a whole portfolio are included;
- correlations of credit quality are taken into account.

The benefits of diversification can be taken into account and quantified. This allows managers to quantify concentrations of risk to individual clients or groups of correlated clients, which can be mitigated through diversification or hedging. Furthermore, portfolios can be viewed along different dimensions such as industry, rating, country, type of instrument, etc.

The measures include both expected losses and VaR. This is uncertainty or volatility of value due to changes in client quality across an entire portfolio and for marginal transactions, which occurs due to changes in credit events or 'migrations'.

Market risk and VaR are significantly different to credit risk. Market distributions are usually reasonably symmetrical and exhibit bell-shaped or normal distributions. Credit portfolio values change little on upgrades and downgrades, but can be substantial on default. This remote possibility gives rise to skewed returns with long downside tails rather than standard normal distributions as shown in Figure 15.1.

Market VaR and other risk models look to a specific horizon and estimate risk across a distribution of estimated market outcomes. Credit VaR constructs a distribution of value given different credit outcomes. The challenge of modelling is not easy in practice since there are two distinct differences:

- Long tails, as in Figure 15.1, where there is a remote possibility of a big loss. More information is needed in addition to the mean (expected value) and standard deviation (volatility).

- Correlations in credit portfolios cannot be directly observed and must be derived indirectly from other sources.

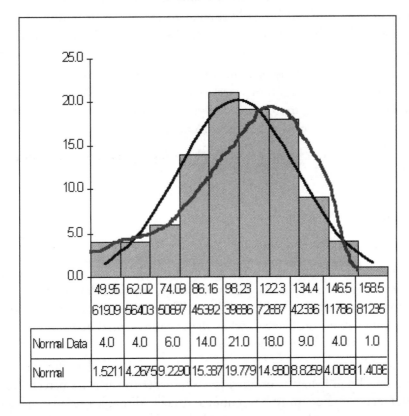

Credit distribution

Figure 15.1

	49.95 61909	62.02 56403	74.09 50897	86.16 45392	98.23 39886	122.3 72887	134.4 42336	146.5 11786	158.5 81235
Normal Data	4.0	4.0	6.0	14.0	21.0	18.0	9.0	4.0	1.0
Normal	1.5211	4.2675	9.2290	15.387	19.779	14.980	8.8259	4.0088	1.4038

OVERVIEW OF COMPONENTS

As stated, Credit Metrics estimates portfolio VaR due to credit events that include upgrades, downgrades and default. The information comes from long-term estimates of migration in order to avoid bias and it is based on probability. This section provides an overview of the components:

- exposures and their distribution;
- VaR framework;
- correlations between individual exposures.

Components

The components are:

- Calculation of different exposure profiles and changes for each exposure type on a comparable basis.
- Derivation of the volatility of value due to credit quality migrations for each individual obligor (VaR framework). This is derived from a transition matrix where each migration results in a change in value. Each value outcome is weighted by its likelihood to create a distribution of value across each credit state from which the asset's expected value and volatility are calculated.
- Calculation of volatility of value due to credit quality migrations across a portfolio and estimation of correlation between the obligors. Individual value distributions are combined to yield a portfolio value, which requires the estimated correlation between the assets.

The sections below explain the principles using a portfolio model with one and then two bonds.

Outputs

The outputs of the model are:

- Standard deviation – this is the standard measure of symmetrical dispersion around the mean. As discussed earlier, standard deviation may not capture the full range of possibilities. The upside may be one standard deviation above the average, while the downside could be many standard deviations below the average.
- Percentile levels – these demonstrate the possibility that the portfolio value will fall below a specified level. In order to calculate percentiles, a full range of values must be computed, usually through a simulation technique such as Monte Carlo simulation. This allows a model to run

through many scenarios and produce either a histogram or cumulative probability graph of possible outcomes.

SINGLE ASSET

This section follows the main calculations with a single asset in the Excel file called FT4_15_01.xls.

Estimating credit exposure amounts

Many different types of instruments encompass credit risk where exposures vary. Variable exposures can change in a way that is related to upgrades and downgrades or due to non-credit-related market moves. These include receivables, bonds and loans. Therefore the features of the model are:

- likelihood (possibility) of credit quality changes;
- changes in value assessed against an exposure amount in the event of each credit quality change.

Receivables are non-interest-bearing debt or trade credit where the exposure is typically less than one year. The exposure on a floating rate note or loan will always be close to face value (par) but the value of fixed-rate bonds and loans moves with market interest rates. The risk horizon is the present value of the remaining coupons and principle and here one can use the yield curve for the category. Figure 15.2 shows yield curves for different credit categories denoted by credit ratings.

Estimating credit quality migrations

There are three key steps to calculating the volatility of value in a stand-alone credit exposure:

- estimating credit quality migrations from one grade to another using a transition matrix;
- estimating changes of value upon credit quality migration across grades;
- computing the distribution of resultant bond values.

Estimating credit quality migrations is based on upgrades, downgrades and defaults, which is represented by a transition matrix (see Figure 15.3). This shows the possibility of moving from one ratings band to another: for example, there is a 7.70 per cent chance that a BB will upgrade to BBB within a year. These matrices are published by the ratings agencies as a result of observing historical patterns and then applying smoothing techniques.

Figure 15.2   **Interest rates**

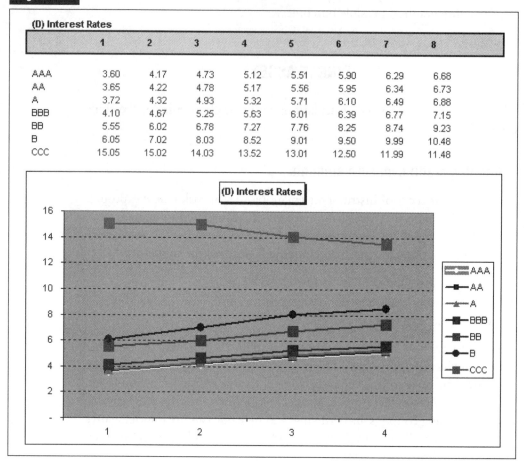

(D) Interest Rates

	1	2	3	4	5	6	7	8
AAA	3.60	4.17	4.73	5.12	5.51	5.90	6.29	6.68
AA	3.65	4.22	4.78	5.17	5.56	5.95	6.34	6.73
A	3.72	4.32	4.93	5.32	5.71	6.10	6.49	6.88
BBB	4.10	4.67	5.25	5.63	6.01	6.39	6.77	7.15
BB	5.55	6.02	6.78	7.27	7.76	8.25	8.74	9.23
B	6.05	7.02	8.03	8.52	9.01	9.50	9.99	10.48
CCC	15.05	15.02	14.03	13.52	13.01	12.50	11.99	11.48

These tables are on the Data sheet.

Estimating changes in value at the end of a forecast period involves re-valuation, it follows, for each credit state:

- upgrade
- downgrade
- default.

In default, the recovery rate depends on the seniority class, but there is great variation (volatility) within a class, as Figure 15.4 suggests. For upgrades and downgrades, the new value is simply the present value of the cash flows at the revised interest rates or yield. Thus, as interest rates go down the value of a bond rises.

Cumulative values show the varying experience of default between the different credit categories. The possibility of a CCC rating defaulting rises from 20 per cent to 45 per cent over a ten-year period (see Figure 15.5).

Transition matrix

Figure 15.3

(A) Transition Matrix

	AAA	AA	A	BBB	BB	B	CCC	Default	Check
AAA	90.80	8.30	0.70	0.10	0.10	-	-	-	100.00
AA	0.70	90.70	7.80	0.60	0.10	0.10	-	-	100.00
A	0.10	2.30	91.10	5.50	0.70	0.30		-	100.00
BBB	-	0.30	6.00	86.90	5.30	1.20	0.10	0.20	100.00
BB	-	0.10	0.70	7.70	80.50	8.80	1.00	1.20	100.00
B	-	0.10	0.20	0.40	6.50	83.50	4.10	5.20	100.00
CCC	0.20	-	0.20	1.30	2.40	11.20	64.90	19.80	100.00
Default									-
Yield	4.00	4.50	4.70	4.90	5.00	12.00	14.00	-	
Recovery	53.00	53.00	51.00	51.00	38.00	32.00	17.00	-	
Uncertainty	26.00	26.00	25.00	25.00	24.00	20.00	11.00		

Default

Figure 15.4

(B) Seniority Class

	Mean %	Standard deviation %
Senior secured	53.00	26.00
Senior unsecured	51.00	25.00
Senior subordinated	38.00	24.00
Subordinated	32.00	20.00
Junior subordinated	17.00	11.00

Computing the distribution of values consists of a probability-weighted value and standard deviation. Figure 15.6 shows a BBB bond together with its transition matrix and the bond values.

Single model

The sheet called 'Single' models the values starting with these inputs. The rating uses a combo box to highlight the available grades (see Figure 15.7). The redemption is 100 and the bond has four years to run and on expiry the final coupon and principal is payable. The coupon rate is 6 per cent.

The value of the bond is calculated using an interest rate table on the Data sheet (see Figure 15.8) and the values are looked up using an OFFSET function:

```
=OFFSET(Data!C68,Base!$C$115,0)
```

The individual values are present valued and added to complete the value of the bond

```
=PV(G22/100,B22,0,-F22,0)
```

Figure 15.5   Cumulative default

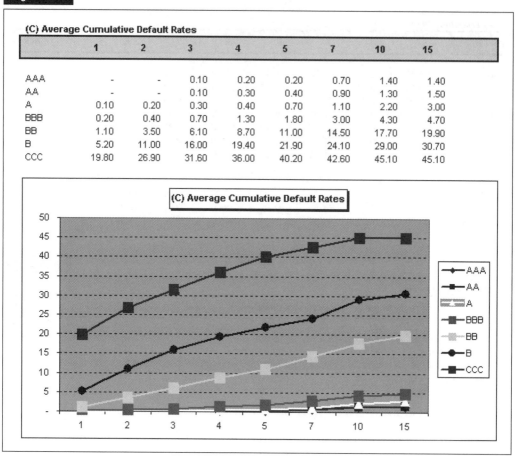

(C) Average Cumulative Default Rates

	1	2	3	4	5	7	10	15
AAA	-	-	0.10	0.20	0.20	0.70	1.40	1.40
AA	-	-	0.10	0.30	0.40	0.90	1.30	1.50
A	0.10	0.20	0.30	0.40	0.70	1.10	2.20	3.00
BBB	0.20	0.40	0.70	1.30	1.80	3.00	4.30	4.70
BB	1.10	3.50	6.10	8.70	11.00	14.50	17.70	19.90
B	5.20	11.00	16.00	19.40	21.90	24.10	29.00	30.70
CCC	19.80	26.90	31.60	36.00	40.20	42.60	45.10	45.10

Figure 15.6   Distribution of value

Distribution of Value

BBB

AAA	AA	A	BBB	BB	B	CCC	Default
-	0.30	6.00	86.90	5.30	1.20	0.10	0.20
109.35	109.17	108.64	107.53	102.01	98.09	83.63	51.00

Inputs

Figure 15.7

Rating:	BBB ▼
Required Confidence %:	95.000
Issue Date:	1-Jan-98
Settlement:	1-Jan-03
Maturity 4 Years:	1-Jan-07
Redemption Value:	100.000
Coupon %:	6.000
Yield to Maturity:	4.900
Price:	0.000
Bond Seniority:	Senior unsecured ▼
Coupons per Annum:	Annual ▼
Basis:	US (NASD) 30/360 ▼

Interest rates

Figure 15.8

(D) Interest Rates	1	2	3	4	5	6	7	8
AAA	3.60	4.17	4.73	5.12	5.51	5.90	6.29	6.68
AA	3.65	4.22	4.78	5.17	5.56	5.95	6.34	6.73
A	3.72	4.32	4.93	5.32	5.71	6.10	6.49	6.88
BBB	4.10	4.67	5.25	5.63	6.01	6.39	6.77	7.15
BB	5.55	6.02	6.78	7.27	7.76	8.25	8.74	9.23
B	6.05	7.02	8.03	8.52	9.01	9.50	9.99	10.48
CCC	15.05	15.02	14.03	13.52	13.01	12.50	11.99	11.48

The probabilities and yields are derived from the transition matrix on the Data sheet using OFFSET functions. The easiest way of calculating the bond values for each credit state is to use a data table based on the number of the rating. The inputs area uses a combo box to generate an index number for the bond. The workings area contains the data table which uses cell C115 as the column input and this approach saves the individual calculation of each of the values (see Figure 15.9).

```
{=TABLE(,C115)}
```

The calculation of standard deviation is thus shown in Figure 15.10.

The distribution of values shows the distinctive 'fat tail' represented by the 51 per cent recovery on default and the relatively small upside to the right of the BBB rating (see Figure 15.11).

Figure 15.9

Projected values

	A	B	C	D	E
113					
114		**Bond Value**			107.53
115		AAA	4	1	109.35
116		AA	BBB	2	109.17
117		A		3	108.64
118		BBB		4	107.53
119		BB		5	102.01
120		B		6	98.09
121		CCC		7	83.63
122		Default			
123					

Figure 15.10

Calculation of standard deviation for a single bond

Number	Year End Rating	Probability %	Yield / Default Recovery	New Bond Value plus Coupon	Probability Weighted Value	Difference of Value from Mean	Probability Weighted Diff. ^2
Price							
1	AAA	-	4.00	109.3529	-	2.2934	-
2	AA	0.30	4.50	109.1724	0.3275	2.1129	0.0134
3	A	6.00	4.70	108.6430	6.5186	1.5835	0.1505
4	BBB	86.90	4.90	107.5309	93.4444	0.4715	0.1932
5	BB	5.30	5.00	102.0064	5.4063	(5.0531)	1.3533
6	B	1.20	12.00	98.0859	1.1770	(8.9736)	0.9663
7	CCC	0.10	14.00	83.6258	0.0836	(23.4337)	0.5491
8	Default	0.20	51.00	51.0000	0.1020	(56.0595)	6.2853
		100.00		107.5309	107.0595		9.5111

Output

The probability-weighted value is the value at the interest rate for the grade multiplied by the probability of moving to the relevant credit state. The variance is a probability-weighted difference squared, which is 9.51 (see Figure 15.12). The standard deviation is the square root of the variance at 3.08.

The input confidence level was 95 per cent and therefore the number of standard deviations is 1.6449. This uses the NORMSINV function:

```
=NORMSINV(1-(D53/100))
```

The standard deviation is multiplied by 1.6449 and subtracted from the

Distribution of values

Figure 15.11

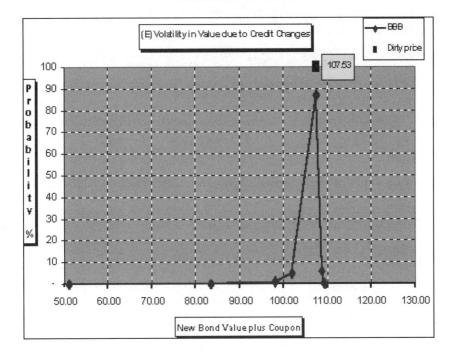

Standard deviation

Figure 15.12

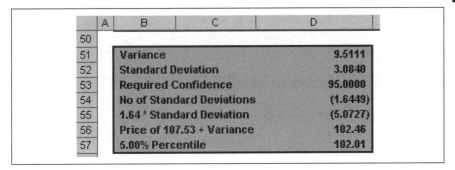

	A	B	C	D
50				
51		Variance		9.5111
52		Standard Deviation		3.0840
53		Required Confidence		95.0000
54		No of Standard Deviations		(1.6449)
55		1.64 * Standard Deviation		(5.0727)
56		Price of 107.53 + Variance		102.46
57		5.00% Percentile		102.01

current bond value of 107.53. This means that using standard deviation as the measure, there is a 5 per cent risk that the value of the bond will fall to 102.46.

It has already been stated that the distribution is not a normal bell curve. The 5 per cent percentile is found by looking up the rows of probabilities from the bottom of the table until 5 per cent is reached. In this case, the probabilities cross 5 per cent at BB, which gives a value of 102.01. This is lower than the standard deviation derived figure confirming the long downside credit tails.

Column M adds the probabilities in column D starting with the 0.20

default (see Figure 15.13). The formula matches the required confidence of 5 per cent to the list in the range M40 : M47. This is declining so the flag is set to −1 in the function.

```
=MATCH(100-$D$53,$M$40:$M$47,-1)
```

The MATCH function finds the answer five and this is used as the row offset in the OFFSET function starting at cell F39. The answer returns as 102.01. Standard deviation overstates the value since it ignores the tail of default and there is a variance of 0.45 between the two results.

Estimating credit quality correlations and calculating portfolio risk

With one bond, there are only eight observable states. With two bonds, the number rises to 64 (8^2) and with N bonds the number is 8^N. To derive the portfolio values, you have to estimate the probabilities of observing the combinations of values. This would be simple if all the values were independent but, in the real world, the outcomes are not completely independent of each other. The correlations have to be estimated from empirical data such as actual rating and default correlations. The next section shows the modelling of a two-bond portfolio.

Figure 15.13   **Cumulative probabilities**

	A	B	C	D	E	F	M
36							
37		Number	Year End Rating	Probability %	Yield / Default Recovery	New Bond Value plus Coupon	Percentiles
38							
39		Price					
40		1	AAA	-	4.00	109.3529	100.00
41		2	AA	0.30	4.50	109.1724	100.00
42		3	A	6.00	4.70	108.6430	99.70
43		4	BBB	86.90	4.90	107.5309	93.70
44		5	BB	5.30	5.00	102.0064	6.80
45		6	B	1.20	12.00	98.0859	1.50
46		7	CCC	0.10	14.00	83.6258	0.30
47		8	Default	0.20	51.00	51.0000	0.20
48							
49				100.00		107.5309	102.01

TWO-BOND PORTFOLIO

The simple analysis above needs to be extended to portfolios containing many individual exposures. This worked example uses two bonds with these characteristics in the file FT4_15_02.xls:

- Bond #1: BBB rated, senior unsecured, 6% annual coupon, five-year maturity;
- Bond #2: A rated, senior unsecured, 5% annual coupon, three-year maturity.

The inputs are shown in Figure 15.14.

The process initially follows the same pattern as the single bond and then combines the values using joint probabilities. The steps are:

- estimating credit quality migrations using transition matrices;
- estimating changes of value upon credit quality migration;
- computing distribution of bond values;
- calculation of all possible portfolio values;
- calculation of joint probabilities;
- summation of a portfolio value;
- outputs – standard deviation and 5 per cent threshold value.

Bond prices

The model calculates the prices of two bonds using the interest rates and

Inputs for two bonds

Figure 15.14

Reference	BBB	A
Amount:	1,000.0	1,000.0
Issue Date:	1-Jan-03	1-Jan-03
Settlement:	1-Jan-03	1-Jan-03
Maturity 5 Years:	1-Jan-08	1-Jan-06
Redemption Value:	100.000	100.000
Coupon %:	6.000	5.000
Yield to Maturity:	4.900	4.760
Price:	0.000	0.000
Required Confidence:	95.000	
Correlation:	0.000	
Bond Rating:	BBB ▼	A ▼
Coupons per Annum:	Annual ▼	Annual ▼
Basis:	US (NASD) ▼	US (NASD) ▼

transition matrix on the Data sheet (see Figure 15.15). Controls are used as on the single bond to ease the inputs and the workings are at the bottom of the schedule. More output is available and the schedule makes use of more advanced functions such as DURATION, MDURATION, COUPON-DAYSNC, COUPONNCD and ACCRINT.

Estimating credit quality migrations and changes in value

Figure 15.16 picks out the probabilities for each rating and then derives a probability-weighted bond value. The standard deviation at the 95 per cent level and the 95 per cent percentile are then calculated. This repeats the calculations in the previous section.

Using the chart in the overview section, the joint likelihood in the credit quality co-movements must be calculated. The objective is to show the probability-weighted value of the portfolio based on the transition matrices and subsequent changes in value. For simplicity, correlation is not included and is assumed to be zero. This means that movement in the rating of one bond has no bearing on the movement in price of another bond. In reality, price movements may be correlated and combinations of bonds lead to a reduced risk (volatility or standard deviation) for an optimized return.

Figure 15.15			Bond price calculations	

(A) Price			Units $'000	
Weighting	50.00	50.00		
Clean price	104.7756	100.6565	Present value of coupons and principal	
Coupon days	0 days	0 days	Days in this coupon period	
Accrued interest at 6%	0.0000	0.0000	Simple interest based on number of days in coupon period	
Dirty price	104.7756	100.6565	Clean price plus accrued interest	
Price amount	104,776	100,657	Nominal value multiplied by amount	
(B) Yield				
Current yield	5.7265	4.9674	Coupon/Price	
Adjusted coupon yield	4.8148	4.7500	[Coupon + ((Redemption-Clean)/Years to Maturity)] / [Clean]	
Yield to maturity	4.9000	4.7600	Calculated yield	
(C) Duration				
Duration	4.4790 yrs	2.8599 yrs	Maturity: 5.00 years	
Modified duration	4.2698 yrs	2.7300 yrs	Duration / [1+(Yield / No of Coupons)] = Slope of series	
Change in price per 0.5%	(2.2368)	(1.3739)	Duration * Price * [1/1+Int] * 1%	
(D) Dates				
Days to next coupon	360 days	360 days	Days remaining in this coupon period	
Interest remaining	(6.0000)	(5.0000)	Interest still to be accrued in period	
Ex dividend price	98.7756	95.6565	Clean price minus interest remaining in period	
Next coupon date	1-Jan-04	1-Jan-04		
No of remaining coupons	5	3	Number until maturity	
Total coupon amount paid	0.0000	0.0000	Coupon amounts pain since issue date	
(E) Portfolio				
Price amount	205,432		Weighted amounts	
Duration	3.6857 yrs			
Modified duration	3.5153 yrs			

Bond BBB

Figure 15.16

Bond BBB

Number	Year End Rating	Probability %	Yield / Default Recovery	New Bond Value plus Coupon	Probability Weighted Value	Difference of Value from Mean	Probability Weighted Difference	Percentage Probability	Standard Deviation
Price				104.7756					
1	AAA	-	4.00	108.9036	-	4.5652	-	100.00%	-
2	AA	0.30	4.50	106.5850	0.3198	2.2465	0.0151	100.00%	-
3	A	6.00	4.70	105.4044	6.3243	1.0659	0.0682	99.70%	2.75
4	BBB	86.90	4.90	104.7756	91.0500	0.4371	0.1661	93.70%	1.53
5	BB	5.30	5.00	104.3295	5.5295	(0.0090)	0.0000	6.80%	(1.49)
6	B	1.20	12.00	78.3713	0.9405	(25.9671)	8.0915	1.50%	(2.17)
7	CCC	0.10	14.00	72.5354	0.0725	(31.8031)	1.0114	0.30%	(2.75)
8	Default	0.20	51.00	51.0000	0.1020	(53.3385)	5.6900	0.20%	(2.88)
		100.00		104.7756	104.3385		15.0423		

Variance	15.0423
Standard Deviation	3.8784
Required Confidence	95.0000
No of Standard Deviatic	(1.6449)
1.64 * Standard Deviatio	(6.3795)
Price of 100.66 + Varianc	98.40
5.00% Percentile	104.33

The standard deviation and 5 per cent level are calculated using the same method as in the first section (see Figures 15.16 and 15.17).

Calculation of all possible portfolio values

Following the calculations for individual bonds, the values can be added

Bond A

Figure 15.17

Bond A

Number	Year End Rating	Probability %	Yield / Default Recovery	New Bond Value plus Coupon	Probability Weighted Value	Difference of Value from Mean	Probability Weighted Difference *2	Percentage Probability	Standard Deviation
Price				100.6565					
1	AAA	0.10	4.00	102.7751	0.1028	2.1780	0.0047	100.00%	6.18
2	AA	2.30	4.50	101.3745	2.3316	0.7774	0.0139	99.90%	3.09
3	A	91.10	4.70	100.6565	91.6981	0.0595	0.0032	97.60%	1.98
4	BBB	5.50	4.90	100.2728	5.5150	(0.3242)	0.0058	6.50%	(1.51)
5	BB	0.70	5.00	100.0000	0.7000	(0.5971)	0.0025	1.00%	(2.33)
6	B	0.30	12.00	83.1872	0.2496	(17.4099)	0.9093	0.30%	(2.75)
7	CCC	-	14.00	79.1053	-	(21.4917)	-	-	-
8	Default	-	51.00	51.0000	-	(49.5971)	-	-	-
		100.00		100.6565	100.5971		0.9395		

Variance	0.9395
Standard Deviation	0.9693
Required Confidence	95.0000
No of Standard Deviatic	(1.6449)
1.64 * Standard Deviatio	(1.5943)
Price of 100.66 + Varianc	99.06
5.00% Percentile	100.27

across and down as shown in Figure 15.18. The values for Bond A are across and the values for Bond BBB are down. The values are a simple summation.

Calculation of joint probabilities

There are eight possible outcomes for each bond, from default to AAA. This multiplies with two bonds to 2^8 or 64 possible states. Thus 79.1659 in the middle of the table is the product of 91.1 per cent for A and 86.9 per cent for BBB (see Figure 15.19).

Row 113 uses the TRANSPOSE function to get the horizontal data for the second bond (see Figure 15.20).

$$\{=TRANSPOSE(\$F\$79:\$F\$86)\}$$

Summation of a portfolio value

The summation of portfolio values is the value multiplied by the probability. 162.6322 in cell F129 in the middle of the table (see Figure 15.21) is the value 205.4321 in cell F104 multiplied by the probability of 86.90 in cell F117.

The portfolio value is derived from the sum of all the probability weighted values and a variance against the initial portfolio value is given. This is the range D126 to K133 and adds up to 204.936 (see Figure 15.21).

Figure 15.18	All possible values

Initial Combined Values: BBB Down A Across

		AAA	AA	A	BBB	BB	B	CCC	Default
		102.7751	101.3745	100.6565	100.2728	100.0000	83.1872	79.1053	51.0000
AAA	108.9036	211.6787	210.2781	209.5602	209.1765	208.9036	192.0908	188.0090	159.9036
AA	106.5850	209.3601	207.9594	207.2415	206.8578	206.5850	189.7721	185.6903	157.5850
A	105.4044	208.1794	206.7788	206.0609	205.6772	205.4044	188.5915	184.5097	156.4044
BBB	104.7756	207.5507	206.1501	205.4321	205.0485	204.7756	187.9628	183.8809	155.7756
BB	104.3295	207.1046	205.7040	204.9860	204.6023	204.3295	187.5167	183.4348	155.3295
B	78.3713	181.1464	179.7458	179.0279	178.6442	178.3713	161.5585	157.4767	129.3713
CCC	72.5354	175.3104	173.9098	173.1919	172.8082	172.5354	155.7225	151.6407	123.5354
Default	51.0000	153.7751	152.3745	151.6565	151.2728	151.0000	134.1872	130.1053	102.0000

Figure 15.19	Joint probabilities

Probabilities

		AAA	AA	A	BBB	BB	B	CCC	Default
		0.1000	2.3000	91.1000	5.5000	0.7000	0.3000	-	-
AAA	-	-	-	-	-	-	-	-	-
AA	0.3000	0.0003	0.0069	0.2733	0.0165	0.0021	0.0009	-	-
A	6.0000	0.0060	0.1380	5.4660	0.3300	0.0420	0.0180	-	-
BBB	86.9000	0.0869	1.9987	79.1659	4.7795	0.6083	0.2607	-	-
BB	5.3000	0.0053	0.1219	4.8283	0.2915	0.0371	0.0159	-	-
B	1.2000	0.0012	0.0276	1.0932	0.0660	0.0084	0.0036	-	-
CCC	0.1000	0.0001	0.0023	0.0911	0.0055	0.0007	0.0003	-	-
Default	0.2000	0.0002	0.0046	0.1822	0.0110	0.0014	0.0006	-	-

Audit trail of calculations

Figure 15.20

Probabilities

		AAA	AA	A	BBB	BB	B	CCC	Default
		0.1000	2.3000	91.1000	5.5000	0.7000	0.3000	-	-
AAA		-	-	-	-	-	-	-	-
AA	0.3000	0.0003	0.0069	0.2733	0.0165	0.0021	0.0009	-	-
A	6.0000	0.0060	0.1380	5.4660	0.3300	0.0420	0.0180	-	-
BBB	86.9000	0.0069	1.9987	79.1659	4.7795	0.6083	0.2607	-	-
BB	5.3000	0.0053	0.1219	4.8283	0.2915	0.0371	0.0159	-	-
B	1.2000	0.0012	0.0276	1.0932	0.0660	0.0084	0.0036	-	-
CCC	0.1000	0.0001	0.0023	0.0911	0.0055	0.0007	0.0003	-	-
Default	0.2000	0.0002	0.0046	0.1822	0.0110	0.0014	0.0006	-	-

Portfolio value

Figure 15.21

Portfolio Value

	AAA	AA	A	BBB	BB	B	CCC	Default
AAA	-	-	-	-	-	-	-	-
AA	0.0006	0.0143	0.5664	0.0341	0.0043	0.0017	-	-
A	0.0125	0.2854	11.2633	0.6787	0.0863	0.0339	-	-
BBB	0.1804	4.1203	162.6322	9.8003	1.2457	0.4900	-	-
BB	0.0110	0.2508	9.8973	0.5964	0.0758	0.0298	-	-
B	0.0022	0.0496	1.9571	0.1179	0.0150	0.0058	-	-
CCC	0.0002	0.0040	0.1578	0.0095	0.0012	0.0005	-	-
Default	0.0003	0.0070	0.2763	0.0166	0.0021	0.0008	-	-

Portfolio value	204.9355
Total value	204,936
Initial portfolio value	205,432
Credit at risk	(497)
Percentage	(0.24%)

Outputs

Figure 15.22

VAR based on Correlation

Interval	0.20					
	(0.40)	(0.20)	-	0.20	0.40
Portfolio variance	3.9954	3.0352	3.6157	4.1962	4.7767	5.3572
Standard Deviation	1.9989	1.7422	1.9015	2.0485	2.1856	2.3146
Required Confidence	95.0000	95.0000	95.0000	95.0000	95.0000	95.0000
No of Standard Deviatic	(1.6449)	(1.6449)	(1.6449)	(1.6449)	(1.6449)	(1.6449)
1.64 * Standard Deviatio	(3.2878)	(2.8656)	(3.1277)	(3.3694)	(3.5949)	(3.8071)
(A) SD Value	202.1443	202.5665	202.3045	202.0627	201.8372	201.6250
Revised Portfolio Value	202,144	202,567	202,304	202,063	201,837	201,625
(B) Percentiles Value	204.9860	(0.4461)				
Revised Portfolio Value	204,986	(446)				

Outputs: standard deviation and 5 per cent threshold

The outputs comprise the standard deviation and the percentiles value. In both cases, the 95 per cent confidence value is used. Due to the skew of credit curves, the values are slightly different (see Figure 15.22).

Figure 15.23   **Offset table for cumulative percentiles**

	A	B	C	O
110				
111		**Probabilities**		
112				**Percentiles**
113				
114		AAA	·	91.10000
115		AA	0.3000	91.10000
116		A	6.0000	90.82670
117		BBB	86.9000	85.36070
118		BB	5.3000	6.19480
119		B	1.2000	1.36650
120		CCC	0.1000	0.27330
121		Default	0.2000	0.18220
122				204.99

The table uses the correlation in cell D15 across the top. The value in Cell D15 is zero and so the schedule provides all the values for positive and negative correlation. The variance in cell D147 uses the formula:

$(((Weighting\_A)\^2)*(SDev\_A)\^2 + ((Weighting\_B)\^2)*(SDev\_B)\^2 + 2*Weighting\_A*SDev\_A*Weighting\_B*SDev\_B*Correlation)$

```
= (D22/100)^2*D68^2+(E22/100)^2*D91^2
  +2*(D22/100)*D68*(E22/100)*D91*D15
```

The standard deviation is the square root of variance and the schedule multiplies out the 95 per cent confidence. The percentile value uses the workings table to the right to match the value along the cumulative probability (see Figure 15.23).

The formula in cell O122 uses OFFSET and MATCH. The OFFSET starts in cell C100 and moves right by the number in cell D238. This is three and therefore the starting point is cell F100. The cumulative probabilities are in the range O114 to O121 and the match reads off the value five cells down in F105.

```
=OFFSET(OFFSET(C100,0,D238),
MATCH(100-$D$14,O114:O120,-1),0)
```

Figure 15.24 shows the cluster of results around the 200 value. This is also evident in the second area chart with the peak between BBB and A (see Figure 15.25).

Combined values

Figure 15.24

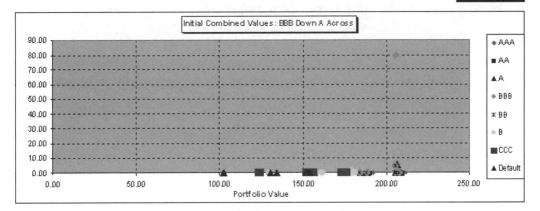

Portfolio chart

Figure 15.25

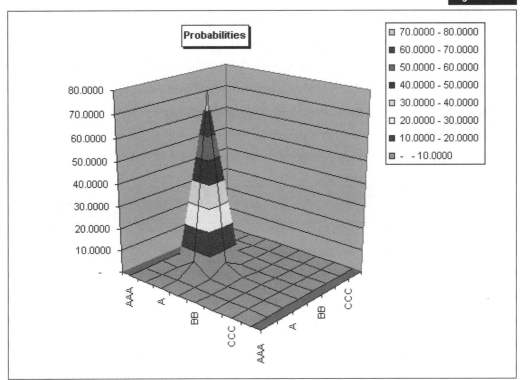

SIMULATION

The method outlined above works for one or two bonds, but large portfolios require a simulation approach and the use of specialized Excel add-ins such as @RISK or Crystal Ball. These generate random numbers with defined distributions and model large numbers of possible scenarios.

The Model_Simulation sheet calculates the values for each bond and then adds up the two values to form the portfolio value (see Figure 15.26).

The random numbers are generated by the macro:

```
=NORMSINV(C7)
```

A RAND function could have been used but this slows down the workbook. The standard deviation uses the NORMSINV function which returns the inverse of the standard normal cumulative distribution. The distribution has a mean of zero and a standard deviation of one and the input is the probability (see Table 15.1).

The next row matches the standard deviation with the position on the list. For example 0.8108 would read off as the fourth item in declining order. Column F provides the rating for the number using an OFFSET function. Therefore the further rating is a BBB.

```
=OFFSET(Data!$B$8,E10,0)
```

The value is also found by an OFFSET function using the values in range Model F56 to F63. This procedure is repeated for the second bond in

Figure 15.26

Simulated bond value

	A	B	C	D	E	F	G
4							
5		Bond: BBB					
6		No	Random No	Standard Deviation	Grade	Rating	Value
7		1	0.8200	0.9154	4	BBB	104.7756
8		2	0.9290	1.4682	4	BBB	104.7756
9		3	0.3211	(0.4647)	4	BBB	104.7756
10		4	0.0522	(1.6235)	5	BB	104.3295
11		5	0.9544	1.6896	3	A	105.4044
12		6	0.4680	(0.0802)	4	BBB	104.7756
13		7	0.1345	(1.1053)	4	BBB	104.7756
14		8	0.0306	(1.8714)	5	BB	104.3295
15		9	0.6751	0.4540	4	BBB	104.7756
16		10	0.1891	(0.8812)	4	BBB	104.7756
17		11	0.7424	0.6509	4	BBB	104.7756
18		12	0.5653	0.1645	4	BBB	104.7756
19		13	0.0586	(1.5668)	5	BB	104.3295
20		14	0.7822	0.7795	4	BBB	104.7756
21		15	0.3543	(0.3738)	4	BBB	104.7756
22		16	0.5416	0.1044	4	BBB	104.7756
23		17	0.0722	(1.4595)	4	BBB	104.7756
24		18	0.9527	1.6720	3	A	105.4044
25		19	0.3201	(0.4674)	4	BBB	104.7756
26		20	0.1102	(1.2253)	4	BBB	104.7756

Rating	Standard deviation
AAA	9.51
AA	4.75
A	2.75
BBB	1.53
BB	(1.49)
B	(2.17)
CCC	(2.75)
Default	(2.88)

columns H to N. Column O adds the two values and there are 1000 lines to provide a range of possible values.

The code for the random numbers is:

```
Sub Model_Simulation()

Dim RandomFactor, Count, StartA, StartB
Range("model_simulation!$C$6").Select

Application.ScreenUpdating = False
Application.Calculation = xlCalculationManual

For Count = 1 To 1000        'START OF LOOP
Application.StatusBar = "Generating random
numbers - " & Count
ActiveCell.Offset(1, 0).Select
ActiveCell.FormulaR1C1 = Rnd
ActiveCell.Offset(0, 5).Select
ActiveCell.FormulaR1C1 = Rnd
ActiveCell.Offset(0, -5).Select
Next Count                   'END OF LOOP

Application.StatusBar = False
Application.ScreenUpdating = True
Application.Calculation
= xlCalculationSemiautomatic

End Sub
```

The Simulation_Results sheet illustrates the results of 1000 scenarios using random number generation (see Figure 15.27). Most of the results reflect

Figure 15.27   **Simulation results**

Grade	Rating	Bond: BBB Value	Bond: BBB No of Results	Bond: A Value	Bond: A No of Results	Portfolio Limits	Portfolio Portfolio
1	AAA	108.90	-	102.78	-	162.90	4
2	AA	106.58	1	101.37	23	171.48	-
3	A	105.68	47	100.82	905	180.50	20
4	BBB	104.78	869	100.27	58	190.00	-
5	BB	104.33	60	100.00	12	200.00	-
6	B	78.37	20	83.19	-	210.00	976
7	CCC	72.54	1	79.11	-	220.50	-
8	Default	51.00	2	51.00	2	231.53	-
Total			1,000		1,000		1,000

the current rating of the bond as A or BBB. The histogram counts the number of results in each sector to shows the peaks for each of the bonds. This is a FREQUENCY function entered as an array using Control and Enter together.

Bond BBB shows 866 results remaining at the same rating against the theoretical value of 869 for each 1000. Similarly Bond A shows 905 against 910. The results of course will vary with each run due to the random numbers. Therefore the results with 1000 scenarios are close the transition matrix.

The next stage is to combine the results to show the portfolio results in values and percentiles. Figure 15.28 shows the values for each bond at a number of confidence levels and then the combined value. The statistics are:

- mean – simple arithmetic average;
- median – number in the middle of a set of numbers; that is, half the numbers have values that are greater than the median, and half have values that are less;

Bond statistics

Figure 15.28

Bond Portfolio Percentiles

	Bond: BBB	Bond: A	Portfolio	Difference	% Diff
Initial Value	104.78	100.66	205.43		
Mean	104.13	100.69	204.82	(0.61)	(0.30%)
Median	104.78	100.82	205.60	0.17	0.08%
Mode	104.78	100.82	205.60	0.17	0.08%
Skew	(7.31)	(22.11)	(8.14)		
Kurtosis	59.14	491.13	78.72		
Interval 5.0%					
Percent 100.0%					
95.0%	104.78	100.82	206.15	0.72	0.35%
90.0%	104.78	100.82	205.60	0.17	0.08%
85.0%	104.78	100.82	205.60	0.17	0.08%
80.0%	104.78	100.82	205.60	0.17	0.08%
75.0%	104.78	100.82	205.60	0.17	0.08%
70.0%	104.78	100.82	205.60	0.17	0.08%
65.0%	104.78	100.82	205.60	0.17	0.08%
60.0%	104.78	100.82	205.60	0.17	0.08%
55.0%	104.78	100.82	205.60	0.17	0.08%
50.0%	104.78	100.82	205.60	0.17	0.08%
45.0%	104.78	100.82	205.60	0.17	0.08%
40.0%	104.78	100.82	205.60	0.17	0.08%
35.0%	104.78	100.82	205.60	0.17	0.08%
30.0%	104.78	100.82	205.60	0.17	0.08%
25.0%	104.78	100.82	205.60	0.17	0.08%
20.0%	104.78	100.82	205.60	0.17	0.08%
15.0%	104.78	100.82	205.60	0.17	0.08%
10.0%	104.78	100.82	205.15	(0.28)	(0.14%)
5.0%	104.33	100.27	205.05	(0.38)	(0.19%)
Lower Percentiles					
5.0%	104.33	100.27	205.05	(0.38)	(0.19%)
4.0%	104.33	100.27	204.78	(0.66)	(0.32%)
3.0%	104.33	100.27	204.77	(0.66)	(0.32%)
2.0%	78.37	100.27	179.19	(26.24)	(12.77%)
1.0%	78.37	100.00	179.19	(26.24)	(12.77%)

- mode – most frequently occurring value;
- skew – degree of asymmetry of a distribution around its mean (a positive skew indicates a distribution with an asymmetric tail extending towards positive values; a negative skew indicates a distribution with an asymmetric tail extending towards negative values);
- kurtosis – a relative peak or flatness of a distribution compared with the normal distribution (positive kurtosis indicates a relatively peaked distribution; negative kurtosis indicates a relatively flat distribution);
- percentiles to show the spread of values; again an array function.

```
{=PERCENTILE(Model_Simulation!$N$7:$N$1006,$C
$50:$C$68)}
```

Figure 15.29 shows the chart of bond values.

Figure 15.30 is the combined values and the count of occurrences with the histogram showing a peak at A and BBB with 786 of the possible results. The combined values table is brought forward from the Model sheet so that there is a portfolio value for each possible eventual value. In the bottom right-hand corner at cell K107 is the result if both bonds default and the recovery is around 50 per cent. Here the portfolio is worth 102.26. The next table uses a COUNTIF function to count the values if the values equal the combined amount in the table. In cell F115, the function counts the number of results in column O that concur with the value 205.59 in cell F103. This is approximately 800.

```
=COUNTIF(Model_Simulation!$O$7:$O$1006,F103)
```

Figure 15.31 is an alternative view of the histogram values showing the peak at the intersection of BBB and A together with the tail of values to default.

Figures 15.32 and 15.33 plot the values and probabilities, to show first the values and second the cumulative probability as percentages.

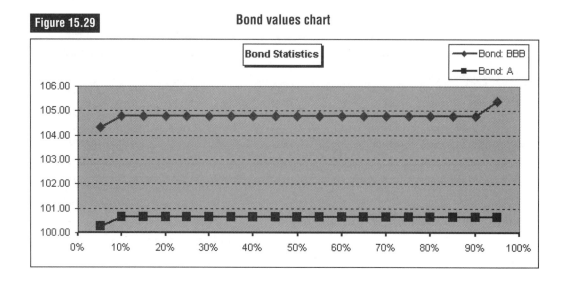

Figure 15.29   **Bond values chart**

Histogram of values

Figure 15.30

Combined Values: BB Down A Across

	AAA	AA	A	BBB	BB	B	CCC	Default
AAA	211.6787	210.2781	209.7252	209.1765	208.9036	192.0908	188.0090	159.9036
AA	209.3601	207.9594	207.4066	206.8578	206.5850	189.7721	185.6903	157.5850
A	208.4504	207.0498	206.4969	205.9481	205.6753	188.8625	184.7806	156.6753
BBB	207.5507	206.1501	205.5972	205.0485	204.7756	187.9628	183.8809	155.7756
BB	207.1046	205.7040	205.1511	204.6023	204.3295	187.5167	183.4348	155.3295
B	181.1464	179.7458	179.1929	178.6442	178.3713	161.5585	157.4767	129.3713
CCC	175.3104	173.9098	173.3569	172.8082	172.5354	155.7225	151.6407	123.5354
Default	153.7751	152.3745	151.8216	151.2728	151.0000	134.1872	130.1053	102.0000

Combined Values: BB Down A Across - Count

	AAA	AA	A	BBB	BB	B	CCC	Default
AAA	-	-	-	-	-	-	-	-
AA	-	-	1	-	-	-	-	-
A	-	1	45	-	1	-	-	-
BBB	-	20	786	51	11	-	-	1
BB	-	2	52	6	-	-	-	-
B	-	-	18	1	-	-	-	1
CCC	-	-	1	-	-	-	-	-
Default	-	-	2	-	-	-	-	-

Count   1,000

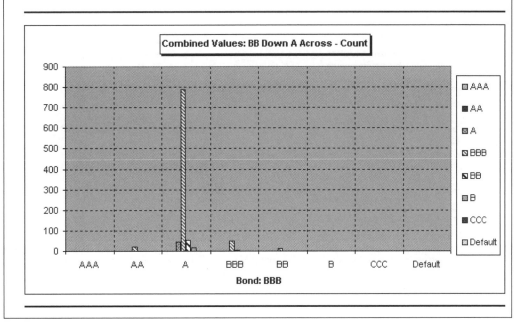

Combined Values: BB Down A Across - Count

Figure 15.31

Portfolio result

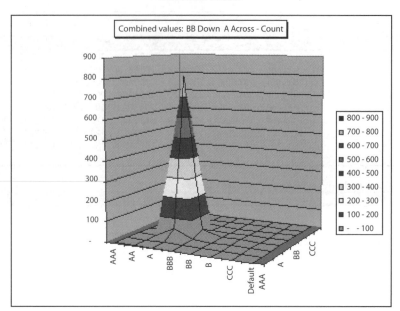

Figure 15.32

Cumulative values

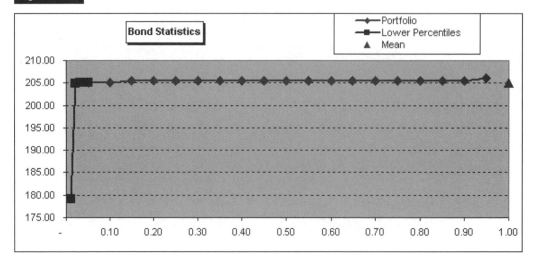

Cumulative probability chart

Figure 15.33

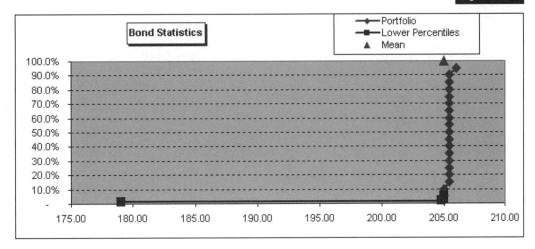

SUMMARY

Credit value at risk is a methodology for encompassing both default and the upgrades and downgrades and produces value at risk scores for portfolios. The method is flexible for a number of different credit exposures and this chapter has illustrated the main principles using a simple portfolio model with one and then two bonds. The main elements are:

- exposures and their distributions;
- the possibility of upgrade, downgrade and default;
- the calculation of a monetary value at the five percentile for a possible portfolio value at the end of a timeframe.

Using this approach provides a framework for considering risk as a monetary value across portfolios and industries and it gives decision makers more information for setting credit limits and managing risk capital.

Appendix: software installation and licence

The appendix contains:

- system requirements
- installation
- accessing the application files
- licence
- file list.

A CD containing the Excel files and templates accompanies this book. The CD contains example files only and complete versions are available for purchase at www.financial-models.com. The file names relate to their chapter numbers and you should refer to the file list. The file notation is FT4 and then the chapter number. For completeness, the files for a particular chapter are quoted at the beginning of each chapter.

Follow the instructions below to install the files and create a program group using the simple SETUP command.

SYSTEM REQUIREMENTS

This section summarizes the requirements for using the application:

- IBM-compatible personal computer with an 804086 or higher processor;
- hard disk with 20 Mb of free space;
- Microsoft Mouse or other compatible pointing device;
- EGA, VGA or compatible display (VGA or higher is recommended);
- 32 MB of random access memory: performance is significantly enhanced with more memory;
- Microsoft Windows and Excel 97 or later.

INSTALLATION

- Insert the CD into your CD-ROM drive.
- Select the Start button in the bottom left of your screen.
- Select Run.
- Write in the space provided: D:\SetUp.exe – then click on OK.
- D is your CD-ROM drive: if this is not correct for your machine then change the letter accordingly.
- The application will now install itself. Follow the instructions on screen to select a destination directory.
- If you are prompted, then restart Windows.

When the installation has finished, open Excel and select Tools – Add-ins. You need to make sure that Analysis Toolpak and solver are selected. This is because the files use some of the advanced functions such as EDATE and XNPV or Solver routines. Analysis Toolpak is often not installed using a typical installation. If this is the case use your original Office disks to install the missing option.

Figure A.1   **Tools Add-Ins**

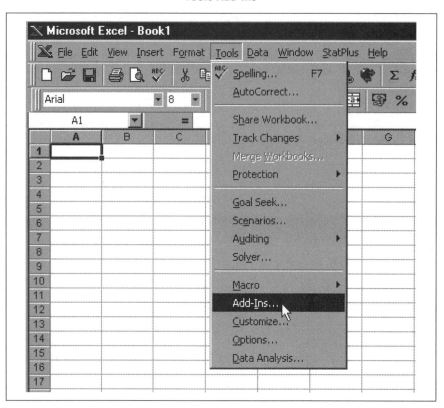

Analysis Toolpak

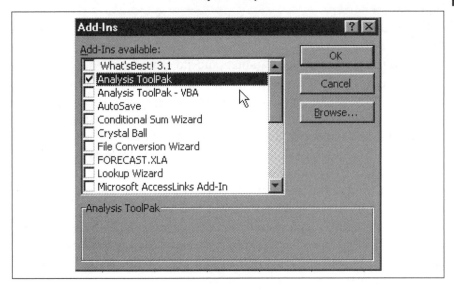

This Toolpak contains extra statistical and financial functions needed by the applications. Click it to select it and press OK. If you do not select it, you will encounter errors on certain files.

ACCESSING THE APPLICATION FILES

- You will see that a program group has been created for you. The application will also now appear under Programs on the Start Menu.
- When installed, the program group should include all the files on the accompanying file list.
- To access any of the files, simply double-click the icons in the program group.
- You can also open a ReadMe file of installation instructions and a file list.
- Press OK to continue and the selected file will open.
- There is a master file list in the form of an Excel model and a list within the book.

LICENCE

This notice is intended to be a 'no nonsense' agreement between you ('the licensee') and Systematic Finance plc ('Systematic'). The software and associated documentation ('software') are subject to copyright law. They are protected by the laws of England. If you use this software, you are deemed to have accepted the terms and conditions under which this software was supplied.

Files accompanying *Mastering Risk Modelling* are copyright © Systematic Finance plc ('Systematic').

The software has not been audited and no representation, warranty or undertaking (express or implied) is made and no responsibility is taken or accepted by Systematic and its directors, officers, employees, agents or advisers as to the adequacy, accuracy, completeness or reasonableness of the financial models and Systematic excludes liability thereof.

In particular, no responsibility is taken or accepted by Systematic and all liability is excluded by Systematic for the accuracy of the computations comprised therein and the assumptions upon which such computations are based. In addition, the recipient receives and uses the software entirely at their own risk and no responsibility is taken or accepted by Systematic and accordingly all liability is excluded by Systematic for any losses which may result therefrom, whether as a direct or indirect consequence of a computer virus or otherwise.

No part of the accompanying documentation may be reproduced, transmitted, transcribed, stored in a retrieval system or translated without the prior permission of the copyright holder. You have a limited licence to use the software for the period stated on the software copyright notice and to make copies of the software for backup purposes. This is a single copy software licence granted by Systematic. You must treat this software just like a book except that you may copy it onto a computer to be used and you may make an archival backup copy of the software for the purposes of protecting the software from accidental loss.

The phrase 'just like a book' is used to give the licence maximum flexibility in the use of the licence. This means, for example, that the software can be used by any number of people, or freely moved between computers, provided it is not being used on more than one computer or by more than one person at the same time as it is in use elsewhere. Just like a book, which can only be read by one person at a time, the software can only be used by one person on one computer at one time. If more than one person is using the software on different machines, then Systematic's rights have been violated and the licensee should seek to purchase further single copy licences by purchasing more copies of the book. (In the case of multiple licences or network licences, then the number of users may only equal the number of licences.)

You may not decompile, disassemble or reverse-engineer the licensed software. You may not rent or lease the software to others or claim ownership. If you wish to pass the software to another person, you may. However, you must provide all original disks, documentation and remove the software from your own computer(s) to remain within the single copy licence agreement. To do otherwise will violate the rights of Systematic.

Systematic does not warrant that the functions contained in the software will meet your requirements or that the operation of the software will be uninterrupted or error free. This warranty does not extend to changes made to the software by third parties, nor does it extend to liability for data loss, damages or lost profits due to the use of the software.

Systematic does not have any responsibility for software failure due to changes in the operating environment of the computer hardware or operating system made after delivery of the software.

FILE LIST

Chapter		Models
1	Overview	FT4_01
2	Review of model design	FT4_02
3	Risk and uncertainty	FT4_03
4	Project finance model	FT4_04
5	Simulation	FT4_05_01
		FT4_05_02
6	Financial analysis	FT4_06
7	Credit risk	FT4_07
8	Equity valuation	FT4_08
9	Bonds	FT4_09
10	Options	FT4_10
11	Real options	FT4_11
12	Equities	FT4_12
13	Risk management	FT4_13
14	Value at risk	FT4_14
15	Credit risk and credit metrics	FT4_15_01
		FT4_15_02

The above files comprise templates and files to allow you to practise building the finished spreadsheets rather than use or modify existing files. This is to allow you to learn by doing and thereby increase your own skill level. Complete versions are available for purchase at www.financial-models.com.

Index